STUDY GUIDE
Volume I

James Schmiechen
Central Michigan University

A History of Western Society
Sixth Edition

John P. McKay
University of Illinois at Urbana-Champaign

Bennett D. Hill
Georgetown University

John Buckler
University of Illinois at Urbana-Champaign

HOUGHTON MIFFLIN COMPANY   BOSTON   NEW YORK

Editor-in-Chief: Jean L. Woy
Assistant Editor: Lisa Rothrauff
Manufacturing Manager: Florence Cadran
Marketing Manager: Sandra McGuire

Printed in the U.S.A.

ISBN: 0-395-90440-4

6 7 8 9 –VG – 05 04 03 02 01

Contents

To the Student

This Study Guide Will Help You Prepare for Exams and Improve Your Grade

The study of history can be rewarding but also perplexing. Most history courses require you to read and understand large bodies of detailed information. The history student is expected to perform many tasks—memorize information, study the reasons for change, analyze the accomplishments and failures of various societies, understand new ideas, identify historical periods, pick out broad themes and generalizations in history, and so forth. These jobs often present difficulties. This study guide has been developed to help you read, study, and review *A History of Western Society,* and regular and systematic use of it will improve your grade in this course. You may use the guide in a variety of ways, but for best results you might choose the following approach.

1. *Preview the entire chapter* by reading the "Learning Objectives" and "Chapter Summary"; then quickly read through the study outline. All of this will take only a few minutes but is an important first step in reading. It is called *previewing.* By pointing out what the chapter is about and what to look for, previewing will make your reading easier and improve your reading comprehension.

2. *Now read your assignment in the textbook.* Pay attention to the chapter title, chapter and section introductions, questions, headings, conclusions, and illustrative material (e.g., maps and photographs). These are clues to what is important.

3. *Think of what you are reading as a story or narrative.* Pay attention to names, events, and ideas. Keep in mind that you want to discover *causes* and *results* and to be able to retell the story in your own words.

4. After reading, *review what you have read* and check your comprehension by going over the chapter outline once again—but this time make sure that you understand all the points and subpoints. If you do not fully understand a particular point or subpoint, then you need to return to the text and reread. It is not at all uncommon to need to read the text at least twice.

5. Continue your review. *Write out answers to the review questions* that follow the study outline. Be sure to include the supporting facts. Reread your answers periodically. This process will help you build a storehouse of information to use at the time of the exam.

6. Now work on the study-review exercises provided in each chapter of the *Study Guide.* This will help you to understand and recall both concepts and specific facts. Know not just who or what,

but also *why* the term is significant. Note that if a particular term appears in the text *and* in your lecture notes, it is of special importance. Do the geography exercises found in all appropriate chapters. This is important because they will enable you to visualize the subject matter and thus remember it better. It will take a few minutes, but the payoff is considerable.

7. Next, *complete the self-test exercises* for the chapter. Some of these questions look for basic facts, while others test your understanding and ability to synthesize material. *The answers are at the end of the guide.* If you miss more than two or three, you need to restudy the text or spend more time working on the *guide*.

8. The section "Major Political Ideas" will help you understand some of the political concepts that are raised in the text. Keep a special section in your notebook where you write out the answers to these questions. By the time you take your exam you will have a good understanding of what these political concepts are and how and why they developed.

9. "Issues for Essay and Discussion" sets out one or two broad questions of the type you may be asked to answer in an essay exam or discuss in a classroom discussion. Answer these by writing a one- to two-page essay in which you address each part of the question with a well-organized answer based on material from the text. Remember, your instructor is looking for your ability to back up your argument with historical evidence.

10. Last, "Interpretation of Visual Primary Sources" is a way for you to better understand the chapter and to help you learn how to use prints, photographs, architectural artifacts, and the like in assessing historical change. Keep a section in your notebook where you answer these questions, but also study the other visuals in the chapter. Don't be reluctant to make reference to these visual sources when you write your examination essays.

Additional Study Hints*

1. *Organize your study time effectively.* Many students fail to do well in courses because they do not organize their time effectively. In college, students are expected to read the material before class, review, and do the homework on their own. Many history teachers give only two or three tests during the semester; therefore, assuming personal responsibility for learning the material is vital. Mark up a semester calendar to show scheduled test dates, when term projects are due, and blocks of time to be set aside for exam study and paper writing. Then, at the beginning of each week, check the calendar and your course outlines and notes to see what specific preparation is necessary for the coming week, and plan your time accordingly. Set aside a block of time each day or once every several days for reading your text or studying your lecture notes and working in the *Study Guide*. Despite what one observes on college campuses, studying is not done most effectively late at night or with background music. Find a quiet place to study alone, one where you can tune out the world and tune into the past.

2. *Take good lecture notes.* Good notes are readable, clear, and above all reviewable. Write down as much of the lecture as you can without letting your pen get too far behind the lecturer. Use

---

*For a complete text and workbook written to meet the needs of students who want to do their best in college, see James F. Shepherd, *RSVP, The Houghton Mifflin Reading, Study, and Vocabulary Program*, Fourth Edition (1992).

abbreviations and jot down key words. Leave spaces where appropriate and then go back and add to your notes as soon after the lecture as possible. You may find it helpful to leave a wide margin on the left side for writing in subject headings, important points, and questions, as well as for adding information and cross-references to the text and other readings. Above all, do not wait until the night before an exam to use lecture notes you have not looked at for weeks or months. Review your lecture notes often and see how they complement and help you interpret your reading.

3. *Underline.* Too often students mark almost everything they read and end up with little else than an entire book highlighted in yellow. Underlining can be extremely helpful or simply a waste of time in preparing for exams; the key is to be selective in what you underline. Use "Studying Effectively—Exercise 2: Learning to Improve Your Understanding Skills" on p. 125. Here are some suggestions:

   a. Underline major concepts, ideas, conclusions, and generalizations. You will be expected to interpret and analyze the material you have read. In many cases the textbook authors themselves have done this, so you need to pinpoint their comments as you read. Is the author making a point of interpretation or coming to a conclusion? If so, underline the key part. The authors do it and you must learn to identify their interpretations and then to make your own. Here is where your study of history can pay big rewards. The historian, like a good detective, not only gathers facts but also analyzes, synthesizes, and generalizes from that basic information. This is the process of historical interpretation, which you must seek to master.

   b. Underline basic facts. You will be expected to know basic facts (names, events, dates, places) so that you can reconstruct the larger picture and back up your analysis and interpretations. Each chapter of this guide includes several lists of important items. Look over these lists before you begin to read, and then underline these words as you read.

   c. Look at the review questions in the *Study Guide*—they will point to the major themes and questions to be answered. Then, as you read, underline the material that answers these questions. Making marginal notations can often complement your underlining.

4. *Work on your vocabulary.* The course lectures and each chapter in the text will probably include words that you do not know. Some of these will be historical terms or special concepts, such as *polis, feudalism,* or *bourgeoisie*—words that are not often used in ordinary American speech. Others are simply new to you but important for understanding readings and discussion. If you cannot determine the meaning of the word from the context in which it appears or from its word structure, then you will need to use a dictionary. *Keep a list of words* in your lecture notebook or use the pages in the back of this guide. Improving your historical and general vocabulary is an important part of reading history as well as furthering your college career. Most graduate-school entrance exams and many job applications, for instance, have sections to test vocabulary and reading comprehension.

5. *Prepare for essay exams.* Essay exams demand that you express yourself through ideas, concepts, and generalizations as well as by reciting the basic narrative. The key to taking an essay exam is preparation. Follow this plan:

a. *Try to anticipate the questions on the exam.* As you read the text, your notes, and this guide, jot down what seem to be logical essay questions. This will become easier as the course continues, partly because you will be familiar with the type of question your instructor asks. Some questions are fairly broad, such as the chapter questions at the beginning of each chapter in this guide; others have a more specific focus, such as the review questions. Study and restudy your lecture notes. Most professors organize their lectures around a particular theme or stage in history. You should be able to invent a question or two from each lecture. Then answer the question. Do the same with the textbook, using the *Study Guide* for direction. Remember, professors are often impressed when students include in their essay textbook material not covered in class.

b. *Aim for good content and organization.* Be prepared to answer questions that require historical interpretation and analysis of a particular event, series of events, movement, process, person's life, and so forth. You must also be prepared to provide specific information to back up and support your analysis. In some cases you will be expected to give either a chronological narrative of events or a topical narrative (for example, explaining a historical movement in terms of its social, political, and economic features). Historians often approach problems in terms of cause and effect, so spend some time thinking about events in these terms. Remember, not all causes are of equal importance, so you must be ready to make distinctions—and to back up these distinctions with evidence. This is all part of showing your skill at historical interpretation.

When organizing your essay, you will usually want to sketch out your general thesis (argument) or point of interpretation first, in an introductory sentence or two. Next move to the substance. Here you will illustrate and develop your argument by weighing the evidence and marshaling reasons and factual data. After you have completed this stage (writing the body of your essay), go on to your conclusion, which most likely will be a restatement of your original thesis. It is often helpful to outline your major points before you begin to write. Be sure you answer all parts of the question. Write clearly and directly. All of this is hard to do, but you will get better at it as the course moves along.

6. *Enhance your understanding* of important historical questions by undertaking additional reading and/or a research project as suggested in the "Understanding History Through the Arts" and "Problems for Further Investigation" sections in the *Study Guide*. Note also that each textbook chapter has an excellent bibliography. Many of the books suggested are available in paperback editions, and all of the music suggested is available in most record-lending libraries and record stores. If your instructor requires a term paper, these sections are a good starting point.

7. *Know why you are studying history.* Nothing is worse than having to study a subject that appears to have no practical value. And indeed, it is unlikely that by itself this history course will land you a job. What, then, is its value, and how can it enrich your life? Although many students like history simply because historical narratives are interesting and exciting, there are a number of solid, old-fashioned reasons for studying it. It is often said that we need to understand our past in order to live in the present and build the future. This is true on a number of levels. On the psychological level, identification with the past gives us a badly needed sense of continuity and order in the face of ever more rapid change. We see how change has occurred in the past and are therefore better prepared to deal with it in our own lives. On another level, it is important for us to know how differing political, economic, and social systems work and what benefits and

disadvantages accrue from them. As the good craftsperson uses a lifetime of experience to make a masterpiece, so an understanding of the accumulated experiences of the past enables us to construct a better society. Further, we need to understand how the historical experiences of peoples and nations have differed, and how these differences have shaped their respective visions. Only then can we come to understand how others view the world differently from the ways in which we do. Thus, history breaks down the barriers erected by provincialism and ignorance.

The strongest argument for the study of history, though, is that it recreates the big picture at a time when it is fashionable and seemingly prudent to be highly specialized and narrowly focused. We live in the Age of Specialization. Even our universities often appear as giant trade schools, where we are asked to learn a lot about a little. As a result, it is easy to miss what is happening to the forest because we have become obsessed with a few of the trees. While specialization has undeniable benefits, both societies and individuals also need the generalist perspective and the ability to see how the entire system works. History is the queen of the generalist disciplines. Looking at change over time, history shows us how to take all the parts of the puzzle—politics, war, science, economics, architecture, sex, demography, music, philosophy, and much more—and put them together so that we can understand the whole. It is through a study of the interrelationships of the parts over a long expanse of time that we can develop a vision of society. By promoting the generalist perspective, history plays an important part in our electronic society.

Therefore, the study of history has a personal and practical application. It is becoming increasingly apparent to many employers and educators that many well-meaning students are unable to think and reason analytically or write and speak effectively. Overspecialized, narrowly focused education has left these students seriously deficient in an understanding of the meaning of Western culture, placing them at a serious disadvantage in the job market. Here is where this course can help. The study of the past enables us to solve today's problems.

James Schmiechen
Mt. Pleasant, Michigan

Chapter 1

Near Eastern Origins

Learning Objectives

After reading and studying this chapter you should be able to:

1. describe the various kinds of sources historians use and define the terms *history, civilization,* and *western.*

2. answer the question: "What is civilization?"

3. describe how nomadic hunters became urban dwellers.

4. describe how and why western culture originated in Mesopotamia.

5. grasp Mesopotamia's and Egypt's contributions to Western society.

Chapter Summary

This chapter defines the terms *history, civilization,* and *western,* and then explores how civilization in the Western world began in the Near East in the area that became modern-day Israel, Iraq, Iran, and Egypt. It was here that agriculture and the first cities emerged, where writing was invented, where law, science, and mathematics developed, and where the central religious beliefs of the modern West evolved. These developments mark the beginning of a distinctively "Western" civilization.

The two prehistoric periods, the Paleolithic, or Old Stone Age, and the Neolithic, or New Stone Age, set the stage for early civilization. Although the invention of tools, the control of fire, and the discovery of the uses of language, art, and agriculture by the Paleolithic peoples were remarkable achievements, it was the Neolithic peoples' use of systematic agriculture and settled life that was one of the most important events in world history.

As these early peoples gave up nomadic life for the settled life of towns and systematic agriculture, civilization—which meant law, government, economic growth, and religion—became possible. By around 3000 B.C., the first urban-agricultural societies had emerged in Mesopotamia, the fertile land between the Tigris and Euphrates rivers. The most important of these early communities of farmers and city builders were the southern Mesopotamians, called the Sumerians. Sumerian society was a mixture of religious ritual, war, slavery, and individual freedom. The Sumerians' greatest achievement was their system of writing, a system called cuneiform. The conquerors of Sumer, people called Semites from the northern part of Mesopotamia, spread

Sumerian-Mesopotamian culture throughout the Near East. They were followed by the Babylonians, whose city, Babylon, dominated the trade of the Tigris and Euphrates. The Babylonians united Mesopotamia and gave the world one of its most important law codes, the Code of Hammurabi. This code tells us how Mesopotamian people lived: how husbands treated their wives, how society dealt with crime, how consumer protection evolved, and so forth.

Egyptian society grew alongside the Nile River, which sheltered and isolated its people more effectively than the rivers of Mesopotamia. Egypt was first united into a single kingdom in about 3100 B.C. The focal point of all life in ancient Egypt was the pharaoh. His tomb, the pyramid, provided him with everything that he would need in the afterlife. Egyptian society was a curious mixture of freedom and constraint. Slavery existed, but ordinary people could rise to high positions if they possessed talent.

Between 2000 and 1200 B.C., Egypt and the entire Near East were greatly influenced by two migrations of Indo-Europeans that disturbed and remolded existing states. While Mesopotamia became unified under the Hittites, Egypt was first influenced by the Hyksos and then by the introduction of monotheism by the pharaoh Akhenaten. During one of the resulting periods of political disintegration, a number of petty kingdoms developed, although the old culture of the Near East—especially that of Mesopotamia—lived on in the kingdoms of the newcomers.

Study Outline

Use this outline to preview the chapter before you read a particular section in your textbook and then as a self-check to test your reading comprehension after you have read the chapter section.

  I. What is history and why do we study it?
      A. History is the effort to reconstruct the past.
          1. The past must be understood so we can understand the factors that shape us today.
          2. Historians reconstruct the past by posing questions about it and then attempting to answer them by studying primary and secondary sources.
              a. Herodotus, the "father of history," joined the two concepts of inquiry and research.
              b. Historians must assess the validity and perspective of each source they study.
      B. The task of the historian is to understand the evidence, then interpret it.
          1. Historians seldom have all of the facts.
          2. Interpretation is often affected by the values and attitudes of the times.
      C. Social history, the study of the basic details of daily life, is a relatively new interpretive process.
      D. *Civilization* means a people's shared way of thinking and believing.
      E. *Western* means the ideas, customs, and institutions that set western civilization apart from others.
  II. The first human beings
      A. Darwin's ideas of human evolution were set forth in two books: *On the Origins of Species* (1859) and *The Decent of Man* (1871).
          1. The discovery of "Neanderthal Man" already proved that man had evolved from lesser forms.

2. Darwin's important theories ushered in a new era in history and science.
3. Darwin believed that human beings and apes are descended from a common ancestor.

B. Paleoanthropologists' search for the "missing link"—the point from which humans and apes went their own evolutionary ways.

III. The Paleolithic and Neolithic ages

A. The Paleolithic or Old Stone Age (ca 400,000-7000 B.C.)
   1. Human survival depended on the hunt; people did not farm.
   2. Paleolithic peoples learned to control fire and make tools from stone and clothes from animal skins.
      a. Social organization allowed them to overpower animals.
      b. They had some knowledge of plants and agriculture.
      c. Kinship and tribal ties were crucial; kinship bonds were strong throughout the extended family.
      d. The tribe was a group of families led by a patriarch.
   3. The greatest accomplishments of Paleolithic peoples were intellectual: thought and language allowed experience to be passed on.
   4. Art, such as cave paintings and small clay statues, dates from this time and may express a desire to control the environment.

B. The Neolithic Age or New Stone Age (ca 7000-3000 B.C.)
   1. The planting of crops and the domestication of animals—the "Agricultural Revolution"—was the age's greatest achievement.
      a. Systematic agriculture ended people's dependence on hunting and allowed them to settle in towns and eventually cities.
      b. Agriculture began in four areas in the Near East: Iran, Iraq, Palestine, and Turkey.
      c. Farming led to walled villages with social-political organization.
      d. Agriculture led to war, population increase, trade, and the division of labor.
   2. The settled lifestyle allowed time to develop new tools and agricultural techniques.
   3. In arid regions, irrigation was undertaken, resulting in the need for a central government.

IV. Mesopotamian civilization

A. The first cities were built in Mesopotamia (ca 3500-1700 B.C.).
   1. Mesopotamia is the level plain between the Euphrates and Tigris rivers.
   2. The peoples of the area, the Sumerians and the Semites, turned to an agricultural-urban way of life.
   3. The Sumerians made Mesopotamia the "cradle of civilization."

B. The role of environment
   1. Geography greatly affected the political life and mental outlook of people in Mesopotamia.
      a. The land is desert; only irrigation made farming possible.
      b. Rivers provided fish and building material but also isolated Sumerian cities—making them into independent city states.
      c. Floods and droughts made life difficult and people pessimistic.

    C. The invention of writing and the first schools
1. Pictograph writing was the forerunner of cuneiform writing.
2. Sumerian cuneiform evolved from a pictographic system to an ideogram system and then to a phonetic system.
3. Scribal schools were centers of learning and culture.
    D. Mesopotamian thought and religion
1. Mathematics
    a. Mesopotamians developed the concept of place value.
    b. They emphasized practical uses for math, such as construction, rather than theorizing.
2. In medicine, evil spirits were believed to cause sickness, and treatment was by magic, prescription, and surgery.
3. Theology, religion, and mythology
    a. The Mesopotamians believed in a hierarchy of anthropomorphic gods who used nature to punish society.
    b. The aim of worship was to appease the gods.
    c. The Mesopotamians created myths and an epic poem—*The Epic of Gilgamesh*—to explain the creation of earth.
    E. Sumerian society
1. Sumerian society was made up of nobles, free clients, commoners, and slaves.
2. The king was supreme, and kingship was hereditary.
3. The nobility—the king and his family, the chief priests, and the high palace officials—controlled most of the wealth and held most of the power.
4. The commoners were free and had a political voice.

V. The spread of Mesopotamian culture
    A. In 2331 B.C., Sargon, a Semitic chieftain, conquered Sumer.
1. He spread Mesopotamian culture throughout and beyond the Fertile Crescent.
2. The Ebla tablets reveal much about Sargon's work and the extent of Mesopotamian influence.
    a. Excavations in 1975 and 1993 show that the Eblaites transmitted the heritage of Mesopotamia to other ports of Syria.
    B. The triumph of Babylon
1. Babylon's position as a center of commerce helped Hammurabi unify Mesopotamia.
    a. He conquered Assyria, Sumer, and Akkad.
    b. He made Marduk the god of all Mesopotamians, thus making Babylon the religious center of Mesopotamia.
2. Hammurabi's genius enabled Babylon to become the cultural center of Mesopotamia.
    C. Life under Hammurabi
1. Hammurabi's code was based on several principles.
    a. Equality before the law did not exist: there were milder penalties for members of the aristocracy than for commoners and slaves.
    b. When criminal and victim were social equals, the punishment was equal to the crime.
    c. Individuals represented themselves, fair trials were guaranteed, and judges could not change a verdict.
    d. The law provided protection for the consumer.

        e.   The code contains many laws about farming, irrigation, crops, and animals.

        f.   Marriage was a business arrangement between the groom-to-be and his future father-in-law.

        g.   Husbands had absolute power; he could sell his wife and children into slavery.

VI. The Kassite Interlude (1500-1200 B.C.)

    A. The Kassites came from the north and conquered Babylonia.

        1.   They gave Babylonia 300 years of peace and prosperity.

        2.   They are of great importance because they spread Mesopotamian culture to others.

VII. Egypt: land of the pharaohs (3100-1200 B.C.)

    A. Geography

        1.   Egypt was known as the "gift of the Nile": annual flooding made crop raising easy and Egypt prosperous.

        2.   The Nile unified Egypt—by 3100 B.C. it had brought 40 communities together.

        3.   Egypt was nearly self-sufficient in raw materials.

        4.   Geography shielded Egypt from invasion and immigration, but not entirely.

    B. The god-king of Egypt

        1.   Egypt was politically unified under a king who was considered to be the god Horus in human form.

        2.   The king-god had a great house, called pharaoh, and great tomb—called pyramid.

            a.   The theory that the Egyptian idea of kingship came from Nubia is probably wrong.

    C. The pharaoh's people

        1.   Social mobility existed, but most people were tied to the land and subject to forced labor.

        2.   Peasants could be forced to work on pyramids and canals and to serve in the pharaoh's army.

        3.   The pharaoh's role was to prevent internal chaos, which could lead to war and invasion.

    D. The Hyksos in Egypt (1640-1570 B.C.)

        1.   About 1800 B.C., Semites (Hyksos) began to push into Egypt, Mesopotamia, and Syria from the Arabian peninsula.

        2.   Their "invasion" of Egypt was probably gradual and peaceful.

        3.   The Hyksos brought new ideas and techniques—such as making bronze.

    E. The New Kingdom: Revival and Empire in Egypt (1570-1200 B.C.)

        1.   The pharaohs of the Eighteenth Dynasty created the first Egyptian empire.

            a.   The pharaoh Akhenaten was interested in religion, not conquests.

            b.   He and his wife, Nefertiti, believed that the sun-god Aton was the only god.

            c.   They attempted to impose monotheism on Egypt, in direct opposition to traditional Egyptian beliefs and the established priesthood.

        2.   Akhenaten's monotheism was unpopular and failed to take hold.

VIII. The Hittite Empire
    A. The Rise of the Hittites
        1. Hittites were a part of the massive Indo-European migrations that began around 2000 B.C.
            a. The term *Indo-European* refers to a large family of languages spoken throughout most of Europe and much of the Near East.
            b. The original home of the Indo-Europeans may have been central Europe.
        2. Hittite diffusion into Anatolia was peaceful, characterized by intermarriage and alliance.
    B. Hittite society
        1. Hattusilis I led the Hittites to conquer Anatolia and then moved eastward as far as Babylon.
        2. Hittite society was headed by a royal family and an often rebellious aristocracy.
        3. The Hittites assimilated the Mesopotamian culture.
    C. The era of Hittite greatness (ca 1475-1200 B.C.)
        1. Through the use of iron for weapons and through wise diplomacy, the Hittites came to control much of the Near East.
            a. They defeated the Egyptians at the battle of Kadesh (ca 1300 B.C.), and then formed an alliance with them to prevent future wars.
            b. The Hittites made peace with the Egyptians and then the Babylonians—all of which made for an important exhange of ideas in the Near East.
        2. The Hittites provided the Near East with an interlude of peace.
IX. The fall of empires and the survival of cultures (1200 B.C.)
    A. Political chaos
        1. In the late thirteenth century B.C. invaders destroyed both the Hittite and the Egyptian empires.
            a. The "Sea Peoples," part of a larger movement of people, dealt both empires a serious blow.
    B. Cultural endurance and dissemination
        1. Palestine, Syria, and Anatolia absorbed Sumerian and Egyptian social, economic, and cultural patterns.
        2. But even before this, Palestine and Syria had walled towns and traded internationally.
        3. The Egyptians found the Phoenicians were advanced in shipbuilding.
        4. In northern Syria, Semite cities were common and cultural exchange with Mesopotamia occurred.
        5. Anatolia also follows this pattern: native cultures that adopted Egyptian and Mesopotamian culture—while introducing new technologies and ideas.

Review Questions

Check your understanding of this chapter by answering the following questions.

    1. What were the major accomplishments of the Paleolithic peoples? Why were their lives so precarious?

2. Why are the artistic creations of Paleolithic and Neolithic peoples so important to historians?

3. Explain the impact that systematic agriculture had on the lives of these early peoples. Why did farming and the domestication of animals constitute a revolution in human life?

4. What effect did the geography of Mesopotamia have on the lives of the people who lived between the Tigris and Euphrates rivers?

5. What importance did the Nile River have in the economic and political development of Egypt?

6. What was the role of the pharaoh in Egyptian society?

7. Why were artistic works placed in the pharaoh's tomb?

8. How much freedom existed in Egyptian society? Was Egypt a slave state?

9. Who unified Mesopotamia and how was unification accomplished? Was it inevitable that Mesopotamia became unified?

10. How did Sumerian writing evolve?

11. What were the Mesopotamian religious beliefs? How did the Mesopotamians explain life and the universe?

12. Define the term *myth*. What role has myth played in Western culture? Does society live by myths today?

13. Describe Mesopotamian family and marriage practices. How were women and children treated in Mesopotamian society? How do you account for their powerlessness?

14. Who were the Kassites and why were they important?

15. What were the religious beliefs of Akhenaten and his wife, Nefertiti? Why were their ideas seen as a threat by some Egyptians?

16. Who were the Indo-Europeans and what impact did they have on the history of the Near East?

17. Who were the Hyksos and what changes did they bring to Egypt? What was the Egyptian response?

18. What were the contributions of the Hittites to Near Eastern history?

19. What was the cause of the coming of the "dark age" in the thirteenth century B.C.?

Study-Review Exercises

Define the following key concepts and terms.

history

civilization

pankus

anthropomorphic gods

monotheism

cuneiform

patriarch

systematic agriculture

place value

pharaoh

Identify and explain the significance of the following people and terms.

Neanderthal Man

Charles Darwin

Marduk

Mursilis I

Amon-Re

Sea Peoples

Ebla tablets

Epic of Gilgamesh

Akhenaten

Nefertiti

Homo sapiens

Sumer

Indo-European

Code of Hammurabi

Sargon

Eighteenth Dynasty pharaohs

Battle of Kadesh

Explain who the following groups of people were and why they were important.
Sumerians

Semites

Kassites

Amorites

Hittites

Hyksos

Test your understanding of the chapter by providing the correct answers.

1. The author of *On the Origin of Species* (1859). _____

2. His law code demanded that the punishment fit the crime. _____

3. A term meaning "king" or "great house." _____

4. The people whom the Egyptians called the "Rulers of the Uplands." _____

5. The pharaoh who advocated monotheism. _____

6. The two empires that fell in the thirteenth century B.C. _____ and _____

7. The capital city of Mesopotamia under Hammurabi. _____

8. Most ordinary people in ancient Egypt *were/were not* tied to the land and subject to forced labor.

9. Under Hammurabi's code, the husband *could/could not* sell his wife and children into slavery.

10. The Agricultural Revolution is the chief event of the *Paleolithic/Neolithic* Age.

11. Mesopotamia was the land between the _____ and _____ rivers.

12. One of the puzzles of ancient history is the identity of the "_____ Peoples" who invaded and destroyed the Hittite and Egyptian empires in the thirteenth century B.C.

13. The Greek researcher who is known as the "father of history." _____

Place the following events in correct chronological order.

Rise of the Hittite Empire
Unification of Mesopotamia under Babylon
Reign of Akhenaten
Establishment of Sumer
Hyksos invasion of Egypt
Establishment of systematic agriculture

1.

2.

3.

4.

5.

6.

Major Political Ideas

1. For thousands of years Paleolithic peoples roamed the earth in search of food. Why did people begin to live in permanent locations and what impact did this have on their political life? What is the difference between a tribal chieftain and an urban king?

2. The focal point of religious and political life in ancient Egypt was the godking pharaoh, who ruled over a unified state. How did geographic and climatic factors contribute to this political structure, and what were the chief features of the pharaoh's power and of Egyptian religion? How did Akhenaten's religious beliefs threaten this system?

Issues for Essays and Discussion

1. Why did Babylon become a cultural center of Mesopotamia? Discuss this by making reference to the origins of Babylon and the contributions of Hammurabi, the Mesopotamians, and the Sumerians in law, language, and religion.

2. Much of the early history of the Near East is that of one culture established and then overthrown by another. Nevertheless, a common civilization emerged. Why? What were the political, social, religious, and economic elements of this civilization?

Interpretation of Visual Sources

Study the photograph of the city of Ur, particularly the ziggurat of Urnammu in the lower right-hand corner. Does the form of the structure indicate its function? What do you know about Mesopotamian environment and culture that would begin to explain the shape of the building and its materials?

Geography

Rivers "acted as a powerful restraining force, particularly on Sumerian political development." Discuss and explain this statement by making reference to the relationship between the physical environment and politics.

On Outline Map 1.1 provided, and using Map 1.1 and Map 1.2 in the textbook as a reference, mark the following:

1. The boundaries of Mesopotamia and the location of Babylon, Ur, Uruk, the cities of Sumer, and the Fertile Crescent.

2. The location of the early Neolithic farming sites of Jericho, Çatal Hüyük, Tepe Yahya, Jarmo, and Hacilar.

3. The Nile River valley, the Nile Delta, the Nubian Desert, and the cataracts of the Nile.

Outline Map 1.1

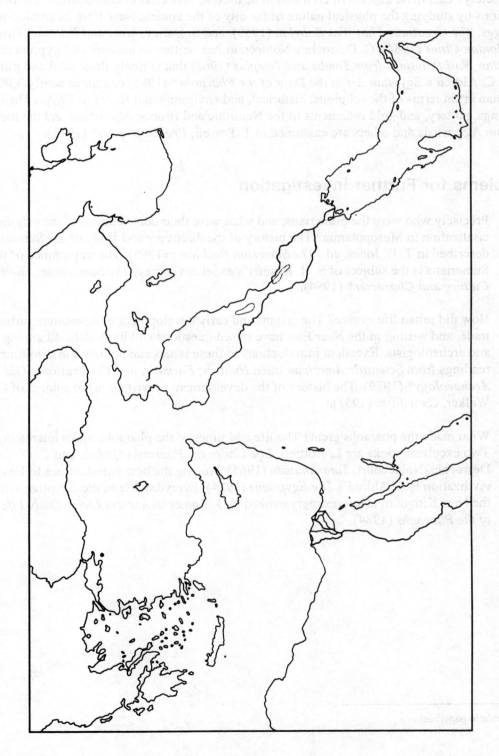

Understanding History Through the Arts

How do ancient Near Eastern art and architecture mirror the economic, social, and political life of that society? Can these aspects of civilization be used as historical documentation? Answer these questions by studying the physical nature of the city of the ancient Near East, beginning with H. W. F. Saggs, *The Greatness That Was Babylon* (1989), and S. Dalley, *Mari and Karana: Two Old Babylonian Cities* (1984). C. Desroches-Noblecourt has written an account of Egyptian art entitled *Egyptian Wall Paintings from Tombs and Temples* (1962) that is richly illustrated and informative, while C. Aldred's *Egyptian Art in the Days of the Pharaohs** (1985) examines nearly 3,000 years of Egyptian art in terms of the religious, historical, and environmental forces of Egypt. The early cave paintings, pottery, and gold ornaments of the Neolithic and Bronze Age artists and the metalwork of the Iron Age artists and others are examined in T. Powell, *Prehistoric Art** (1985).

Problems for Further Investigation

1. Precisely who were the Sumerians, and what were their contributions to the origins of civilization in Mesopotamia? The history of the discovery and study of the Sumerians is described in T. B. Jones, ed., *The Sumerian Problem** (1969). The importance of the Sumerians is the subject of S. H. Kramer's excellent survey, *The Sumerians: Their History, Culture and Character** (1984).

2. How did urban life evolve? The origins and early development of agriculture, urban life, trade, and writing in the Near East have raised questions still hotly debated among historians and archeologists. Excellent introductions to these issues can be found in a volume of readings from *Scientific American* titled *Hunters, Farmers, and Civilizations: Old World Archaeology** (1979). The history of the development of writing is the subject of C. B. F. Walker, *Cuneiform* (1987).

3. What made the pharaohs great? The life and times of the pharaohs make interesting reading. Two excellent books are L. Cottrell, *Life Under the Pharaohs* (1964), and C. Desroches-Noblecourt, *Tutankhamen* (1965). Among the best introductions to Egyptian civilization is C. Aldred's *The Egyptians* (1984). Everyday life in the Egyptian village during the New Kingdom is interestingly evoked by J. Romer in *Ancient Lives: Daily Life in Egypt of the Pharaohs* (1984).

---

*Available in paperback.

Self-Test Multiple-Choice Questions

<u>Do</u> <u>not</u> assume that these questions will appear on any examination. It is recommended that you <u>not</u> memorize these questions, but use them only as a self-test. Answers are at the end of this book.

1. Which of the following characterized Paleolithic society?
    a. Urban life
    b. Hunting technology and primitive art
    c. Written language
    d. Farming and irrigation

2. The most influential ancient Near Eastern culture was the
    a. Egyptian.
    b. Mesopotamian.
    c. Assyrian.
    d. Hittite.

3. Amon-Re was the Egyptian god (king) of
    a. the dead.
    b. fertility.
    c. the gods.
    d. agriculture.

4. Part of the Hittite success in war against Egyptians was due to
    a. their refusal to adapt to Egyptian culture.
    b. their refusal to use diplomacy to gain power.
    c. their use of iron to make weapons.
    d. their rejection of Mesopotamian culture.

5. According to the Code of Hammurabi, tavernkeepers who watered down drinks were
    a. sent to jail.
    b. sold into slavery.
    c. drowned.
    d. dragged through a field.

6. The Ebla tablets, discovered in 1976, prove
    a. the close connection between Mesopotamia and Syria, plus the presence of a written language.
    b. that there was no Mesopotamian influence on the Bible.
    c. that Mesopotamian culture remained only in Mesopotamia.
    d. that no link existed between Mesopotamian literature and religion and Old Testament theology.

7. Which of the following was the goal of King Hammurabi of Babylon?
   a. To completely erase the concept of tribal kingship
   b. To unify Mesopotamia with Babylon at its head
   c. To replace the worship of the god Marduk with himself
   d. To live at peace with his neighbors, regardless of the cost

8. The Semitic chieftain who conquered Sumer in 2331 B.C. was
   a. Hammurabi.
   b. Marduk.
   c. Osiris.
   d. Sargon.

9. The law code of King Hammurabi
   a. included much legislation on agriculture and irrigation canals.
   b. handed down mild punishments for almost all crimes.
   c. treated all social classes equally.
   d. did not protect the consumer.

10. Irrigation was an essential agricultural method of all of the following *except*
    a. Egypt.
    b. Anatolia.
    c. Syria.
    d. Assyria.

11. Geography influenced Sumerian society by
    a. making communication within the region easy.
    b. making communication within the region difficult.
    c. providing the inhabitants with everything they needed.
    d. providing an abundance of precious metals.

12. Rivers in Mesopotamia were important because they
    a. were a unifying factor.
    b. drained off excess water.
    c. kept out invaders.
    d. made irrigation possible.

13. The Sumerians responded to their environment by
    a. achieving rapid political unification.
    b. developing a pessimistic view of life.
    c. appreciating the value of floods.
    d. developing an appreciation of nature.

14. After 155 years the dynasty established by Hammurabi fell to a conquering group called the
    a. Semites.
    b. Kassites.
    c. Egyptians.
    d. Sumerians.

15. The *lugal* in Mesopotamia was the
    a. secular war leader and administrator.
    b. chief priest of the temple.
    c. council of elders.
    d. legal owner of a slave.

16. Marduk was the chief god of the
    a. Sumerians.
    b. Egyptians.
    c. Amorites.
    d. Hittites.

17. The common people of Egypt were
    a. completely without legal rights.
    b. at the bottom of the social scale.
    c. divided on the basis of color.
    d. related to the Mesopotamians.

18. The hero of the first epic poem, produced by the Sumerians, was
    a. Enlil.
    b. Osiris.
    c. Gilgamesh.
    d. Khunanup.

19. The Hittites were
    a. Persian.
    b. Semites.
    c. Akkadians.
    d. Indo-Europeans.

20. The Egyptian god Osiris was closely associated with
    a. Isis.
    b. Aton.
    c. Amon-Re.
    d. Serapis.

21. Akhenaten was interested in fostering
    a. military expansion.
    b. worship of Aton.
    c. agricultural improvements.
    d. a return to traditional values.

22. The real transformation of human life occurred when
    a. iron was discovered.
    b. religion replaced mythology.
    c. nomadic life was replaced by systematic agriculture.
    d. free citizenship evolved in Sumer.

23. The earliest known attempts to answer the question "how did it all begin" were undertaken by
    a. the lawgiver Hammurabi in his codes.
    b. the early myths.
    c. Egyptian religion.
    d. Akhenaten's monotheism.

24. Although the common folk in Egypt were often exploited, they did have
    a. release from taxation.
    b. freedom from forced labor.
    c. release from military service.
    d. the right to appeal the actions of their landlord.

25. Because of its natural resources and geography, ancient Egypt
    a. was nearly self-sufficient in raw materials.
    b. could use the Nile to gain raw materials from the south.
    c. turned to conquest to make up for its lack of resources.
    d. established trading networks along its Mediterranean coast for necessary food and raw materials.

Studying Effectively—Exercise 1

The Best Way to Underline or Highlight Your Textbook

Underlining (or highlighting with a felt-tipped pen, as many students prefer) plays an important part in the learning process in college sources. Underlining your textbook provides you with a permanent record of what you want to learn. It helps in your efforts to master the material and prepare for exams.

Further Suggestions

1. *Read an entire section through before you underline or highlight it.* Then, as you read it a second time, pick out and underline key facts, main points, concepts, ideas, and conclusions.

2. *Identify the major points in each paragraph.* Then number *the main points* in the margin to help you remember them. Numbering helps make the main points stand out clearly, which is a major purpose of all underlining or highlighting.

3. *Avoid false economies.* The alternative to marking your books is making detailed written notes, which is more difficult and much more time consuming. Some students do not mark their books because they are afraid that the bookstores will not buy them back. This is an unwise way to try to save money because by refusing to mark your books, you are reducing your chances of doing your best and thus endangering your whole college investment.

    Carefully underlined books are *an important personal record of your study of western history. Your* books become valuable reference works, helping you recall important learning experiences and forming the core of your library in future years.

Exercise

1. Read the following passage once as a whole.

2. Read it a second time to underline or highlight it. Number the points.

3. On completion, compare your underlining with the model on the next page, which is an example of reasonable and useful underlining.

4. Finally, compare the underlined section with the chapter outline in the *Study Guide*. You will see how the outline summary is an aid in learning how to underline major points.

Egypt, The Land of the Pharaohs (3100-1200 B.C.)

The Greek historian and traveler Herodotus in the fifth century B.C. called Egypt the "gift of the Nile." No other single geographical factor had such a fundamental and profound impact on the shaping of Egyptian life, society, and history as the Nile. Unlike the rivers of Mesopotamia it rarely brought death and destruction by devastating entire cities. The river was primarily a creative force. The Egyptians never feared the relatively calm Nile in the way the Mesopotamians feared their rivers. Instead they sang its praises:

> *Hail to thee, O Nile, that issues from the earth and comes to keep Egypt alive! . . .*
> *He that waters the meadows which Re created,*
> *He that makes to drink the desert . . .*
> *He who makes barley and brings emmer [wheat] into being . . .*
> *He who brings grass into being for the cattle.*
> *He who makes every beloved tree to grow . . .*
> *O Nile, verdant art thou, who makest man and cattle to live.*

In the mind of the Egyptians, the Nile was the supreme fertilizer and renewer of the land. Each September the Nile floods its valley, transforming it into a huge area of marsh or lagoon. By the end of November the water retreats, leaving behind a thin covering of fertile mud ready to be planted with crops.

The annual flood made the growing of abundant crops almost effortless, especially in southern Egypt. Herodotus, used to the rigors of Greek agriculture, was amazed by the ease with which the Egyptians raised crops:

> *For indeed without trouble they obtain crops from the land more easily than all other men. . . .*
> *They do not labor to dig furrows with the plough or hoe or do the work which other men do to raise grain. But when the river by itself inundates the fields and the water recedes, then each man, having sown his field, sends pigs into it. When the pigs trample down the seed, he waits for the harvest. Then when the pigs thresh the grain, he gets his crop.*

As late as 1822, John Burckhardt, an English traveler, watched nomads sowing grain by digging large holes in the mud and throwing in seeds. The extraordinary fertility of the Nile valley made it easy to produce an annual agricultural surplus, which in turn sustained a growing and prosperous population.

Whereas the Tigris and Euphrates and their many tributaries carved up Mesopotamia into isolated areas, the Nile unified Egypt. The river was the principal highway, promoting easy communication throughout the valley. As individual bands of settlers moved into the Nile Valley, they created stable agricultural communities. By about 3100 B.C. there were some forty of these communities in constant contact with one another. This contact, encouraged and facilitated by the Nile, virtually ensured the early political unification of Egypt.

Egypt was fortunate in that it was nearly self-sufficient. Besides the fertility of its soil, Egypt possessed enormous quantities of stone, which served as the raw material of architecture and sculpture. Abundant clay was available for pottery, as was gold for jewelry and ornaments. The raw materials that Egypt lacked were close at hand. The Egyptians could obtain copper from Sinai and timber from Lebanon. They had little cause to look to the outside world for their essential needs, which helps to explain the insular quality of Egyptian life.

Geography further encouraged isolation by closing Egypt off from the outside world. To the east and west of the Nile valley stretch grim deserts. The Nubian Desert and the cataracts of the Nile discouraged penetration from the south. Only in the north did the Mediterranean Sea leave Egypt exposed. Thus, geography shielded Egypt from invasion and from extensive immigration. Unlike the Mesopotamians, the Egyptians enjoyed centuries of peace and tranquility during which they could devote most of their resources to peaceful development of their distinctive civilization.

Yet Egypt was not completely sealed off. As early as 3250 B.C., Mesopotamian influences, notably architectural techniques and materials and perhaps even writing, made themselves felt in Egyptian life. Still later, from 1680 to 1580 B.C., northern Egypt was ruled by foreign invaders, the Hyksos. Infrequent though they were, such periods of foreign influence fertilized Egyptian culture without changing it in any fundamental way.

The God-King of Egypt

The geographical unity of Egypt quickly gave rise to political unification of the country under the authority of a king whom the Egyptians called "pharaoh." The details of this process have been lost. The Egyptians themselves told of a great king, Menes, who united Egypt into a single kingdom around 3100 B.C. Thereafter the Egyptians divided their history into *dynasties,* or families of kings. For modern historical purposes, however, it is more useful to divide Egyptian history into periods. The political unification of Egypt ushered in the period known as the Old Kingdom, an era remarkable for its prosperity, artistic flowering, and the evolution of religious beliefs.

Egypt, The Land of the Pharaohs (3100-1200 B.C.)

Geography

1

The Greek historian and traveler Herodotus in the fifth century B.C. called Egypt the "gift of the Nile." No other single geographical factor had such a fundamental and profound impact on the shaping of Egyptian life, society, and history as the Nile. Unlike the rivers of Mesopotamia it rarely brought death and destruction by devastating entire cities. The river was primarily a creative force. The Egyptians never feared the relatively calm Nile in the way the Mesopotamians feared their rivers. Instead they sang its praises

> *Hail to thee, O Nile, that issues from the earth and comes to keep Egypt*
> *alive! . . .*
> *He that waters the meadows which Re created,*
> *He that makes to drink the desert . . .*
> *He who makes barley and brings emmer [wheat] into being . . .*
> *He who brings grass into being for the cattle.*
> *He who makes every beloved tree to grow . . .*
> *O Nile, verdant art thou, who makest man and cattle to live.*

1a

In the mind of the Egyptians, the Nile was the supreme fertilizer and renewer of the land. Each September the Nile floods its valley, transforming it into a huge area of marsh or lagoon. By the end of November the water retreats, leaving behind a thin covering of fertile mud ready to be planted with crops. The annual flood made the growing of abundant crops almost effortless, especially in southern Egypt. Herodotus, used to the rigors of Greek agriculture, was amazed by the ease with which the Egyptians raised crops:

> *For indeed without trouble they obtain crops from the lend more easily*
> *than all other men. . . . They do not labor to dig furrows with the plough*
> *or hoe or do the work which other men do to raise grain. But when the*
> *river by itself inundates the fields and the water recedes, then each man,*
> *having sown his field, sends pigs into it. When the pigs trample down the*
> *seed, he waits for the harvest. Then when the pigs thresh the grain, he gets*
> *his crop.*

2

As late as 1822, John Burckhardt, an English traveler, watched nomads sowing grain by digging large holes in the mud and throwing in seeds. The extraordinary fertility of the Nile valley made it easy to produce an annual agricultural surplus, which in turn sustained a growing and prosperous population.

Whereas the Tigris and Euphrates and their many tributaries carved up Mesopotamia into isolated areas, the Nile unified Egypt. The river was the principal highway, promoting easy communication throughout the valley. As individual bands of settlers moved into the Nile Valley, they created stable agricultural communities. By about 3100 B.C. there were some forty of these communities in constant contact with one another. This contact, encouraged and facilitated by the Nile, virtually ensured the early political unification of Egypt.

3   <u>Egypt was fortunate in that it was nearly self-sufficient</u>. Besides the fertility of its soil, Egypt possessed enormous quantities of stone, which served as the raw material of architecture and sculpture. Abundant clay was available for pottery, as was gold for jewelry and ornaments. The raw materials that Egypt lacked were close at hand. The Egyptians could obtain copper from Sinai and timber from Lebanon. They had little cause to look to the outside world for their essential needs, which helps to explain the insular quality of Egyptian life.

4   <u>Geography further encouraged isolation by closing Egypt off from the outside world</u>. To the east and west of the Nile valley stretch grim deserts. The Nubian Desert and the cataracts of the Nile discouraged penetration from the south. Only in the north did the Mediterranean Sea leave Egypt exposed. Thus, geography shielded Egypt from invasion and from extensive immigration. Unlike the Mesopotamians, the Egyptians enjoyed centuries of peace and tranquility during which they could devote most of their resources to peaceful development of their distinctive civilization.

5   <u>Yet Egypt was not completely sealed off</u>. As early as 3250 B.C., Mesopotamian influences, notably architectural techniques and materials and perhaps even writing, made themselves felt in Egyptian life. Still later, from 1680 to 1580 B.C., northern Egypt was ruled by foreign invaders, the Hyksos.

6   <u>Infrequent though they were, such periods of foreign influence fertilized Egyptian culture without changing it in any fundamental way</u>.

The God-King of Egypt

The geographical unity of Egypt quickly gave rise to political unification of the country under the authority of a king whom the Egyptians called "pharaoh." The details of this process have been lost. The Egyptians themselves told of a great king, Menes, who united Egypt into a single kingdom around 3100 B.C. Thereafter the Egyptians divided their history into *dynasties,* or families of kings. For modern historical purposes, however, it is more useful to divide Egyptian history into periods. The political unification of Egypt ushered in the period known as the Old Kingdom, an era remarkable for its prosperity, artistic flowering, and the evolution of religious beliefs.

Chapter 2

Small Kingdoms and Mighty Empires in the Near East

Learning Objectives

After reading and studying this chapter you should be able to:

1. describe the factors that led to the dissolution of Egypt and the creation of small kingdoms in the wake of Egypt's decline.

2. distinguish Hebrew life and thought from that of the other peoples of the ancient Near East.

3. describe the factors that led to Assyrian dominance in the ninth and eighth centuries B.C.

4. explain how Zoroastrian beliefs influenced both Judaism and Christianity.

Chapter Summary

Between the time when the empires of the Hittites and the Egyptians were destroyed by invaders, and the time when Assyrian rule was imposed on the area, the Near East existed as a patchwork of small, independent kingdoms. This chapter opens with a description of how a weakened Egypt was given new life when overrun by its African neighbors, the Nubians and the Libyans, who, at the same time, assimilated Egyptian culture. By 700 B.C., Egypt was reunited, but it did not re-emerge as an empire.

The power vacuum that followed the fall of the great empires was significant because it allowed less powerful peoples to settle and prosper independently and, as a result, make particularly important contributions to Western society. Foremost among these peoples were the Phoenicians, who explored the Mediterranean Sea and built a prosperous commercial network, and the Hebrews. Modern archeology confirms the Old Testament account of the Hebrews' move from Mesopotamia into Canaan, their enslavement in Egypt and subsequent liberation, and the establishment of a homeland in Palestine. Important in this process was the Hebrews' vision of their god, Yahweh. A covenant with Yahweh—centering on the Ten Commandments—formed the basis of Hebrew life and law. The kings Saul, David, and Solomon, along with the great prophets, unified the Hebrews into a prosperous society based on high standards of mercy and justice. Their unique monotheism, combined with settled agriculture and urban life, provided the framework for the Hebrews' daily life.

A turning point in the Near East occurred in the ninth century with the rise of the Assyrians, the most warlike peoples the Near East had yet known. For two hundred years the Assyrians ruled an empire that stretched from the Persian Gulf across the Fertile Crescent and westward through northern Egypt. Despite their brutality, the Assyrians owed their success less to calculated terrorism than to efficient military organization. The Assyrian empire fell swiftly in 612 B.C., and had it not been for modern archeological work, may have remained unknown.

The Persian Empire began in 550 B.C. with the first conquests of Cyrus the Great. The next two hundred years of Persian rule in the Near East were marked by efficient administration and respect for the diverse cultures of conquered states. Out of this benevolent rule came an important new religion, Zoroastrianism, which gave to Western society the idea of individual choice in the struggle between goodness and evil.

Study Outline

Use this outline to preview the chapter before you read a particular section in your textbook and then as a self-check to test your reading comprehension after you have read the chapter section.

    I. Phoenicia and its neighbors
      A. The Phoenicians were Semites who lived in coastal cities in today's Lebanon
        1. They were merchants and explorers of Tyre, Sidon, and Byblos who founded Carthage in 813 B.C.
        2. They developed an alphabet based on one letter for one sound.
        3. Their port city of Ugacit shows us how a small state increased trade contacts and preserved culture.
    II. Egypt, a shattered kingdom
      A. The invasions of the thirteenth century B.C. inaugurated an era of weakness and confusion.
        1. The Third Intermediate Period (eleventh to seventh centuries B.C.) was characterized by political fragmentation and loss of power.
        2. From 950 to 730 B.C. northern Egypt was ruled by the Libyans, while southern Egypt came under the control of the Africans of Nubia.
        3. Both the Nubians and the Libyans adopted the Egyptian culture.
      B. In the eighth century B.C., Egypt was reunified by the African Kingdom of Kush.
        1. The king of Kush, Piankhy, brought unity and peace to Egypt, but not a revival of empire.
        2. Egyptian culture had a massive impact on northeastern Africa.
   III. The children of Israel
      A. The power vacuum created by the fall of the Hittite and Egyptian states allowed lesser states, such as Syria, Phoenicia, and Palestine, to thrive.
        1. The Philistines settled along the coast of Palestine and became farmers.
        2. The small kingdom of the ancient Jews or Hebrews arose south of Phoenicia.
        3. They migrated into the Nile Delta and were enslaved and then escaped to the Sinai and to Palestine.
        4. The Bible is a religious document that contains historical material as well as myths and legends.
        5. Despite war, at times the Hebrews had friendly contact with their neighbors, and some even worshiped Baal.
      B. Hebrews struggled against the Philistines.
        1. Under Saul and David, the twelve tribes became united under a monarchy.

2. David led them to defeat the Philistines and capture Jerusalem.
3. King Solomon built a great temple in Jerusalem and extended Hebrew power.
   a. He replaced the tribal division of Israel with twelve administrative units.
   b. In addition to the temple, he built cities, palaces, fortresses, and roads.
4. At Solomon's death the kingdom was divided in two.
   a. The northern half became Israel, while the southern half was Judah, with its capital still at Jerusalem.
   b. War broke out between these two Hebrew kingdoms.
   c. The northern half of the kingdom was destroyed by the Assyrians, but the southern half became the center of Judaism.
   d. This kingdom of Judah survived until it was crushed by the Babylonians and its survivors were sent into exile; many were freed by the Persians in 538 B.C.
   e. During and just after this "Babylonian Captivity," the exiles redefined their beliefs into the law of Yahweh—these believers are called *Jews*.

C. The evolution of Jewish religion
1. The Hebrew religion was monotheistic, centered on the covenant between Yahweh and the Hebrew people.
   a. Yahweh was unique in that he was eventually defined as having no human form and as the only god.
   b. The Hebrews did not proselytize as the later Christians did.
2. Jewish law and ethics, with their stress on justice and mercy, evolved from the Ten Commandments of Yahweh and the words of the prophets.
   a. The early codes (the Torah) originated from Moses and were harsh, while the later codes of the prophets were more humanitarian.
   b. The prophet Jeremiah's emphasis on mercy and justice represents a positive shift in Hebrew thinking to a god of forgiveness and mercy.
   c. The religions of the modern West are deeply rooted in Judaism.

D. Daily life in Israel
1. The end of nomadic life and coming of urban life changed family and marriage customs.
   a. Communal landownership gave way to family ownership.
   b. The extended tribal family gave way to the nuclear family, and women became less free, confined to the home, and religion became male-oriented.
   c. The typical marriage was monogamous, and a virtuous wife was highly respected and honored.
   d. Jewish society placed strong emphasis on rearing children; both parents played a role in the child's education.
2. Land was precious to the family, but peace and prosperity brought about a decline of the family farm and a rise of large estates and slave labor.
3. The rise of urban life brought new job opportunities and increased trade.
   a. Craft and trade specialization thrived, often under guilds.
   b. Under Solomon trade and commerce was dominated by the king and/or foreigners.
   c. The Torah is basically the Mosaic law, while the Talmud is a record of civil and ceremonial law begun during the Babylonian Captivity.
   d. The Talmud states regulations with regard to diet and food preparation—because of concern about eating dangerous food.

IV. Assyria, the military monarchy
   A. The power of Assyria followed the rise of militarism and political cohesion among the Assyrians.
      1. King Shalmaneser unleashed the first of the Assyrian attacks on Syria and Palestine in 859 B.C.
      2. Under Tiglath-pileser III and Sargon II, the Assyrians created an empire that extended from Mesopotamia to central Egypt.
      3. Conquest bred revolt, which in turn led to brutal Assyrian retaliation.
      4. Assyrian success was due to and effective military organization and new military techniques and equipment.
   B. Assyrian rule and culture
      1. The Assyrians organized an empire with provinces and dependent states.
      2. The Babylonians and the Medes destroyed the Assyrian Empire in 612 B.C.
      3. The Assyrians disappeared from history until Nineveh was excavated in 1839. Archeologists have unearthed many artistic masterpieces (palace reliefs) that convey detailed information about Assyrian life.
      4. Many Assyrian innovations were taken over by the Persians.

V. Chaldean Babylonia (626-539 B.C.)
   A. The decline of Assyria led to a new "Chaldean" dynasty in Babylonia.
      1. The Chaldean kin Nebuchadrezzar led Babylonia to take Syria and Judah—and destroy Jersualem and deport its people.
      2. Babylonia underwent great religious and economic revival—but it eventually fell.

VI. The empire of the Persian kings
   A. The Persians were Indo-European Iranians who unified many cultures under a tolerant and humane empire.
   B. Persia (modern Iran) was a land of mountains and plateau.
      1. The chief geographical feature of Persia is a central plateau between the Tigris-Euphrates valley and the Indus valley surrounded by high mountains.
      2. This explains Iran's position as the highway between East and West.
   C. The first Iranians—the coming of the Medes and Persians
      1. The first Iranians were nomadic Medes and Persians whose use of horses allowed them to conquer the natives.
      2. They established a patchwork of small kingdoms centered on agricultural towns.
      3. These towns became centers for agriculture, mineral extraction, and horsebreeding.
      4. The Iranians of the north, the Medes, grew strong enough to help overthrow the Assyrian Empire.
   D. The creation of the Persian Empire
      1. The founder of the Persian Empire, Cyrus the Great (559-530 B.C.), held enlightened views.
         a. He viewed Persia and Medea as the state of Iran.
         b. His empire gave respect, toleration, and protection to its conquered peoples.
         c. His first act after conquering the Medes was to unite them with the Persians.
      2. Next Cyrus won control of the west as far as the Greek coast of Anatolia.
      3. Then Cyrus marched to eastern Iran (Parthia and Bactria) to secure Iran from the pressure of warring nomads.
      4. He conquered Babylonia and gave protection to the Jews.

E. Thus spake Zarathustra: the religion of Iran
   1. At first Iranian religion was polytheistic, simple, and primitive.
   2. Zoroaster gave Iranian religion new ideas.
      a. Most information about Zoroaster comes from a collection of hymns and poems called *Zend Avesta*.
      b. Zoroaster preached that life is a battleground between good and evil.
      c. A person's eternal fate would be decided on the basis of his or her deeds in life.
      d. The conversion of King Darius to Zoroastrianism led to its spread throughout the empire.
F. Persia's world empire
   1. Cyrus's successors rounded out the Persian Empire by adding part of India in the east, and Anatolia, Egypt, and Libya in the west.
      a. The empire was divided into twenty *satrapies,* each ruled by governors—or *satrap*.
      b. Roads were built so that royal couriers could enable the king to keep in touch with his officials and subjects.
   2. For over two hundred years the Persians gave the Near East a period of peace.

Review Questions

Check your understanding of the chapter by answering the following questions.

1. Explain how the peoples of Nubia, Libya, and the Kingdom of Kush interacted with Egypt and its culture. What were the results?

2. Why is the Old Testament such an important source for historians in reconstructing Hebrew society? Provide examples.

3. What are the main features of Judaism? How important was religion in the daily life of the people?

4. What effect did the end of nomadic life have on Hebrew property and marriage practices?

5. Describe Hebrew attitudes toward children. What was childhood like for Hebrew sons and daughters?

6. What changes did prosperity and urbanization bring to Hebrew life?

7. What impact did Assyria have on the Near Eastern world? Was its influence long-lasting?

8. Describe the extent of the Assyrian Empire. What were the secrets of Assyrian success?

9. How did the discoveries of A. H. Layard shed new light on Assyrian history?

10. What made Iran the "highway between East and West"?

11. Describe the accomplishments of Cyrus the Great. Why was this conqueror regarded by many non-Persians as a liberator and benefactor?

12. Zoroaster gave the Near East some novel ideas about divinity and human life. What were these ideas?

13. Describe the Persian system of imperial rule. In what ways is it different from or similar to that of the Assyrians?

Study-Review Exercises

Define the following key concepts and terms.

nuclear family

monotheism

polygamy

monogamy

Yahweh

Covenant

Zoroastrianism

satrap

Torah

Identify and explain the significance of the following people and terms.

Sargon II

Nubians

Solomon's Jerusalem temple

Jews

Libyans

Phoenicians

Ten Commandments

Moses

Chaldians

Zend Avesta

Kingdom of Kush

Jeremiah

Ark of the Covenant

Old Testament

Nineveh

Cyrus the Great

Ugarit

Ahura

Medes

Persians

Magi

Test your understanding of the chapter by providing the correct answers.

1. With the coming of peace, more settled conditions, and prosperity, many Jewish farmers *increased/broke up* their landholding.

2. Compared with the early Hebrew law (the Torah) later legal tradition of the prophets in Hebrew society tended to be *more/less* humanitarian.

3. The one god of Jewish religion. _____

4. The African invaders of Egypt in the thirteenth century B.C. *did/did not* admire and adopt Egyptian culture.

5. The two groups of Iranian peoples united by Cyrus the Great. _____ and _____

6. With the rise of the Persian Empire, the balance of power in the Near East shifted *east/west* of Mesopotamia.

7. The provinces into which the Persians divided their empire. _____

Major Political Ideas

Hebrew law grew out of the covenant between the god Yahweh and the Hebrew people. Discuss this covenant in relationship to the Ten Commandments and the law that evolved from it. Explain how Hebrews thought about their god and the law changed through time.

The Assyrians dominated the Near East. How did they do this? What were their political and military methods and techniques? How did they differ from the views of Cyrus the Great? Be specific.

Issues for Essays and Discussion

1. Compare and contrast the ideas and beliefs of Judaism, the monotheism of Akhenaten (see Chapter 1), and Zoroastrianism.

2. What evidence exists to support the claim that the power vacuum resulting from the fall of the Hittite and Egyptian empires encouraged cultural advance among less powerful peoples?

3. The end of nomadic life and the rise of urban living in Israel led to some important changes in Jewish life. Discuss the changes affecting landownership, family life, marriage, the position of children, work, and slavery.

4. Describe the Jewish religion and how it evolved. What made it unique and is it important in the study of the history of the West?

Interpretation of Visual Sources

1. Study the photograph of the relief titled "Siege of the City". What does this tell us about Assyrian warfare—including practices, tactics, and weapons?

Geography

On Outline Map 2.3 provided, and using Map 2.2, Map 2.3, and Map 1.3 in the textbook as references, mark the following:

1. The boundaries of the Assyrian Empire and the location of Anatolia, Nineveh, Kalah, Ashur, Syria, Palestine, and Jerusalem.

2. The Persian Empire, the Caspian Sea, the Persian Gulf, the Indus Valley, the Tigris-Euphrates Valley, the central plateau of Iran, the region of Persis, Ecbatana, Lydia, and Sardis.

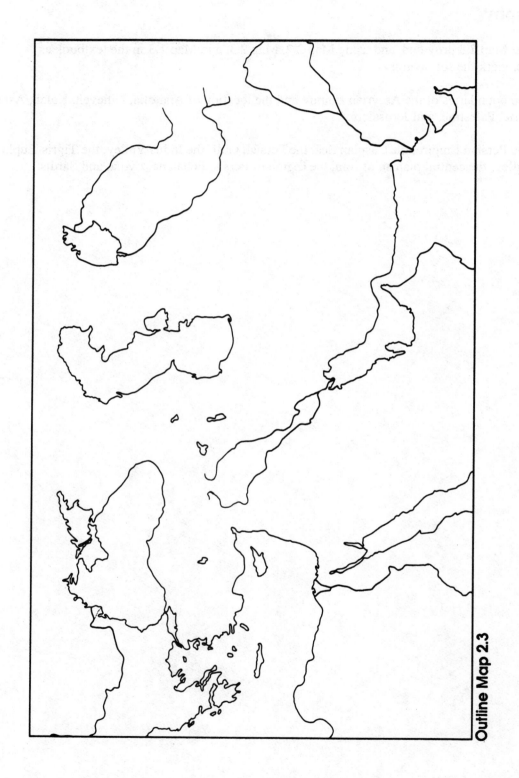

Outline Map 2.3

Understanding History Through the Arts

1. What were the accomplishments of the Babylonians, the Assyrians, and the Sumero-Akkadians in the arts? How did the artistic works of these people mirror the environments in which they lived? Begin your inquiry with A. Moortgat, *The Art of Ancient Mesopotamia: The Classical Art of the Near East* (1969).

2. Were the artists of Persia imitators of their neighbors, or did they produce an original art? This and many other aspects of Persian art are explored in R. W. Ferrier, ed., *Arts of Persia* (1989).

Problems for Further Investigation

1. How did monotheism evolve? Students interested in ancient Near Eastern monotheism should start with R. J. Christen and H. E. Hazelton, eds., *Monotheism and Moses** (1969), or the more general work, *A History of Religious Ideas,** 3 vols. (1978-1985), by M. Eliade. For Egyptian beliefs see C. Elmahdy, *Mummies, Myth and Magic* (1989), C. Hobson, *The World of the Pharaohs* (1987), and C. Aldred, *Akhenaten: King of Egypt* (1988).

2. What was life like in the ancient Near East? Problems of interpretation and investigation in the history of the ancient Near East are set forth, along with an excellent bibliography, in M. Coven Sky, *The Ancient Near Eastern Tradition** (1966). The impact of infectious diseases on ancient civilization is considered in W. McNeill, *Plagues and Peoples* (1976). For insight into the Assyrian character, see H. W. F. Saggs, *The Might That Was Assyria* (1984).

3. What was the position of women in Egyptian society? This and other issues are discussed in B. S. Lesko, ed., *Women's Earliest Records from Ancient Egypt and Western Asia* (1989).

4. Is it true that the biblical flood story did not originate with the Hebrews and that Hammurabi's law code is not the oldest? The sources of the story and the code and other subjects relating to the ancient Near East are considered in S. N. Kramer, *History Begins at Sumer: Twenty-Seven "Firsts" in Man's Recorded History** (1959), and S. Dalley, *Myths from Mesopotamia: Creation, the Flood, Gilgamesh and Others* (1989).

5. How can the Bible be used to understand culture and daily life in Hebrew society? The Old Testament is one of the best sources for learning about the history and culture of the Near East. See especially the major history books of the Old Testament: Joshua, Judges, Ruth, I and II Samuel, I and II Kings, Nehemiah, and Esther. Archeological data do not always agree with the biblical accounts. For a good introduction, read K. Kenyon, *Archaeology in the Holy Land** (1979). Also informative is D. J. Wiseman, ed., *Peoples of Old Testament Times* (1973). M. Grant, *The History Of Ancient Israel* (1984), provides an eminently readable discussion of early Hebrew society and the rise of the Hebrew monarchy. A briefer summary is H. M. Orlinsky, *Ancient Israel** (1960). Hebrew law and morality are described in G.

---

*Available in paperback.

Mendenhall, *Law and Covenant in Israel and the Ancient Near East* (1955). J. Goldwin, *The Living Talmud: The Wisdom of the Fathers and Its Classical Commentaries** (1954), offers an interesting essay on Jewish life and religion.

Self-Test Multiple-Choice Questions

<u>Do</u> <u>not</u> assume that these questions will appear on any examination. It is recommended that you <u>not</u> memorize these questions, but use them only as a self-test. Answers are at the end of this book.

1. For women, the evolution of Jewish society led to
   a. Less freedom of action—especially in religious life.
   b. Women were seen as ritually pure.
   c. Little participation in raising children.
   d. Greater participation in religious life.

2. King Solomon is important in Hebrew history for which of the following reasons?
   a. He failed to attend to Hebrew unity and economic growth.
   b. He encouraged the division of Israel into a tribal system.
   c. He removed the religious temple, which stood as the symbol of Hebrew unity.
   d. He imposed far greater taxes than any levied before.

3. The most brutal and militaristic of all the Near Eastern cultures was that of the
   a. Persians.
   b. Assyrians.
   c. Phoenicians.
   d. Hebrews.

4. The Persian king Cyrus the Great carried out a foreign policy based on
   a. torture and submission to Persian traditions.
   b. tolerance of other cultures.
   c. universal acceptance of the Zoroastrian religion.
   d. the tradition of the warrior-king.

5. The Zoroastrian religion stressed which of the following?
   a. The rejection of individual free will
   b. The constant battle between evil and good
   c. The impossibility of eternal life
   d. The absence of a Last Judgment

6. Egypt was reunified in the eighth century by the African Kingdom of
   a. the Nile.
   b. Phoenicia.
   c. Kush.
   d. Ethiopia.

---

*Available in paperback.

7. The power vacuum following the fall of the Hittite and Egyptian empires in about the thirteenth century B.C. was important because it
   a. resulted in the end of Egypt's cultural influence in the Near East and Africa.
   b. led to the unification of the Near East under Hebrew rule.
   c. allowed less powerful peoples, such as the Phoenicians and the Hebrews, to settle and prosper independently.
   d. led to four centuries of backwardness and cultural regression.

8. The Hebrew family pattern evolved
   a. from an extended family to an urban nuclear family.
   b. from a nuclear family to an extended family.
   c. from a strong emphasis on monogamy to an emphasis on polygamy.
   d. from a matriarchy to a patriarchy.

9. Peace and prosperity in Israel brought about
   a. increased landholding for small farmers.
   b. a breakup of the large estates.
   c. the end of slave labor.
   d. the decline of the small family farm.

10. Zoroastrianism was adopted by
   a. the early Hebrews.
   b. the Egyptians.
   c. Darius, the Persian king.
   d. most of the Mediterranean world.

11. The successors of Cyrus the Great divided his empire into
   a. three separate kingdoms.
   b. twenty *satrapies*.
   c. an east and a west province.
   d. six military districts.

12. The founder of the Persian empire was
   a. King Darius.
   b. Zoroaster.
   c. Cyrus the Great.
   d. Siyalk.

13. Which of the following statements about marriage in early Hebrew society is *not* true?
   a. Divorce was available to the husband only.
   b. Marriage was most often arranged for family and economic reasons.
   c. Restrictions against mixed marriages existed.
   d. Children were not seen as an important reason for marriage.

14. Iran's chief geographical feature is
    a. a great central plateau between the Tigris-Euphrates and the Indus valleys.
    b. a central mountainous region.
    c. a dense tropical coastal area at its western edge.
    d. the eastern portion of the Fertile Crescent.

15. The wealth of Iran was based on all of the following *except*
    a. iron production.
    b. horse breeding and overland trade.
    c. small-farm agriculture.
    d. the mining and trading of gold.

16. The Persians acquired many of their military and political practices and organizational genius from the
    a. Hebrews.
    b. Sumerians.
    c. Assyrians.
    d. Philistines.

17. As rulers of conquered territory and peoples, the Persians preferred to rely on
    a. diplomacy.
    b. brutal repression.
    c. forced assimilation of Persian ways.
    d. democratic strategies.

18. The Phoenicians are best known as
    a. great militarists.
    b. prosperous urban merchants and sea traders.
    c. religious innovators.
    d. rulers of the entire Near East after the fall of Persia.

19. The Phoenicians
    a. overthrew the Egyptian kingdom.
    b. developed a thriving agricultural community.
    c. waged large-scale wars against the Hebrews.
    d. became merchants and explorers.

20. Which of the following empires of the ancient Near East was the largest?
    a. The Hebrew
    b. The Hittite
    c. The Egyptian
    d. The Persian

21. The priestly class that officiated at sacrifices, chanted prayers, and tended to the sacred flame of early Iranian religion was the
    a. Magi.
    b. *satrapy*.
    c. Medes.
    d. scribes.

22. *Monotheism* means
    a. adherence to the Ten Commandments.
    b. the worship of nature.
    c. marriage within one's race.
    d. worship of one god alone.

23. During the sixth century B.C., Iranian religion was given new life by the religious thinking of
    a. Ahuramazda.
    b. Mithra.
    c. Zarathustra.
    d. Ahriman.

24. The Hebrew god was known as
    a. Moses.
    b. Solomon.
    c. Yahweh.
    d. Zoroaster.

25. Iran's geographical position and topography explain its
    a. isolation from its neighbors.
    b. role as the highway between East and West.
    c. absence of any urban culture.
    d. failure to attract peoples migrating from elsewhere.

Chapter 3

The Legacy of Greece

Learning Objectives

After reading and studying this chapter you should be able to:

1. explain how geography influenced the development of Greece.

2. identify the Minoans and the Mycenaens.

3. describe the distinguishing characteristics of the Greek polis, and the differences between the city-states of Athens and Sparta.

4. discuss the impact of the Persian War and the Peloponnesian War on ancient Greek civilization.

5. describe the achievements of the Greeks in the so-called Classical Age.

Chapter Summary

Ancient Greece was the home of many aspects of Western civilization. Greek society explored a remarkable range of the problems that beset men and women of all ages: the nature of God and the universe, the dimensions of human sexuality, the challenges of war and imperialism, the proper relationship between the individual and the state. The Greeks were also great thinkers and actors. They have become an example of both human excellence and human frailty, for the Greeks eventually destroyed themselves through war and imperialism. An important question this chapter seeks to answer is why the Greek experiment failed.

The chapter stresses the importance of geographical isolation and proximity to the sea in the political and economic development of the city-state, or polis. It also describes how Greek (Hellenic) religion, art, and life were interwoven. Because the Greek gods were attributed human qualities, the Greeks honored the human spirit and sought human excellence. For the Greeks, the search for truth and meaning in life was pursued not only through mythology and religious experience but through rational philosophy—by great thinkers such as Socrates, Plato, and Aristotle—and through the arts as well. The plays of the great dramatists Aeschylus, Sophocles, and Euripides have led generations of people to examine life's basic conflicts. The Greeks saw drama, comedy, sculpture, and philosophy as ways to relate to their gods and discover the truth about life.

Why did much of Greek history center on war between the two Greek superpowers, Sparta and Athens? These two states represented opposing political systems and different philosophies of life.

Daily life in Athens included sophisticated art and great literature, but the economic system was simple and based to a large extent on slavery. Although it was war that saved Greece (and the West) from the Eastern monarchy of the Persians, it was also war within Greece—especially among Sparta, Athens, and Thebes—that destroyed the freedom of the Greeks and brought on their conquest by the ambitious Philip II of Macedonia. Only the city-state of Thebes, through its sponsorship of federalism, was able to set forth a resolution to internecine war—a resolution that was adopted by the conqueror Philip II.

Study Outline

Use this outline to preview the chapter before you read a particular section in your textbook and then as a self-check to test your reading comprehension after you have read the chapter section.

    I. Hellas: the land
        A. The islands of the Aegean served as stepping stones between the Greek peninsula and Asia Minor.
        B. The mountains both inspired the Greeks and isolated them from one another, hindering unity.
   II. The Minoans and Mycenaeans (ca 1650-ca 1100 B.C.)
        A. The Greeks had established themselves in Greece by ca 1650 B.C.
            1. The first Greek-speaking culture was possibly at Cnossus in Crete.
                a. Archeologists have used Homer's *Iliad* and *Odyssey* to locate this and other sites.
                b. H. Schliemann excavated many sites in order to discover the lost past of the Greek people.
                c. Minoans developed a written language called "Linear A."
            2. The head of Crete was a king; its political-economic centers were a series of palaces.
                a. The Minoan society was wealthy and apparently peaceful.
                b. They used bronze implements.
            3. By 1650 B.C. Greek speaking cities existed at Mycenae, Thebes, Athens, Tiryns, and Pylos.
                a. The king and his warrior-aristocracy exercised political and economic control.
                b. Scribes kept records, but little is known of the ordinary people except that an extensive division of labor existed.
                c. "Linear B" tablets tell us about Greek religion.
            4. Minoan-Mycenaean contacts were originally peaceful but turned to war ca 1450 B.C.
                a. The Minoan capital of Cnossus was destroyed for unknown reasons.
                b. The Mycenaeans grew rich, but eventually were destroyed, probably by internecine war.
            5. The fall of the Mycenaean kingdoms led to a "Dark Age" in Greece from 1100 to 800 B.C.—although religion and social organization remained unchanged.
                a. Some Greeks left to settle in Crete or Asia Minor—and thus spread Greek culture.
  III. Homer, Hesiod, and the heroic past (1100-800 B.C.)
        A. The poems of Homer and Hesiod idealized the past.
            1. The *Iliad* recounts an expedition of Mycenaeans to besiege the city of Troy.

2. The *Odyssey* narrates the adventures of Odysseus during his voyage home from Troy.
3. Hesiod's *Theogony* traces the descent of Zeus.
4. *Works and Days* offered advice on how to live a good life.

B. The great poets taught men and women how to live.

IV. The polis

A. During the Dark Age, the polis, or city-state, evolved throughout Greece.

1. Athens, Sparta, and Thebes were the chief city-states.
2. The polis was a town that grew up around a palace.
3. The polis was walled, with an "agora" (marketplace and political center), and an acropolis that was the religious center of the polis.
4. The polis had important links to the countryside.
5. The average polis relied on its citizens for protection; the backbone of the army was the hoplites, who were wealthy landowners who were well armed.
6. The polis was an intimate community of citizens that tended to exclude outsiders and maintain its independence jealously; there was little room for women to exert a voice in politics.
7. The polis could be governed as a monarchy, aristocracy, oligarchy, democracy, or tyranny.

V. The Lyric Age (800-500 B.C.)

A. Overseas expansion accompanied the rise of the polis.

1. The expansion of Greeks throughout the Mediterranean was due to land shortage and the desire for adventure.
2. Greek colonies extended from the Black Sea to North Africa and into Spain and the Atlantic.
   a. In Sicily the Greeks shared land with the native Sicels.
   b. They established port towns in Sardinia and then founded Marseilles in France.
   c. They took their culture to the Canary Islands in the Atlantic.
3. The Greeks grafted foreign (Near Eastern and Egyptian) ideas and artistic styles onto their own culture.
   a. They then spread their art and culture beyond the Aegean as far as Italy and Carthage.
   b. They created a large new market for agricultural and manufactured goods and imported wheat and other goods.
4. Greek colonization led to greater power for the colonizing polis (called *Metropolis*) and spread its values far beyond the shores of Greece.

B. The lyric poets encouraged individualism, energy, and adventure.

1. Archilochus typifies the restlessness and self-reliance of the era.
2. Erotic, bisexual love is portrayed in the work of Sappho.

C. The growth of Sparta into a powerful polis

1. Sparta's victories in the Messenian wars extended its boundaries and enslaved the Messenians.
2. The warriors demanded and received political rights.

    3. The Lycurgan regime was a new political, economic, and social system.
        a. All citizens became legally equal, and oligarchy replaced aristocracy.
        b. Executive power rested in five elected *ephors,* or overseers.
        c. Land was divided among all citizens and worked by *helots,* or state serfs.
        d. Spartan women were more emancipated than women in other Greek states.
        e. Spartan men disdained wealth and luxury, glorified war and patriotism, and suppressed individualism.
  D. The evolution of Athens
    1. Athens moved from aristocracy to democracy.
        a. Poor peasants demanded legal reforms.
        b. Draco's code—Athens's first law code—established that the law belonged to all citizens.
    2. Solon became *archon* in ca 594 B.C. and enacted sweeping reforms.
    3. Pisistratus became tyrant in 546 B.C. and reduced the power of the aristocracy.
    4. Beginning in 508 B.C., Cleisthenes reorganized the state and created the Athenian democracy.
        a. *Demes* were the basis of the political system.
        b. The demes were grouped into tribes.
        c. The central government included an assembly of all citizens and a council of five hundred members.
        d. Ostracism was used to rid the state peacefully of potentially dangerous politicians.
    5. "Democracy" was based on the idea of rule by all—although practicality dictated that power be delegated to representatives, called archons, and a council called the Areopagos.
        a. Legislation was in the hands of two bodies, the boule (council) and the ecclesia (assembly); the boule administered government while the ecclesia voted on bills and reflected public opinion.
        c. Athenian democracy proved that a large group of people could rule—although the rich and well-born still had greater influence.
VI. The Classical period (500-338 B.C.)
  A. The Persian wars (499-479 B.C.)
    1. The struggle began when the Ionian Greeks rebelled against the Persians—causing the Persians to strike at Athens.
    2. The Greeks won at Marathon (490 B.C.), but the Persian king Xerxes invaded Greece in 480 B.C.
    3. The Persians were defeated at Salamis (480 B.C.) and Plataea (479 B.C.)—and the Greeks formed a united pan-hellenic alliance.
  B. The growth of the Athenian Empire (478-431 B.C.)
    1. The Athenians and others established the Delian League (478 B.C.) as a naval alliance to continue the fight against Persia.
        a. Led by Cimon, the Athenians drove the Persians out of the Aegean.
        b. Cimon and the Athenians turned the league into a tool of their own empire.
        c. Athenian aggressiveness alarmed Sparta and its allies.
    2. Athens's conflict with Corinth led to war with Sparta.

C. The Peloponnesian War (431-404 B.C.)
   1. The long war brought death, destruction, stalemate, and a new breed of self-serving Athenian politicians.
   2. The opportunist Alcibiades led Athens in an invasion of Sicily, which led to war between Athens and Sparta.
   5. The Spartans defeated Athens in 404 B.C.
D. The birth of historical awareness
   1. Herodotus, the "father of history," covered the major events of the Near East and Greece in *The Histories*.
   2. Thucydides chronicled the history of the Peloponnesian War.
E. Athenian arts in the age of Pericles
   1. In the last half of the fifth century B.C., Pericles turned Athens into the showplace of Greece.
   2. The Athenian Acropolis became the center of Greek religion and art.
      a. The entrance building (the Propylaea) led to small temples that honored the goddess Athena and Athenian victories.
      b. The Parthenon, a Doric temple, was an architectural masterpiece and the epitome of Greek art and its spirit.
   3. The development of drama was tied to the religious festivals of the city.
   4. Aeschylus, Sophocles, and Euripides were the three greatest dramatists of Athens.
      a. Aeschylus wrote a trilogy of plays about humans in conflict, stressing the themes of betrayal, reconciliation, reason, and justice.
      b. Sophocles' masterpieces (the three *Oedipus* plays) deal with the interplay of human actions, justice, and the will of the gods.
      c. Euripides' plays focus on humans who face disaster because they allow their passions to overwhelm them.
F. Daily life in Periclean Athens
   1. Material life was simple, and most goods were produced at home.
   2. Houses were a series of rooms built around a central courtyard—some with bedrooms on the upper floor.
      a. The two main rooms were a dining room for men and a workroom for women.
      b. Food was from grains, fruits, garlic, and wine—but not much meat.
   3. Slavery was common.
   4. Agriculture and small crafts were the major types of labor.
   5. Women were protected by law but did not have equal rights with men.
      a. Because the historical evidence is largely military or political, women's role is often underestimated.
      b. Women held a *liminal* position—that is, one of considerable unofficial power.
      c. Courtesan women were the most free—some gained intellectual status.
      d. Women's main functions were to raise the children, oversee the slaves, and work wool into cloth.
   5. Acceptance of homosexuality was a distinctive feature of Athenian life.
      a. Many believed that warriors who were lovers would fight harder.

6. Greek religion was individualistic and lacked organized creeds and sacred books.
   a. Religion was a matter of ritual and a way to honor the polis.
   b. The Olympic games were held for the glory of Zeus and were a unifying factor in Greek life.
   c. Some Greeks turned to mystery religions, which united individuals within exclusive societies with secret cults and ritual.
   d. For most Greeks, religion was simple and close to nature—a world of gods and goddesses such as Hestia, Pan, Zeus, Europa, and others.
   e. The farmer-poet Hesiod reminds us how Greek religion linked people with nature.

G. The flowering of philosophy
   1. The Greeks of the Classical period viewed the universe in terms of natural law, not mythology.
   2. Thales, Anaximander, and Heraclitus made important contributions to the sciences.
   3. Aesop used fables to teach ethics (moral behavior)—often using animals as the main characters—such as the fox in the vineyard.
   4. Hippocrates was the founder of modern medicine.
   5. The Sophists taught excellence and believed that nothing is absolute.
   6. Socrates attempted to discover truth and happiness by continuous questioning; he believed that true happiness could be found in the pursuit of excellence.
   7. Plato's philosophy is based on the idea that reality exists only in the immaterial world.
      a. He founded a philosophical school, the Academy, to ask how to create the ideal polis.
      b. In *The Republic,* Plato sought to define the ideal polis.
   8. Aristotle's range of philosophical inquiry was staggering.
      a. He wrote about the ideal polis in his book *Politics* and criticized Plato.
      b. He developed a new school of scientific discussion based on the syllogism; he often discussed topics with students in the "peripatos" manner (discussing while walking).
      c. In his books *Physics* and *Metaphysics* he developed a theory of nature based on the four principles of matter, form, movement, and goal.
      d. His book *On the Heaven* wrongly asserted that the earth is the center of the universe.

H. The final act (404-338 B.C.)
   1. With the end of the Peloponnesian War, a century of further warfare left the Greek states exhausted and vulnerable to the Macedonian conquest of Greece.
   2. Philip II king of Macedonia was a brilliant leader who won control of the northern Aegean and then defeated a combined Theban-Athenian army at Chaeronea in 338 B.C.

Review Questions

Check your understanding of this chapter by answering the following questions.

1. What were the early Greek Minoan and Mycenaean cultures like? What caused their eventual destruction?

2. What impact did climate and population size have on the polis?

3. How did the Greeks use the gods to help explain the makeup of the universe and how man should live?

4. What were the causes of Greek expansion from ca 750 to 550 B.C.?

5. In what ways does Archilochus represent the spirit of Greek colonization?

6. How did the Spartans settle the problems of overpopulation and land hunger?

7. What was life like in Sparta in terms of (a) the military, (b) the family, and (c) economic needs?

8. What were the accomplishments of Draco, Solon, Pisistratus, and Cleisthenes?

9. What were the causes of the conflict between Athens and Sparta? The outcome?

10. What role did architecture and building play in the age of Pericles?

11. What role did drama and comedy play in the life of the polis and the people?

12. What was the position of women in Greek society? Were they completely powerless?

13. How widespread and important was homosexuality in Greek society? Did the Greeks regard homosexuality as deviant behavior?

14. How would you judge Hippocrates' views on illness?

15. What were the causes and the outcome of the Theban-Spartan conflict?

Study-Review Exercises

Define the following key concepts and terms.

polis

rationalism in art and architecture

natural laws versus mythological explanations of the universe

deme

Sophist relativism

Hippocrates' theory of four humors

Aristotelian logic

empirical knowledge

Aesop's fables

Common Peace

Identify and explain the significance of the following people and terms.
Mycenaeans

Minoans

Cnossus

Messenian wars

helot

Parthenon

Draco's law code

Marathon

Delian League

Peloponnesian War

ostracism

hoplites

Sacred War

Second Athenian Confederacy

Identify the following people and explain their importance.

Aesop

Hesiod

Homer

Thucydides

Hippocrates

Socrates

Sappho

Solon

Lysander

Plato

Zeus

Aristotle

Cimon

Sophocles

Xerxes

Pericles

Philip II of Macedonia

Epaminondas

Odysseus

Aspasia

Fill in the following blank lines with the letter of the correct answer.

1. _____ He thought that the basic element of the universe is water.

2. _____ This Pre-Socratic thinker was the first to use general concepts.

3. _____ He theorized that the earth is made of invisible, indestructible atoms.

4. _____ He is known as the father of medicine.

5. _____ He thought that excellence and happiness could be learned through continuous questions.

6. _____ He believed that visible things are merely copies of ideas.

7. _____ He claimed that the universe revolves and is spherical.

8. _____ She is best known for erotic poetry.

a. Hippocrates
b. Democritus
c. Socrates
d. Anaximander
e. Plato
f. Sappho
g. Thales
h. Pericles
i. Aristotle

Test your understanding of the chapter by providing the correct answers.

1. The three major Greek city-states were _____, _____, and _____.

2. The Olympian gods *were/were not* seen as having human qualities.

3. The democratic Athenians *did/did not* conquer other people and force them to submit to their rule.

4. He defeated a Theban-Athenian army in 338 B.C. to win control of Greece. _____

5. Sophocles' character Antigone supports the idea of the influence of *divine law/the state* on human conduct.

6. The hoplites of Sparta *were/were not* successful in gaining political rights.

7. In general, the peasants of Athens *supported/opposed* rule by the tyrants.

8. The city-state of _____ defeated Sparta and successfully blended the three concepts of hegemony, federation, and Common Peace.

Major Political Ideas

Define the terms *monarchy, aristocracy, oligarchy, tyranny,* and *democracy.* How does each differ in terms of the placement of authority within society? Describe the transition from aristocracy to tyranny to democracy in Athens. How did the system of democracy evolve and what were its principal features? In what sense was Athenian democracy similar to or different from modern democracy?

Issues for Essays and Discussion

1. The Greek polis was a dramatic break from the past. Explain this by discussing what the polis was and what its major political and cultural achievements were. Was the polis, in your view, a failure or a success?

2. Compare and contrast Pre-Socratic and Socratic philosophy. In your discussion make reference to specific thinkers, their method of acquiring knowledge, and how they explained human experience and the origins of the universe.

3. What characteristics of Athenian daily life made it distinctive? Discuss this by referring to such things as Athenian religion, sport, sexual attitudes, drama, and the role of women. Include examples.

4. Compare and contrast Athenian culture to that of the Hebrews discussed in the previous chapter. Make particular reference to religion, politics, and social and sexual/gender attitudes. Do you believe that geographic differences made any difference in the manner in which these two cultures evolved?

Interpretation of Visual Sources

Study the painting of women working on the Greek vase. Describe the scene and its participants. What types of information does this provide with regard to womanhood, industry, and the purpose of art?

Geography

1. On Outline Map 3.1 provided, mark the approximate location of the following: Athens, Crete, Asia Minor, Mount Olympus, Sparta, the Mediterranean Sea, Lesbos, Marathon, Thebes, the Aegean Sea, Peloponnesus, Mycenae, Troy, the Ionian Sea, Ionia.

2. The geography of Greece encouraged political fragmentation. Explain.

3. Using Map 3.2 as a reference, describe the area that came under Greek control as a result of its overseas expansion. What were the causes of this expansion?

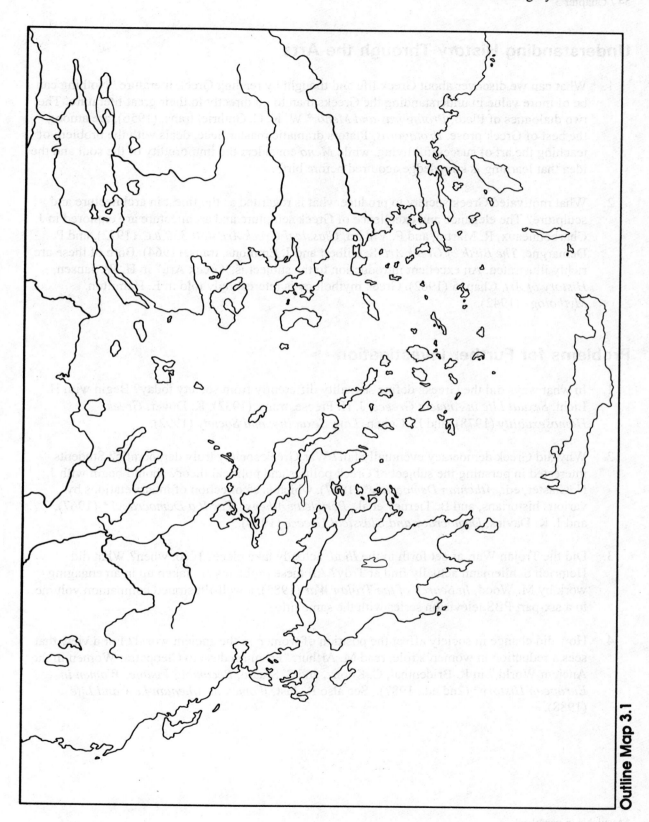

Outline Map 3.1

Understanding History Through the Arts

1. What can we discover about Greek life and thought by reading Greek literature? Nothing can be of more value in understanding the Greeks than to go directly to their great literature. The two dialogues of Plato, *Protagoras and Meno,** W. K. C. Guthrie, trans. (1956), are among the best of Greek prose. *Protagoras,* Plato's dramatic masterpiece, deals with the problem of teaching the art of successful living, while *Meno* considers the immortality of the soul and the idea that learning is knowledge acquired before birth.

2. What motivated Greek society to produce what is regarded as the finest in architecture and sculpture? The elegance and excellence of Greek sculpture and architecture are explored in J. Charbonneaux, R. Martin, and F. Villard, *Classical Greek Art, 480-330 B.C.* (1972), and P. Demargne, *The Birth of Greek Art,* S. Gilbert and J. Emmons, trans. (1964). Both of these are richly illustrated. An excellent introduction to the subject is "Greek Art," in H. W. Jansen, *History of Art,* Chap. 5 (1962). Greek mythology is interestingly told in E. Hamilton, *Mythology* (1942).

Problems for Further Investigation

1. In what ways did the Greeks define sexuality differently from society today? Begin with H. Licht, *Sexual Life in Ancient Greece,* J. H. Freese, trans. (1932), K. Dover, *Greek Homosexuality* (1978), and D. Cohen, *Law, Sexuality, and Society* (1992).

2. Why did Greek democracy eventually fail? Was Greek society truly democratic? Students interested in pursuing the subject of Greek politics and political theory should begin with J. N. Claster, ed., *Athenian Democracy** (1967), which is a collection of interpretations by various historians, and B. Tierney et al., *Periclean Athens: Was It a Democracy?** (1967), and J. K. Davies, *Democracy and Classical Greece* (1993).

3. Did the Trojan War, as set forth in the *Iliad,* actually take place? If so, when? What did Heinrich Schliemann actually find at Troy? All these problems are taken up in an engaging work by M. Wood, *In Search of the Trojan War* (1985), a well-illustrated companion volume to a six-part PBS television series with the same title.

4. How did change in society affect the position of women in the ancient world? For a view that sees a reduction in women's role, read M. Arthur, "From Medusa to Cleopatra: Women in the Ancient World," in R. Bridenthal, C. Koonz, and S. Stuard, *Becoming Visible: Women in European History** (2nd ed., 1987). See also R. Just, *Women in Athenian Law and Life* (1988).

---

*Available in paperback.

Self-Test Multiple-Choice Questions

Do not assume that these questions will appear on any examination. It is recommended that you not memorize these questions, but use them only as a self-test. Answers are at the end of this book.

1. The two main historians of ancient Greece were
   a. Homer and Hesiod.
   b. Herodotus and Thucydides.
   c. Sophocles and Aristotle.
   d. Plato and Socrates.

2. Mycenaean Greece was most probably destroyed by
   a. foreign invaders.
   b. famine.
   c. internecine war.
   d. a volcano.

3. The Delian League was transformed into a means of imperialistic expansion by which of the following city-states?
   a. Sparta
   b. Thebes
   c. Athens
   d. Delos

4. Which of the following statements about the Mycenaeans is true?
   a. They were the ancestors of the ancient Egyptians.
   b. Their political unit was the polis.
   c. Few social distinctions existed, and slavery was prohibited.
   d. The economic center of the society was the royal palace.

5. Two poems written by Homer during the Heroic Age were
   a. *Theogony* and *Works and Days*.
   b. *Iliad* and *Odyssey*.
   c. *The Histories*.
   d. *The Agamemnon* and *The Libatian Bearers*.

6. The polis included all of the following *except*
   a. a public square or marketplace.
   b. a citadel or acropolis.
   c. agricultural land and pastureland.
   d. land reserved for the king and priesthood.

7. The polis can be best described as
   a. a community of citizens.
   b. a religious community.
   c. a community of merchants.
   d. a community of warriors.

8. The Acropolis and the Parthenon are two buildings still standing that were built during the Age of
   a. Solon.
   b. Pericles.
   c. Alcibiades.
   d. Aristophanes.

9. The *Iliad* and *Odyssey* were
   a. sacred writings.
   b. collections of laws.
   c. historical records.
   d. epic poems.

10. A woman best known for her erotic poetry was
    a. Tyrtaeus.
    b. Archilochus.
    c. Lesbos.
    d. Sappho.

11. Solon was an Athenian
    a. tyrant.
    b. reformer.
    c. king.
    d. priest.

12. Greeks at first used the word *tyrant* to denote a
    a. leader who ruled without legal right.
    b. cruel leader who oppressed the poor.
    c. champion of the commercial classes.
    d. leader whose efforts destroyed all forms of democracy.

13. Cleisthenes was famous because he
    a. made Athens a major commercial center.
    b. suppressed popular unrest.
    c. was the most successful Athenian tyrant.
    d. created the Athenian democracy.

14. Athens used the Delian League
    a. to colonize the Mediterranean.
    b. to fight the Persians.
    c. to promote Mediterranean trade.
    d. to spread Greek culture.

15. Thucydides wrote in order to
    a. analyze the Peloponnesian War.
    b. describe the Athenian democracy.
    c. record events in the Persian wars.
    d. defend Athenian foreign policy.

16. Which of the following statements does *not* describe the drama *Oresteia* by Aeschylus?
    a. The trilogy deals with the themes of betrayal, murder, and reconciliation.
    b. The use of reason and justice is urged to reconcile fundamental conflicts.
    c. The trilogy ends with a plea that civil dissension not be allowed to destroy societal stability.
    d. The trilogy's major theme is the societal taboo of incest.

17. Aristophanes was popular because
    a. the government tried to censure his plays.
    b. he was the most religious Athenian poet.
    c. he justified Athenian imperialism.
    d. he was a critic of political and social life.

18. Most Greeks supported themselves by
    a. fishing.
    b. trading.
    c. warfare.
    d. farming.

19. Athenian women
    a. had the status of slaves.
    b. had full citizens' rights.
    c. had protection under the law.
    d. had greater rights than men.

20. Greek homosexuality was considered
    a. the curse of the lower classes.
    b. a threat to family life.
    c. an insult to religion.
    d. for many a normal practice.

21. First and foremost the Athenian Acropolis was
    a. an economic and trade center.
    b. a series of temples in honor of Athena.
    c. the monumental gateway to the Athenian harbor.
    d. the center of Greek political activity.

22. The aristocrat and writer Thucydides believed that the fate of men and women was
    a. left to the gods.
    b. entirely in their own hands.
    c. determined by nature.
    d. not to be understood or determined.

23. The power of free women in Greek society is defined as *liminal,* which means that
    a. women had limited power in society.
    b. they had considerable political power through office holding.
    c. they had significant unofficial power.
    d. their influence began only after their husbands died.

24. The Macedonian king who took advantage of the internecine Greek struggle and thereby conquered Greece was
    a. Alexander the Great.
    b. Philip II.
    c. Cleon.
    d. Cleisthenes.

Chapter 4

Hellenistic Diffusion

Learning Objectives

After reading and studying this chapter you should be able to:

1. discuss Alexander the Great's ideas of a political state.

2. explain how the meeting of Greek and eastern ideas had an impact on philosophy, religion, science, and society.

3. compare the role of women in Hellenistic and Hellenic times.

Chapter Summary

This chapter describes how the ancient Near Eastern cultures and the Greek ("Hellenic") culture came together to form a new, "Hellenistic" culture during the time of Alexander the Great, the son of Philip II. This Hellenistic age was a period of both political confusion and cultural unity that lay the groundwork for the triumph of Roman imperialism. The culture of this age is called "Hellenism."

Alexander the Great, who was given a Greek education by Aristotle, conquered most of the known world by 324 B.C. He defeated and conquered Persia and then marched on to India, part of which was incorporated into his Macedonian state. Along the way he founded new cities and military colonies, all of which became agencies by which Hellenistic culture spread throughout most of the Mediterranean and Near Eastern world. When he died, his empire was divided into four kingdoms, which became frontiers of opportunity for large numbers of Greeks in search of jobs, wealth, and power. Thus, Greek men and women settled throughout the East, forming an elite class of professionals and administrators. These Greek settlers also carried Greek literature, law, engineering, architecture, and philosophy into every corner of the Near East and the Mediterranean. These cities differed greatly from the former Greek polis in that the new city was the possession of the king and thus was not the basis of the political rights of the citizen.

Like in the earlier Greek culture, the Hellenistic kings were not interested in the spread of their religion among their new subjects. Important new discoveries in science and medicine were made in the Hellenistic period. Philosophy became extremely creative, led by the competing doctrines of the Cynics, the Epicureans, and the Stoics. There were also important advances in food production, trade, and mining. Women enjoyed new opportunities as they entered the professions and commerce. Thus, the Hellenistic age was a time of change and creativity.

Study Outline

Use this outline to preview the chapter before you read a particular section in your textbook and then as a self-check to test your reading comprehension after you have read the chapter section.

    I. Alexander and the great crusade to conquer Asia Minor
       A. Alexander the King
          1. The son of King Philip, Alexander was tutored by Aristotle.
          2. Alexander became king in 336 B.C. and invaded Asia in 334 B.C.
          3. By 330 B.C., he had defeated the Persians to avenge the Persian invasion of Greece.
          4. He then set out to conquer the rest of Asia.
   II. Alexander's legacy
       A. Alexander became a legend in his own time.
          1. Historians still disagree over his character.
          2. The record shows him as a violent and savage person.
          3. The "philosopher-king" interpretation of Alexander is based on a misunderstanding of his intentions at a banquet in 324 B.C.
          4. The practical result of his role was to open the East to Hellenism.
       B. The political legacy
          1. After his death in 323 B.C., Alexander's empire was divided among four dynasties: the Antigonids, the Ptolemies, the Seleucids, and the Pergamenes; a kingdom of Bactria was founded in the far northeast.
          2. In Greece the polis system was replaced by leagues of city-states.
          3. The Hellenistic world was politically fragmented and constantly at war.
       C. The cultural legacy of Alexander
          1. The colonies founded by Alexander and his successors brought many Greeks into Asia, thereby bringing East and West together; this culture is called Hellenism.
             a. Over 70 cities were founded by Alexander, and his successors established at least 250 colonies—making the Mediterranean basin into a Greek-speaking region.
             b. The newly discovered Hellenistic city of Ay Khanoum is an example of Greek influence—far away from Greece.
          2. Alexander's empire spread Greek culture as far east as India.
          3. Hellenism became a common bond for the Mediterranean.
  III. The spread of Hellenism
       A. Cities and kingdoms of the Hellenistic age
          1. The creation of new kingdoms accompanied the resurgence of monarchy; this was a method of uniting diverse peoples—often linking the ruler with the gods.
          2. The new cities were not politically independent (or *sovereign*) but rather a part of a kingdom.
             a. Legal and social inequality existed in the Hellenistic city; Greeks had greater rights and thus formed an elite and the city was fully the possession of the king.
       B. The Hellenistic kings were frequently at war as they attempted to solidify their kingdoms and gain the loyalty of subjects.
       C. Hellenistic cities formed the cultural foundation on which Roman and Christian cultures were to spread and flourish.
       D. The warfare to change: Hellenistic soldiers were paid to remain loyal.

E. Greeks and Easterners: the Hellenistic cities became centers of Hellenism
1. The spread of Greek culture was uneven.
2. A Greco-Egyptian culture evolved slowly in Egypt under the Ptolemies.
3. Under the Seleucid kings, Greek and Eastern culture merged in Asia Minor.
4. Most Easterners took only the external trappings of Greek culture, such as the Greek dialect called *koine,* while retaining their own way of life.
F. Hellenism and the Jews
1. The Greeks allowed the Jews political and religious freedom.
2. Despite adoption of some Hellenistic culture, Jews remained Hebrew at heart.
IV. Developments in the western Mediterranean
A. A large variety of peoples and cultures were creating important settlements in the western part of the Mediterranean.
1. For example, Berbers in Algeria, Morocco, and Tunisia and Iberians and Celts in Spain and Portugal.
2. Most of these people had some contacts with the Greek world—but it would be Rome (later) that would bring them together.
V. The economic scope of Hellenism
A. Commerce
1. Alexander's conquests brought the East and the West together for trade.
2. Overland trade to India was conducted by caravan.
a. Silk, tea, and other luxuries came by way of two camel caravan routes—the northern Dura route and the southern Arabia route.
b. In return, Mediterranean people traded manufactured goods (weapons, cloth, etc.) and wine and oil.
c. Ideas passed along these routes.
d. The Greek cities depended on seaborne trade (largely from Egypt) for grain.
4. The slave trade flourished because slavery was important to the Hellenistic economy.
B. Industry
1. Cheap labor left no incentive to invent machinery.
2. The only change in mining was the introduction of the Archimedean screw for pumping water into irrigation ditches and out of the mines.
3. Labor in the gold, silver, and iron mines was harsh; many of the workers were political prisoners and slaves.
4. Important changes in pottery style took place, but production methods remained unchanged.
C. Agriculture
1. The Ptolemies made advances in seed development and produced handbooks on farming.
2. The Ptolemies also made great strides in irrigating the land, partly because of their strong central government.
VI. Religion in the Hellenistic world
A. The Greek religious cults centered on the Olympian gods.
1. The cults, consisting mainly of rituals, did not fill the religious needs of the people.
B. Many people turned to a belief in *Tyche* (fate or chance).

    C. There was a growth in mystery religions to fill emotional and ethical needs.
       1. These religions promised life for the soul after death and union with a god who had himself risen from the dead.
       2. Isis was the most important goddess of the new mystery cults.

  VII. Philosophy and common people
    A. Common people became interested in philosophy, because of the decline of the polis, the decline of religion, and increased mobility, all of which left people in need for something permanent.
       1. The new philosophies taught that people could be truly happy only when they rejected the world and focused their attention on enduring things.
       2. The Cynics believed in the rejection of the material life.
         a. Diogenes, the greatest of the Cynics, stressed living according to nature and without allegiance to a particular city or monarchy.
         b. The Cynics influenced all the other major schools of philosophy.
       3. The Epicureans taught that pleasure was the chief good and advocated political passivity.
       4. The Stoics stressed the unity of man and universe and resignation to one's duty.
         a. Zeno made Stoicism the most popular Hellenistic philosophy.
         b. Participation in worldly affairs was encouraged, but leading a virtuous life was most important.
         c. The Stoic concept of natural law—one law for all people—was of great importance, particularly later in Rome.

 VIII. Hellenistic science
    A. Aristarchus developed the heliocentric theory of the universe, although Aristotle's earth-centered view remained dominant.
    B. Euclid compiled a textbook on geometry.
    C. Archimedes, an inventor and theoretician, sketched out basic principles of mechanics.
    D. Eratosthenes made advances in mathematics and geography—and was the head of a great museum.
    E. Theophrastos founded the study of botany.

  IX. Hellenistic medicine
    A. The Dogmatic school of medicine, under Herophilus and Erasistratus, used vivisection and dissection to gain knowledge of the body, including the nervous system.
    B. The Empiric school stressed observation and the use of medicine and drugs, including opium.
    C. Many quacks did untold harm, but they were popular.

  X. Meander, a playwright for a new world.
    A. Hellenistic theater in Athens developed the "New Comedy" style.
       1. The playwright Meander brought theater down to earth with themes of love and ordinary domestic life.

Review Questions

Check your understanding of this chapter by answering the following questions.

1. What were Alexander's major achievements? Does he deserve to be called "the Great"?

2. Trace the expansion of the Macedonian kingdom into Asia. What were the reasons for this movement?

3. Explain why Alexander's empire began disintegrating at the time of his death. Why could the empire not remain intact?

4. How did the Hellenistic polis differ from the earlier Greek polis? Why?

5. What did the new Hellenistic kingdoms offer the Greeks? Why couldn't these kingdoms gain the loyalty of the Greek immigrants?

6. How successful was Greek culture in penetrating Egypt and the East?

7. What was the impact of Hellenistic policies and culture on the Jews who resided in Hellenic areas?

8. Trace the developments in agriculture and industry in Hellenistic society. Why was there so little technological innovation?

9. Explain the interregional trade patterns of the Hellenistic world. What products did the various parts of the Hellenistic world specialize in?

10. What kinds of commodities made up the caravan trade?

11. How did the position and power of women in Hellenistic society change from those of earlier periods?

12. Discuss the religious and philosophical trends in the Hellenistic world. Why did the common person become interested in philosophy?

13. Trace the development of medical science in the Hellenistic era. What advances were made over the Hellenic period?

14. Describe how and why the nature of warfare changed from the time of the Greek polis to the time of the Hellenistic cities ruled by kings. In what important way was the Macedonian army different?

Study-Review Exercises

Define the following key concepts and terms.

Hellenism

politeuma

Tyche

natural law

heliocentric theory

empirical tradition

Meander

Explain the major ideas and accomplishments of the following people.

Aristarchus of Samos

Euclid

Archimedes

Eratosthenes

Theophrastos

Herophilus

Explain the principal ideas and beliefs of the following Hellenistic philosophers.

Cynics

Epicureans

Stoics

Identify and explain the significance of the following people and terms.

Hellenistic period

Aetolian League

Ptolemy

koine

Alexander the Great

Zeno

Isis

Dogmatic school of medicine

Empiric school of medicine

Test your understanding of the chapter by providing the correct answers.

1. Epicurus taught that the gods had *no/great* effect on human life.

2. The most popular philosophy of the Hellenistic world was _____.

3. The Cynics advised men and women to *accept/discard* traditional customs and conventions.

4. The founder of the Cynics was _____, who believed that nothing natural was dirty or shameful.

5. The Hellenistic world *did/did not* see much trade in manufactured goods.

6. Alexander the Great's conquest of Persia was completed by about the year _____.

7. The Greek immigrants in the Hellenistic kingdoms generally *did/did not* develop a strong loyalty to the state.

8. After Alexander's death the empire was broken into four parts, the _____, _____, _____, and _____ kingdoms.

9. The political and economic power of women tended to *increase/decrease* during the Hellenistic period.

10. To the Hellenists, *Tyche* meant _____.

11. Generally, the Greeks tended to be *tolerant/intolerant* toward other religions.

12. _____ was the goddess of marriage, conception, and childbirth.

Major Political Ideas

1. What is the relationship between political and philosophical thought? The Hellenistic period is particularly interesting because it stressed philosophy for the common people. What did Cynicism, Epicureanism, and Stoicism have to say about the relationship between the individual and the state?

2. Define the stoic concept of *natural law*. Why is this an important idea? What are its political implications?

Issues for Essays and Discussion

During the Hellenistic period, much of the Near East was transformed by new ideas. What was Hellenism and what did it mean for society? Describe Hellenism in terms of the exchange of ideas in the fields of culture, political administration, philosophy, science, industry-commerce, and medicine. Was Hellenism successful in creating a unified society?

Interpretation of Visual Sources

Study the picture of the relief titled "Religious Syncretism." Describe what is happening here. Why is this significant? Why is the place this object was found a significant piece of information for the historian?

Geography

On Outline Map 4.1 provided, and using Map 4.1 and Map 4.2 in the textbook as a reference, mark the following:

1. The location of India, Mesopotamia, the Mediterranean Sea, Asia Minor, Persia, the Nile River, the Black Sea, Alexandria, Macedonia, Persepolis, Egypt, the Arabian Desert.

2. The area conquered by Alexander the Great.

3. The boundaries of the four kingdoms established after Alexander's death. Label each kingdom.

4. A route by which goods might have moved between Greece, Asia Minor, Egypt, and the Far East.

Outline Map 4.1

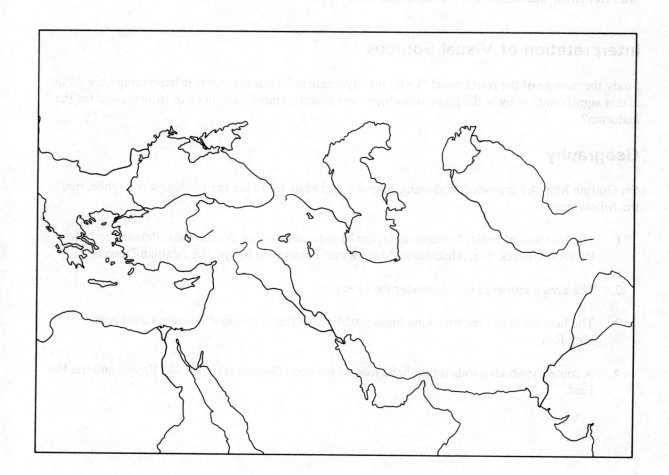

Understanding History Through the Arts

1. What do ancient coins tell us about Hellenistic life? Many of the remarkable personages of the Hellenistic age—including Cleopatra and Ptolemy of Egypt—are featured in N. Davis and C. Kraay, *The Hellenistic Kingdoms: Portrait Coins and History* (1973).

2. What was the social and political function of art in Hellenistic cities? For developments in architecture see J. Charbonneaux, R. Martin, and F. Villard, *Hellenistic Art, 330-50 B.C.* (1973), and T. Fyfe, *Hellenistic Architecture* (1963). For painting and sculpture, see C. Havelock, *Hellenistic Art* (1970). The traditions of Hellenistic literature and culture are explored in T. Webster, *Hellenistic Poetry and Art* (1964).

Problems for Further Investigation

1. Has Alexander the Great been turned into a myth by historians? What was the real Alexander like? Alexander the Great is the subject of a number of biographies, including R. L. Fox, *Alexander the Great* (1974), J. R. Hamilton, *Alexander the Great* (1973), and N. G. L. Hammond, *Alexander the Great*, 3rd ed. (1994). A fascinating historical novel about life, love, and adventure with Alexander is M. Renault, *The Persian Boy** (1972).

2. Did the Hellenists make any significant contributions to science and medicine? To pursue this question begin with E. Hamilton, *The Greek Way to Western Civilization** (1943).

3. What were the reasons for Alexander the Great's conquest of the Near Eastern world? Begin your research with A. R. Burn, *Alexander the Great and the Hellenistic World** (1964).

4. How did Greek philosophy change in this period? What are Stoicism and Cynicism? Those interested in Greek thought should see a book of essays, interpretations, and source material entitled *The Greek Mind** (1957) by W. R. Agard; also A. Long, *Hellenistic Philosophy* (1974), and R. W. Sharples, *Stoics, Epicureans, Sceptics* (1996).

5. Did women enjoy a new kind of individualism in the Hellenistic city? This is the argument set forth in M. Arthur, "From Medusa to Cleopatra: Women in the Ancient World," in R. Bridenthal, C. Koonz, and S. Stuard, *Becoming Visible: Women in European History** (1987). A bibliography on women in antiquity is included for further study.

*Available in paperback.

Self-Test Multiple-Choice Questions

<u>Do</u> <u>not</u> assume that these questions will appear on any examination. It is recommended that you <u>not</u> memorize these questions, but use them only as a self-test. Answers are at the end of this book.

1. The Epicureans believed that one could find happiness
    a. by becoming involved in politics.
    b. through pain.
    c. by retiring within oneself.
    d. by pleasing the gods.

2. The most important achievement of the Stoics was the
    a. idea of rejecting the state.
    b. cult of Isis.
    c. education of Alexander.
    d. concept of natural law.

3. Which of the following statements about Hellenized Easterners is true?
    a. They rejected everything Greek except Greek religion.
    b. They adopted much but retained the essentials of their own culture.
    c. They became thoroughly assimilated into Greek culture.
    d. They had no culture of their own.

4. Within the Hellenistic world Greeks formed the
    a. middle class of merchants.
    b. favored class.
    c. slave class.
    d. priest class.

5. Alexander's troops refused to proceed farther after they reached
    a. Persia.
    b. India.
    c. Bactria.
    d. China.

6. Alexander made his greatest contribution toward understanding between West and East when he
    a. forced Greeks to marry barbarians.
    b. established the Greek church in India.
    c. established colonies for Greek emigration.
    d. encouraged the adoption of barbarian food and dress.

7. Women's position improved during the Hellenistic age because of
    a. the Greeks' belief that women were equal.
    b. full citizenship rights conferred by law.
    c. their increased activity in economic affairs.
    d. their noble and self-sacrificing deeds.

8. During the Hellenistic period, the greatest strides in agriculture were made by the
   a. Ptolemies in Egypt.
   b. Macedonians.
   c. Seleucids.
   d. Athenians.

9. The Greek word *Tyche* means
   a. revelation.
   b. honor.
   c. to be strong.
   d. fate.

10. The author of *The Elements of Geometry* was
    a. Euclid.
    b. Archimedes.
    c. Aristarchus of Samos.
    d. Eratosthenes.

11. After Alexander's death, his empire was divided into all of the following dynasties except the
    a. Seleucid dynasty.
    b. Ptolemaic dynasty.
    c. Antigonid dynasty.
    d. Athenian dynasty.

12. In the Hellenistic period philosophy was
    a. the pastime of the wealthy.
    b. the profession of specialists.
    c. a propaganda tool of kings.
    d. an outlet for common people.

13. The Cynics thought that
    a. people should avoid pain.
    b. people should live according to nature.
    c. people should uphold the norms of society.
    d. people should enjoy luxury in moderation.

14. Epicurean philosophy taught
    a. the overthrow of monarchies.
    b. the virtue of self-discipline.
    c. the value of religion.
    d. the value of pleasure.

15. The Stoics evolved the idea of
    a. might makes right.
    b. pain against pleasure.
    c. the unity of mankind and the universe.
    d. the unity of mankind and the state.

16. Aristarchus of Samos is important because he thought that
    a. the sun revolved around the earth.
    b. the moon revolved around the earth.
    c. the earth revolved around the sun.
    d. the sun and moon were fixed bodies.

17. Which of the following sciences got its start in the Hellenistic period?
    a. Economics
    b. Physics
    c. Botany
    d. Geology

18. The discoverer of the nervous system was
    a. Herophilus.
    b. Erasistratus.
    c. Heraclides.
    d. Serapion.

19. The Empiric school of medicine emphasized
    a. the study of anatomy.
    b. the study of physiology.
    c. the use of vivisection and dissection.
    d. the cure of sickness through observation and drugs.

20. Hellenistic industry relied chiefly on
    a. labor-saving machines.
    b. new techniques of production.
    c. increased use of animal power.
    d. use of manual labor.

21. In the Hellenistic period, for the most part, the polis
    a. was totally abandoned.
    b. remained unchanged.
    c. became more independent.
    d. was less independent and active than in earlier time.

22. Jews living in Hellenistic cities
    a. often embraced a good deal of Hellenism.
    b. rejected Hellenism.
    c. adopted only the Greek gods.
    d. usually abandoned their religion in favor of Stoicism.

23. The real achievement of Alexander and his successors in the economic realm was
    a. an industrial revolution.
    b. a switch to a sophisticated consumer society.
    c. blocking the overland trade with India and Arabia.
    d. the creation of a broad commercial network linking East and West.

24. After Alexander's conquest of the Persian Empire, the only commodity listed below that did *not* increase in economic importance because of stimulated trade was
    a. luxury items.
    b. slaves.
    c. raw materials, grain, and industrial products.
    d. manufactured goods.

25. Which of the following statements about the relationship between industrial growth and the labor supply in Hellenistic Greece is true?
    a. The demand for products fell; therefore, unemployment rose.
    b. A limited supply of labor led to technological innovation.
    c. An abundance of labor caused many technological advances.
    d. Human labor was cheap; therefore, there was little incentive to invent machinery.

Chapter 5

The Rise of Rome

Learning Objectives

After reading and studying this chapter you should be able to:

1. describe the factors that contributed to Rome's conquest of the Italian Peninsula.

2. explain the challenges Rome faced in its conquest of the Mediterranean world.

3. describe how the Romans become imperialists and how they acquired their empire.

4. explain the problems that Rome faced as the result of her acquisition of empire.

Chapter Summary

How and why did the city of Rome become an enormous world state? Whereas the Greeks gave the Mediterranean world cultural unity, Rome gave it political unity and a political heritage. This chapter traces the origins of that legacy from the Etruscans in the eighth century B.C. through the troubled but dynamic days of the republic in the first century B.C. Between these two periods the Romans built an enormous empire, gave the world important lessons in politics, and established some new concepts in law.

There are three major themes in this chapter. The first is assimilation. The Romans assimilated many of the customs of the ancient Etruscans and then, like the Macedonians before them, readily adopted the culture of Hellenic Greece. Conquest and imperialism is the second theme. The Romans became empire builders almost by accident. A conflict in southern Italy led to foreign involvement, first in Sicily and then in North Africa during the Punic wars between Rome and Carthage. The third theme is the impact of imperialism on Rome. Did imperialism bring more harm than blessings? The chapter evaluates the economic and political changes that military victory brought, noting how the coming of empire meant a change in lifestyle and, according to some Romans, such as Cato, a general moral deterioration. Certainly, foreign conquests created large standing armies and veterans who played a growing role in Roman politics. Once this happened, government by constitution was doomed.

Study Outline

Use this outline to preview the chapter before you read a particular section in your textbook and then as a self-check to test your reading comprehension after you have read the chapter section.

I. The land and the sea
   A. The geography and early settlement of Rome
      1. Italy's lack of navigable rivers discouraged trade, but the land was fertile and productive and the mountains not as divisive as those of Greece.
      2. The two great fertile plains of Italy are Latium and Campania.
      3. The Romans established their city on seven hills along the Tiber River in Latium.
II. The Etruscans and Rome (750-509 B.C.)
   A. Between 1000 and 875 B.C., many Indo-European peoples moved into Italy from the north.
   B. The Etruscans
      1. Etruscans were probably in Italy since time immemorial.
         a. They had their own language based on the Greek alphabet.
         b. Etruscan urban life came to dominate much of Italy.
   C. The Celts were fierce fighters who migrated throughout Europe from the upper Danube.
   D. The Romans
      1. According to legend, Romulus and Remus founded Rome in 753 B.C.
      2. The Etruscans passed many customs and practices on to the Romans.
      3. The Etruscans turned Rome into an important city and brought it into contact with the Mediterranean world.
      4. The Capitoline Hill became Rome's religious center (Temple of Jupiter).
      5. Much of early Roman history is based on legends and tales of war, brought together by the historian Livy long after the founding of Rome.
      6. According to tradition, the Romans expelled the Etruscan rulers and founded a republic in 509 B.C.
         a. They used alliances and soldiering to grow and prosper.
      7. In 390 B.C., invading Celts—or Gauls—destroyed Rome but the Romans reorganized their army and rebuilt the city.
      8. One reason for Rome's success in subduing Italy was the Roman concept of citizenship.
         a. The Romans frequently granted citizenship to those they conquered, thereby strengthening Rome.
         b. In their willingness to extend citizenship, the political genius of the Romans triumphed where Greece had failed.
         c. Building a vast road system also helped keep Rome united with her colonies.
III. The Roman state
   A. In the early republic, power resided in the hands of the members of the aristocracy, called the patricians; commoners were called plebeians.
      1. Rome was ruled by people's assemblies, elected magistrates, and—most important—the senate.
         a. The senate advised the consuls and magistrates, and its advice had the force of law.
         b. The senate gave the republic stability and ʼntinuity.

      c. The *comitia centuriata,* which was dominated by the patricians, decided Roman policy.

      d. In 471 B.C. the plebeians gained their own assembly, the *concilium plebis.*

      e. Two elected consuls and the senate ran the state.

      f. In 366 B.C. the office of praetor was created.

  2. Rome's greatest achievement was its development of the concept of law.

      a. Civil law developed to protect people and property.

      b. Gradually, the concept of universal law applicable to all societies developed.

IV. Social conflict in Rome

  A. The plebeians' desire for equality and justice led to a conflict with the patricians known as the Struggle of the Orders.

    1. A general strike led to concessions being granted to the plebeians—partly because of patrician fears of hostile neighbors.

    2. The plebeians won legal and land reforms.

      a. The *lex Canuleia* allowed for intermarriage between plebeians and patricians.

      b. The Law of the Twelve Tables, a codification of previously unpublished law, was a result of plebeian pressure for legal reform.

      c. Later, the patricians were forced to publish legal procedures, too, so plebeians could enjoy full protection under the law.

    3. Licinius and Sextus brought about further reform for the plebeians, but the struggle did not end until the passage of *lex Hortensia* in 287 B.C.

    4. The end result of the Struggle of the Orders was greater political opportunities for the plebeians and a new ruling nobility made up of both plebeians and patricians.

V. Roman Expansion

  A. Italy becomes Roman

    1. Between 282 and 262 B.C. the Romans colonized nearly all of Italy.

      a. They created two classes of citizenship—one for those close to Rome, another, with less rights, as allies.

      b. Therefore, all Italians were included in making Italy Roman.

  B. Overseas conquest (282-146 B.C.)

    1. When the Romans reached southern Italy, they became involved in a series of wars.

    2. The Romans did not have a pre-existing strategy for world conquest.

    3. Roman imperialism took two forms: aggression in the West and patronage in the East.

    4. They imposed a "Pyrrhic victory" on the Greeks in southern Italy.

    5. Rome's need to control Sicily led to war with Carthage—the economic giant of the western Mediterranean.

  C. The Punic wars

    1. The First Punic War, fought over Sicily, was won by Rome in 241 B.C.

    2. The Second Punic War found Carthage attacking Rome by way of Spain, with a major victory at Cannae in 216 B.C.

      a. Hannibal led the Carthaginian forces over the Alps into Italy.

      b. He then spread devastation throughout Italy, yet failed to crush Rome.

    3. Rome's commander, Scipio, took Spain from the Carthaginians in 207 B.C.

    4. A victory by Scipio over Hannibal at Zama in 202 B.C. meant that the western Mediterranean would be Roman.

     5. Fear of Carthage led to the Third Punic War.
       a. In 146 B.C. Carthage was defeated, but Spain was not conquered until 133 B.C.
       b. By 146 B.C. the Mediterranean had become for the Romans *mare nostrum*—"our sea."

VI. Old values and Greek culture
   A. The acquisition of an empire was the beginning of Rome's troubles.
     1. The building of empire brought about the end of traditional values and encouraged a new materialism.
     2. The Romans had to change their institutions, social patterns, and way of thinking to meet their new responsibilities as world rulers.
   B. Marcus Cato represented the traditional ideal of a simple and virtuous life.
     1. In traditional Rome the *paterfamilias* held immense power within the family.
     2. The virtues of chastity and modesty among women were valued.
     3. Children began their formal education at the age of seven.
     4. The agricultural year followed the traditional farmer's calendar.
     5. Slavery was common; relations between master and slave were often good.
     6. Religion played an important role in Roman life; Romans believed that if they honored the gods, they could grant them divine favor.
   C. Scipio Aemilianus represented the new spirit of wealth and leisure.
     1. For the new Romans victory in war meant materialism and the pursuit of pleasure.
     2. Greek culture—Hellenism—came to dominate roman life.
     3. Scipio Aemilianus introduced to Rome the art of personal politics.
     4. He was the center of a circle of Hellenists and helped make the culture of Greece an integral part of Roman life.
     5. Hellenism stimulated the growth of Roman art, literature, and leisure activities such as bathing.
       a. The "baths" were gyms and pools for exercise and social interaction.
       b. Women had separate facilities.

VII. The late republic (133-31 B.C.)
   A. War and the demands of the new empire created serious political problems.
     1. The republican constitution no longer suited Rome's needs.
     2. Powerful generals became a threat.
     3. Rome's Italian allies agitated for the rights of citizenship.
   B. Unrest in Rome and Italy
     1. War and the new empire also caused economic problems; many veterans sold their war-ruined farms to the big landowners and migrated to the cities.
     2. A large number of urban poor emerged.
     3. The Gracchus brothers sought a solution to the problem of the veterans and the urban poor.
       a. Tiberius Gracchus angered aristocrats and the senate by proposing land reform.
       b. The murder of Tiberius Gracchus by the senators initiated an era of political violence.
       c. Gaius Gracchus demanded citizenship for all Italians, but was killed by the senate.

    4. Consul Marius used the army as his tool by recruiting landless men and promising land to the volunteers.
       a. But the Senate refused to give the troops land.
       b. Henceforth, army troops looked to their commanders for their rewards—not the state.

C. The Civil War (91-88 B.C.).
    1. Marius changed the military so that the army was virtually a private army and no longer made up of loyal citizens.
    2. Marius and then Sulla fell into warring against each other and into a civil war.
       a. Sulla used his troops to take Rome and make the Senate stronger.
       b. Marius, in turn, returned to Rome and killed Sulla's supporters.
    3. Sulla became dictator but allowed a return to the constitutional republic; then, however, fifty more years of civil war led to the end of the Republic.
    4. A slave revolt led by Spartacus in 73 B.C. was put down by the military under Crassus and Pompey—who in turn became dictators.

D. The Triumph of Julius Caesar
    1. Caesar, a military genius and an intellectual, conquered all of Gaul by 50 B.C.
    2. Conflict between Caesar and Pompey resulted in more civil war.
    3. Caesar defeated Pompey in 45 B.C. and made himself dictator.
    4. Caesar founded colonies to absorb Rome's poor and extended citizenship to many of the provincials.
    5. Caesar was assassinated in 44 B.C., setting off another round of civil war.
    6. The Second Triumvirate (Augustus, Antony, and Lepidus) defeated Caesar's murderers but soon came into conflict themselves.
    7. In 31 B.C., Augustus put an end to civil war by defeating Antony and Cleopatra at the battle of Actium.

Review Questions

Check your understanding of this chapter by answering the following questions.

1. Who were the Etruscans and of what importance were they to the early Romans?

2. What were the causes and the outcome of the Struggle of the Orders?

3. What were the motives and events that caused Rome to become an expansionist state?

4. What were the causes and results of the Punic wars?

5. Why did Sicily and Spain become battlegrounds for the Punic wars? What was Hannibal's military strategy?

6. Trace the territorial expansion of Rome that followed the Punic wars. By what year could the Romans declare the Mediterranean to be *mare nostrum*?

7. Describe the role of the *paterfamilias* in Roman life. How were women and children treated in Roman society?

8. Discuss the institution of slavery in Roman society. Is slavery ever a humane institution?

9. How did the Romans regard their gods? Was religion important to the Romans? Did Christianity completely replace Roman religion?

10. Contrast the interests and lifestyles of Marcus Cato and Scipio Aemilianus. Do you believe that Greek culture corrupted the Romans? What causes certain elements within society to break with their past?

11. What impact did the imperial expansion of Rome have on the economic and political conditions of Roman people? Who were the winners and the losers?

12. What did the Gracchus brothers intend to do for Rome? Why was there so much opposition? What were the results?

13. What were the reasons for instability in Rome from about the time of Gaius Marius in 107 B.C. to Augustus in 31 B.C.? Why did dictatorship come about?

Study-Review Exercises

Define the following key concepts and terms.

Pyrrhic victory

ius naturae

mare nostrum

paterfamilias

pax Romana

latifundia

senatus populusque Romanus

imperialism

Identify and explain the significance of each of the following.
Romulus and Remus

Livy

Gauls

Punic wars

First Triumvirate

comitia centuriata

concilium plebis

Law of the Twelve Tables

The festival of Anna Perenna

lex Hortensia

patricians

plebeians

Roman senate

Hannibal

Cincinnatus

Marcus Cato

Scipio Aemilianus

Sciponic Circle

Etruscans

Explain who the following people were and what role each played in the troubled years of the late republic.

Gracchus brothers

Cicero

Sulla

Pompey

Julius Caesar

Octavian (Augustus)

Antony and Cleopatra

Test your understanding of the chapter by providing the correct answers.

1. The Punic wars were between Rome and _____.

2. The general strike of the plebeians in 494 B.C. *did/did not* gain them rights.

3. Once the Romans had conquered southern Italy, they found themselves in need of controlling _____ and then _____.

4. The Romans *did/did not* hold racist attitudes toward their slaves.

5. After the wars of conquest the Romans began to express *more/less* interest in Hellenism.

6. The Roman sky god _____ became the equivalent of the Greek Zeus.

7. Roman art tended to be more *idealistic/realistic* than Greek art.

8. Prior to 90 B.C., all Italians *did/did not* hold Roman citizenship.

9. The wealthy landowning aristocracy in Rome was known as the _____ class.

Place the following events in correct chronological order.

End of the First Punic War
Roman conquest of Spain
Invasion of Italy by the Gauls
Defeat of Hannibal at Zama
Completion of the Roman conquest of the eastern Mediterranean
Invasion of Italy by Pyrrhus

1.

2.

3.

4.

5.

6.

Major Political Ideas

1. How did Roman ideas about the state, citizenship, and participation in the state differ from those of the Greeks? What did it mean to live in a "republic" at the time of Rome and why did the republican constitution form of government fail?

2. Define *ius civile, ius gentium,* and *ius naturae.* Where did political power lie in republican Rome?

Issues for Essays and Discussion

What geographical, political, military, and economic factors contributed to Rome's rise to greatness? Was this rise an inevitable result of military-economic strength , or did the Romans exhibit imagination and inventiveness?

Interpretation of Visual Sources

Study the photograph of the mosaic tile depiction of "Roman Table Manners." What does this tell us about Roman life—in terms of diet, sense of humor, and art?

Geography

1. Study Map 5.1 in your textbook and then answer the following questions: how did geography encourage Italy to "look to the Mediterranean"? What geographic features of Italy encouraged the growth and development of Rome? What was special about the area where Rome was established?

2. On Outline Map 5.2 provided, and using Map 5.2 in your textbook as a reference, mark the following: North Africa, Farther and Nearer Spain, Gaul, Cisalpine Gaul, Dalmatia, Germany, Britain, Macedonia, the Mediterranean Sea, Thrace, Phrygia, Cappadocia, Cilicia, Syria, Parthia, Armenia, the Black Sea. Now outline the area held by Rome by 133 B.C. and the territories added to Rome by 44 B.C.

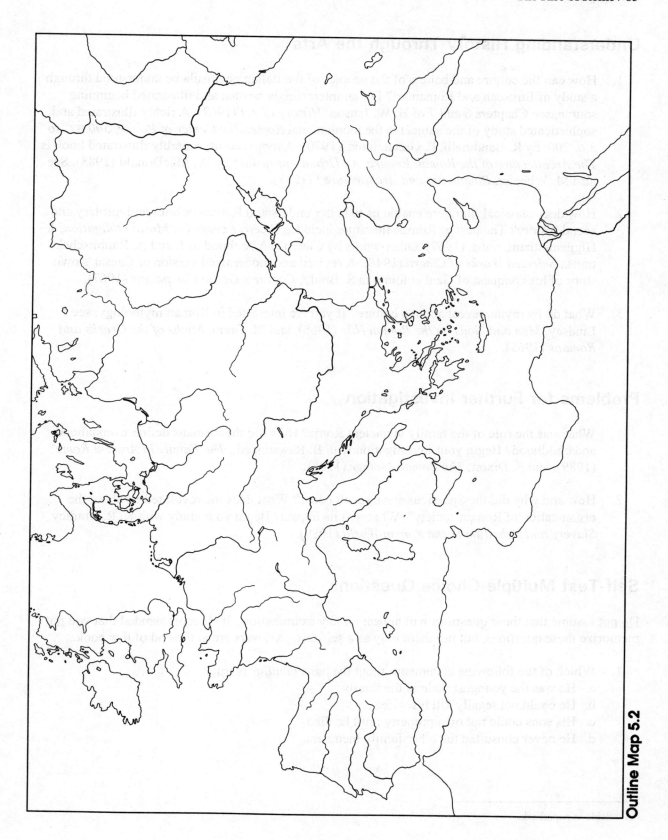

Outline Map 5.2

Understanding History Through the Arts

1. How can the culture and beliefs of the peoples of the Italian peninsula be understood through a study of Etruscan and Roman art? For an interestingly written and illustrated beginning source, see Chapters 6 and 7 of H. W. Janson, *History of Art* (1962). A richly illustrated and sophisticated study of the subject is the monumental *Rome: The Center of Power, 500 B.C. to A.D. 200,* by R. Bandinelli, P. Green, trans. (1970). A more recent, superbly illustrated book is *The Architecture of the Roman Empire, An Urban Appraisal** by W. MacDonald (1988). See also M. Wheeler, *Roman Art and Architecture** (1985).

2. How does classical literature enable us to better understand Roman politics and military and social history? The best of Roman literature includes Cicero's essay *On Moral Obligation,* J. Higgenbotham, trans. (1967). Other works by Cicero can be found in J. and A. Raubitschek, trans., *Selected Works of Cicero* (1948). A revised and modernized version of Caesar's own story of his conquest of Gaul is found in S. Brady, *Caesar's Gallic Campaigns* (1967).

3. What do its myths reveal about a culture? If you are interested in Roman mythology, see J. Lindsay, *Men and Gods on the Roman Nile* (1968), and M. Grant, *Myths of the Greeks and Romans* (1965).

Problems for Further Investigation

1. What was the role of the family in ancient Rome? How did the Romans define womanhood and childhood? Begin your investigation with B. Rawson, ed., *The Family in Ancient Rome** (1989), and S. Dixon, *The Roman Mother* (1988).

2. How and why did the Spartacus slave revolt occur? What does the revolt tell us about the organization of Roman society? What was its impact? Begin your study with K. R. Bradley, *Slavery and Rebellion in the Roman World* (1989).

Self-Test Multiple-Choice Questions

Do not assume that these questions will appear on any examination. It is recommended that you not memorize these questions, but use them only as a self-test. Answers are at the end of this book.

1. Which of the following statements about the *paterfamilias* is true?
   a. He was the youngest male in the family.
   b. He could not legally kill his wife.
   c. His sons could not own property until he died.
   d. He never consulted the other family members.

---

*Available in paperback.

2. As a result of the wars of conquest, the small, independent Roman farmers
   a. gained vast new markets for their grain.
   b. found their farms in ruins.
   c. became an important political power.
   d. got rich.

3. Overall, the Romans' greatest achievements were in the field of
   a. empire building.
   b. agriculture.
   c. the arts.
   d. literature.

4. Rome succeeded where Greece had failed because it
   a. conquered peoples and let them govern themselves.
   b. always lived peacefully with its neighbors.
   c. always peacefully incorporated peoples into the Roman system.
   d. conquered peoples and incorporated them into the Roman system.

5. Which of the following was *not* a Roman republican office?
   a. Emperor
   b. Quaestor
   c. Praetor
   d. Consul

6. The Struggle of the Orders resulted in all of the following *except*
   a. the office of the tribune.
   b. the ascendancy of the patricians.
   c. the Law of the Twelve Tables.
   d. a stronger and more united Rome.

7. The goal of the Gracchi was to
   a. exploit the urban poor and the peasant farmers.
   b. join the patricians.
   c. aid the urban poor and the peasant farmers.
   d. deny citizenship to certain Romans.

8. All but which of the following are principal geographical characteristics of Italy?
   a. Hilly, but not inhospitable, land
   b. The division of the peninsula into northern and southern halves by the Appenine mountains
   c. Few navigable rivers
   d. Two large fertile plains

9. According to Roman legend, the founders of Rome were
   a. the Greeks.
   b. the tribe of Autun.
   c. Livy and his family.
   d. Romulus and Remus.

10. The Roman citizen appointed dictator for fifteen days who returned to his farm after defeating his country's enemy was
    a. Tarquin the Proud.
    b. Cincinnatus.
    c. Servius Tullius.
    d. Pyrrhus.

11. The chief magistrates of republican Rome—the officials who administered the state and commanded the army—were known as
    a. consuls.
    b. quaestors.
    c. praetors.
    d. senators.

12. During the Second Punic War the Carthaginian leader who attempted to conquer Rome was
    a. Philip of Carthage.
    b. Hannibal.
    c. Alexander.
    d. Menenius Agrippa.

13. Most ordinary Roman women
    a. had little influence in family affairs.
    b. spent most of their time performing religious rituals.
    c. had considerable influence and responsibility in the family economy.
    d. exercised total control of their children's upbringing.

14. Which of the following statements best describes the status of Roman slaves?
    a. Slaves were considered to be inferior human beings.
    b. Slaves suffered from racial bias.
    c. Slaves were conscripted into the Roman army.
    d. Slaves were often granted freedom by their masters.

15. The father of Latin poetry was
    a. Gaius Marius.
    b. Ennius.
    c. Scipio Aemilianus.
    d. Cato.

16. The conservative, traditional elements of Rome regarded the public baths as
    a. the only way to encourage reform in public health.
    b. a good way of using Greek culture for the benefit of Rome.
    c. a waste of time and an encouragement to idleness.
    d. important as places for political discussion.

17. The wars during the time of republican Rome
    a. left Rome a strong and prosperous agricultural base.
    b. left Roman farms in a state of decay.
    c. caused Rome to look elsewhere for its food supply.
    d. caused a decentralization of landownership.

18. The Roman leader who was murdered because he proposed that public land be given to the
    poor in small lots was
    a. Sulla.
    b. Tiberius Gracchus.
    c. Cato.
    d. Caesar.

19. The consul who recruited an army by allowing landless men to serve in the regions was
    a. Cincinnatus.
    b. Tiberius.
    c. Sulla
    d. Marius.

20. By the time of the late republican period in Rome, most industry and small manufacturing
    was in the hands of
    a. plebeians.
    b. slaves.
    c. Christians.
    d. the army.

21. The Etruscans amassed extensive wealth by
    a. military conquest in Gaul.
    b. moving the center of their community away from Rome.
    c. perfecting agriculture and rural community life.
    d. trading their manufactured goods in Italy and beyond.

22. The status of one who held *civitas sine suffragio* was that of
    a. slavery.
    b. full citizenship, but for Romans only.
    c. citizenship without the right to vote or hold office.
    d. military service.

23. The geographic area described as the "wrestling ground for the Carthaginians and Romans" was
    a. western Greece.
    b. Gaul.
    c. North Africa.
    d. Sicily.

24. Manumission in Roman society was
    a. infrequent.
    b. against all laws.
    c. only common among Christian Romans.
    d. common.

25. The latifundia was
    a. a large farming estate.
    b. a client kingdom of Rome.
    c. a law that provided for equality between plebeians and patricians.
    d. a form of citizenship.

Chapter 6

The Pax Romana

Learning Objectives

After reading and studying this chapter you should be able to:

1. discuss Augustus's goals for the Roman republic and how he tried to implement them.

2. discuss the appeal and influence of Christianity.

3. discuss the attempted reforms of Diocletian and Constantine I.

Chapter Summary

This chapter tells the story of Rome in the age of empire and emperors. When Julius Caesar's nephew Augustus became "the First Citizen of the State" in 31 B.C., Rome began a new era of constitutional monarchy called the Augustan Age. This was the "golden age" of Rome in terms of economy, literature, and imperial expansion. Under the Roman Empire the Mediterranean and European peoples enjoyed a long tradition of firmly established personal freedom. The *Pax Romana,* or peace of Rome, encouraged the spread of Roman law, justice, and administration as well as the further diffusion of Greek culture, especially into the European world. This era of peace occurred in part because of the constitutional monarchy Augustus established, which lasted until the third century A.D., when once again Rome became wracked by civil war. The emperor's power, however, rested mainly with the army, which he controlled. Indeed, control of the army became a growing problem for Augustus and his successors, many of whom owed their power to some military rebellion in the provinces. In the long run, Augustus's political settlement was not successful, but his contributions were great.

Augustus treated imperial subjects in the conquered provinces justly, and his expansion of the empire into Europe was enormously important for European history. His reign also ushered in a great age of Latin literature. It is through the works of Virgil, Livy, and Horace that we are able to gain a sense of what Roman people were like and what they expected of life.

The development and spread of Christianity also occurred during this era. Paul of Tarsus turned the Jewish cult of Jesus into a universal religion based on the ethics of love and forgiveness. Finally, in the fourth century A.D., Christianity was made the official religion of Rome. Oddly, what had begun as a Jewish hope for salvation from Rome became Rome's state religion.

In the third century A.D., the breakdown of government and order ushered in an age of civil war and barbarian invasions from which Rome never fully recovered. The reforming emperors Diocletian and Constantine were able to restore the old system only partially. They were not able to turn around the depression and decline in trade and agriculture.

Why did Rome "fall"? Gibbon's famous theory, that Christianity was the primary cause, is flawed, and although economic and political explanations are important, they do not tell the entire story. In a real sense there is no answer because the Roman Empire did not actually fall but slowly merged into a new medieval world. It was Rome and Christianity that provided Europe with the framework for a new age.

Study Outline

Use this outline to preview the chapter before you read a particular section in your textbook and then as a self-check to test your reading comprehension after you have read the chapter section.

I. Augustus's settlement (31 B.C.-A.D. 14)
   A. Augustus's goal was to re-establish the republic after years of civil war, to demobilize the army, and to meet the threat of the barbarians.
   B. The principate and the restored republic
      1. Augustus created a constitutional monarchy but did not give the senate power equal to his own.
      2. Augustus became *princeps civitatis,* "the First Citizen of the State," and held other offices, particularly that of magistrate.
      3. His control of the army was the main source of his power.
         a. Augustus controlled deployment of the soldiers and paid their wages.
         b. He founded colonies of soldiers, which helped unite the Mediterranean world and spread Greco-Roman culture.
   C. Augustus's administration of the provinces
      1. Augustus encouraged self-government and urbanism.
      2. The cult of *Roma et Augustus* gave the empire unity.
   D. Roman expansion into northern and western Europe
      1. Augustus continued Caesar's push into Europe.
         a. In Gaul he founded towns and built roads.
         b. He extended Roman rule into Spain, Germany, and eastern Europe.
      2. The Romans' relations with barbarians varied from cooperation to hostility.
   E. Literary flowering
      1. The Augustan Age was a golden age of Latin literature.
      2. Roman writers celebrated the dignity of humanity and the range of its accomplishments.
         a. Virgil wrote about the greatness and virtue of Rome in his masterpiece, the *Aeneid.*
         b. Ovid's poems tell of festivals, religious rites, and other aspects of popular religion.
         c. Livy's history of Rome is one of Rome's great legacies to the modern world.
         d. Horace praised the simple life and the pax Romana.
   F. By sharing power with his adopted son, Augustus created a dynasty.

II. The coming of Christianity
   A. The colony of Judaea suffered during the Roman civil wars, and Jewish resentment of Rome increased.
   B. Hatred of King Herod and Roman taxes, harsh enforcement of the law, and religious interference led to civil war in Judaea.
   C. Two anti-Roman movements existed: Zealot extremists, who fought Rome, and militant believers in the apocalypse, who believed that the coming of the Messiah would end Roman rule.
   D. Pagan religious cults were numerous, including the official state cults, the old traditional cults, and the new mystery cults, which met the needs of the people for security and emotional release.

III. The life and teachings of Jesus
   A. Jesus was raised in Galilee—which was exposed to many peoples, ideas, and trade.
      1. People have long disagreed as to who Jesus was and what he intended to do.
         a. The main records of his life are the four gospels of the New Testament.
         b. But they were written long after his death and do not agree.
   B. Jesus was a teacher who claimed to be the Messiah of a spiritual kingdom.
      1. His teachings were in the Jewish tradition, but he refused to preach rebellion against Rome.
      2. Pontius Pilate, the Roman prefect, was worried about maintaining civil order, so he sentenced Jesus to death.
   C. Jesus's followers claimed that he had risen from the dead—to promise immortality to Christians.
      1. His followers met in congregations to discuss the meaning of the life of Jesus.
   D. Paul of Tarsus transformed the Jesus cult and made it applicable to all.
      1. He broadened Christianity's appeal to non-Jews ("Gentiles") and women.
      2. He taught that Jesus died to save sinners.
      3. Paul taught that Jesus was sent to save Gentiles, not Jews.
   E. Christianity was attractive for many reasons.
      1. It was open to common people.
      2. It held out the promise of salvation and forgiveness.
      3. It gave each person a role and a sense of importance in working for God's plan.

IV. The Julio-Claudians and the Flavians (27 B.C.-A.D. 96)
   A. For fifty years after Augustus's death, all emperors of Rome came from the Julio-Claudian dynasty.
      1. Claudius created a system of imperial bureaucracy so he could delegate power.
      2. The army, especially the Praetorian Guard, began to interfere in politics. The Year of the Four Emperors proved the Augustan settlement a failure.
   B. The Flavian dynasty
      1. Vespasian created a monarchy and suppressed rebellions, destroying the state of Judaea in the process.
      2. Domitian won additional new territory for the empire.

V. The Age of the "Five Good Emperors" (A.D. 96-180)
   A. The age of the Antonines was one of unparalleled prosperity.

B. The Antonines were emperors in fact as well as theory—the emperor became an indispensable part of the imperial system.
   1. The emperors were the source of all authority in the empire.
   2. Hadrian reformed the bureaucracy by making it more professional and organized.
C. Changes in the army
   1. Under the Flavians the boundaries of the empire became fixed.
   2. More and more soldiers came from the provinces closest to the frontiers.

VI. Life in the "golden age"
A. Imperial Rome
   1. The city was huge, and fire and crime were ongoing problems.
   2. The government provided the citizens of Rome with free grain, oil, and wine to prevent riots.
   3. Free, often brutal, entertainment was provided, but the most popular entertainment was chariot racing.
   4. Most Romans worked hard and lived average lives.
B. Rome and the provinces
   1. Roman *cultural* influence was limited to urban areas while its influence in rural areas was largely *economic.*
   2. Agriculture flourished on large tracts of land cultivated by free tenant farmers.
   2. Romans left rural native culture alone.
   3. The biggest impact on provinces was the growth of manufacturing.
   4. Manufacturing, such as glass and pottery making, tended to move from Italy to the provinces, especially to northern Europe.

VII. Civil wars and invasion in the third century
A. Commodus's reign led to civil war; over twenty emperors ascended the throne between 235 and 284.
B. Migrating barbarians on the frontiers found gaps in the Roman defenses.
   1. In A.D. 258, the Goths burst into Europe.
   2. The Alamanni, Franks, Saxons, and other tribes invaded the empire.
C. Turmoil and impoverishment in farm and village life
   1. The breakdown of the system led to crime and corruption.
   2. Much of the damage was done by officials and soldiers.

VIII. Reconstruction under Diocletian and Constantine (A.D. 284-337)
A. The end of political turmoil under Diocletian's reign
   1. Diocletian claimed that God had chosen him to rule; his power became absolute.
   2. Because the empire was too big for one person to govern well, Diocletian reorganized it.
     a. Imperial authority was split between two emperors—Diocletian in the east and an *augustus* in the west.
     b. Each emperor was assisted by a *caesar.*
     c. The power of the provincial governors was reduced.
     d. Diocletian's division between east and west became permanent.
B. Inflation and taxes
   1. The monetary system was in ruins and highly inflated.
   2. Diocletian attempted to curb inflation through wage and price controls.
   3. The new imperial taxation system led to a loss of freedom as people became locked into their jobs.

  C. The decline of small farms
    1. Worsening conditions fostered the growth of large, self-sufficient villas.
    2. Small farmers turned to big landlords for protection, in exchange for their land.
  D. The acceptance of Christianity
    1. The emperor Constantine legalized Christianity—he died a Christian in 337.
    2. Scholars today believe that the Christians exaggerated the degree of pagan hostility to them and that most of the stories about martyrs were fictitious.
    3. Many Romans misunderstood Christianity, thinking, for example, that Christian rejection of their gods would harm Rome or that Christians engaged in cannibalism.
      a. They thought the Christians were atheists because they denied the existence of pagan gods.
      b. Because Roman religion was linked to the state; a token ritual to pagan gods was expected.
      c. Hostility to Christians decreased; Emperor Trajan forbade hunting down Christians.
    5. The desperation and stress of the third century caused a short-lived upswing in persecutions.
      a. In 380 Emperor Theodosius made Christianity the official religion of the Roman Empire; henceforth the Christians began to persecute the pagans for their beliefs.
  E. The construction of Constantinople
    1. Constantine built a new capital for the empire at the site of Byzantium.
    2. The focus of the empire shifted to the east.
 IX. Classical Antiquity and Late Antiquity
  A. How had the world changed since the creation of Pax Romana?
    1. During Pax Romana the Romans had created security and order—with a uniform culture and rule by educated oligarchies.
    2. By 500 B.C., however, the East and West were divided and in the West cities and commerce declined and society had become rural and agricultural.
  B. How did Christianity differ from the state religion?
    1. Christianity demanded conversion and was intolerant of other faiths.
    2. Christianity claimed that all people are equal in the eyes of Jesus.
    3. When Roman administration fell, the Christian bishops assumed public responsibilities.
    4. Christianity eventually pushed classical culture aside and substituted all of it with Christian culture.

Review Questions

Check your understanding of this chapter by answering the following questions.

 1. What were the sources of Augustus's power? Was Augustus a "dictator" in the modern sense?

 2. What were Augustus's accomplishments with regard to the administration and expansion of the empire?

3. What does the work of the writers during Rome's golden age of literature tell us about Roman life and what the Romans thought important?

4. Why was the relationship between Rome and Judaea so strained in the age of Augustus? What were the motives and responses of both Jews and Romans?

5. Describe the political climate in Judaea during the life of Jesus of Nazareth. Did this climate influence the course of religious history?

6. Did Jesus intend to found a new religion? Explain by evaluating his work.

7. What role did Paul of Tarsus play in the evolution of Christianity, and what might have happened if Peter of Jerusalem had kept control over the cult?

8. Why was Christianity so attractive? How was this religion unlike that of the Greeks and Romans?

9. Under what circumstances did the Flavian dynasty come about and what were its contributions?

10. What is meant by the term *barracks emperors*?

11. What were the causes and the results of the civil wars between A.D. 235 and 284?

12. Discuss the impact the barbarians had on the empire. Were the invasions the cause or the result of a political breakdown?

13. Why did the number of small farmers and the amount of personal freedom decrease during and after the period of civil war?

14. What did Diocletian and Constantine do to restore and strengthen the empire?

15. Why were many Romans distrustful of Christianity?

Study-Review Exercises

Define the following key concepts and terms.

Messiah

paganism

princeps civitatis

Pax Romana

imperator

Julio-Claudian dynasty

gospels

Eucharist

villa

Identify and explain the significance of each of the following people and terms.

Goths

Jesus

Paul of Tarsus

Antonines

Apocalypse of Baruch

King Herod of Judaea

Zealots

gladiatorial fighting

"five good emperors"

Mithraism

Commodus

barracks emperors

Constantine

Virgil

Theodosius

Explain the contributions of each of the following to Rome and the Roman Empire.

Augustus

Claudius

Hadrian

Vespasian

Diocletian

Constantine

Explain the subject matter and the central theme of each of the following works.

Georgics

Aeneid

Ab Urbe Condita

Test your understanding of the chapter by providing the correct answers.

1. Augustus *did/did not* believe that the colonies should be self-governing and culturally independent.

2. The capital of the Roman Empire was eventually moved to the new eastern city of _____ .

3. The great Roman historian who believed that history should be applied to the present was _____ .

4. From the time of Augustus, the power of the principate tended to *increase/decrease.*

5. Christianity was made the official religion of Rome in the year _____ .

6. The Roman government *did/did not* provide free food and entertainment for the citizens of Rome.

7. During the reign of Augustus, free farming tended to *increase/decrease*.

8. For the most part, Roman persecution of Christians was *minor/widespread*.

9. Under the "five good emperors" northern and western Europe underwent a period of economic *expansion/decline*.

Place the following events in correct chronological order.

First barbarian invasion
"Year of the Four Emperors"
Execution of Jesus of Nazareth
Ending of the republican civil wars by Augustus
Golden age of Rome under the "five good emperors"
Building of Constantinople

1.

2.

3.

4.

5.

6.

Major Political Ideas

1. Describe the two Jewish responses to Roman rule, the Zealots and the growth of a militant apocalyptic sentiment. Which one was more successful? Was Jesus a revolutionary?

2. What was the *princeps civitatis* and what was the system of picking him after the death of Augustus? Did the system work?

3. What was the source of Augustus's power? Was he a dictator? Explain how the concept and power of the emperor changed under Diocletian and Constantine. Why did these changes occur?

Issues for Essays and Discussion

1. What is meant by the term *Pax Romana*? What was the secret of Roman success? Answer these questions by making reference to the particular accomplishments of the Romans in the areas of law, administration, politics, literature, and religion. Did the Romans create anything new, or did they simply build on the accomplishments of others, such as the Greeks?

2. What were the results of the period of civil war between A.D. 235 and 284? Could it have been prevented? What is meant by the claim that it was in this period of disruption that the medieval world had its origin?

3. Was the rise of Christianity simply a reaction on the part of Jews to Roman rule? Describe the life and teachings of Jesus. What was Christianity's appeal to so many people in the Roman world? How did it evolve from an outlawed religion to the state religion of Rome?

4. What caused the "decline and fall" of the Roman Empire? Was it self-inflicted? Was it destroyed by some outside forces? Was it inevitable?

Geography

1. On Outline Map 6.1 provided, and using Map 6.1 and Map 6.4 in the textbook as a reference, mark the following: the boundaries of the Roman Empire under Augustus, the empire's division under Diocletian, Rome, Sicily, Britain, the Rhine River, Byzantium, Crete, the Danube River, Carthage, Jerusalem, the Teutoburger forest.

2. Describe the Roman penetration into northern and western Europe. What kinds of problems did the Romans face, and what techniques did they use in their successful conquests?

Outline Map 6.1

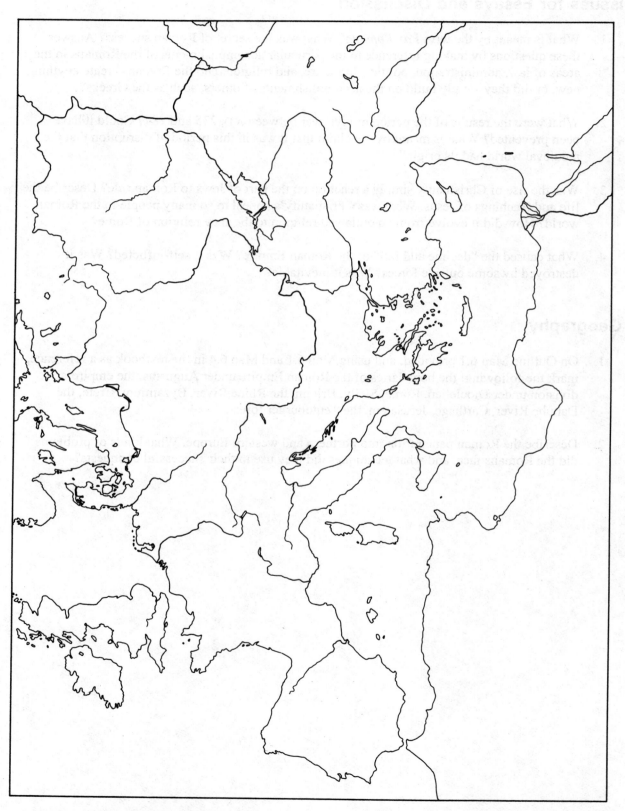

Understanding History Through the Arts

1. Were the Romans innovators or mimics in the realm of art? Since the source of much Roman art was Greece, many argue that there is hardly such a thing as a "Roman" style and that only in architecture were the Romans truly original. The arch and vault and the construction of sewers, bridges, roads, and aqueducts were among Rome's great enterprises. Chapter 7, "Roman Art," in H. W. Janson's *History of Art* (1962) is an excellent review. A more detailed account is G. Rivoira, *Roman Architecture* (1930), and R. Bandinelli, *Rome: The Late Empire. Roman Art, A.D. 200-400,* P. Green, trans. (1971).

2. Why was Virgil's poetry so popular? For insight into the works of this poetic genius, see W. Knight, *Roman Virgil** (1966). Other works of interest include *On the Nature of the Universe,** R. Latham, trans. (1967), by Lucretius, a poet, and Epicurean; and Ovid's *The Love Poems of Ovid,** H. Gregory, trans. (1964).

Problems for Further Investigation

Reading biography can be an interesting and rewarding way of discovering the past. A. Schweitzer's *The Quest of the Historical Jesus* (1948) is a superb work; more recently is J. D. Crossan, *The Historical Jesus* (1992). A. D. Nock's *St. Paul* (1938) is an interesting study of one of the most important men in world history. *Rome in the Augustan Age* (1962) by H. Rowell is about Augustus, the man whose imprint on the empire was immense. Also recommended is R. Warner, *The Young Caesar* (1958). R. Graves's *I, Claudius** (1934) is an exciting account of the families, the work, and the loves of the emperors from Augustus to Claudius, and A. Ferrill, *Caligula, Emperor of Rome* (1992) is an interesting recent biography.

Self-Test Multiple-Choice Questions

Do not assume that these questions will appear on any examination. It is recommended that you not memorize these questions, but use them only as a self-test. Answers are at the end of this book.

1. Which of the following statements about Jesus of Nazareth is true?
   a. Jesus was a Persian teacher.
   b. Jesus sought to lead a rebellion against the hated Romans.
   c. Jesus wished to build an independent Christian state.
   d. Jesus's teachings and cult were basically Jewish.

---

*Available in paperback.

2. This "good emperor" reformed the Roman bureaucracy—including giving talented men the chance to serve government without having to rise up through the military.
   a. Trajan
   b. Diocletian
   c. Pontius Pilate
   d. Hadrian

3. The government that developed under Augustus is best described as a
   a. dictatorship.
   b. constitutional monarchy.
   c. republic.
   d. democracy.

4. The man most responsible for the spread of Christianity to non-Jews was
   a. Emperor Diocletian.
   b. St. Peter.
   c. Livy.
   d. Paul of Tarsus.

5. Which of the following statements about farm and village life during the turmoil of the third century A.D. is true?
   a. Crime decreased.
   b. Corruption increased.
   c. The villas disintegrated.
   d. Small landholdings increased.

6. In the restored republic, Augustus became
   a. *Res Gestae.*
   b. *Sanhedrin.*
   c. *dominus.*
   d. *princeps civitatis.*

7. Augustus's attitude toward the provinces was one of
   a. neglect.
   b. oppression.
   c. prejudice toward minorities.
   d. respect for local customs.

8. Which of the following was an anti-Roman group in Judaea?
   a. Zealots
   b. Baruch
   c. Essenes
   d. Hittites

9. Many people in the Roman era were attracted to Christianity because
   a. Christianity didn't discriminate by class or sex.
   b. Christianity did not share any of the features of mystery religions.
   c. Christianity was passive.
   d. Christianity would not have anything to do with the worldly and the sinner.

10. The backbone of Roman agriculture in the Augustan Age was
    a. slave labor.
    b. imported foods from the empire.
    c. captured barbarian labor.
    d. small free farmers.

11. Before Constantine legalized Christianity, the Romans demanded that the Christians
    a. worship the Roman gods.
    b. observe the ritual of sacrifice to the gods.
    c. deny Christ as a god.
    d. go back to their Jewish beliefs.

12. The city that Constantine made the capital of the eastern Roman Empire was
    a. Kiev.
    b. Constantinople.
    c. Alexandria.
    d. Athens.

13. *The Decline and Fall of the Roman Empire* was written by
    a. Constantine.
    b. Livy.
    c. Gibbon.
    d. Paul of Tarsus.

14. During the reign of Augustus, the direction of Roman conquest was toward
    a. Judaea.
    b. northern Europe.
    c. Britain.
    d. the Black Sea.

15. Above all, Virgil's *Aeneid* is
    a. a plea for Christianity.
    b. an argument against Roman imperialism and war.
    c. a vision of Rome as the protector of good in the world.
    d. the history of the fall of Athens.

16. The Roman-appointed king of Judaea was
    a. Herod.
    b. Jesus.
    c. Philip Augustus.
    d. Cato.

17. All except which of the following were characteristic of the third-century period of the barracks emperors?
    a. Civil war
    b. Barbarian invasions
    c. Severe economic decline
    d. Expansion of the empire into northern and western Europe

18. A villa was
    a. a Jewish military district.
    b. the Roman banking system.
    c. a Roman civil service district.
    d. a large, self-sufficient estate.

19. Rome's greatest poet was
    a. Horace.
    b. Livy.
    c. Caligula.
    d. Virgil.

20. To solve problems resulting from the empire's vast and unmanageable size, Diocletian
    a. reduced the empire's size by declaring the frontiers independent.
    b. tripled the number of local rulers to maintain better control.
    c. divided the territory among four emperors.
    d. divided the empire into an eastern and western half, appointing a colleague to rule in the western part.

21. The Flavian period came about largely because of
    a. military interference in the selection of the emperor.
    b. the Flavian control of the banking system.
    c. military defeat of Rome by the Goths.
    d. revolution in Judaea.

22. When the Roman general Decius bid for the emperorship by invading Rome in A.D. 249, the result was
    a. a strengthening of the frontiers.
    b. the expansion of the empire.
    c. greater military attention to imperial defenses.
    d. invasion by the Goths.

23. The Roman solution to the problems of food shortages and the ensuing food riots in the city of Rome was
    a. a free market economy with regard to food.
    b. new and improved crowd-control measures.
    c. land reform in order to improve productivity in the countryside.
    d. free grain for all citizens and cheap grain for noncitizens.

24. Hadrian's major contribution to Roman government was
    a. the merger of the civil service with the military.
    b. the creation of a professional, efficient government bureaucracy.
    c. the establishment of a constitutional monarchy.
    d. the conquest of Gaul.

25. In contrast to the Greek system of colonies, Roman colonies were
    a. independent.
    b. not influenced by the culture of the conqueror.
    c. not linked together by any economic ties.
    d. part of a tightly linked imperial system.

Chapter 7

The Making of Europe

Learning Objectives

After reading and studying this chapter you should be able to:

1. describe the main features of Germanic, Christian, and Greco-Roman life which came together as a new "European" culture.

2. explain how Christianity assimilated pagan culture.

3. discuss how both Byzantine and Islamic culture influenced western Europe in the Middle Ages.

Chapter Summary

Between 400 and 900, a distinctly "European" society evolved. The basic ingredients of this new European civilization were the Greco-Roman culture, the customs and traditions of the Germanic peoples, and Christianity.

Diocletian had divided the Roman Empire into two major parts. The capital of the western half was Rome; the capital of the eastern half was Constantinople. The eastern (Byzantine) empire lasted for nearly a thousand years after the disintegration of the western empire in the fifth century. Imperial administration in the West had, by 476, given way to massive Germanic invasions. Within Europe the strongest power and the only stabilizing force was the Roman church, which, largely by default, came to be the major political as well as spiritual power. In the eastern empire the emperor held supreme authority over the church. In Rome, however, the bishops formulated the theory of the church's ultimate power over the state. The church in the West assimilated much of the Greco-Roman culture and used its intellectual passion and administrative talent to tame and transform the Germanic tribes. Of equal importance in the making of Europe were the monastic orders, which after about 529 were unified under the *Rule* of Saint Benedict.

While Germans were being baptized and were consolidating themselves into great kingdoms, the new threat of Islam pushed into Europe. Founded by Muhammad in the early seventh century, the religion of Islam united the Arabs and in a short period produced one of the most expansionist cultures the world has ever witnessed. By the early eighth century, Muslims had conquered Spain and were pushing into France.

Both the Byzantine and the Islamic empires were important for European development. Both preserved much Greco-Roman knowledge, a great deal of which was not rediscovered in the West until much later, and they made important contributions to law, science, and medicine. Germanic tradition and custom were also important in that development. But above all, it was Christianity that gave Europe its strength and unity.

Study Outline

Use this outline to preview the chapter before you read a particular section in the textbook and then as a self-check to test your reading comprehension after you have read the chapter section.

I. The growth of the Christian church
  A. Christianity was a *syncretic* faith—that is, one that absorbed and adapted many ideas from other religions.
  B. While the Empire declined, the Church grew. The word *church* can mean several things, but at this time it was often applied to the officials, or *papa,* who presided over all Christians.
     1. The church adopted the Roman system of organization and succeeded in assimilating many peoples.
     2. The church possessed able administrators and literate, creative thinkers.
  C. The church and the Roman emperors
     1. Constantine supported and legalized Christianity in 312.
        a. He helped settle theological disputes.
     2. Theodosius increased the power of the church and made Christianity the official religion of the Roman Empire.
     3. The emperors were important in enforcing theological uniformity in the church.
        a. Constantine summoned the Council of Nicaea in 325 to combat the Arian heresy, which denied that Christ was divine.
        b. The council produced the Nicene Creed—the doctrine that Christ was of the same substance as God, and this became the orthodox position, supported by the state.
     4. Bishop Ambrose formulated the theory that the church was supreme over the state.
  D. Inspired leadership in the early church
     1. Many talented Romans, such as Ambrose, became administrators and workers in the church.
        a. The church adopted the empire's system of dioceses.
        b. Bishops came to preside over dioceses.
     2. The bishop of Rome eventually became the "Patriarch of the West," while other patriarchs sat at Antioch, Alexandria, Jerusalem, and Constantinople.
     3. Because the position of emperor disappeared in the West, the Roman bishop became the chief civil authority in Italy.
        a. It was said that Pope Leo I saved Rome from Attila.
        b. Pope Gregory acted as civil authority.
  E. The missionary activity of the early Christians
     1. The Roman soldier Martin of Tours brought Christianity to Gaul, while Saint Patrick brought Christianity and Roman culture to Ireland.
        a. Under Saint Columba, Iona in Scotland became an important Christian center.
        b. In 597, Pope Gregory I sent a delegation of monks to Britain, under the leadership of Augustine, to convert the English.

      2. Two forms of Christianity—Roman and Celtic—clashed, but the Roman tradition won out at the Synod of Whitby in 664.

      3. Between the fifth and tenth centuries, most people living in Europe were baptized.

         a. Religion influenced tribal life.

         b. Participating in religious observances was a social duty.

      4. Because of the Germans' warlike customs and different culture, their assimilation into Christianity was slow.

         a. The Christian emphasis on poverty, universal brotherhood, and love of enemies was difficult for German warriors to accept.

         b. The Christian concepts of sin and repentance were also hard for them to understand.

  F. Conversion and assimilation

      1. The missionaries pursued a policy of preaching and assimilating pagan customs and beliefs into Christianity.

      2. Penitentials—manuals used to examine one's conscience—were used by priests to teach people Christian virtue.

         a. The penitentials tell about the ascetic ideals of early Christianity and about crime in Celtic and Germanic societies.

         b. The penitential system helped religion become a private, personal matter.

II. Christian attitudes toward classical culture

  A. Adjustment: Despite early hostility, the Christians eventually adjusted to Roman culture.

      1. Early Christians believed that Roman culture was useless, immoral, and that the end of the world was near.

      2. They hated the Romans because they had crucified Christ and persecuted his followers.

  B. Nevertheless, Christianity compromised and adjusted to Roman culture.

      1. Saint Paul and Saint Jerome and others incorporated pagan thought into Christianity.

         a. Early Christians encouraged adjustment to the existing social, economic, and political establishment.

         b. Christians adopted the views of their contemporary world.

         c. Jesus had regarded women as equal to men but other (often later) influences were to cause Christianity to view women as inferior and sexual intercourse as undesirable.

         d. Early Christians treated homosexuality no differently than heterosexuality; objections came later, as Greco-Roman urban culture gave way to rural medieval culture.

  C. Saint Augustine and the synthesis of pagan and Christian thought

      1. Augustine, one of the most brilliant thinkers of Western culture, had a major impact on Christian thought.

         a. *The Confessions* describes Augustine's conflict between his spiritual self and his sensual self.

         b. He set forth what became a basic Christian belief: that all humans have an innate tendency to sin.

         c. In *City of God,* Augustine argued that the state is a necessary evil, but it can work for the good by providing the peace, justice, and order that Christians need to learn to live according to their religion.

     d.   Contrary to the Donatist Christians, Augustine believed that Christians should live in and transform society and that the Church was not simply for an elite.

     e.   Augustine believed that the function of the state is to protect people, and that ultimate authority in society lies with the church.

III. Christian Monasticism

   A. With the growth of Christianity as a city religion, materialism, sexual promiscuity, and political corruption caused some Christians to become nonconformists and escape urban life.

     1.   Monks took the place of martyrs as those who could speak for God.

   B. Western Monasticism: Early monasticism began in Egypt with people called hermits (from the Greek word *eremos*).

     1.   When this *eremitical* life spread to Western Europe it faced some problems:

        a.   The climate discouraged isolated living.

        b.   Church leaders feared and distrusted eremitical life.

     2.   Communal monasticism, first set forth by Pachomius in Egypt, was a way to overcome these objections; many experiments in communal living, which the church encouraged, followed in the fifth and sixth centuries.

        a.   John Cassian established monasteries in Gaul; the abbey of Lerins encouraged extremely ascetic behavior, such as fasting and self-flagellation.

        b.   Cassiodorus started the association of monasticism with scholarship and learning.

   C. The *Rule* of Saint Benedict became the guide for all Christian monastic life.

     1.   The *Rule* outlined a life of regularity, discipline, and moderation applicable to varying physical and geographical conditions.

        a.   Monks made a vow of stability, conversion of manners, and obedience.

        b.   The *Rule* is an expression of the assimilation of the Roman spirit into Western monasticism.

     2.   The Benedictine form of monasticism succeeded because it was balanced and it suited the social circumstances of early medieval society.

        a.   It provided for both intellectual and manual activity.

        b.   Benedict's twin sister adapted the *Rule* for the use of her community of nuns.

        c.   It provided local young people with education.

        d.   It generated great wealth and made substantial contributions to agricultural development.

   D. Eastern monasticism was influenced by the *Long Rules* of Saint Basil.

     1.   Severe asceticism was discouraged, and urban monasteries were encouraged.

        a.   Seventy abbeys were erected in Constantinople.

        b.   Monasteries grew wealthy from gifts and from engaging in industry and agriculture.

        c.   Revenues were spent on social services, such as food, hospitals, homes for the mentally ill, and so on.

     2.   The primary duty of the monk or nun was to pray; a central person was the holy and charismatic elder.

3. This eastern (Greek Orthodox) monasticism differed from that of the West in that each house developed its own rules, called *typikon*.
 a. Monks often moved from one monastery to another.
 b. Unlike in the West, monasteries never became a central feature of Greek monastic houses.

IV. The migration of the Germanic peoples
 A. The migrations of the Germanic peoples was important in the decline of the Roman Empire and the making of European civilization.
  1. Germanic tribes had been pushing against the Roman Empire's frontiers since about 150.
  2. The Germans migrated into Europe not because they were overpopulated—but because of war and the attraction to Roman wealth and work.
 B. Romanization and barbarization
  1. From the third century the Roman army was the chief agent of barbarization.
  2. Barbarian people entered the empire as army recruits, as *laeti* (refugees or prisoners of war), or as *foederati* (free barbarian units).
  3. The arrival of the Huns in the West in 376 caused the entry of entire peoples, the *gentes,* into the empire.
  4. The Visigoths crushed a Roman army at Adrianople in 376, making further invasions possible.
  5. Except for the Lombards, barbarian conquests on the continent ended about 600.
  6. The Visigoths, Vandals, Burgundians, and other tribes established a number of kingdoms.
   a. Theodoric, an Ostrogoth king, established control over Italy and Sicily and pursued a policy of assimilation between the Germans and the Romans.
  7. The kingdom of the Franks was the most important
   a. These Germanic-speaking people settled at Rome's northeast Rhine frontier.
   b. The Salien Franks issued a law code; Chlodio's wife founded the Merovingian dynasty.
   c. The era of Clovis saw Franks conquer much of Gaul and adopt Gallo-Roman culture.
   d. The conversion of Clovis to Roman Christianity was crucial for Frankish power.

V. Germanic society
 A. Kinship, custom, and class
  1. The basic Germanic social unit was the tribe, or *folk*.
   a. Law was unwritten custom, handed down orally from generation to generation.
   b. Tribes were bound by shared peace and led by kings or chieftains.
  2. The *comitatus,* or war band, fought with the chieftain; gradually, a warrior-nobility evolved.
 B. Law
  1. In the sixth century, during the process of Christianization, Germanic law began to be written down.
  2. Under Salic Law each person had a *wergeld,* or monetary value, and each offense had a fine.
  3. German law aimed at the reduction of violence; it was not concerned with abstract justice.

C. German life
   1. Germans lived in small villages.
       a. German males engaged in animal husbandry.
       b. The women raised grain and were responsible for the weaving and spinning.
       c. The number of cattle a man possessed indicated his wealth and determined his social status.
       d. German society was patriarchal.
   2. Ironworking was advanced, but the goods were produced for war and the subsistence economy, not for trade.
   3. Warfare constituted the main characteristic of Germanic society.
   4. The law codes show that women were regarded as family property and fines existed to protect women from rape and abduction.
   5. Widows had considerable power and wealth; women were regarded as being spiritually inferior.
   6. Some women exercised considerable influence; some used their beauty and their intelligence to advance their positions.

D. Anglo-Saxon England
   1. The Romans conquered Britain, built towns, and brought their religion.
   2. Celtic people were fully assimilated into Roman culture.
   3. When Rome withdrew from Britain in 407, the island was open to plundering Picts, Saxons from Denmark, and Germans, and the Britons fled to Wales.
       a. The period 500-1066 is the "Anglo-Saxon" era.
       b. The Anglo-Saxon invasion gave rise to the Arthurian legends; Roman culture disappeared.
       c. By the seventh and eighth centuries there were seven Germanic kingdoms, which were united under Alfred of Wessex in the ninth century.

VI. The Byzantine East
A. Justinian's failed wars against the Ostrogoths led to conquest of Italy by the Lombards.
   1. Despite Hun, Slav, Avar, Persian, and Greek attacks, the eastern Roman-Byzantine empire survived.
       a. One reason was strong military leadership under Priskos and others; another was the strength and position of the city of Constantinople.
   2. This Byzantine empire survived and grew rich under Greek rule—and protected ancient culture.

B. Byzantine east and Germanic west: The western and eastern halves of the empire drifted apart.
   1. In the West, civic functions were performed first by church leaders and then by German chieftains; the Church grew away from the empire.
       a. The popes were too preoccupied with conversion of the Germans and issues of classical culture to concentrate on church organization.
       b. Disputes developed between church officials and secular officials over administration of the church; Gelasius claimed that sacred authority was greater than secular authority.
   2. In the East, the emperor's jurisdiction over the church was fully acknowledged.
       a. Religion was seen as a branch of the state in the East.

3. Much of the difference between the Eastern and Western churches was how each received classical culture.
   a. Classical culture was condemned in the West; in the East, apologists, or defenders, of Christianity demanded harmony between classical culture and Christianity.
4. In 1054, a theological dispute led the bishop of Rome and the patriarch of Constantinople to excommunicate each other—the two churches split apart.
5. Despite religious differences, the Byzantine Empire protected the West against invasions from the East.
6. The Byzantines civilized the Slavic people and converted them to Christianity.
   a. The Byzantine missionary Cyril invented a Slavic alphabet using Greek characters (the Cyrillic alphabet).
   b. Byzantine art and architecture became the basis of Russian forms.

B. The law code of Justinian
1. The law codes of the emperors Theodosius and Justinian are among the most important contributions of the Byzantine Empire.
2. The *corpus juris civilis*—based on the *Code, Digest,* and *Institutes*—is the foundation of European law.

C. Byzantine intellectual life
1. The Byzantines kept scholarship alive, especially history.
2. They passed Greco-Roman culture on to the Arabs.
3. Although they made no advances in science or mathematics, they did make contributions to medicine and military technology.

VII. The Arabs and Islam

A. The Arabs
1. The Hejaz Arabs were urban and commercial, while the Bedouin Arabs were nomadic and rural.
2. All Arabs, however, were tribal and followed similar religious rules.

B. Muhammad and the faith of Islam
1. Muhammad was a merchant who became a preacher-prophet.
   a. He described his visions in verse form—his Qur'an (prayer recitation).
   b. After Muhammad's death, scribes organized these revelations into chapters.
2. Muhammad was a reformer of the Old Testament—the religion he reformed is called Islam.
3. The Qur'an outlines the monotheistic theology of Islam.
   a. Islam means "submission to the word of God," and its central idea is the Day of Judgment.
   b. Islam is a strict religion that condemns such things as immorality, alcoholic beverages and gambling, and usury; it insists on regular prayer and alms giving, and condemns *usury*.
   c. Muslims believed that following their religion's basic rules would automatically gain them salvation, as would dying for their faith in battle.
   d. The Qur'an sets forth austere sexual morality; it allowed polygamy.
   e. Muslim women were more emancipated than women in the West.
   f. It was believed that salvation is by way of God's grace, which is predestined; there are many similarities between the Muslin, Jewish, and Christian faiths.
4. The doctrines of Islam superseded tribal ties and bound all Arabs.

    C. When the caliph Ali (successor to Prophet Muhammad) was assassinated in 661, Islam split into the Shi'ite (or Shi'a) and the Sunni factions.

        1. The Shi'ites claimed to be the blood descendants of Ali and to possess divine knowledge.

        2. The Sunnis, the majority of the faith, claimed that the *Sunna* was a source of truth.

    D. The expansion of Islam

        1. Islam united the Arabs and encouraged expansion and conquest; much of the old Roman Mediterranean empire came under Muslim control.

        2. Spain was held until the *reconquista* of the tenth to the fourteenth centuries.

        3. The Muslims were stopped at Tours in 733, but successfully carried their conquest to India and Africa.

            a. But a Muslim kingdom was established in Spain under the Umayyad dynasty.

            b. In Spain and elsewhere the Muslims had enormous impact on agricultural development—through new crops and new agricultural techniques.

            c. They established intellectual centers, such as at Toledo.

            d. They advanced the use of algebra and made other contributions to mathematics, such as the concept of zero.

            e. They excelled in medical knowledge and preserved Greek philosophical thought.

    E. Muslim-Christian relations

        1. Muslim assault on Christian Europe and the Christian intolerance and misunderstanding of Muslim teaching caused a barrier between the two peoples.

        2. Muslims and Christians shared the belief that the state existed to allow its people to find God.

            a. But Muslims did not regard the state as a territorial entity.

            b. They saw the world in terms of the House of Islam and the House of War.

            c. The *jihad* was the struggle to spread Islam—by war if necessary.

        3. By the thirteenth century, Western literature regarded the Muslims both sympathetically and as the worst enemies of Christian society.

        4. Muslims rejected European culture and avoided going to Europe; they viewed Christianity as a flawed religion.

        5. All in all, Muslim expansion meant that Mediterranean civilization would be divided into three spheres of influence: Byzantine, Arabic, and Western.

Review Questions

Check your understanding of this chapter by answering the following questions.

1. What was the role of the Roman emperors and the empire in the growth of Christianity from an outlawed movement to the most important power in Rome?

2. Why did Rome become the capital of the Christian church in the West?

3. How did Christian missionaries convert the pagans? What devices and techniques did they use in the assimilation of Germanic peoples into Christianity?

4. What ideas did Saint Augustine contribute to Christian thought?

5. What was happening to Rome at the time Saint Augustine wrote *City of God*? How could this have influenced his philosophy that the City of God is more important than the city of man?

6. What was the purpose of monasticism? Why is Benedict of Nursia one of the most important figures in the history of Christian monasticism?

7. Describe the Benedictine *Rule*. Why was it successful?

8. Why was the defeat of the Roman army by the Visigoths in 378 a turning point in European history?

9. What patterns of social and political life existed in German society and what was the economy like?

10. How and why did Germanic law evolve and how did it work?

11. Name the kingdoms of the English Heptarchy. What were their origins and what role did King Alfred of Wessex play in this development?

12. How did the Byzantine Empire serve the West as both a protector from the East and as a preserver of ancient culture?

13. What are the similarities and differences between Christianity and Islam?

14. What was Muhammad's message?

15. What impact did the Muslims have on the politics and culture of the Mediterranean world?

Study-Review Exercises

Define the following key concepts and terms.

ekklesia

Justinian's *Code*

catholic

penitentials

Salic Law

City of God

Rule of Saint Benedict

coenobitic monasticism

Arianism

Islamic Day of Judgment

wergeld

heresy

diocese

jihad

Identify and explain the significance of the following people and terms.
Dooms of Ethelbert

Theodosius

Byzantine Empire

King Alfred of Wessex

Augustine the missionary

Muhammad

Bishop Ambrose

Pope Leo I

Saint Martin of Tours

Saint Patrick

Saint Augustine

Saint Jerome

Clovis

Saint Benedict

Saint Basil

Qur'an

Toledo

Tell why the following events are important.

Synod of Whitby, 664

Battle of Tours, 733

Council of Nicaea, 325

Theodosius-Ambrose dispute

Test your understanding of the chapter by providing the correct answers.

1. Overall, the Benedictine monastic movement *did/did not* result in economic and material benefits to Europe.

2. This emperor legalized Christianity in the year 312. _____

3. Each person's monetary value to the tribe. _____

4. Of the two parts of the old Roman Empire—East and West—it was the _____ that was politically and culturally more stable and progressive.

5. The early church fathers believed that the church *was/was not* ultimately superior to the state.

6. The author of *The Confessions* and an important Christian philosopher. _____

7. After the year 476 it was _____, not emperors, who held power in the western Roman world.

8. This book, written at the time of Rome's destruction, argues that humanity is divided between those who live the earthly life of selfishness and those who live according to the spirit of God. _____

9. The head of the Byzantine church was the *emperor/pope.*

Major Political Ideas

1. According to Saint Augustine, what is the origin of the state and the purpose of government? How does this view fit into his philosophy of history?

2. What was Saint Ambrose's position with regard to authority within society? Which was, in his view, the ultimate power—the church or the state?

Issues for Essays and Discussion

By 476 the western Roman Empire had given way to massive invasions. What sort of new culture grew out of this disruption? Discuss this by making reference to the role of the Christian church and the role of the Germanic peoples. What were the strengths and contributions of each?

Interpretation of Visual Sources

Study the photograph that shows the interior of the Pantheon in Rome. What is the function of this building? What architectural and cultural influences can you detect in it? In what way does this building reflect the adaptability and flexibility of early Christianity?

Geography

1. On Outline Map 7.3 provided, and using Map 6.1, Map 7.3, and Map 7.4 in the textbook as guides, mark the following: the boundaries of the Roman Empire at the time of Hadrian, the invasion routes of the seven Germanic invasion groups, the battle site of Tours, Constantinople, the Red Sea, Paris, Rome, Jerusalem, the Black Sea, Egypt.

2. Using Map 7.4 in the text as a guide, (a) show the extent of Muslim expansion by 733, and (b) locate and explain the significance of the following Muslim cities: Mecca, Damascus, Cordova, Toledo.

Outline Map 7.3

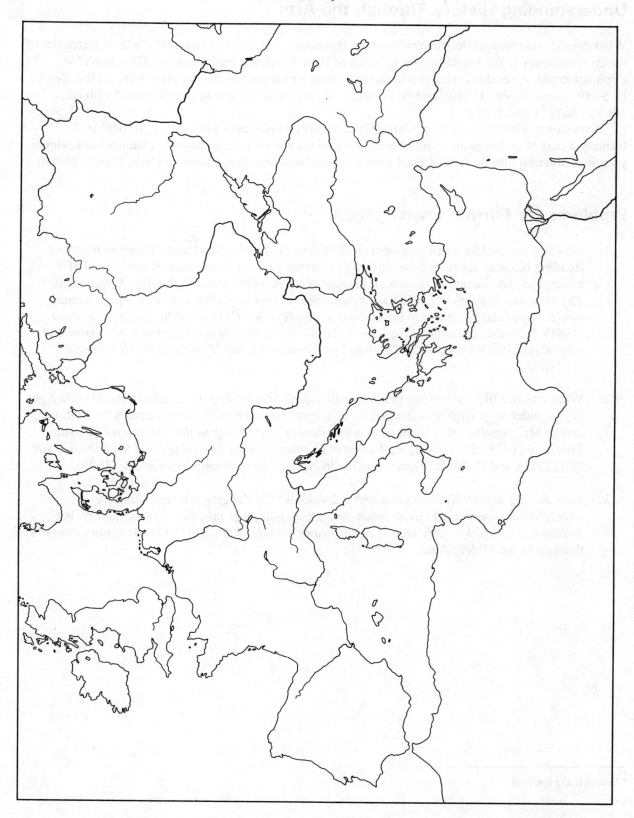

Understanding History Through the Arts

What does Byzantine architecture reveal about Byzantine culture? The best architectural statement of the Byzantine age is the Hagia Sophia (Church of Holy Wisdom), built between 532 and 637 in Constantinople. After the Turkish conquest it became a mosque and the minarets were added. See E. H. Swift, *Hagia Sophia* (1940), and N. Pevsner, *An Outline of European Architecture** (7th ed., 1963), Chaps. 1 and 2.

A mosaic is a picture made up of an infinite number of pieces of glass, stone, or pebble—forming a part of architecture. A number of mosaics are shown in this chapter in the textbook. Begin your investigation into this brilliant art form with the book *Mosaics,* edited by Carlo Bertelli (1988).

Problems for Further Investigation

1. How did people like Saint Augustine and Muhammad both reflect and change their times? Reading biographies is an excellent way to further your understanding of this period of expansion and change. P. Brown, *Augustine of Hippo* (1967), and T. Andrae, *Mohammed: The Man and His Faith** (1970), are biographies of two important men of the post-Roman world. If you are interested in the Germanic invaders, see C. D. Gordon, *The Age of Attila* (1961). E. S. Duckett, *Alfred the Great** (1956), about the life and times of that warrior and scholar, is filled with drama and action. For Mohammed, see M. Rodinson, *Mohammed* (1974).

2. What was life like for women in the Middle Ages? Scholarship on women in the Middle Ages is just under way. Highly acclaimed by undergraduates is a collection of essays by R. Reuther and E. McLaughlin, eds., *Women of Spirit: Female Leadership in the Jewish and Christian Tradition* (1979). S. F. Wemple, *Women in Frankish Society: Marriage and the Cloister, 500-900* (1981), and P. Ranft, *Women and the Religious Life in Premodern Europe* (1996).

3. How did life in the Middle Ages affect individuals? Challenging but rewarding for undergraduates, especially those interested in psychology or interdisciplinary history, is C. Redding, *A World Made by Men: Cognition and Society, 400-1200* (1985). It applies Piaget's theories to the Middle Ages.

---

*Available in paperback.

Self-Test Multiple-Choice Questions

<u>Do</u> <u>not</u> assume that these questions will appear on any examination. It is recommended that you <u>not</u> memorize these questions, but use them only as a self-test. Answers are at the end of this book.

1. At the Council of Nicaea in 325 it was decided that
   a. the Arians were correct.
   b. emperors should not participate in theological disputes.
   c. Christ was of the same substance as God.
   d. God and Christ were of different substances.

2. Writers of penitentials tended to be most concerned about people's
   a. faith in God.
   b. rejection of Roman authority.
   c. baptism and the end of fighting.
   d. sexual behavior.

3. Which of the following statements about the Benedictine *Rule* is true?
   a. It applied to men alone.
   b. It was quite flexible.
   c. It emphasized love of self.
   d. It encouraged intellectual labor only.

4. The greatest intellectual contribution of Islam to the West is in
   a. literature.
   b. mathematics and medicine.
   c. law.
   d. music.

5. The major accomplishment of Alfred the Great was
   a. the unification of the Anglo-Saxon kingdoms.
   b. the conversion of Britain to Christianity.
   c. the defeat of Rome's last emperor.
   d. a new law code.

6. Which of the following statements about the Muslim religion is true?
   a. It is polytheistic.
   b. Its adherents believe that Muhammad is the successor to Abraham and Christ.
   c. It rejects the idea of a Day of Judgment.
   d. It states that good behavior can bring salvation.

7. The word *church* was first used in the New Testament Letter to the Christians of Thessalonica and referred to
   a. officials of the Christian religion.
   b. the local community of Christian believers.
   c. the pope.
   d. the international Christian communities.

8. Saint Augustine is important in European history because he
   a. worked out the theory of papal supremacy.
   b. compiled the writings of Jesus into a new testament.
   c. assimilated Greco-Roman thought into Christianity.
   d. was the first bishop of Rome.

9. The Benedictine *Rule* was primarily designed to
   a. spread Christianity to the Germans.
   b. draw the individual away from love of self.
   c. encourage new economic ventures.
   d. train officials for government.

10. The Qur'an is the
    a. sacred book of Islam.
    b. Germanic practice of infanticide.
    c. Islamic religious center at Mecca.
    d. leading Muslim official.

11. Collections of early Germanic laws dealt primarily with
    a. sex.
    b. civil rights.
    c. property rights.
    d. fines for criminal offenses, such as theft, murder, rape, and so forth.

12. The basic Germanic social unit was the
    a. *laeti.*
    b. *comitatus.*
    c. *foederati.*
    d. *folk.*

13. The most important ecclesiastical statement about church-state relations was formulated by
    a. Arius of Alexandria.
    b. the emperor Theodosius.
    c. the emperor Diocletian.
    d. Ambrose of Milan.

14. Which of the following did *not* provide political and social leadership in the early Christian era?
    a. Giaseric
    b. St. Paul
    c. Leo I (440-461)
    d. Gregory I (590-604)

15. Religious conversion means
    a. baptism.
    b. a turning of the heart and mind to God.
    c. confession.
    d. confirmation.

16. Missionaries used all of the following methods to get pagan peoples to accept Christianity *except*
    a. preaching.
    b. edification through stories about Christ.
    c. the adaptation of pagan places and practices to Christian use.
    d. group penitentials and baptisms.

17. Church organization was closely associated with local monastic life in
    a. Germany.
    b. Scotland.
    c. Ireland.
    d. Italy.

18. Cassiodorus identified monasticism entirely with
    a. prayer and mortification.
    b. study and learning.
    c. manual labor.
    d. service to the poor and orphaned.

19. The monastic vows in the *Rule* of Saint Benedict were
    a. poverty, chastity, and obedience.
    b. the Work of God.
    c. stability, conversion of manners, and obedience.
    d. designed to spread the Gospel through missionary activity.

20. Benedictine monasticism replaced other forms of early Christian monasticism largely because
    a. of its moderation, flexibility, and balanced life.
    b. the emperors encouraged it.
    c. Benedictine monks were clever.
    d. Europeans were especially suited to the eremitical life.

21. The Byzantine emperor Justinian secured a permanent place in European history for his
    a. defeat of the Slavs and Turks.
    b. production of the *corpus juris civilis*.
    c. marriage to Theodora.
    d. invention of the Cyrillic alphabet.

22. The *corpus juris civilis* was
    a. snippets of the works of Herodotus, Procopius, and Aristotle.
    b. Russian, Roman, and Greek laws.
    c. Roman law and Greek practices.
    d. the body of civil law of Justinian.

23. *Islam* literally means
    a. "the Day of Judgment is at hand."
    b. "submission to the word of God."
    c. "the Qur'an is a sacred book."
    d. "Muhammad is Allah's prophet."

24. Which of the following statements about Islam, Christianity, and Judaism is false?
    a. All three religions teach predestination.
    b. Members are called People of the Book by Muslims.
    c. All three religions are monotheistic.
    d. Members of all three religions worship the same God.

25. The center of Spanish learning was
    a. Mecca.
    b. Madrid.
    c. Iona.
    d. Toledo.

Studying Effectively — Exercise 2

Learning to Improve Your Underlining Skills

Read the following paragraphs, in which some words are printed in italic type to help you find the major points. Read the passage a second time and underline or highlight one or two sentences in each paragraph that best summarize the paragraph's major point. Now study and review these points. Finally, close the book and on a piece of notepaper summarize the major points with a few words under the heading "The Success of Benedictine Monasticism." Compare your summary with that found at the end of the exercise.

The Success of Benedictine Monasticism

Why was the Benedictine form of monasticism so successful? Why did it eventually replace other forms of Western monasticism? The answer lies partly in its *spirit of flexibility and moderation,* and partly in the *balanced life* it provided. Early Benedictine monks and nuns spent part of the day in prayer, part in study or some other form of intellectual activity, and part in manual labor. The monastic life as conceived by Saint Benedict did not lean too heavily in any one direction; it struck a balance between asceticism and idleness. It thus provided opportunities for persons of entirely different abilities and talents—from mechanics to gardeners to literary scholars. Benedict's *Rule* contrasts sharply with Cassiodorus's narrow concept of the monastery as a place for aristocratic scholars and bibliophiles.

Benedictine monasticism also *suited the social circumstances of early medieval society.* The German invasions had fragmented European life: the self-sufficient rural estate replaced the city as the basic unit of civilization. A monastery, too, had to be *economically self-sufficient.* It was supposed to produce from its lands and properties all that was needed for food, clothing, buildings, and the liturgical service of the altar. The monastery fitted in—indeed, represented—the trend toward localism.

Benedict monasticism also succeeded partly because it was so *materially successful.* In the seventh and eighth centuries, monasteries pushed back forest and wasteland, drained swamps, and experimented with crop rotation. For example, the abbey of Saint Wandrille, founded in 645 near Rouen in northwestern Gaul, sent squads of monks to clear the forests that surrounded it. Within seventy-five years, the abbey was immensely wealthy. The abbey of Jumièges, also in the diocese of Rouen, followed much the same pattern. Such Benedictine houses made a *significant contribution to the agricultural development of Europe.* The communal nature of their organization, whereby property was held in common and profits pooled and reinvested, made this contribution possible.

Finally, *monasteries conducted schools* for local young people. Some learned about prescriptions and herbal remedies and went on to provide medical treatment for their localities. A few copied manuscripts and wrote books. This training did not go unappreciated in a society desperately in need of it. Local and royal governments drew on the services of the *literate men and able administrators* the monasteries produced. This was not what Saint Benedict had intended, but the effectiveness of the institution he designed made it perhaps inevitable.

Answer

The Success of Benedictine Monasticism

1. A flexible and balanced life

2. Economically self-sufficient

3. Economically successful, especially in agriculture

4. Provided education for young and able administrators for governments

Chapter 8

The Carolingian World: Europe in the Early Middle Ages

Learning Objectives

After reading and studying this chapter you should be able to:

1. explain how Merovingian and Carolingian rulers govern their kingdoms and empire.

2. describe the relations between the Carolingian rulers and the church.

3. discuss the breakup of the Carolingian Empire and its role in the development of medieval feudalism.

4. explain how Viking expansion led to the establishment of the Kievan principality.

Chapter Summary

For about a century after the Franks defeated the Muslims at the Battle of Tours in 733, Europe enjoyed a period of political and economic regeneration and unity. A principal reason for this regeneration was the Frankish Carolingian family. It was the Carolingian Charles Martel who won at Tours, and it was his son, Pippin III, and grandson, Charlemagne, who molded western Europe into a unified Christian empire—the Carolingian Empire.

The Carolingian era was a high point of stability and creativity in the early Middle Ages, which was generally a precarious time. The Carolingians struck up a mutually beneficial relationship with the church. They supported church missionaries and enforced Christian moral codes. In return, the pope recognized and strengthened Carolingian political authority. Charlemagne extended the boundaries of his empire and brought peace to Europe. Within this climate of peace a meaningful renaissance in learning and the arts took place. The center for both the intellectual renaissance and the Carolingian Empire was northern Europe. The very fact that this Carolingian Empire and culture developed in the north, or even at all, was due to the forced isolation of Europe from the Islamic-Mediterranean world, as the great historian Henri Pirenne first argued.

While these changes related to the Carolingian era were taking place, Europe continued to experience the economic-political transformation that historians call feudalism. Beginning as a natural response of insecure people to the disappearance of the protection the strong Roman government had provided, feudalism became a means for communities to defend themselves. Over time, as discussed in Chapter 6, freemen gave up their personal rights and their property to local lords. These lords provided protection, in return, and built their own little empires. Essential to the feudal system was the fief—the land a lord received from the monarch. Charlemagne was able to manage the feudal lords, but his grandsons could not keep control of the feudal system. When they divided Charlemagne's empire into three parts in 843, it was already soaked in blood because of the ambitions of petty lords. The division was an invitation to invasion from the outside. The Vikings, Magyars, and Muslims then threw Europe back into a period of violence and fear.

Study Outline

Use this outline to preview the chapter before you read a particular section in the textbook and then as a self-check to test your reading comprehension after you have read the chapter section.

I. The Frankish kingdom and the rise of the Carolingians
   A. The Franks, under Clovis
      1. Acquired Roman Gaul, defeated other tribes, and won over the church.
      2. The Frankish kingdom included most of France and southwestern Germany.
      3. Clovis divided his kingdom among his four sons.
   B. After Clovis's death in 511, the Merovingians fell into a long period of civil war.
      1. Civil war was caused by unsure succession to the throne and desire for booty (land) and plunder.
      2. Queen Brunhilda encouraged war.
   C. How did the Merovingians rule?
      1. The *civitas* ruled over by the *comites* served as the basis of rule in the Frankish kingdom.
      2. Royal income came from royal estates, taxes, new lands, plunder, fines, and minting coins.
      3. Kings traveled to check on their estates, but also relied on their duxs (dukes) to defend the land.
      4. Capitularies—or laws—to regulate the kingdom
         a. These related to property, robbery, arson, etc.
         b. Capitularies were influenced by Roman law and the Roman idea of effective central rule.
      5. The king also used and consulted his aristocracy in the form of a royal court.
         a. The aristocratic Carolingian family emerged to replace the Merovingians.
         b. Pippin I had been the head (mayor) of the royal palace.
         c. Pippin II, Charles Martel, and Pippin III acquired great land and wealth, and defeated other contenders and outside tribal threats such as the Saxons and the Arabs.
      6. The Carolingians acquired the support of the church by their support of missionary activity, including that of Boniface.
         a. Pippin III's acquisition of the kingship was aided by Pope Zacharias.
         b. Pippin created strong ties between the church and the Carolingian dynasty.
         c. Pippin was annointed by Saint Boniface and Pope Stephen II.
         d. The pope Leo III regarded Pippin's son Charles as emperor.

II. The imperial coronation of Charlemagne
   A. The church supported Charlemagne, and in 800 the pope crowned him the emperor.
   B. Charlemagne consciously perpetuated old Roman imperial notions while at the same time identifying with the new Rome of the Christian church.
   C. The coronation gave rise to theories of both imperial and papal supremacy.
III. The empire of Charlemagne
   A. The warrior-ruler Charlemagne is described in Einhard's biography as both an intellectual and a strong, brutal man.
   B. Territorial expansion
      1. Charlemagne continued the Carolingian tradition by building a large European kingdom.
      2. He checked Muslim expansion by establishing *marches* (strongly fortified areas) and conquered the Saxon German tribes.
      3. He incorporated Lombardy into the Frankish kingdom.
      4. He added northern Italy to his kingdom, but his Spanish campaign failed, inspiring the *Song of Roland.*
   C. The government of the Carolingian Empire
      1. The empire of Charlemagne was mainly a collection of agricultural estates.
      2. The political power of the Carolingians depended on the cooperation of the Frankish aristocracy.
      3. Charlemagne divided his empire into counties, ruled by counts and viscounts.
      4. Charlemagne appointed *missi dominici* as links between local authorities and the central government.
      5. *Margraves* ruled in the frontier regions.
IV. The Carolingian intellectual revival
   A. The revival of learning began with Irish-Celtic influence in Anglo-Saxon Britain.
   B. Northumbrian culture in Britain
      1. Under Saint Benet Biscop and others, Irish-Celtic culture permeated Roman Britain and Europe, partly by way of monastic missals and other books.
      2. The Lindisfarne book, in a Celtic script, is a high point in the Northumbrian artistic renaissance.
      3. The noblewoman Hilda and others established "double monasteries" that were governed by women and were intellectual centers.
      4. The Venerable Bede wrote a history—*The Ecclesiastical History of the English Nation*—that is the chief source of information about early Britain.
      5. The epic poem *Beowulf* was written in vernacular Anglo-Saxon.
      6. The physical circumstances of life were grim.
         a. Learning took place in an atmosphere of violence.
         b. Food was not scarce, but the climate was harsh, and disease was frequent.
   C. The Carolingian Renaissance
      1. A new culture based on Christian sources emerged. Its purpose was primarily the promotion of Christianity.
      2. Charlemagne fostered an intellectual revival that centered on his court at Aachen.
      3. His scholars (the most important being Alcuin) encouraged interest in the classics and preserved Greek and Roman knowledge.
      4. Basic literacy was established among the clergy, and Christianity was spread.

V. Health and medical care in the early Middle Ages
   A. No rational understanding of disease existed among the Germanic peoples.
      1. Drug and prescription therapy was common.
      2. Physicians knew little about disease, and their treatments were primitive and often harmful.
      3. Christianity had a beneficial effect on medical knowledge and treatment.
   B. The Italian school at Salerno was an important medical center, and several female physicians played a key role in medical writings.
   C. Most people had no access to physicians; death came early and most people had a fatalistic acceptance of death.

VI. Aristocratic Resurgence
   A. Charlemagne left his empire to his son, Louis the Pious.
   B. Louis was tough and ruthless but he could not retain the loyalty of the warrior-aristocracy.
      1. He drew up the *Arrangement of the Empire* to divide his empire.
      2. The huge empire lacked an efficient bureaucracy.
      3. Lothar received the crown.
         a. Dissatisfied with their portions, Louis's sons—Lothair, Louis the German, and Charles the Bald—fought bitterly.
         b. Finally, in the Treaty of Verdun in 843, they agreed to divide up the empire.
   C. But fratricidal warfare among Charlemagne's descendants was not the main reason for disintegration of the empire.
      1. The strength and self-interest of the greedy aristocrats (magnates) were the main cause of disintegration.
      2. Many count's holdings had become hereditary—thereby weakening the crown.

VII. Feudalism and the historians
   A. "Feudalism" is a confusing term which appears to have come into use only recently; no current definition is satisfactory.
      1. Much discussion of feudalism revolves around the terms fief, lord, and vassal.
      2. The historian Bloch defines feudalism as a whole system of life—economic, political, cultural, and even religious.
   B. The two levels of early feudalism
      1. The alternative to Bloch is to see feudalism as a political and legal system.
      2. Feudalism was a type of government in which power was considered private and was divided among many lords, and was the main type of government in Europe from 900 to 1300.
      3. Feudalism existed at two social levels, that of armed retainers (knights) and of royal officials such as counts.
         a. The adoption of the stirrup made the cavalry a potent weapon, and armed retainers became very valuable.
         b. Retainers took an oath of fealty, and some, called vassals, were given estates by their lords.
         c. Counts held power at the local level and came to rule independently.
      4. Because of the premium placed on physical strength, women were subordinate to men, although they occasionally held positions of power.

C. Manorialism, which was the economic and social side of feudalism, centered on the relationship between peasant (or serf) and the lord's estate.
   1. Peasants exchanged their labor and land for protection from the lord to become serfs.
   2. The free farmers became serfs—bound to the land and to the lord.
   3. By 800 perhaps 60 percent of the population had been reduced to serfdom.

VIII. The great invasions of the ninth century
   A. Disunity in Europe after Charlemagne's death was an invitation to aggression from the outside.
   B. Assaults on western Europe
      1. The Vikings from the north overran Europe.
         a. Their superb seamanship gave them an overwhelming advantage.
         b. Reasons for their attacks include overpopulation, crop failures, and trade.
         c. They did not take slaves, but held powerful people for ransom.
         d. Between 876 and 954 their control extended from Ireland to France, and perhaps even New York.
   D. The Magyars, or Hungarians, pushed into Europe from the east, and the Muslims pushed up from the south.
   E. These invasions accelerated the growth of feudalism.
   F. The invaders brought with them some important advances in agriculture, law, and industry.

IX. The Vikings and the Kievan principality
   1. The Slavs lived as a single people until the mass migrations of the late Roman times when they moved in different directions—splitting into three groups, the Ukrainians, the Russians, and the White Russians.
      a. Their lands were great forests and prairie grasslands on which they lived by the "slash and burn" method.
   2. Vikings from Scandinavia moved up and down Slav lands and linked Scandinavia to the Black Sea and Constantinople; the Slavs became "slaves."
   3. The Viking Ruirik founded the Varangian dynasty, and then his successor Oleg made Kiev the center of a confederation of Slavic territories—the Kievan state.
      a. The Vikings and the Slavs were converted to Eastern Orthodox Christianity; trade was the major interest of the rulers.
      b. The Slavified Vikings had no way to pass power from one generation to the next; therefore, much strife occurred.
      c. To avoid chaos, Kiev was divided into competing units (beginning in 1054)—the result was a system of estates worked by slaves called *kholops* and princely owners, and a warrior class called *boyers*.

Review Questions

Check your understanding of this chapter by answering the following questions.

1. What was the relationship between the Carolingians and the pope? How did both sides benefit from the relationship?

2. How successful was Charlemagne in expanding the power of the Frankish state?

3. What techniques and methods did Charlemagne use to govern his vast empire? How well did his empire function?

4. What was the church's attitude toward Charlemagne and the political value of the "state"?

5. What were the probable reasons for Charlemagne's quest for the title of emperor? The results?

6. Describe the Northumbrian cultural revival. What were its sources of inspiration and its goals?

7. Why did Charlemagne's empire break up? Was it the fault of his son Louis?

8. What was the "Carolingian Renaissance"? Who were its participants and what did they accomplish?

9. How much did people, in the early medieval period, understand about disease, and what kind of health care existed?

10. Define feudalism and describe its origins. What impact did it have on the peasants?

11. Who were the Vikings? What were their motives and why were they able to terrorize Europe so well after 814?

12. Describe the Magyar and Muslim invasions in terms of motives, areas terrorized, methods, and impact.

Study-Review Exercises

Define the following key concepts and terms.

citivas

capitularies

Missals

dux

fief

feudalism

missi dominici

vassal

polygamy

Carolingian Renaissance

Pirenne thesis

Charlemagne's *marches*

double monasteries

Identify and explain the significance of each of the following people.
Saint Hilda

Queen Brunhilda

the Venerable Bede

Pippin of Landen

Pippin III

Saint Boniface

Charles Martel

Charlemagne

Alcuin

Louis the Pious

Pope Leo

Benet Biscop

Louis the German

Charles the Bald

Lothair

the Vikings

the Varagian Dynasty

Explain what the following events were, who participated in them, and why they were important.

Northumbrian cultural renaissance

coronation of Charlemagne

Battle of Tours

Treaty of Verdun

Test your understanding of the chapter by providing the correct answers.

1. Charlemagne's biographer. _____

2. In general, the economic and political power and status of aristocratic women in the early Middle Ages tended to *increase/decrease.*

3. In the eighth and ninth centuries, the population of western Europe tended to become *more/less* free.

4. In general, the relationship between the Carolingian emperor Charles and the Christian church was *good/warlike.*

5. This Northumbrian was an important scholar and educator and the major adviser to Charlemagne. _____

6. The foundation of a medical school at _____ in the ninth century gave tremendous impetus to medical study.

Place the following events in correct chronological order.

Beginning of Magyar tribal invasions across the Danube
Battle of Tours
Coronation of Charlemagne
Founding of Wearmouth and Jarrow monasteries by Biscop
Charlemagne's Spanish campaign
Life of the Venerable Bede
Death of Louis the Pious
Pope Zacharias confirms that Pippin III is king of the Franks

1.

2.

3.

4

5.

6.

7.

8.

Major Political Ideas

1. Define *feudalism*. Was it primarily a political, military, or social system? What were the reasons for its emergence? Was it, in your analysis, a source of order or a source of instability in Europe? What impact did it have on the peasants?

2. What is an aristocracy? What was the aristocrats' source of wealth and power, and why were they looked upon as dangerous by the Merovingian kings?

Issues for Essays and Discussion

1. It is said that between 733, when the Muslims were defeated at Tours, and the division of Charlemagne's empire in 843, a distinctly European society emerged. Three of the main developments of this new society were Charlemagne's empire, the rise of feudalism, and an intellectual revival. Discuss this new Europe by describing each of these developments. Was this a unique new society? In what ways was this society different from that of Roman times?

2. Who or what was more important in the development of European society in the Carolingian era, the warrior-rulers or the men and women of the church? Support your argument with historical evidence.

Interpretation of Visual Sources

Study the "Plan for an Ideal Monastery". What were the different classes or groups of residents at the monastery? What was the diet of the community? What seems to have occupied most of the time of the residents?

Geography

On Outline Map 8.1 provided, and using Map 8.1, Map 8.2, and Map 8.3 in the textbook as a reference, mark the following: the geographic boundaries of Charlemagne's empire, the location of the Spanish and Danish *marches,* Aachen, Rouen, Strasbourg, Paris, the Rhine, and the Elbe, the division of Charlemagne's empire in 843, and the invasionary routes of the Vikings, the Magyars, and the Muslims.

Outline Map 8.1

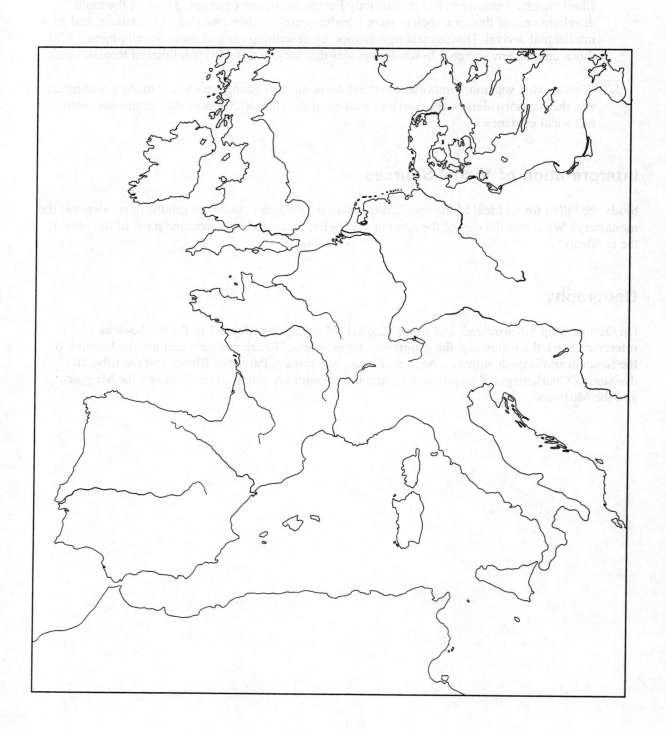

Understanding History Through the Arts

What were the architectural and artistic achievements of this age? For architecture, see K. Conant, *Carolingian and Romanesque Architecture, 800-1200** (1978). A good general introduction to the illuminated manuscripts and religious treasures of the period is J. Beckwith, *Early Medieval Art** (1979), and on the Anglo-Saxon church and cathedral building and life, see P. Collinson et al. eds., *A History of Canterbury Cathedral* (1995).

Problems for Further Investigation

1. What can be learned about early medieval life from works like *Beowulf*? Paperback editions of several early medieval works are available: L. Sherley-Price, trans., *Bede: A History of the English Church and Peoples** (1962); M. Alexander, trans., *The Earliest English Poems** (1972); D. L. Sayers, trans., *The Song of Roland**; and D. Wright, trans., *Beowulf* (1957). Einhard's biography of Charlemagne is available in a 1960 edition with a foreword by Sidney Painter.

2. How did Merovingian and Carolingian government work? How did the concept of kingship evolve? Was Christianity as important as claimed? These and other questions are answered in P. Wormald et al., *Ideal and Reality in Frankish and Anglo-Saxon Society* (1984), and I. Wood, *The Merovingian Kingdoms* (1991).

3. What were the motives of the pope and Charlemagne at the time of the coronation on Christmas Day in 800? Of what significance is it that the church gave the title to the king? These and other questions are considered in a collection of interpretations entitled *The Coronation of Charlemagne** (1959), edited by R. E. Sullivan.

4. How much did the Islamic movement shape the course of European history? The classic statement on this is Henri Pirenne, *Mohammed and Charlemagne** (1958).

Self-Test Multiple-Choice Questions

<u>Do</u> <u>not</u> assume that these questions will appear on any examination. It is recommended that you <u>not</u> memorize these questions, but use them only as a self-test. Answers are at the end of this book.

1. Saint Boniface, the missionary monk
   a. refused to support the Carolingian kings.
   b. encouraged monasteries to develop their own religious rule.
   c. attacked Germanic sexual and marriage customs.
   d. was a staunch enemy of Roman ideas and Roman traditions.

---

*Available in paperback.

2. The most important source of Northumbrian (and Carolingian) cultural revival was
    a. Muslim society.
    b. Jewish society.
    c. Irish-Celtic society.
    d. Frankish society.

3. The *missi dominici* of Charlemagne were
    a. missionaries.
    b. peasant farmers.
    c. royal legal officials.
    d. military outposts.

4. Charlemagne was crowned emperor by
    a. himself.
    b. his father Pippin.
    c. the pope.
    d. the Frankish council.

5. Which of the following peoples were *not* part of the great invasions of the ninth century?
    a. The Vikings
    b. The Franks
    c. The Magyars
    d. The Muslims

6. Which of the following was *not* one of Charlemagne's accomplishments?
    a. The establishment of the *missi dominici*
    b. The creation of *marches*
    c. The encouragement of literature and art
    d. The destruction of papal power

7. The Northumbrian period of creativity was centered in
    a. Charlemagne's court.
    b. the monasteries of Britain.
    c. the courts of feudal lords.
    d. Pavia in Lombardy.

8. When Charlemagne's son, Louis the Pious, died, the empire
    a. was divided into three parts.
    b. remained intact under Charles Martel.
    c. was united with the Anglo-Saxon kingdoms.
    d. remained a unified but weak state.

9. The monk-historian who wrote *The Ecclesiastical History of the English Nation* was
    a. Louis the German.
    b. Pippin III.
    c. Bede.
    d. Augustine.

10. The Battle of Tours (733)
    a. aided the spread of Christianity in the Frankish kingdom.
    b. checked the advance of the Muslims in Europe.
    c. made Pippin II mayor of the palace.
    d. ended the Viking attacks.

11. Saint Boniface is famous as
    a. the biographer of Charlemagne.
    b. the author of *Beowulf*.
    c. the apostle of Germany.
    d. the author of a great medical treatise.

12. Historians consider the narrative poem *Beowulf* useful for
    a. an illustration of early Germanic marriage laws.
    b. its information on eighth-century monastic life.
    c. an early example of Germanic fairy tales.
    d. the picture it provides of Anglo-Saxon society and ideals.

13. The Carolingian Empire collapsed because
    a. it was too large and lacked an effective bureaucracy.
    b. it was overrun by Arabs and Turks.
    c. Charlemagne's grandsons were lazy and incompetent.
    d. Charlemagne failed to make a will.

14. The first major medical center in Europe was at
    a. Aix-la-Chapelle.
    b. Bologna.
    c. Salerno.
    d. Strasbourg.

15. Constantine the African advanced medical knowledge by
    a. founding hospitals.
    b. researching gynecological problems.
    c. recommending heroin as an anesthetic.
    d. translating Arabic medical treatises.

16. Viking expansion in the eighth century was probably due to
    a. underpopulation.
    b. the search for a colder climate.
    c. the search for new trade and commercial outlets.
    d. their desire to learn Carolingian shipbuilding techniques.

17. Feudalism was a form of government concerned with the rights and powers of
    a. the church.
    b. peasants.
    c. the military elite.
    d. absolute monarchs.

18. A feudal lord exercised all of the following rights *except*
    a. judicial.
    b. religious.
    c. political.
    d. economic.

19. The famous noblewoman who ruled the double monastery of Whitby was
    a. Queen Brunhilda.
    b. Martha of Aachen.
    c. Saint Hilda.
    d. Abbess Marie.

20. The medieval rebirth of interest in and preservation of achievements of classical Greece and Rome was
    a. the Carolingian Renaissance.
    b. feudalism.
    c. the Danelaw.
    d. *rex et sacerdos.*

21. Charlemagne's fortified areas in northeastern Spain were known as
    a. *missi.*
    b. villas.
    c. courts.
    d. *marches.*

22. The *Song of Roland* was based on Charlemagne's crusade in
    a. Spain.
    b. Greece.
    c. England.
    d. Germany.

23. "On the very day of the most holy nativity of the Lord, when the king at Mass had risen from prayer . . . Pope Leo placed the crown on his head. . . ." The person who was crowned in this event was
    a. King Leopold.
    b. Charlemagne.
    c. Charles Martel.
    d. Boniface.

24. The Norse word *vik* means
    a. "boat."
    b. "feudalism."
    c. "creek."
    d. "red."

25. Manorialism is concerned with
    a. the economic side of feudalism.
    b. the way the military was organized.
    c. the spread of ancient texts.
    d. the conversion of manors to centers of learning.

Chapter 9

Revival, Recovery, Reform, and Expansion

Learning Objectives

After reading and studying this chapter you should be able to:

1. discuss causes of the revival of Europe and the establishment of a more stable political environment.

2. explain the reasons for the church reform of the eleventh and twelfth centuries and the role of monasticism in that reform.

3. describe the Crusades and what caused them. Were they successful?

4. describe the "Gregorian Revolution" and the investiture issue. Who won?

Chapter Summary

When Charlemagne died in 814, Europe was thrown into a century and a half of disorder. Then, around the year 1000, Europe began to recover from this long, bitter winter of violence. This chapter deals with two of the most important signs of that European springtime: political recovery and the spiritual and political revival of the church. These two revivals were of great importance for the evolution of individual freedom and for the political and intellectual growth of Europe. The chapter begins with an account of events in one part of France—Normandy, which had come under the control of the Northmen, and which by 1066 under William was a well-ordered principality.

One of the earliest signs of revival was the success of feudalism in bringing peace and unity to Europe in the tenth and eleventh centuries. The reduced level of warfare in this period, together with favorable changes in climate, resulted in both population expansion and agricultural improvement, and medieval engineers made significant advances in harnessing both waterpower and windpower. More forceful testimony to the dynamism of the age was the Crusades. Growing out of the influence of the papacy and religion in medieval society, and the efforts of the *reconquista* in Spain, the Crusades provided an outlet for the spiritual and political energy of Europe, although their cultural and economic effects remain debatable.

The religious revival also began, with monastic reform at the abbey of Cluny in the eleventh century, and spread across Europe. When monastic life was subsequently threatened by materialism and lay interference, there were fresh demands for reform by the Cistercians at the abbey of Cîteaux.

146

At the same time, and partly as a result of the Cistercian reforms, the papacy set out to purify itself and to redefine its relationship with the emperors, kings, and other lay political authorities of Europe. This led to the investiture controversy, which reached its height in the conflict between Pope Gregory VII and the German emperor Henry IV. The struggle between the popes and the emperors turned out to be one of the most important and long-lasting political conflicts in European history.

Between 1000 and 1300 great numbers of people moved to Europe's frontiers—to Ireland, to eastern and northern Europe, and to Spain. Much of this migration activity was led by restless knights looking for land and by bishops and missionaries looking to spread Christianity. Many German settlers followed German knights into the east, and hence a Germanization of Poland and elsewhere was set in motion. In Spain, the king of Castile and Leon and the Cistercian monks led the movement, called the *reconquista,* to take over the Muslim settlements in Spain. Building on the Muslim city-life, Spain became the most urbanized part of Europe.

All in all, by 1300 Europeans identified themselves first and foremost as belonging to a unified Christian race.

Study Outline

Use this outline to review the chapter before you read a particular section in your textbook and then as a self-check to test your reading comprehension after you have read the chapter section.

    I. Political revival in western Europe in the tenth and eleventh centuries
      A. The decline of invasions and civil disorder
        1. Medieval France was an area of diverse languages and cultures, with the northern counties being the center of French feudalism, and with the king of France king in name only.
        2. The Northmen Rollo and William made Normandy a strong territory.
          a. Rollo was given more land in return for allegiance to the king; Rollo and his men became Christianized.
          b. Duke William, his successor, was successful in defeating King Henry, united his Norman nobility, and built many castles at his frontier.
        3. The nobles elected Hugh Capet king in 987, laying the foundation for future political stability.
        4. In England, the victory of Alfred of Wessex over the Danes in 878 slowly led to English unity.
        5. The Danish king Canute made England part of a large Scandinavian empire.
        6. The German king Otto halted the Magyars in 955.
          a. The base of Otto's power was his alliance with the church, which he used to weaken the feudal lords.
          b. Otto's coronation in 962 laid the foundation for the future Holy Roman Empire.
        7. The Italian cities of Venice, Genoa, and Pisa broke Muslim control of Mediterranean trade.
      B. Population, climate, and mechanization
        1. The decline in war and plague meant a rise in population.
        2. The warmer climate meant better agricultural production—hence, improved diet and an increase in female fertility.

      3. An ancient energy system, the water mill, was used on a more widespread basis for food production and industry.

      4. Windmills also came into use.

II. Revival and reform in the Christian church in the eleventh century

    A. The monastic revival

      1. Monastic activity had declined as the Carolingian Empire disintegrated.

      2. The abbey of Cluny led the way in a tenth-century monastic revival.

         a. Cluny provided strong leadership for reform of abuses such as simony, for high religious standards, and for sound economic management.

         b. The Cluniac reform spread throughout Europe.

      3. The monastic reform led by the abbey of Gorze emphasized literary culture, simple lifestyle, and lay authority.

      4. By the eleventh century, wealth and lay interference caused corruption.

      5. The Cistercians (beginning in 1098) isolated themselves from laymen and elaborate ritual.

         a. Their reform movement centered on farming and a simple communal life.

         b. The Cistercians founded 525 new monasteries in the twelfth century and had a profound influence on European society.

    B. The reform of the papacy

      1. The tenth-century papacy was corrupt and materialistic and provided little leadership to the people of Europe.

         a. Factions in Rome sought to control the papacy for their own gain.

         b. The office of pope was frequently bought and sold.

         c. There were many married priests.

      2. Leo IX made the first sweeping reforms.

      3. Later reforms stipulated that the college of cardinals would henceforth elect the pope.

III. The Gregorian revolution in church reform

    A. Pope Gregory VII's ideas for reform of the church

      1. Gregory believed that the pope could hold kings accountable.

      2. He wanted the church to be free from lay control.

    B. The controversy over lay investiture

      1. The church outlawed the widespread practice of lay investiture (the appointment of church officials by secular authority) in 1075.

      2. Emperor Henry IV of the Holy Roman Empire protested Pope Gregory's stand on investiture.

         a. The decree raised the question of who had the ultimate authority in a Christian society, the king or the pope.

         b. In 1076, Gregory excommunicated Henry.

      3. Their conflict was resolved by Henry's submission to the pope at Canossa in 1077.

      4. In 1080 Gregory again excommunicated Henry; in return, Henry invaded Rome.

      5. In 1122, the lay investiture controversy was finally settled in a conference at Worms.

         a. The emperor surrendered the right to choose bishops.

         b. However, lay rulers retained a veto over ecclesiastical choices.

      6. In the long run, the investiture crisis perpetuated the political division of Germany and encouraged the rise of a very strong noble class.

C. The papacy in the High Middle Ages
1. Pope Urban II laid the foundation for the papal curia, which henceforth administered the church and was its court of law.
   a. The papal curia developed into the court of final appeal for all of Christian Europe.
   b. Most of the cases involved property disputes, ecclesiastical elections, and marriage and annulment.
2. By the early thirteenth century, papal reform had succeeded, but in the following decades the papal bureaucracy became greedy and indifferent.

IV. The Crusades of the eleventh and twelfth centuries
A. The Crusades reflect papal influence in society and the church's new understanding of the noble warrior class.
1. The Crusades, or holy wars, to recover the Holy Land from the Muslims grew out of the Christian-Muslim conflict in Spain.
2. Many knights participated in the Crusades, which manifested both the religious and chivalric ideals of medieval society.
3. The Crusades began with Pope Urban II's plea in 1095 for a crusade to take Jerusalem from the Turks.
4. The Crusades offered a variety of opportunities for many people.
   a. Religious convictions inspired many.
   b. The lure of foreign travel and excitement was also strong.
   c. The Crusades also gave kings an opportunity to get rid of troublesome knights.
   d. The Crusades encouraged prejudice against European Jews.
B. The results of the Crusades
1. The First Crusade (1096) was marked by disputes among the great lords and much starvation and disease.
   a. The Crusaders captured Jerusalem in 1099.
   b. Crusader kingdoms were founded in Jerusalem, Edessa, Tripoli, and Antioch.
2. There were eight papally approved expeditions to the East between 1096 and 1270, but none of the later ones accomplished much.
   a. The Third Crusade was precipitated by the recapture of Jerusalem in 1187.
   b. The Fourth Crusade made the split between the Western and Eastern churches permanent when the Crusaders sacked Byzantium.
3. Crusades were also fought against the heretical Albegensians and against Emperor Frederick II.
4. A crusading religious order, the Knights Templars, waged war against pagans in eastern Europe and established a Christian Prussia.
5. Some women, such as Eleanor of Aquitaine, went on Crusades, while many found that the Crusades brought new economic opportunities.
6. The Crusades brought few cultural changes, since strong economic and intellectual ties with the East had already been made.
7. The long struggle between Christians and Muslims left a legacy of deep bitterness.
8. However, the Christian West benefited from commercial contact with the Middle East.

V. The expansion of Latin Christendom
A. Between 1000 and 1300 the frontiers of Europe were populated by peoples of Europe—including many restless knights looking for land.

B. Northern and eastern Europe
1. An Anglo-Norman takeover of Ulster led to English towns and a new type of church in Ireland.
2. Similarly, immigrant knights entered Scotland and established feudal society.
3. Bishoprics were organized in Scandinavian and Baltic regions, by Otto I and others.
4. Pagan peoples (the Balts) in the east and north were conquered and christianized by Otto I and Albert the Bear.
   a. Albert the Bear founded a dynasty in Brandenburg and carried out Ostiedlung to the east.
   b. He pushed his kingdom eastward to the Oder River—ruled by his knights with castles to crush the slavs.
   c. German knights and monks moved elsewhere including Silesia under Duke Boleslaw I.
   d. From Prague in Bohemia missionaries moved to convert Poland; Otto I established an archbishop at Gniezno, Poland.
   e. Many German settlers accompanied these knights and missionaries, and Germanization followed.

C. Spain
1. Caliph Rahman III's descendents fell into civil war, thus making a Christian *reconquista* easier.
2. Alfonso VI of Castile and Leon conquered Toledo and brought French monks and knights to settle the meseta.
   a. Alfonso VIII crushed the Muslims in 1212 and James of Aragon captured Valencia and turned the chief mosque into a cathedral.
   b. Ferdinand of Castile and Leon captured Cardoba and Seville and converted mosques to churches.
3. By 1299 Spain had 51 bishoprics and many Cistercian monasteries for military and religious use.
   a. Alcobaca in Portugal became a great intellectual center, led by Cistercian monasteries.
   b. Foreign businessmen came to Spain to take over the many former Muslim towns. Spain became the most urbanized part of Europe.
   c. Huge migration of people accompanied the reconquista.

D. Toward a Christian society
1. Cultural unity of new and old parts of Europe came about through and by the Roman papacy.
   a. One religious rite took place in all of Europe.
   b. Europeans identified themselves first and foremost as belonging to the "Christian race."

Review Questions

Check your understanding of this chapter by answering the following questions.

1. Describe the political revival that took place in the ninth and tenth centuries. Who were the chief participants in this revival and what did they accomplish?

2. What role did the church play in the recovery of Europe from a period of war and invasion?

3. Why did the population of Europe begin to increase in the eleventh century?

4. What were the goals of the Cluniac reformers? Why were they interested in isolation from lay society?

5. Describe the condition of the clergy and church leadership prior to Leo IX's reform movement. What were the major abuses?

6. Was it inevitable that Pope Gregory would come into conflict with the monarchs of Europe? Explain.

7. What was the investiture controversy? Who held ultimate power in medieval society?

8. Describe the conflict between Pope Gregory VII and Henry IV. What was the outcome?

9. In the long run who were the winners in the investiture controversy? How did this controversy affect the political development of Germany?

10. What were the role and function of the papal curia?

11. What were the various reasons for the Crusades? Were they primarily theological, economic, or imperialistic?

12. In what sense were the Crusades a "steam valve" for late medieval society?

13. What changes did the Crusades bring to western European society? Did the benefits outweigh the disadvantages?

14. What were the motives of those peoples who migrated into eastern Europe from western Europe between 1000 and 1300?

15. Describe how the *reconquista* worked in Spain. What were the motives of its leaders?

Study-Review Exercises

Define the following key concepts and terms.

simony

lay investiture

curia

cardinals

excommunicate

indulgence

Identify and explain the significance of the following terms.

Treaty of Saint Claire-sur-Epte

investiture controversy

Cluniac reforms

Gorze reforms

Cistercians

Canossa

college of cardinals

reconquista

Worms conference of 1122

Identify and explain the significance of the following people.

Canute

Hrotswitha

Rollo

Henry IV

King Otto

Pope Leo IX

Pope Gregory VII

Albert the Bear

Duke Bolslaw I

Alfonso VI

Test your understanding of the chapter by providing the correct answers.

1. The Crusades resulted in an *increase/decrease* in greed and social-religious intolerance, while they *improved/eroded* relations between Christians and Muslims.

2. It appears that between the ninth and eleventh centuries the European climate became significantly *warmer/cooler.*

3. The *increase/decrease* of warfare in the eleventh century led to an *increase/decrease* in the population of Europe.

4. The important monastic revival began in the tenth century at the _____ in Burgundy.

5. According to the Worms settlement of 1122, bishops were henceforth to be chosen by the _____ but veto power was to be held by the _____.

6. The German monastic reform movement was centered at the abbey of _____.

Major Political Ideas

Describe the idea of "freedom of the church," which emerged from the Gregorian reform movement, and how it was connected to the practice of lay investiture. Discuss and define the terms *freedom of the church* and *lay investiture.* Include in your discussion an account of the conflict between Henry IV and Pope Gregory VII.

Issues for Essays and Discussion

The High Middle Ages were a period of growth and achievement. What were the chief political and religious changes of the age? Make specific reference to increased political stability in western Europe, the monastic revival, and the Gregorian revolution.

Refute or defend this statement: The Crusades were essentially a noble and idealistic enterprise aimed at creating a better and more free world.

Interpretation of Visual Sources

Study the illustration entitled "The Capture of Jerusalem in 1099". Who were the combatants in this event? What does this picture tell us about offensive and defensive military tactics? Do any of the scenes here suggest that this is in any way a propaganda piece?

Geography

Study Map 9.1 in the textbook and then answer the following questions: Why did the First Crusade begin in France? Approximately how many miles did the Crusaders travel before they reached Jerusalem? What is the significance of the cities of Edessa, Antioch, Tripoli, Damascus, and Acre? Why did the Third Crusade take three different routes? Where did the Fourth Crusade end? Why?

Understanding History Through the Arts

1. How did the Crusades affect the art and architecture of the High Middle Ages? To begin a study of the art and architecture of the Crusades, see the chapter titled "Crusader Art and Architecture" in J. R. Strayer, ed., *The Dictionary of the Middle Ages,* vol. 4 (1984).

2. What were the ideas and stories that inspired the imagination and dreams of medieval people? Who were their heroes? The myths of any period are important because they make up the backbone of the culture. Seven myths and hero stories of the Middle Ages are retold in N. L. Goodrich, *The Medieval Myths** (1961).

3. What contributions did the Cistercian monks make to architecture? For discussion of this subject, begin with R. Stalley, *The Cistercian Monasteries of Ireland* (1988).

Problems for Further Investigation

1. How did knights, churchmen, and migrants from western Europe succeed in taking over so much of eastern Europe? Begin your study with L. R. Johnson, *Central Europe: Enemies, Neighbors, Friends* (1996).

2. How did Cluny come to exert such a strong religious influence? B. Rosenwein, *To Be the Neighbor of Saint Peter: The Social Meaning of Cluny's Property, 909-1049* (1989), is an interesting study for anyone interested in the power of the papacy and the Cluniac movement.

3. Were the Crusades a success or a failure? Was it a military blunder? A great expression of religious faith? Come up with your own theory—backed up with historical fact. Students interested in further research in this area should begin with *Soldiers of the Faith: Crusaders and Muslims at War* (1983).

---

*Available in paperback.

Self-Test Multiple-Choice Questions

<u>Do</u> <u>not</u> assume that these questions will appear on any examination. It is recommended that you <u>not</u> memorize these questions, but use them only as a self-test. Answers are at the end of this book.

1. The curia was
   a. the headquarters for the Italian bishops.
   b. the papal financial office.
   c. the location of the imperial court.
   d. the papal bureaucracy and court of law.

2. Emperor Henry IV challenged Pope Gregory VII because
   a. the pope wanted ownership of Germany.
   b. the pope was a peasant.
   c. the pope restricted lay investiture.
   d. Henry wanted control over all of Italy.

3. The Battle of Edington in 878 marked
   a. West Saxon political revival and unity.
   b. the rise of Normandy.
   c. Danish control of northern Europe.
   d. the fall of Anglo-Saxon law and culture in England.

4. The sale of church offices, including the office of pope, is called
   a. lay investiture.
   b. the chancery.
   c. excommunication.
   d. simony.

5. The real winner of the eleventh-century investiture controversy was
   a. the nobility.
   b. the papacy.
   c. the emperor.
   d. the college of cardinals.

6. A new religious order founded in the late eleventh century that avoided involvement with secular feudal society was the
   a. Nicolaites.
   b. Cistercians.
   c. cardinals.
   d. curia.

7. In 962 which German king was crowned Holy Roman Emperor, thereby reviving imperial authority in central Europe?
   a. William
   b. Otto
   c. Gregory
   d. Charles V

8. As king of Germany and successor to Charlemagne, Otto I used the resources of the church in all of the following ways *except*
   a. to control ecclesiastical appointments.
   b. in his army.
   c. to assume the role of pope.
   d. in his administration.

9. At which Burgundian abbey did the tenth-century monastic reform and religious revival have its origins?
   a. Cluny
   b. Canossa
   c. Flanders
   d. Worms

10. The Lateran Synod of 1059 decreed that the power and authority to elect the pope rest solely in the
    a. emperor.
    b. college of cardinals.
    c. townspeople.
    d. Roman citizens.

11. The duchy of Normandy became strong under William I partly because he
    a. turned over the control of the currency to the church.
    b. forbade the construction of private castles.
    c. allowed vassals to avoid military obligations.
    d. allowed the church autonomy.

12. The power of the German emperor Otto I rested on
    a. an alliance with William of Normandy.
    b. heavy taxation of the merchants of his territories.
    c. papal approval.
    d. the support of ecclesiastical officials in Germany.

13. The church reform during the eleventh century included all of the following *except*
    a. new religious orders.
    b. increased practice of lay investiture.
    c. "freedom of the church."
    d. reform of the papacy.

14. In the tenth and eleventh centuries, Nicolaites were
    a. reformed monks.
    b. married priests.
    c. priests who bought and sold church offices.
    d. none of the above.

15. The Crusades originated as reaction to
    a. Christian-Muslim conflict in Spain.
    b. the decline of Christian influence in Turkey.
    c. the decline of Christian influence in Italy.
    d. new economic opportunities in southern Italy.

16. The goal of the Gregorian reform movement was
    a. the end of Philip I's adulterous marriage.
    b. the abolition of simony.
    c. the moral reform of the clergy and the centralization of the Catholic church under papal authority.
    d. the excommunication of William of Normandy.

17. Emperor Henry IV opposed Pope Gregory VII because
    a. the pope was too inflexible.
    b. Gregory VII was a peasant.
    c. the pope wanted Henry's strict obedience.
    d. Henry relied on the services of churchmen whom the pope wanted to make responsible solely to papal authority.

18. The pontificate of Innocent III represents the high point of medieval papal authority because
    a. Innocent launched the Crusades.
    b. he composed important legal treatises.
    c. he exerted power all over Europe.
    d. he secured the end of clerical marriage.

19. The papal curia was important as
    a. a symbol of papal power and authority.
    b. the first strong monarchical bureaucracy.
    c. a final court of appeals for Christians all over Europe.
    d. all of the above.

20. The crusade that resulted in Christian fighting Christian was the
    a. Fourth Crusade.
    b. Second Crusade.
    c. Eastern Crusade.
    d. First Crusade.

21. The tenth- and eleventh-century advance in energy use centered on
    a. coal mining.
    b. the building of dams.
    c. the development of the steam engine.
    d. the water wheel and the windmill.

22. By the last quarter of the eleventh century, monastic observance and spiritual fervor declined because of
    a. the economic depression of the monasteries.
    b. war.
    c. the increased wealth of the monasteries.
    d. competition from the Cistercian orders.

23. The investiture struggle between church and state had its largest impact on
    a. Germany.
    b. France.
    c. England.
    d. Italy.

24. Compared to the dukes of Normandy and Aquitaine, the first Capetian kings of France were
    a. rich and powerful.
    b. able to use royal law and coinage to unify France.
    c. weak.
    d. militarily superior but not hereditary.

25. Which of the following statements best describes the effect of the Crusades on the women of Europe?
    a. They made it impossible for any women to experience foreign travel.
    b. They further limited the possibilities of female independence.
    c. They lowered the birthrate.
    d. They provided greater economic opportunities for women.

Chapter 10

Life in Christian Europe in the High Middle Ages

Learning Objectives

After reading and studying this chapter you should be able to:

1. describe the everyday life of serfs and peasants and their connections to the land.

2. describe the power and function of noble families—including men, women, and children.

3. discuss the nature of feudal society as it pertained to peasants, women, and other groups.

4. describe the "popular" religion of the people and the religious life of monastic people.

Chapter Summary

This chapter describes and analyzes life in medieval society. It focuses on the three most representative groups within medieval society: the peasants, who worked; the nobles, who fought; and the monks, who prayed. Despite the rise of towns and the beginning of a merchant class, most of the people were peasants or serfs, who lived and labored on the land. These men and women toiled on the land of the manors to scratch out a meager existence for themselves and to support their noble lords in noble fashion. The agricultural productivity of the average manor was low because there was a lack of fertilizer and it was necessary to leave as much as half of the land fallow each year. Between the ninth and thirteenth centuries, however, it appears that agricultural productivity doubled—a remarkable achievement. Nonetheless, the diet of the peasantry was very limited and seldom adequate. A major problem of the Middle Ages was that the birthrate tended always to outpace the food supply.

The manor was the center of medieval rural life, and Christianity was the center of the day-to-day world on the manor. The church provided an explanation for the meaning of life, and it also supplied the community with much of its entertainment and political leadership. Women held a pivotal position in the family and village economy.

The aristocratic nobility was a class with special power and legal status. It had its own lifestyle and goals. The size of noble families; aristocratic patterns of child rearing, marriage, and sex; and women's role were determined by the fact that males were the holders of property.

The monasteries of Europe had a great civilizing influence and provided important opportunities for aristocratic men and women. They contributed to both literacy and agricultural improvement in the Middle Ages. Monastic life varied from order to order and from district to district, but daily life in all monasteries centered around the liturgy.

Study Outline

Use this outline to preview the chapter before you read a particular section in your textbook and then as a self-check to test your reading comprehension after you have read the chapter section.

   I. Those who work
      A. The condition of the peasantry varied according to geographic location, and there were many levels of peasantry.
      B. Slavery, serfdom, and upward mobility
         1. The church did not take a strong stand in opposing the enslavement of Christians.
         2. The distinction between slave and serf was not always clear. Although serfs could not be bought and sold, they were property of the lord.
         3. Serfs had to perform labor services on the lord's land.
            a. Serfs often had to pay fees to the lord.
            b. Serfs were tied to the land, and serfdom was a hereditary condition.
            c. Serfs could obtain freedom in several ways: from their lord, by purchase by a third party, or by being in a town guild for a year and a day.
         4. Settlement on new land meant opportunities for social mobility and freedom.
      C. The manor—the estate of the lord—was the basic unit of medieval rural life.
         1. Manors varied in size.
         2. A manor usually contained a village.
         3. All the arable land of the manor was divided into strips.
         4. The demesne was cultivated for the lord. The other part was held by the peasantry.
         5. Each manor usually had pastures and forests.
      D. Agricultural methods
         1. The land was usually divided into two or three fields—with fields being divided into strips assigned to individual peasants.
            a. Usually one of the two fields were left fallow.
         2. Animal manure was the major form of fertilizer.
         3. The increase in iron production after 1100 meant better tools.
         4. The development of the padded horse collar led to the use of horses in agriculture and thus a great increase in productivity.
         5. Yields were low, but they improved from the ninth to the thirteenth centuries; the amount for sheer survival was thought to be three times the amount sown—the average thirteenth century manor got a 5 to 1 yield.
      E. Life on the manor
         1. Medieval village life was provincial and dull but secure.
         2. Most peasant households consisted of a nuclear family.
         3. Women worked the fields, managed the household, and dominated in the production of beer and ale.

4. Diet included vegetables, some fruit, grains, beer, cheese, some fish, and wild meat—with possibly a great increase in meat consumption by the mid-thirteenth century—but the mainstay was bread.
5. Children helped with the family chores.

F. Health care
1. People who survived to adulthood were generally strong and tough.
2. Midwives were non-professionals who occasionally performed Cesarean births.
3. Hospitals were established in the twelfth century.
4. Urban people had greater access to doctors—who were usually men.

G. Popular religion
1. The Christian religion infused and regulated daily life.
2. Religious ritual and practice synthesized many elements—Jewish, pagan, Roman, and Christian.
3. The church was the center of village social, political, and economic life.
4. Popular religion consisted largely of symbolic rituals and ceremonies.
5. In the eleventh century a great emphasis on the devotion to Mary evolved.
6. Peasants believed that God intervened directly in human affairs, and that sin was caused by the Devil.
7. Few peasants lived beyond the age of forty; pilgrimages offered adventure and hope in a world of gloom.
   a. The church granted indulgences (remissions of penalties for sin) to those who visited the shrines of great saints.
   b. Indulgences and pilgrimages came to be equated with salvation.

II. Those who fight
A. The nobility strongly influenced all aspects of medieval culture.
1. The social structure of Europe varied from region to region; overall the nobility was an elite, self-conscious social class.
   a. Nobles held political power and had a special legal status.
2. Nobles were professional fighters.
   a. Their function was to protect the weak, the poor, and the churches.
   b. Nobles were supposed to display the chivalric virtues of courage, courtesy, loyalty, generosity, and graciousness.
3. The medieval nobility developed independently of knighthood—all nobles were knights, but not all knights were noble.
   a. In France and England, the term *knight* connoted moral values, consciousness of family, and participation in a superior hereditary caste.
   b. In Germany, a large caste of nonnoble knights, or *ministerials*, existed.

B. Infancy and childhood in aristocratic families
1. Ignorant medical care contributed to the high infant mortality rate.
2. Infanticide probably decreased during this period, but abandonment of infants, which was socially acceptable, increased.
3. Children were often sold or given to monasteries as oblates.
4. Other family-planning strategies, such as primogeniture, late marriages, and birth control were used to preserve family estates.
5. Most young aristocratic children had a great deal of playtime and freedom.

6. At about age seven, aristocratic boys served in a lord's household and received formal training in arms.
   a. Learning to read and write was not common until the eleventh and twelfth centuries.
   b. Formal training concluded at age twenty-one with the ceremony of knighthood.
C. Youth in aristocratic families
   1. Unless a young man's father was dead, he was still considered a youth and could not marry.
   2. Knighted men whose fathers were alive had to find activities, such as travel, tournaments, and carousing, to occupy themselves.
   3. Aristocratic women married early; their families provided large marriage portions, or dowries.
   4. Generational disputes were common in aristocratic families in the twelfth and thirteenth centuries.
   5. Sexual tensions arose from aristocratic marriage practices, which brought together young wives, older husbands, and young, unmarried men.
D. Power and responsibility in the aristocracy
   1. A male member of the nobility became an adult when he came into possession of his property.
   2. Aristocrats saw lavish living as a sign of status and power, but it often meant debt.
   3. As a vassal, a noble was required to fight for the lord or for the king when called on to do so.
   4. He was also obliged to attend his lord's court on important occasions.
   5. He had to look after his own estates, which usually required frequent travel.
   6. Holding the manorial court was one of his major duties.
   7. Women played an important role in running the estate—partly because men were frequently away.
      a. Because of frequent warfare, many women became widows, and thus came to control land and exercise great authority.
   8. All in all, the constant warfare among the nobility was a constant source of trouble for the monarchy—causing the monarchy to turn to the middle classes for support; the Crusades eliminated some the most dangerous problems for the monarchs.

III. Those who pray
   A. Prayer was a vital social service performed by monks; they also performed other important cultural and economic services.
   B. Recruitment
      1. Many who became monks did so because of their parents' decision to give them to the church as oblates.
      2. Monasteries provided careers for aristocratic children.
      3. In the later Middle Ages the monasteries recruited from the middle class.
   C. The nuns
      1. Convents were established for women of the noble class.
         a. The abbess or prioress was customarily a woman of high social standing.
         b. Some abbesses achieved national prominence.

2. The duties of a nun varied from religious duties to administration to sewing and perhaps manuscript copying.
   a. Hildegard of Bingen represents the scholarly life of many nuns.
   b. Isabella of Lancaster represents the type of prioress who was active in court life and travel.
D. Prayer and other work
   1. Daily life in the monasteries centered around the liturgy.
      a. The need to praise God justified the spending of a great deal of money on objects to enhance the liturgy.
      b. The liturgy thus inspired a great deal of art.
   2. The lords gave the monasteries land.
   3. Aristocratic monks, or choir monks, did not till the land, but relied on lay brothers supervised by a cellarer for this.
   4. The almoner took care of the poor; the precentor, the library; the sacristan, the liturgy materials; and the novice master, the training of recruits.
   5. Law and medicine were studied and practiced—sometimes in the royal court.
   6. Raising and breeding of horses were undertaken, as was the conversion of wasteland to agriculture.
   7. The Cistercians were important in agricultural developments in the Low Countries, Germany, France, and England.
   8. Some monasteries got involved in iron and lead mining.
   9. Most monasteries were involved in providing social services such as schools, hospitals, and hostels for travelers.
E. Economic difficulties
   1. By the late Middle Ages many monasteries, such as Cluny, did not have enough income to support their lavish lifestyle.
   2. Many fell into debt and agricultural recession led to less endowment.

Review Questions

Check your understanding of this chapter by answering the following questions.

1. How could a serf obtain freedom?

2. Describe a medieval manor. How did it work and what agricultural methods governed its existence? Was it "efficient"?

3. What was the role of women in medieval society? What evidence exists to suggest that women might have held considerable power within the family unit?

4. How important was religion in medieval manor life?

5. What do you believe to have been the worldview of the average medieval peasant? How would peasant men and women have thought about themselves and their environment?

6. What was the function of the nobility? What were its characteristics as a class?

7. How did medieval people treat their children? Why was child abandonment so widespread and what were the responses of society to it?

8. Why did aristocratic men marry late and aristocratic women marry early?

9. Why was aristocratic society marked by sexual tension and generational conflict?

10. What were the responsibilities and lifestyles of aristocratic men and women?

11. What was the social background of most medieval monks? How did this tend to change in the later Middle Ages?

12. What were the major functions of the medieval monasteries? Were they solely spiritual institutions?

13. Why was the monastic movement important to the aristocratic families of Europe?

14. Describe the economic dilemma that many monasteries faced in the late Middle Ages.

Study-Review Exercises

Define the following key concepts and terms.

slave

serf

villein

manor (demesne)

open-field system

child abandonment

oblate

nobility

almoner

choir monks

lay brothers

Identify and explain the significance of the following people and terms.

ministerials

abbey of Cluny

Cistercian Order

Orderic Vitalis

The Leech Book of Bald

chevaliers

knighthood

"Salve Regina"

Describe each of the following aspects of medieval life.

monastic recruitment

medieval agricultural system

aristocratic marriage patterns

medieval peasants' diet

Test your understanding of the chapter by providing the correct answers.

1. The evidence about infanticide makes it *certain/uncertain* that it increased in the Middle Ages.

2. The use of horses rather than oxen in farming meant *greater/less* productivity.

3. In medieval society, women *did/did not* play an important economic role in the manor and the family.

4. The word _____ derives from a Latin term meaning "dwelling," "residence," or "homestead."

5. In medieval society women were *frequently/never* raised to the nobility.

6. By the late Middle Ages it was the *groom/bride* who provided the marriage dowry.

7. Most noblemen married relatively *early/late* in life.

8. Formal military training for the medieval aristocratic boy was concluded with the ceremony of _____.

9. Slavery *was/was not* common in medieval European society.

10. Some scholars believe that the use of the _____ in agriculture was one of the decisive ways in which Europe advanced over the rest of the world.

Major Political Ideas

1. Compare and contrast the concepts of serfdom and freedom. How was freedom acquired in medieval society?

2. What political role did the nobility play in medieval society? What was the relationship between the nobility and the monarchy in terms of power and the dispensing of justice? Who was more important in medieval society, the nobles or the monarch?

Issues for Essays and Discussion

Describe the opportunities for social and economic mobility for both men and women in the three general groups within the High Middle Ages—those who fought, those who prayed, and those who worked. Who among these people had the greatest opportunities? In what way did these opportunities tend to expand or contract during this period, and who made the greatest contribution to society?

Interpretation of Visual Sources

Study the reproduction of the painting *The Siege of Antioch*. Describe the types of weapons depicted. What military advantages do those inside the castle seem to enjoy? How might their defenses be weakened? What advantages do the aggressors appear to have? What factors might result in their loss of the siege?

Understanding History Through the Arts

1. How do the illuminated manuscripts created in the Carolingian, Byzantine, and Norman empires compare with one another? Begin your study with H. Buchthal et al., *The Place of Book Illumination in Byzantine Art* (1975), J. J. G. Alexander, *Norman Illumination at Mont St. Michael* (1970), and G. Braziller, *Carolingian Painting* (1976). For the relationship between Russian and Byzantine art, see A. Voyce, *The Art and Architecture of Medieval Russia* (1967), and for the remarkable artistic developments in Ireland, see P. Harbison et al., *Irish Art and Architecture: From Pre-History to the Present* (1978).

2. How does poetry help us understand medieval life? *Carmina Burana* by C. Orff is a series of songs based on poems written in the thirteenth century by wandering students and

disillusioned monks in Germany, who celebrated their carousing and lovemaking in verse. Orff put these intensely physical, scenic, and entertaining poems to vibrant music in 1937, and it is available in many recordings.

3. How aware were medieval women poets of the issue of womanhood? A recent study of feminine poetry, *Sister of Wisdom: St. Hildegard's Theology of the Feminine* (1987), by B. Newman, shows how one woman of the twelfth century used symbolic theology to explore the issue of gender.

Problems for Further Investigation

1. Did the peasants really starve? What are some of the modern world's mistaken beliefs about sex, marriage, and family in medieval times? These and other questions are considered in a ground-breaking social history, *The World We Have Lost** (1965) by P. Laslett.

2. Did aristocratic women have any power in the churches or households of this military society? Were children mistreated in the medieval family? Historians are just beginning to investigate how childhood and the status of women in society have changed over the course of history. Some good starting points for research on childhood are L. de Mause, ed., *The History of Childhood** (1974); *The History of Childhood Quarterly*; and a collection of essays, *Women as Mothers in Pre-Industrial England*, V. Fildes, ed. (1990). For medieval women, see E. Power, *Medieval Women,** M. M. Postan, ed. (1976), and S. Shahar, *The Fourth Estate: A History of Women in the Middle Ages* (1984). Much of the work on medieval women is on women in the world of religion. The best of these works is G. Nichols and L. Shank, *Medieval Religious Women*, vol. l: *Distant Echoes* (1984). A good place to begin a study on women as mystics and the masculine-feminism issues in religion is C. Bynum, *Jesus as a Mother: Studies in the Spirituality of the High Middle Ages* (1982).

Self-Test Multiple-Choice Questions

Do not assume that these questions will appear on any examination. it is recommended that you not memorize these questions, but use them only as a self-test. Answers are at the end of this book.

1. Which of the following statements about the medieval village church is *false*?
    a. It was often a business center.
    b. It was often a center for medieval drama.
    c. It was the chief educational center.
    d. It was often open only to aristocratic participation.

---

*Available in paperback.

2. In the twelfth century many of the older monastic houses found themselves in economic difficulties because
   a. they could no longer recruit monks.
   b. peasants refused to pay their levies.
   c. building and living expenses increased faster than revenue.
   d. knights no longer placed their estates under their authority when they went on Crusades.

3. Which of the following statements about medieval nobility is *false*?
   a. All nobles were knights.
   b. Their function was primarily military and political.
   c. Father-son ties tended to be strong and loving.
   d. A castle was an aristocratic status symbol.

4. Generally, the monasteries recruited their members from
   a. the middle class.
   b. the aristocracy.
   c. the peasantry.
   d. village church schools.

5. For noblemen, adulthood came with
   a. knighthood.
   b. the age of eighteen.
   c. the acquisition of property.
   d. the demonstration of military prowess.

6. The difference between a free person and a serf was that the
   a. free person was tied to the land and the serf was not.
   b. serf had no obligations to the lord, while the free person had many.
   c. serf paid rent to his lord, while the free person paid nothing at all.
   d. serf was bound to the land by the obligations he owed his lord, while the free person usually just paid rent.

7. Medieval farmers
   a. generally farmed the land in strips scattered throughout the manor.
   b. did not use any kind of fertilizer.
   c. never used iron for tools.
   d. were unable to show any improvement in agricultural output in nearly a thousand years.

8. Medieval peasants
   a. traveled widely and visited many foreign countries.
   b. had a sense of community and pride of place.
   c. hardly ever drank alcoholic beverages.
   d. refused to let women work in the fields.

9. Peasants usually did not consume
   a. vegetables, particularly cabbage.
   b. large quantities of meat.
   c. bread.
   d. beer.

10. Medieval treatment of infants and children was characterized by
    a. a low rate of mortality.
    b. an increase in infanticide.
    c. legal prohibitions on sale of children.
    d. widespread child abandonment.

11. In medieval society, noblewomen
    a. usually married late in life.
    b. had the right to select their husbands.
    c. were customarily required to present a dowry to the groom and his family.
    d. generally married men younger than themselves.

12. Monastic life in general was
    a. a combination of attention to liturgy and manual work.
    b. devoted exclusively to prayer.
    c. so different from place to place that it is impossible to generalize about it.
    d. centered exclusively on manufacturing and farming.

13. Which of the following statements about medieval serfs and freedom is *true*?
    a. There were very few immigration possibilities within Europe for serfs.
    b. Serfs had little chance of purchasing freedom with cash.
    c. Serfs could obtain freedom by fleeing from the manor and living in town for a year and a day.
    d. Serfs had no possibility of freedom as long as they remained on the manor.

14. Chevaliers were
    a. wealthy monks.
    b. members of a religious order that stressed agricultural reform.
    c. horsemen, or knights.
    d. court painters and architects.

15. A medieval manor was
    a. an estate of at least ten villages.
    b. a plantation.
    c. the estate of a lord and his dependent tenants.
    d. an estate of at least three villages.

16. To provide food for all the people on the manor, the land had to yield at least
    a. six times the amount of seeds planted.
    b. ten times the amount of seeds planted.
    c. three times the amount of seeds planted.
    d. five times the amount of seeds planted.

17. A person became a noble by
    a. thrift, hard work, and sobriety.
    b. clever business acumen.
    c. birth or remarkable service to king or lord.
    d. buying a patent of nobility.

18. Most of the education of medieval aristocrats was in
    a. the Bible.
    b. the Latin classics.
    c. canon law.
    d. the arts of war and chivalry.

19. The opportunities and responsibilities of aristocratic women in the Middle Ages were
    a. significant, particularly in terms of the administration of the manorial estate.
    b. limited to bearing and raising children.
    c. considerable, but only at times of crusade when the husband was away.
    d. centered on noneconomic activities, such as music and reading.

20. Until the fourteenth century, most monks were drawn from the
    a. business classes.
    b. peasantry.
    c. petty bourgeoisie.
    d. nobility.

21. Management of the monastic estate was the basic responsibility of the
    a. abbot.
    b. novices.
    c. cellarer.
    d. almoner.

22. The monastic order that excelled in the development of new agricultural techniques and methods was the
    a. Dominicans.
    b. Benedictines.
    c. Franciscans.
    d. Cistercians.

23. In general, the monasteries regarded their major social responsibility to be
    a. academic work.
    b. providing for the poor.
    c. educating the children of the nobility.
    d. prayer.

24. The opinion of most scholars is that medieval peasant households were
    a. usually composed of unmarried couples.
    b. extended families with many grandparents and married children present.
    c. mostly small nuclear families.
    d. on average composed of teen parents and five to seven children.

25. English serfs were called
    a. *ministerials.*
    b. *miles.*
    c. *villeins.*
    d. *chevalier.*

Chapter 11

The Creativity and Vitality of the High Middle Ages

Learning Objectives

After reading and studying this chapter you should be able to:

1. discuss how the kingdoms of England, France, and Germany welded themselves into proto-modern states.

2. explain the significance of the Norman impact on Anglo-Saxon England, Philip II's importance in the development of medieval France, and the developments in medieval Germany.

3. list factors that led to the revival of commerce, the revitalization of towns and cities, and the appearance of universities.

Chapter Summary

The High Middle Ages—roughly, the twelfth and thirteenth centuries—was an era of remarkable achievement in law, the arts, philosophy, and education. The modern idea of the sovereign nation-state took root in this period. By means of war, taxation, and control over justice, the kings of England and France were able to strengthen royal authority and establish a system of communication with all of their people.

The Normans were important in bringing a centralized feudal system to England by using the sheriff, the writ, and other devices to replace baronial rule with royal power. Out of this process emerged the concept of common law and, with the Magna Carta, the idea of supremacy of the law. The process, however, was not altogether smooth, as the conflict between Henry II and Becket illustrates. The evolution of the territorial state in France was not quite as rapid as in England. France was less of a geographical unit than England, and the creation of strong royal authority involved more armed conflict between king and barons. And in Germany, royal power failed to develop at all, despite a good start by Emperor Frederick Barbarossa. Part of the reason was the historic connection between Germany and Italy. The church-state struggle was another major reason that royal authority in Germany was destined to remain weak.

The rise of the universities accompanied the emergence of the strong secular states because the new states needed educated administrators to staff their bureaucracies. The new universities became centers for the study of law and medicine.

Improvement in agriculture, coupled with a reopening of the Mediterranean to Christian traders, fostered the growth of towns and commerce. Flanders and Italy led the way in this urban revival. The growth of towns was one of the most important developments in Western history. Towns meant a new culture and social order, increased economic opportunities, and the beginnings of modern capitalism.

Religious heresy grew as the traditional Christian religion was unable to meet the needs of urban dwellers. The result of the heretical crisis was the evolution of several new religious orders of Friars, which counteracted the heretical movement by putting emphasis on a nonmaterialistic clergy that could preach to the needs of the people and at the same time manage the process of reconversion.

Few periods in history can claim as many artistic achievements as the High Middle Ages. The Gothic cathedrals, shimmering in stone and glass, stand not only as spiritual and artistic testimony to the age but also as a reflection of the economic power and civic pride of the great cities. By 1300, the energy of the High Middle Ages had been spent.

Study Outline

Use this outline to preview the chapter before you read a particular section in your textbook and then as a self-check to test your reading comprehension after you have read the chapter section.

I. The medieval origins of the modern state
   A. England
      1. England's seven kingdoms were united under one king under the pressure of the Danish (Viking) invasions of the ninth and tenth centuries.
         a. England was divided into shires, each under the jurisdiction of an unpaid sheriff appointed by the king.
         b. All the English thegns (local chieftains) recognized the central authority of the king.
      2. William the Conqueror replaced the Anglo-Saxon sheriffs with Normans.
      3. Sheriffs, the writ, the Norman inquest, and *Domesday Book* were used to centralize royal power.
      4. The Angevin dynasty began with William's grandson, Henry II.
   B. France
      1. In the early twelfth century, France consisted of virtually independent provinces; the king's goal was to increase the royal domain and extend his authority.
      2. Philip II began the process of unifying France.
      3. By the end of the thirteenth century, most of the provinces of modern France had been added to the royal domain through diplomacy, marriage, war, and inheritance, and the king was stronger than his nobles.
      4. Philip Augustus devised a system of royal agents called baillis and seneschals to help enforce royal law.
      5. Unlike England, where administration was based on unpaid local officials, royal administration in France rested on a professional bureaucracy.
   C. Germany
      1. Unlike England and France, Germany moved toward multiple independent principalities—or *landesherrschaft.*

2. The emperor shared power with the princes, dukes, archbishops, etc.—built great castles.
3. Frederick Barbarossa tried to unify Germany by creating royal officials, called ministerials, to enforce his will.
   a. He supported local judicial authority by way of the *landfrieden*.
   b. He tried to subdue Italian cities but was defeated at Legnano in 1176.

D. Finance
1. Growth of territory and authority led medieval kings to seek new sources of revenue and better systems of administration.
   a. Henry I of England established a bureau of finance called the Exchequer to keep track of income.
   b. French kings relied on royal taxes, mostly from the church, the tallage, and the conversion of feudal dues to cash payments.
2. Medieval people believed that royal taxation should be imposed only in times of emergency.
3. Sicily is a good example of an efficient financial bureaucracy.
   a. Roger de Hauteville introduced feudalism to the island.
   b. Frederick II Hohenstaufen centralized royal power in Sicily by taxing regularly, building bureaucracy, controling local government, founding a university, and regulating the economy
   c. He granted huge concessions to the local rulers in Germany.

E. Law and justice in medieval Europe
1. The legal system by the twelfth century was a hodgepodge of customs practices—very often differing from one locale to another. Medieval kings sought to blend these into a uniform system under their control.
   a. A system of royal justice, founded by Louis IX, unified France.
   b. He established the Parlement of Paris as a kind of supreme court.
   c. He sent royal judges to all parts of the country.
   d. He was the first French monarch to publish laws for the entire kingdom.
2. Beginning with Henry II the English kings developed and extended the common law, which was accepted by the whole country.
   a. Henry II established a jury system and improved procedure in criminal justice.
   b. Courts sought witnesses and evidence—but sometimes judged guilt or innocence by trial by ordeal.
3. Becket and Henry II quarreled over legal jurisdiction.
   a. Becket claimed that crimes by clerics should be tried in church courts ("benefit of clergy").
   b. He was assassinated by the king's friends in 1170.
   c. Henry gave up his attempt to bring clerics under the authority of the royal court.
4. King John's conflict with church and barons led to the Magna Carta (1215), which claims that everyone, including the king, must obey the law.
5. In the German empire justice was administered by local and regional authorities.
   a. Crimes were first seen as acts against the individual, but later as acts against the public interest.

6. The English common law system was strikingly different from the system of continental (Roman) law.
   a. The common law relied on precedents and thus was able to evolve.
   b. The Roman law tradition used the fixed legal maxims of the Justinian Code.
7. The extension and centralization of the law, along with economic and agricultural competition and fear of foreigners, led to discrimination and pressure for social conformity.
   a. Many towns in Europe had a small Jewish population; they were forbidden to own land and hence they became important in finance and commerce; they even managed the papal affairs.
   b. By the late twelfth century, anti-Semitism was on the rise; the king of France used hostility against Jews to raise royal revenue.
   c. Likewise, the king of England expelled Jews in order to gain new revenues from parliament.
   d. It may be that some of this discrimination resulted from the general xenophobia that spread across Europe and that grew out of the Crusades.
8. Homosexuality, which had been accepted for centuries, had (by 1300) been declared illegal.
   a. The early Christians displayed no special prejudice against homosexuals; some important church leaders and kings were publicly known homosexuals.
   b. It is probable that the Crusades resulted in raising fears of minorities and that the centralization of the law and the state led to intolerance of religious and sexual distinctiveness.

II. Economic revival
   A. The rise of towns
      1. Some historians believe that towns began as fortifications (boroughs).
      2. The historian Henri Pirenne claimed that towns resulted from trade and commerce.
      3. Others believe that towns sprang up around religious centers.
      4. All towns had a few common characteristics: a town wall, a central market, a court, and a monetary system.
      5. The bourgeoisie, or townspeople, became a new class in medieval society.
   B. Town liberties
      1. Townspeople worked hard to acquire social, political, and legal liberties, or special privileges.
         a. The most important privilege a medieval townsperson could gain was personal freedom.
         b. The liberty of personal freedom that came with residence in a town contributed greatly to the emancipation of the serfs in the High Middle Ages.
      2. Merchant and craft guilds evolved to provide greater economic security; they bargained with kings and lords for political independence.
      3. Women played an important role in the household, the guilds, and the town economy.

    C. Town life
1. Medieval towns served as places of trade and protection.
    a. The place where a product was made and sold was also usually the merchant's residence.
    b. Towns grew without planning or regulation.
    c. Air and water pollution were serious problems.
2. As the bourgeoisie grew wealthier, more and more churches were built.
    D. The revival of long-distance trade in the eleventh century
1. Groups of merchants would pool capital to finance trading expeditions.
2. Italian and Flemish cities dominated the trade market.
    a. Venice led the West in trade and controlled the Oriental market.
    b. Flanders controlled the cloth trade.
3. England was the major supplier of wool for Flanders.
    a. Wool was the cornerstone of the English medieval economy.
    b. Eventually cloth manufacture was taken up in English towns.
    E. The commercial revolution of the eleventh through thirteenth centuries
1. Huge new supplies of silver led to increased trade in consumer products.
    a. This led to new business practices and a "road revolution."
2. The Hanseatic League developed new trade routes and established new "factories" (foreign trading centers) and business techniques like the business register.
3. The commercial revolution meant a higher standard of living and new opportunities.
4. Kings allied with the middle classes to defeat feudal lords and build modern states, while many serfs used the commercial revolution to improve their social position.
5. The slow transformation of European society from rural isolation to a more urban sophistication was the commercial revolution's greatest effect.
  III. Medieval universities
    A. Origins
1. Prior to the twelfth century, only monasteries and cathedral schools existed, and there weren't very many of them.
2. During the twelfth century, cathedral schools in France and municipal schools in Italy developed into universities.
    a. The first universities were at Bologna and Salerno in Italy.
    b. Bologna became a law school, while medicine was studied in Salerno.
    c. The cathedral school at Notre Dame in Paris became an international center of learning.
    B. Instruction and curriculum
1. The Scholastic method of teaching was used.
    a. In this method of reasoning and writing, questions were raised and authorities cited on both sides of the question.
    b. Its goal was to arrive at definite answers and provide a rational explanation for what was believed on faith.
    c. Arabic thought encouraged people to study Aristotle.
    d. By asking questions about nature and the universe, Scholastics laid the foundations for later scientific work.

        e.   Scholastic philosophers dealt with many theological issues.

        f.   They published *summa,* or reference books, on many topics, the most famous of which—Aquinas's *Summa Theologica*—became the fundamental text of Roman Catholic doctrine.

   2. The standard method of teaching was the lecture accompanied by a gloss, or interpretation.

   3. Oral examinations came when students applied for their degree.

IV. Gothic art

  A. After 1000, church building increased greatly; most churches were in the Romanesque style, with thick walls, small windows, and rounded arches.

  B. From Romanesque gloom to "uninterrupted light"

    1. Political stability and the increase in church wealth led demands for better buildings.

       a.   The Gothic style was created by Suger, the abbot of St. Denis, who reconstructed the abby church at Saint Denis beginning in 1137.

       a.   The Gothic style has several distinct features: the pointed arch, the ribbed vault, flying buttresses, and interior brightness.

       b.   The Gothic style spread rapidly throughout Europe—with French architects invited to design new churches in places such as Canterbury in England.

  C. The creative outburst of cathedral building

    1. Bishops, nobility, and the commercial classes supported cathedral building.

    2. Cathedrals became symbols of bourgeois civic pride, and towns competed to build the largest and most splendid church.

    3. Cathedrals served many purposes, secular as well as religious.

    4. The architecture of the cathedrals was a means of religious instruction.

    5. Tapestry making and drama were first used to convey religious themes to ordinary people, then emerged as distinct art forms.

       a.   Early tapestries depicted religious themes, but the later ones, produced for the knightly class, bore secular designs.

       b.   Mystery plays, which combined farce and serious religious scenes, were very popular.

    6. In music the *organum* style of singing began; *counterpoint* was introduced, and the system of *notation* evolved.

       a.   Also, new instruments came into use: stringed instruments such as the lute and clavichord; and reed and brass instruments (the trumpet).

  D. Troubadour Poetry

    1. In southern France a new art of singing poetry blossomed in the twelfth and thirteenth centuries.

       a.   This was known as "troubadour" music and poetry—and it took up a great variety of themes, including courtly love, bawdy experiences, and beauties of nature.

       b.   Troubadours often focused on love affairs within the noble courts; however, the idea and practice of courtly love is hotly debated among modern scholars.

       c.   Troubadours were greatly influenced by Hispano-Arabic influences—perhaps by way of slave girls who brought sung poetry to France from Andalusia.

       d.   In northern France this music influenced the epic poems of the *trouvères* who wrote in the Old French language.

       e.   Overall, troubadour music and verse stimulated vernacular languages in Europe, such as in Germany with the "Minnesangers" (love singers).

V. Heresy and the friars

A. Heresy flourished most in the most economically advanced and urbanized areas.
   1. Neither traditional Christian theology nor the isolated monastic orders addressed the problems of mercantile society.
   2. Townspeople desired a pious clergy who would meet their needs.

B. Heresy, originally meaning "individual choosing," was seen as a threat to social cohesion and religious unity.
   1. The Gregorian injunction against clerical marriage made many priests vulnerable to the Donatist heresy, which held that sacraments given by an immoral priest were useless.
   2. Various heretics, such as Arnold of Brescia, Peter Waldo, the Albigensians, and others denounced wealth, the sacraments, and material things.
      a. The Albigensian heresy grew strong in southern France and was the subject of a political-religious crusade.
      b. Heretical beliefs became fused with feudal rebellion against the French crown.

C. As a response to heretical cults, two new religious orders were founded.
   1. Saint Dominic's mission to win back the Albigensians led to the founding of a new religious order of "Preaching Friars" (the Dominicans).
   2. Saint Francis of Assisi founded an order (the Franciscans) based on preaching and absolute poverty of the clergy.
   3. These new orders of friars were urban, based on the idea of poverty, and their members were drawn from the burgher class.

D. The friars met the spiritual and intellectual needs of the thirteenth century.
   1. The friars stressed education and intellectual pursuit.
   2. Their emphasis on an educated and nonmaterialistic clergy won them the respect of the bourgeoisie.
   3. The friars successfully directed the Inquisition, and heresy was virtually extinguished.

E. A challenge to religious authority
   1. Pope Boniface VIII refused to let King Edward I of England and Philip the Fair of France tax the clergy to finance their war.
   2. In the *Unam Sanctam* (1302), Boniface declared that all Christians are subject to the pope, whereupon French mercenaries arrested him.

Review Questions

Check your understanding of this chapter by answering the following questions.

1. Define the modern state. What are its characteristics and goals?

2. Describe the unification and centralization of royal power in England. Who were the participants and what methods did they use?

3. What problems did the French kings face in unifying France under royal authority? What techniques did they use?

4. Why was unification in Germany so much more difficult than in England or France? What were the factors that weakened and divided Germany?

5. Why was Frederick II Hohenstaufen called "The Transformer of the World"? What was so modern about him? What effect did he have on Germany?

6. Describe the evolution of common law and royal justice in England. Who were the important participants and what were their methods and accomplishments?

7. The later twelfth and the thirteenth centuries saw a notable increase in hostility toward minorities, including Jews and homosexuals, and a drive toward social conformity. Why?

8. Evaluate the various theories advanced to explain the rise of towns in late medieval society. Which do you believe to be the most plausible?

9. How did the new townspeople manage to gain political status and liberty for their towns?

10. Why did Venice and the Flemish towns become leaders in long-distance trade?

11. What were the purpose and origins of the medieval universities?

12. Who were the medieval Scholastics? What were their basic beliefs about knowledge and education and what were their methods of acquiring knowledge?

13. What were the chief features of the Gothic style?

14. How did architecture become the servant of theology in the High Middle Ages? Give examples.

15. What were the reasons for the rise of heretical cults? Why and how were they extinguished?

Study-Review Exercises

Define the following key concepts and terms.

Landesherraft

thegn

Gothic

scholasticism

universitas

common law

Roman law

Hanseatic League

burgher

Define each of the following terms and explain how it contributed to the evolution of the modern state.

writ

sheriff

baillis and seneschals

Exchequer

jury

tallage

Identify and explain the significance of the following people and terms.
cult of Saint Denis

merchant guild

heresy

Frederick II Hohenstaufen

Philip II of France

Saint Thomas Aquinas

Suger, abbot of St. Denis

Henry II of England

Peter Abelard

Summa Theologica

Louis IX of France

Saint Dominic

Saint Francis of Assisi

Explain what the following events were and why they are important in understanding the High Middle Ages.

Domesday survey

crusade against the Albigensians

Inquisition

Frederick Barbarossa's Italian wars

William of Normandy's conquest of England

Conflict between Pope Boniface VIII and King Philip the Fair of France

Test your understanding of the chapter by providing the correct answers.

1. This letter declared that everyone must submit to the papacy. _____

2. The English royal bureau of finance. _____

3. The emperor of Germany who tried to unify Germany. _____

4. William the Conqueror's survey of English wealth. _____

5. The European country best known for its common law. _____

6. The area that underwent development by Frederick II Hohenstaufen. _____

7. This document implied that in English society the law is above the king. _____

8. The method of teaching at medieval universities. _____

9. The architectural style that reflects Roman and early Christian models. _____

10. Medieval reference books. _____

11. A league of German cities with its center at Lübeck. _____

12. Author of *Sic et Non*. _____

13. The bishop who was murdered as the result of a church-state struggle. _____

14. A kind of French supreme court. _____

Major Political Ideas

1. Define and describe the concept of the sovereign nation-state. How does it contrast to the early medieval idea of government?

2. What is meant by common law? How and why did it evolve?

3. The history of towns is also the history of merchants' efforts to acquire liberties. What does *liberties* mean and what role did the merchant and craft guilds and their members play in its evolution?

Issues for Essays and Discussion

The High Middle Ages witnessed remarkable achievements in the areas of political organization, law and justice, the evolution of the town, and art. What were the major developments in these areas? How did they differ in England, France, Germany, and elsewhere? What were the reasons for these developments and were there any negative effects?

Interpretation of Visual Sources

Study the section of the Bayeaux Tapestry. What is the subject of this tapestry? What information about medieval life does it provide? What is the political significance of the event depicted?

Geography

1. The *Domesday Book* of 1086 is one of the most famous population surveys in history and an important source of information for historians and geographers. What was the purpose of the "book" and who undertook the survey? Use the Map 11.1 in your textbook (which shows the *Domesday* results) to determine (1) which parts of England were most/least populated (north, south, east, west); (2) which parts had the highest concentration of agricultural activity; and (3) how many towns had a population over 5,000.

2. On Outline Map 11.2 provided, and using Map 11.2 in the textbook as a reference, mark the following: the royal domain, or crown lands, of France as they existed in 1180, the names of the territories added by Philip Augustus, the territories added from 1223 to 1270, and the territories added from 1270 to 1314.

3. Study Map 11.4 in the textbook. In the space below (1) list the four largest cities in Europe in about the late thirteenth century, (2) indicate what part of Europe was the most urbanized, and (3) use Map 11.5 to explain the evolution of the urban concentration indicated on Map 11.4.

   _____

   _____

   _____

   _____

4. Using Map 11.5 and the text discussion as your sources, describe the various trade routes used by the Italians, the Flemish, and the Hanseatic League.

   _____

   _____

   _____

   _____

5. Undertake your own survey of intellectual activity in Medieval Europe by using Map 11.6 in your textbook. State the following:

   1. Total number of schools of higher learning _____

   2. Number of each type: University _____; Monastery school _____; Cathedral school _____;

   3. Distribution: Spain _____; France _____; Holy Roman Empire _____; Italian states _____; England _____; Scotland _____; Denmark _____.

Outline Map 11.2

Understanding History Through the Arts

1. Your textbook tells you that eighty cathedrals were built in France (a country of eighteen million people) between 1180 and 1270. Why was France the center of Gothic achievement? Begin your investigation with J. Evans, *Art in Medieval France, 987-1498* (1969), and J. Harvey, *The Medieval Architect* (1972). See also Chapters 3 and 4 of N. Pevsner, *An Outline of European Architecture** (7th ed., 1963).

2. What does the Bayeaux Tapestry reveal about medieval life? This problem of historical interpretation is dealt with in D. Bernstein, *The Mystery of the Bayeaux Tapestry* (1987).

Problems for Further Investigation

1. What are the origins of the modern state? How does the rise of great cities fit into this picture? New interpretations and ideas for research on the rise of the modern state are found in a collection of essays edited by H. Lubasz, *The Development of the Modern State** (1964), and in C. Tilly and W. P. Blockmans, eds., *Cities and the Rise of States in Europe* (1994). Did urbanization force Christianity to re-evaluate its traditional antimaterialistic position? A good place to begin your investigation is with L. Little, *Religion, Poverty, and the Profit Economy in Medieval Europe* (1978).

2. Why was Thomas Becket murdered? Many possible research and term-paper topics are suggested in T. M. Jones, ed., *The Becket Controversy* (1970). The conflict between King Henry II and Archbishop Becket has produced some interesting literature, such as Jean Anouilh, *Becket, or the Honor of God*, L. Hill, trans. (1960), and T. S. Eliot, *Murder in the Cathedral* (1935).

3. What was life like for aristocratic women during this period? One of the most fascinating women of the Middle Ages was Eleanor of Aquitaine, wife to the king of France and the king of England and mother to two kings of England. She is the subject of a spellbinding biography, *Eleanor of Aquitaine and the Four Kings** (1950) by A. Kelly. See also E. Amt, ed., *Women's Lives in Medieval Europe* (1993).

---

*Available in paperback.

Self-Test Multiple-Choice Questions

<u>Do</u> <u>not</u> assume that these questions will appear on any examination. It is recommended that you <u>not</u> memorize these questions, but use them only as a self-test. Answers are at the end of this book.

1. The Jewish members of most medieval towns had the reputation of being
   a. rich landowners who retired to the town.
   b. the town's military class.
   c. semibarbaric.
   d. rich and learned.

2. By origin and definition, a burgher, or bourgeois, was
   a. a person involved in trade or commerce.
   b. a person who lived within town walls.
   c. a resident of Hamburg, Germany.
   d. a person who lived on hamburgers.

3. The modern scholar who identified the growth of medieval towns with the development of trade was
   a. Josiah Cox Russell.
   b. Eileen Power.
   c. Henri Pirenne.
   d. Marc Bloch.

4. Towns were most successful in gaining rights in the area of
   a. political freedom from the monarchy.
   b. emancipation from the influence of religion and the church.
   c. judicial independence.
   d. military influence in the larger state.

5. Artisans and craftspeople in medieval towns formed
   a. courts to try corrupt businessmen.
   b. craft guilds.
   c. merchant guilds.
   d. the *scutage*.

6. The French government, as conceived by Philip Augustus, was characterized by
   a. centralization at the local level and diversity at the top.
   b. diversity at the local level and centralization at the top.
   c. complete local government.
   d. a system identical to England's.

7. Frederick Barbarossa's success in restoring order to the Holy Roman Empire was spoiled by his involvement in
   a. France.
   b. Germany.
   c. England.
   d. Italy.

8. The principle implied in the Magna Carta was
   a. democracy.
   b. that all people, even the king, are subject to the law.
   c. that the king is above the law.
   d. that the people rule the monarch.

9. Which of the following is *not* a characteristic of a Gothic cathedral?
   a. Pointed arches
   b. Ribbed vaults
   c. Thick walls
   d. Flying buttresses

10. The surge of cathedral building in the twelfth and thirteenth centuries was closely associated with
    a. the increase of university-trained architects.
    b. financial hard times, which caused people to turn to religion.
    c. the low cost of building materials.
    d. the growth of towns and the increase of commercial wealth.

11. The university in the Europe of the High Middle Ages
    a. was borrowed from the Muslims.
    b. was a unique contribution of western Europe.
    c. was copied from the Greek model.
    d. was copied from the Roman model.

12. The duties of sheriffs in Norman England included all of the following *except*
    a. maintaining law and order.
    b. collecting taxes when instructed by the king.
    c. raising infantry at the king's request.
    d. supervising the remaining Anglo-Saxon sheriffs.

13. Heresy flourished
    a. in the most economically advanced and urbanized areas.
    b. in backward rural areas.
    c. only in southern France.
    d. in urban areas suffering from plague and economic depression.

14. The two European states that first developed efficient state bureaucracies were
    a. England and Sicily.
    b. England and France.
    c. England and Italy.
    d. Sicily and France.

15. Which of the following financial problems eventually forced England's King John to sign the Magna Carta?
    a. The debts incurred from Richard the Lionhearted's crusading zeal
    b. The ransom paid for Richard the Lionhearted
    c. The war debt caused by John in his attempt to regain Normandy from France
    d. John's attack on Scotland

16. The first European universities were located in
    a. England.
    b. France.
    c. Italy.
    d. Germany.

17. Prior to the systematization of law in the thirteenth century, homosexuality was
    a. socially accepted.
    b. outlawed.
    c. uncommon.
    d. unknown.

18. The origin of Western universities was
    a. manor schools.
    b. monasteries.
    c. cathedral schools.
    d. medieval public schools.

19. The standard method of teaching in medieval universities was
    a. *summa*.
    b. a gloss.
    c. reading assignments in books.
    d. lecture.

20. Common law differed from the system of Roman law in that it
    a. applied only to the peasant class.
    b. was more permanent and static.
    c. relied on precedents.
    d. relied heavily on torture.

21. By the end of the twelfth century, the general European attitude toward the Jews in society
    a. became increasingly intolerant.
    b. moved in the direction of greater acceptance.
    c. led to political emancipation of the Jews.
    d. had not changed from that of the previous generations.

22. The major function of the medieval city was that of
    a. an ecclesiastical center.
    b. a political center.
    c. a royal stronghold.
    d. a vast marketplace.

23. The *Summa Theologica* was written by
    a. John of Salisbury.
    b. Peter Abelard.
    c. Thomas Aquinas.
    d. William of Sens.

24. The Waldensians were
    a. a heretical group that attacked the sacraments and church hierarchy.
    b. the political and financial supporters of the German princes.
    c. the merchant bankers of Hamburg.
    d. the religious order that built the abbey church at Saint Denis.

25. The followers of Domingo de Guzman became known as the
    a. Albigensians.
    b. bourgeois.
    c. masters of the Cathedral School at Paris.
    d. "Preaching Friars."

Chapter 12

The Crisis of the Later Middle Ages

Learning Objectives

After reading and studying this chapter you should be able to:

1. explain what the Black Death was, why it occurred, and how it spread throughout Europe.

2. discuss the role of Dante, Chaucer, and Villon in the transition from Latin to vernacular languages and literature.

3. explain the reasons for the decline of the influence of religion and the Church.

4. explain why the Black Death left some people better off, and why greater ethnic-racial conflict occurred.

Chapter Summary

The fourteenth century was a time of disease, war, crime, violence, and ethnic-racial conflicts. The art and literature of the period are full of the portrayal of death, just as the historical accounts are full of tales of conflict and violence. There were several major causes for this century of human suffering. Natural disaster—including changes in climate and horrible new diseases—attacked Europe. A long series of wars between France and England not only brought death and economic ruin but increased personal violence and crime as well. In addition, a serious shortage of labor, created by the bubonic plague, resulted in intense social conflict among landlords. Economic crisis during the century also resulted in a bitter struggle between urban workers and their guild masters.

Amid such violence the church lost power and prestige, partly because of the religious disillusionment that accompanied the plague. In short, the institutional church failed to fill the spiritual vacuum left by the series of disasters. A more immediate reason for the decline of the church's influence and prestige was the Babylonian Captivity and the Great Schism. The call for reform, often in the form of the conciliar movement, by people such as Marsiglio of Padua and John Wyclif, was a signal of things to come in the sixteenth century. The disillusionment with the organized church also led to greater lay independence and, ultimately, ideas of social and political equality. The wars actually fostered the development of constitutionalism in England.

But the century of disaster was also a century of change, some of it for the good of ordinary people. It is in this light that the chapter examines some important changes in marriage practices, family relations, and the life of the people. The decline in population meant that those who survived had better food and higher wages. Peasants in western Europe used the labor-shortage problem to demand higher wages and freedom from serfdom. Meanwhile, landlords tried to shift the cost of war and the increase in expenses to their peasants. These circumstances often resulted in conflict with their lords.

The migrations of peoples from European heartland to the frontier regions of Ireland, the Baltic, eastern Europe, and Spain led to ethnic frictions between native peoples and new settlers. Economic difficulties led to ethnic consciousness and spawned a vicious racism.

Study Outline

Use this outline to preview the chapter before you read a particular section in your textbook and then as a self-check to test your reading comprehension after you have read the chapter section.

I. Prelude to disaster
   A. Poor harvests led to famines in the years 1315-1322.
      1. Fewer calories meant increased susceptibility to disease and less energy for growing food.
   B. Diseases killed many people and animals.
   C. Economies slowed down and population growth came to a halt.
   D. Weak governments were unable to deal with these problems.
      1. Starving people turned against rich people and Jews.
      2. English kings tried to regulate the food supply, but failed.
II. The Black Death
   A. Genoese ships brought the bubonic plague—the Black Death—to Europe in 1347.
      1. The bacillus lived in fleas that infested black rats.
      2. Some claim that it came from the east by way of the Crimea.
   B. Pathology and care
      1. The bubonic form of the disease was transmitted by rats; the pneumonic form was transmitted by people.
         a. Unsanitary and overcrowded cities were ideal breeding grounds for the black rats.
      2. Most people had no rational explanation for the disease, and out of ignorance and fear many blamed it on Jews, causing thousands of Jews to be murdered.
      3. The disease, which killed millions, recurred often and as late as 1700.
         a. It spread to central Europe and eastward—although its toll was less in Poland.
         b. In Hungary, type-D blood people may have been immune.
         c. Its last occurrence was in France in 1721.
         d. A vaccine was not developed until 1947.
   C. The social and cultural consequences of the Black Death
      1. The plague hit the poor harder than the rich, but all classes suffered; the clergy was particularly affected.
      2. Labor shortages meant that wages went up and social mobility increased, as did per capita wealth, and the demand for slaves increased.

3. The psychological consequences of the plague were enormous: pessimism, gross sensuality, religious fervor, and flagellantism.
   a. Society became divided and full of fear.
   b. Artists and writers became obsessed with death.

III. The Hundred Years' War (ca 1337-1453)
  A. The causes of the war
    1. Edward III of England, the grandson of the French king Philip the Fair, claimed the French crown by seizing the duchy of Aquitaine in 1337.
    2. French barons backed Edward's claim as a way to thwart the centralizing goals of their king.
    3. Flemish wool merchants supported the English claim to the crown.
    4. Both the French and the English saw military adventure as an excuse to avoid domestic problems.
  B. The popular response to the war
    1. Royal propaganda for war and plunder was strong on both sides.
    2. The war meant opportunity for economic or social mobility for poor knights, criminals, and great nobles.
  C. The Indian summer of medieval chivalry
    1. Chivalry, a code of conduct for the knightly class, enjoyed its final days of glory during the war.
    2. Chivalry and feudal society glorified war.
  D. The course of the war to 1419
    1. The battles took place in France and the Low Countries.
    2. At the Battle of Crécy (1346), the English disregarded the chivalric code and used new military tactics: the longbow and the cannon.
    3. The English won major battles at Poitiers (1356) and Agincourt (1415) and had advanced to Paris by 1419.
  E. Joan of Arc and France's victory
    1. Joan of Arc participated in the lifting of the British siege of Orléans in 1429.
    2. She was turned over to the English and burned as a heretic in 1431.
  F. Costs and consequences
    1. The war meant economic and population decline for both France and England.
    2. Taxes on wool to finance the war caused a slump in the English wool trade.
    3. In England, returning soldiers caused social problems.
    4. The war encouraged the growth of parliamentary government, particularly in England.
      a. The "Commons" (knights and burgesses) acquired the right to approve all taxes and developed its own organization.
      b. In France, neither the king nor the provincial assemblies wanted a national assembly.
    5. The war generated feelings of nationalism in England and France.
IV. The decline of the church's prestige
  A. The Babylonian Captivity (1309-1377)
    1. The pope had lived at Avignon since the reign of King Philip the Fair of France and thus was subject to French control.
      a. The Babylonian Captivity badly damaged papal prestige.
      b. It left Rome poverty-stricken.

    2. Pope Gregory XI brought the papacy back to Rome in 1377, but then Urban VI alienated the church hierarchy in his zeal to reform the church.

    3. A new pope, Clement VII, was elected, and the two popes both claimed to be legitimate.

B. The Great Schism (1378-1417)

    1. England and Germany recognized Pope Urban VI, while France and others recognized the antipope, Clement VII.

    2. The schism brought the church into disrepute and wakened the religious faith of many.

C. The conciliar movement

    1. Conciliarists believed that church authority rested in councils representing the people—not the authority of the pope.

    2. Marsiglio of Padua had claimed in 1324, in Defensor Pacis, that authority within the church should rest with a church council and not the pope and that the church was subordinate to the state.

    3. John Wyclif attacked papal authority and called for even more radical reform of the church.

      a. He believed that Christians should read the Bible for themselves, prompting the first English translation of the Bible.

      b. His followers, called Lollards, disseminated his ideas widely.

    4. Wyclif's ideas were spread to Bohemia by John Hus.

    5. An attempt in 1409 to depose both popes and select another led to a threefold schism.

    6. Finally, the council at Constance (1414-1418) ended the schism with the election of Pope Martin V.

V. The life of the people in the fourteenth and fifteenth centuries

A. Marriage and the family

    1. Marriage usually came at 16 to 18 years for women and later for men.

    2. Legalized prostitution existed in urban areas and was the source of wealth for some women.

    3. Economic factors, rather than romantic love, usually governed the decision to marry.

    4. Divorce did not exist.

    5. Many people did not observe church regulations and married without a church ceremony.

B. Life in the parish

    1. The land and the parish were the centers of life.

    2. Opportunities to join guilds declined in the fourteenth century.

      a. Strikes and riots became frequent.

      b. Women were increasingly excluded from guilds.

    3. Cruel sports, such as bullbaiting and bearbaiting, and drunkenness reflect the violence and frustrations of the age.

      a. The execution of William Wallace illustrates the violence in society.

    4. Because of the crisis within the church, lay people increasingly took over church management from the clergy.

C. Fur-collar crime
1. Fur-collar crime was crime committed by nobility—a phenomenon on the increase in the fourteenth and fifteenth centuries.
   a. In England, nobles returning from war had little to do and were in need of income; thus they resorted to crime.
   b. Kidnapping, extortion, and terrorism by the upper classes were widespread.
2. Because governments were not able to stop abuses, outlaws such as Robin Hood sought to protect the people.
   a. The popularity of the Robin Hood legends symbolized the deep resentment of aristocratic corruption and abuse.
D. Peasant revolts
1. Major peasant revolts against the nobility occurred in France in 1358 (the Jacquerie), 1363-1484, 1380, and 1420, and in England in 1381.
   a. French peasants were angry about taxes, food shortages, fur-collar crime, and other circumstances.
   b. One cause of the Revolt of 1381 was the lords' attempt to freeze wages.
   c. In general, peasants were better off; the revolts were due to rising expectations.
   d. The 1381 revolt in England was due to economic grievances, anti-aristocratic sentiment, and protest against taxes.
   e. King Richard II and his nobles tricked the peasants into ending the revolt.
2. Workers in Italy (the *ciompi*), Germany, and Spain also revolted.
VI. Race and ethnicity on the frontiers
A. Earlier (12th and 13th century) migrations led to peoples of different ethnic-racial background living side by side.
1. "Race" meant language, custom, and law—not biological anthropological classification.
2. In the early period, newcomers were given separate but equal rights (legal pluralism).
   a. The great exception to this was Ireland where the English practiced extreme racial discrimination.
   b. The Irish had no access to law courts and were considered unfree.
3. In the later Middle Ages legal pluralism disappeared and emphasis on legal homogeneity, language, and blood descent led to ethnic tension.
   a. Language differences between clergy and people led to tension in Poland, Ireland, and elsewhere.
   b. The arrival of new monastic groups led to conflicts between language groups.
   c. Towns were dominated by immigrants while the countryside was dominated by natives.
   d. Famine and the Black Death led to ghettoization and racial savagery.
   e. Intermarriage was often forbidden and discriminatory laws were applied to certain language groups.
4. This discrimination had its basis in the effort of privileged groups to protect their economic interests.
VII. Vernacular literature
A. The emergence of national consciousness is seen in the rise of literature written in national languages—the vernacular.

B. Many literary masterpieces manifest this new national pride.
1. Dante's *Divine Comedy,* a symbolic pilgrimage through Hell, Purgatory, and Paradise to God, embodies the psychological tensions of the age and contains bitter criticism of some church authorities.
2. Chaucer, in the *Canterbury Tales,* depicts the materialistic, worldly interests of a variety of English people in the fourteenth century.
3. Villon used the language of the lower classes to portray the reality, beauty, and hardships of life here on earth.
4. Christine de Pisan's poems and books on love, religion, and morality celebrate the historical accomplishments of women and provide advice for all women.
5. Vernacular literature emerged in eastern Europe, partly as a result of new national self-consciousness.
6. Overall, the number of laypersons who could read and write increased but society continued to be based on oral culture.

Review Questions

Check your understanding of this chapter by answering the following questions.

1. What were the causes of the population decline that began in the early fourteenth century?

2. What was the source of the bubonic plague and why did it spread so rapidly in Europe?

3. What impact did the plague have on wages and the demand for labor? What happened to land values?

4. Describe the psychological effects of the plague. How did people explain this disaster?

5. What were the immediate and other causes of the Hundred Years' War?

6. Why did the people support their kings in war?

7. What were the results of the Hundred Years' War? Who were the winners and losers within both countries?

8. How did the Babylonian Captivity weaken the power and prestige of the church? Why were there three popes in 1409?

9. What was the conciliar movement and who were its advocates? Was this a revolutionary idea?

10. Why was Wyclif a threat to the institutional church?

11. What was fur-collar crime and why did it occur?

12. Did peasants' lives improve or deteriorate in the fourteenth and fifteenth centuries? In what ways?

13. What were the reasons for the French of 1358 and the English Peasants' Revolt of 1381?

14. Why did a great amount of conflict and frustration among guild members develop in the fourteenth century?

15. Describe and explain the increase in ethnic-racial tensions in the frontier areas of Europe in the late Middle Ages.

Study-Review Exercises

Define the following key concepts and terms.

Pasteurella pestis

fur-collar crime

English Statute of Labourers

conciliar movement

vernacular literature

craft guild

Identify and explain the significance of the following people and terms.

Queen Isabella of England

Hundred Years' War

Robin Hood

Marsiglio of Padua

Battle of Crécy (1346)

Martin V

Joan of Arc

Babylonian Captivity

Margaret Paston

Lollards

House of Commons

Edward III

John Hus

John Wyclif

the *Jacquerie*

Christine de Pisan

Explain the importance of each of the following concepts in late medieval life and describe what changes it was subject to in this period.

legal pluralism

marriage

feudal chivalry

individual Christian faith

leisure time

nationalism

Test your understanding of the chapter by providing the correct answers.

1. In reaction to the calls for reform in the fourteenth century, the church *did/did not* enter into a period of reform and rejuvenation.

2. Prior to the plague in 1348, Europe experienced a period of unusually *good/bad* harvests.

3. The Hundred Years' War was between the kings of _____ and _____.

4. The followers of the English theologian Wyclif. _____

5. Up to the nineteenth century, *economic/romantic* factors usually determined whom and when a person married.

6. For the most part, job mobility within the late medieval guilds tended to *increase/decrease*.

Place the following events in correct chronological order.

First instance of the bubonic plague in Europe
Babylonian Captivity
Start of the Hundred Years' War
Council of Constance
Battle of Crécy
the *Jacquerie* in France
Dante's *Divine Comedy*
Great Schism

1.

2.

3.

4.

5.

6.

7.

8.

Major Political Ideas

1. Define nationalism. How did the Hundred Years' War encourage nationalism? What is the purpose and function of a national assembly? Why did a national representative assembly emerge in England but not in France?

2. What were the ideas set forth by Marsiglio of Padua in his Defensor Pacis? What were the political implications of these ideas?

Issues for Essays and Discussion

Some historians have argued that war is the engine of change. Does this theory have any validity for the fourteenth century? Discuss this in terms of the political, economic, and social experience of the fourteenth century.

Interpretation of Visual Sources

Study the reproduction of the painting *Procession of Saint Gregory*. How did people respond to this mysterious disease? Look carefully at the figures in this painting. Who is represented in this procession? What role did the church play in fighting the plague?

Geography

Use Map 12.1 to explain the timing and the spread of the Black Death. Where did it begin, how far did it spread, and why do you believe some areas were spared its destruction?
    Use Map 12.2 and Map 12.3 in the textbook to complete the following:

1. Locate the extent of the English possessions in France. What were the origins of English claims to French land?

2. Why was it unlikely that England could have held these territories permanently?

3. Locate the main centers of popular revolt in France and England.

4. Why were so many of the English revolts in the highly populated and advanced areas of the country?

Understanding History Through the Arts

1. What was the music of this period like? An excellent introduction is a recording, *Instruments of the Middle Ages and Renaissance,* with an accompanying illustrated book by David Munro (Angel recording number SB2-3810 [1976]). For the French chansons and the English madrigals, listen to the recording titled *The King's Singers Sing of Courtly Pleasures,* which includes text and translations (Angel recording number s-37025 [1974]).

2. How did the Black Death affect art? While some members of society responded to the plague with religious fervor, others merely looked to enjoy life as best they could. The fourteenth-century Italian writer Boccaccio wrote the *Decameron,* a series of bawdy tales told by a group of Florentine men and women who fled to the countryside to escape the plague.

Problems for Further Investigation

1. How can a single disease affect the course of history? Students interested in the plague should begin with P. Zeigler, *The Black Death: A Study of the Plague in Fourteenth Century Europe* (1969); W. McNeill, *Plagues and Peoples* (1976), and D. Herlihy, *The Black Death and the Transformation of the West* (1977).

2. What was the cause of the Hundred Years' War? What effect did it have on English and French society? E. Perroy, *The Hundred Years' War** (1951), and M. M. Vale, *The Origins of the Hundred Years War* (1996), is a good start for anyone interested in that subject.

3. Why did the peasant revolts start? Those interested in popular protest during this age should consult M. Mullett, *Popular Culture and Popular Protest in Medieval and Early Modern Europe* (1987). The fourteenth century is analyzed in the interesting book *A Distant Mirror: The Calamitous Fourteenth Century* (1978) by B. W. Tuchman.

4. What was the cause of the conflict between Philip the Fair of France and the pope? Was the French king out to destroy the power of the papacy? These and other questions are debated by a number of historians in C. T. Wood, ed., *Philip the Fair and Boniface VIII** (1967).

5. What was medieval chivalry and how did it reflect changes in medieval society? Begin your study with R. Barber, *The Knight and Chivalry** (1990). You may want to supplement this with M. W. Thompson, *The Decline of the Castle* (1988).

Self-Test Multiple-Choice Questions

<u>Do</u> <u>not</u> assume that these questions will appear on any examination. It is recommended that you <u>not</u> memorize these questions, but use them only as a self-test. Answers are at the end of this book.

1. The conciliar movement was
   a. an effort to give the pope the power to use councils to wipe out heresy.
   b. the effort by the French lords to establish a parliament.
   c. a new monastic order vowing poverty.
   d. an attempt to place ultimate church authority in a general council.

2. The plague was probably brought into Europe by
   a. Chinese soldiers.
   b. Spanish warriors returning from South America.
   c. English soldiers pushing into France.
   d. Genoese ships from the Crimea.

---

*Available in paperback.

3. In general, farm laborers who survived the bubonic plague faced
   a. higher wages.
   b. food shortages.
   c. the need to migrate.
   d. excommunication from the church.

4. Generally, the major new source of criminals after the Hundred Years' War was
   a. the urban mobs.
   b. the rural peasants.
   c. the nobility.
   d. the bourgeoisie.

5. Which of the following statements about the fourteenth century is *false*?
   a. The population declined.
   b. The standard of living fell drastically.
   c. The power of the church declined.
   d. War between England and France was frequent.

6. Most people in the fourteenth century believed that the Black Death was caused by
   a. bad air.
   b. poor sanitation and housing.
   c. a bacillus living in fleas.
   d. black rats.

7. Generally, the plague disaster of the fourteenth century resulted in all but which of the following for European society?
   a. Higher wages for most workers
   b. A severe decline in the number of German clergymen
   c. A decline in flagellantism
   d. An obsession with death

8. Which of the following did *not* participate in the Hundred Years' War?
   a. Edward III of England
   b. King Philip the Fair
   c. Joan of Arc
   d. The Dauphin Charles of France

9. One reason for peasant-landlord conflict in the fourteenth century was
   a. peasants' opposition to declining wages and inflation.
   b. landlords' attempts to legislate wages.
   c. land scarcity.
   d. peasants' refusal to be drafted for war service.

10. The author of *Defensor Pacis* and proponent of the idea that authority in the Christian church rested in a general council rather than in the papacy was
    a. Cardinal Robert of Geneva.
    b. Pope Urban V.
    c. John Wyclif.
    d. Marsiglio of Padua.

11. Which of the following statements about the Hundred Years' War is true?
    a. It discouraged representative government.
    b. It depressed the English wool trade.
    c. It increased the amount of arable land in England.
    d. It created a surplus of manpower.

12. The followers of the English theologian-reformer Wyclif were called
    a. Protestants.
    b. outlaws.
    c. Lollards.
    d. flagellants.

13. Fur-collar crime is a term used to describe
    a. the robbery and extortion inflicted on the poor by the rich.
    b. the criminal activity carried out by bandits such as Robin Hood.
    c. crimes committed by churchmen.
    d. the illegal activities of noblewomen.

14. After 1347, the Black Death generally moved
    a. from north to south.
    b. from west to east.
    c. from south to north.
    d. from east to west.

15. Initially the Hundred Years' War was fought over
    a. Aquitaine.
    b. King Edward III's claim to the French crown.
    c. the control of the Flemish wool trade.
    d. religion.

16. English military innovation(s) during the Hundred Years' War included
    a. the crossbow.
    b. the cannon and the longbow.
    c. cavalry.
    d. the pike.

17. Which of the following statements about marriage during the Middle Ages is true?
    a. Most marriages were based on romantic love.
    b. Most marriages were arranged.
    c. Divorce was common.
    d. Marriage without the church's sanction was unheard of.

18. Which of the following was a writer of vernacular literature?
    a. Dante
    b. Jacques de Vitry
    c. Clement VII
    d. Marsiglio of Padua

19. Which of the following statements about Joan of Arc is *false*?
    a. She dressed like a man.
    b. The English king was her greatest supporter.
    c. She was accused of being a heretic and was burned.
    d. She was from a peasant family.

20. For the French, the turning point of the Hundred Years' War was
    a. the relief of Paris.
    b. the defeat of the English fleet in the English Channel.
    c. the relief of Orléans.
    d. the Battle of Poitiers.

21. Prostitution in late medieval society
    a. did not exist.
    b. existed only among the lower classes.
    c. was not respected but was legalized.
    d. existed in the countryside but not the city.

22. In the fourteenth century craft guilds began to change in that
    a. master and journeyman distinctions began to disappear.
    b. the guilds lost control over the production process.
    c. apprenticeship was abandoned.
    d. membership became more restrictive and master-journeyman relations deteriorated.

23. Chaucer's *Canterbury Tales* is important because
    a. it depicts the impact of the plague on Italian life.
    b. it reflects the cultural tensions of the times.
    c. it illustrates the highly religious interests of most people.
    d. it shows how people were obsessed with the next world.

24. The effect of the Hundred Years' War on England was that it
    a. brought great wealth in the form of cash reserves to England.
    b. caused a great increase in wool exports.
    c. allowed many English knights to become very rich.
    d. resulted in a great net loss in cash.

25. The English Peasants' Revolt most probably
    a. was the largest single uprising of the entire Middle Ages.
    b. was an event of little significance at the time.
    c. affected only a very small number of people.
    d. was engineered by the landowners.

Chapter 13

European Society in the Age of the Renaissance

Learning Objectives

After reading and studying this chapter you should be able to:

1. discuss the meanings of the term *renaissance*.

2. compare the significant features of the so-called Italian Renaissance with other renaissances, such as the Carolingian and twelfth-century renaissances.

3. explain how the Italian Renaissance affected politics, the economy, and society.

4. elaborate on the evolution of medieval kingdoms into early modern nation-states, on the spread of Renaissance humanism northward, and on the effects of the Wars of the Roses.

Chapter Summary

The Renaissance was an era of intellectual and artistic brilliance unsurpassed in European history. It is clear that some thinking people in this era, largely a mercantile elite, saw themselves living in an age more akin to that of the bright and creative ancient world than that of the recent dark and gloomy Middle Ages. Although many of the supposedly "new" Renaissance ideas are actually found in the Middle Ages, scholars generally agree that the Renaissance was characterized by a number of distinctive ideas about life and humanity—individualism, secularism, humanism, materialism, hedonism, and even the identification of popular homoerotic activity.

The Renaissance began in Florence, Italy, in the late thirteenth century. It subsequently spread to the rest of Italy—particularly Rome—and then to northern Europe, where it developed somewhat differently. The best-known expressions of the bold new Renaissance spirit can be seen in the painting, sculpture, and architecture of the period. New attitudes were also found in education, politics, and philosophy; in Northern Europe new ideas of social reform developed. Although the Renaissance brought some benefits to the masses of people, such as the printing press, it was basically an elitist movement. People of wealth began to spend less on war and more on art and architecture. A negative development of the age was a deterioration in the power and position of women in society.

In politics, the Renaissance produced an approach to power and the state that historians often call "new monarchies." The best known and most popular theoretician of this school was the Florentine

Niccolò Machiavelli. Its most able practitioners were the fifteenth- and sixteenth-century monarchs of France, England, and Spain. In Italy, the city-state system led to wealthy and independent cities that were marvelously creative but also vulnerable to invasion and control from the outside by powerful Spanish and French kings. Unfortunately, nationalism in Spain led to attacks on Jewish converts *(conversos)* to Christianity.

Study Outline

Use this outline to preview the chapter before you read a particular section in your textbook and then as a self-check to test your reading comprehension after you have read the chapter section.

I. The evolution of the Italian Renaissance
  A. Beginnings
    1. The Renaissance was a period of commercial, financial, political, and cultural achievement in two phases, from 1050 to 1300 and from 1300 to about 1600.
    2. The northern Italian cities led the commercial revival, especially Venice, Genoa, and Milan.
      a. Venice had a huge merchant marine; improvements in shipbuilding enhanced trade.
      b. These cities became the crossroads between northern Europe and the East.
    3. The first artistic and literary flowerings of the Renaissance appeared in Florence.
      a. Florentine mercantile families dominated European banking.
      b. The wool industry was the major factor in the city's financial expansion and population increase.
  B. Communes and republics
    1. Northern Italian cities were communes—associations of free men seeking independence from the local lords.
      a. The nobles, attracted by the opportunities in the cities, often settled there and married members of the mercantile class, forming an urban nobility.
      b. The *popolo,* or middle class, was excluded from power.
      c. *Popolo*-led republican governments failed, which led to the rule of despots *(signori)* or oligarchies.
      d. In the fifteenth century, the princely courts of the rulers were centers of wealth and art.
  C. The balance of power among the Italian city-states
    1. Italy had no political unity; it was divided into city-states such as Milan, Venice, and Florence, the Papal States, and a kingdom of Naples in the south.
    2. The political and economic competition among the city-states prevented centralization of power.
    3. Shifting alliances among the city-states led to the creation of permanent ambassadors.
    4. After 1494 a divided Italy became a European battleground.
II. Intellectual hallmarks of the Renaissance
  A. Many, like the poet and humanist Petrarch, saw the fourteenth century as a new golden age and a revival of ancient Roman culture.

B. Individualism
   1. Literature specifically concerned with the nature of individuality emerged.
   2. Renaissance people believed in individual will and genius.
C. Humanism
   1. Italians collected ancient manuscripts and monuments, and copied the ancient Roman lifestyle.
   2. The study of the classics led to humanism, an emphasis on human beings.
      a. Humanists sought to understand human nature through a study of pagan and classical authors *and* Christian thought.
      b. The humanist writer Pico della Mirandola believed that there were no limits to what human beings could accomplish.
   3. Ancient Latin style was considered superior to medieval Latin.
D. Secular spirit
   1. *Secularism* means a concern with materialism rather than religion.
   2. Unlike medieval people, Renaissance people were concerned with money and pleasure.
      a. In *On Pleasure,* Lorenzo Valla defended the pleasure of the senses as the highest good.
      b. In the *Decameron,* Boccaccio portrayed an acquisitive and worldly society.
   3. The church did little to combat secularism; in fact, many popes were Renaissance patrons and participants.
III. Art and the artist
A. The *quattrocento* (1400s) and the *cinquecento* (1500s) saw dazzling artistic achievements, led by Florence and Rome.
B. Art and power
   1. In the early Renaissance, powerful urban groups commissioned works of art, which remained overwhelmingly religious.
   2. In the later fifteenth century, individuals and oligarchs began to sponsor works of art as a means of self-glorification.
   3. Wealthy people began to spend less on warfare and more on art and architecture.
      a. At first the bed chamber room was the most important, but later many other rooms were even more decorated.
      b. The home's private chapel was the most elaborate and expensive.
   4. As the century advanced, art became more and more secular, and classical subjects became popular.
   5. The style of art changed in the fifteenth century.
      a. The individual portrait emerged as a distinct genre.
      b. Painting and sculpture became more naturalistic and realistic, and the human body was glorified, as in the work of the sculptors Donatello and Michelangelo.
      c. A new "international style" emphasized color, decorative detail, and curvilinear rhythms.
      d. In painting, the use of perspective was pioneered by Brunelleschi and della Francesca.
   6. The status of the artist
      a. The status of the artist improved during the Renaissance; most work was done by commission from a prince.

   b. The creative genius of the artist was recognized and rewarded.
   c. The Renaissance was largely an elitist movement; Renaissance culture did not directly affect the middle classes or the urban working class.
IV. Social change during the Renaissance
  A. Education and political thought
   1. Humanists were interested in education, particularly the training of rulers, and moral behavior.
      a. Vergerio wrote a treatise on education that stressed the teaching of history, ethics, and rhetoric (public speaking).
      b. Castiglione's *The Courtier,* which was widely read, describes the model Renaissance gentleman as a man of many talents, including intellectual and artistic skills.
      c. Machiavelli's *The Prince* describes how to acquire, maintain, and increase political power.
      d. Machiavelli believed that the politician should manipulate people and use any means to gain power.
      e. Machiavelli did not advocate amoral behavior but believed that political action cannot be governed by moral considerations.
  B. The printed word
   1. The invention in 1455 of movable type by Gutenberg, Fust, and Schöffer made possible the printing of a wide variety of texts.
   2. Printing transformed the lives of Europeans by making propaganda possible, encouraging a wider common identity, and improving literacy.
  C. Clocks
   1. By about 1320 some Europeans had learned how to quantify time by use of the mechanical "clock"—meaning "bells."
   2. Clocks were important for understanding and controlling urban-economic life.
  D. Women in Renaissance society
   1. Compared to women in the previous age, the status of upper-class women declined during the Renaissance.
   2. Although the Renaissance brought improved educational opportunities for women, they were expected to use their education solely to run a household.
      a. Education became the factor that separated upper- from lower-class women.
   3. Women's status declined with regard to sex and love.
      a. Renaissance humanists laid the foundations for the bourgeois double standard.
      b. The rape of women by upper-class men was frequent and not considered serious.
   4. Sex crimes occurred and were punished, but women appear to be victims in fewer cases than earlier.
  E. Gender and culture
   1. The repetition of anti-sodomy laws in the fifteenth century suggests that homosexuality was widespread, difficult to outlaw, and important in shaping masculine gender identity.
      a. Most cases of sodomy to come to court were that of an active adult male and an adolescent under 18 as the passive partner.

       b. Society did not see the active adult sodomite as unmasculine—perhaps because marriage and women were not available for many men.

       c. For some, homoerotic activity was part of male bonding; for others it was for economic, social, or sexual needs.

   F. Blacks in Renaissance society

      1. Beginning in the fifteenth century, black slaves were brought into Europe in large numbers.

      2. Blacks as slaves and freemen filled a variety of positions, from laborers to dancers and actors and musicians.

      3. The European attitude toward blacks was ambivalent—blackness symbolized both evil and humility.

      4. In the Renaissance, blacks were displayed as signs of wealth.

V. The Renaissance in the north began in the last quarter of the fifteenth century.

   A. It was more Christian than the Renaissance in Italy, and it stressed social reform based on Christian ideals.

   B. Christian humanists sought to create a more perfect world by combining the best elements of classical and Christian cultures.

      1. Humanists like Lefèvre believed in the use of the Bible by common people.

      2. Thomas More, the author of *Utopia,* believed that society, not people, needed improving.

       a. More was a Christian lawyer and minister of King Henry VIII.

       b. His *Utopia* was a socialistic society based on common ownership and social equality.

      3. The Dutch monk Erasmus best represents Christian humanism in his emphasis on education as the key to a moral and intellectual improvement and inner Christianity.

   C. The stories of the French humanist Rabelais were distinctly secular but still had a serious purpose.

      1. Like More, Rabelais believed that institutions molded individuals and that education was the key to moral life.

      2. His books on the adventures of Gargantua and Pantagruel were spoofs on French social life.

   D. Northern art and architecture were more religious than in Italy and less influenced by classical themes and motifs.

      1. Van Eyck painted realistic works with attention to human personality.

      2. Bosch used religion and folk legends as themes.

VI. Politics and the state in the Renaissance (ca 1450-1521)

   A. Fifteenth-century rulers began the process of order through centralization of power.

      1. The result was the rise of many powerful and ruthless rulers interested in the centralization of power and the elimination of disorder and violence.

      2. Many of them, such as Louis XI of France, Henry VII of England, and Ferdinand and Isabella of Spain, seemed to be acting according to Machiavelli's principles.

      3. These monarchs invested kingship with a strong sense of royal authority and national purpose.

      4. The ideas of the new monarchs were not entirely original—some of them had their roots in the Middle Ages.

B. France after the Hundred Years' War
  1. Charles VII ushered in an age of recovery and ended civil war.
      a. He expelled the English, reorganized the royal council, strengthened royal finances, reformed the justice system, and remodeled the army.
      b. He made the church subject to the state.
  2. Louis XI expanded the French state and laid the foundations of later French absolutism.
C. England also suffered from disorder.
  1. Feudal lords controlled the royal council and Parliament in the fifteenth century.
  2. Between 1455 and 1471, the houses of York and Lancaster fought a civil war called the Wars of the Roses that hurt trade, agriculture, and domestic industry.
  3. Edward IV and his followers began to restore royal power, avoided expensive war, and reduced their reliance on Parliament for funds.
  4. The English Parliament had become a power center for the aristocracy but was manipulated by Henry VII into becoming a tool of the king.
  5. Henry VII used the royal council and the court of Star Chamber to check aristocratic power.
  6. Henry VII and his successors won the support of the upper middle class promoting their interest in money, trade, and stability.
D. Spain
  1. The *reconquista* was the centuries-long attempt to unite Spain and expel Muslims and Jews.
  2. The marriage of Ferdinand and Isabella was the last major step in the unification and Christianization of Spain.
      a. Under their reign, however, Spain remained a loose confederation of separate states.
      b. They used the *hermandades,* or local police forces, to administer royal justice.
  3. They restructured the royal council to curb aristocratic power.
  4. The church was also used to strengthen royal authority.
  5. Ferdinand and Isabella completed the *reconquista* in 1492, but many Jews remained because they aided royal power.
      a. Jews were often financiers and professionals; many (called *conversos*) had converted but were still disliked and distrusted.
      b. Needing a scapegoat during the Black Death, Spanish mobs killed many Jews.
      c. Ferdinand and Isabella revived the Inquisition and used its cruel methods to unify Spain and expel the Jews.
  6. Spanish Christians rejected *conversos* on the basis of race—out of fear of *conversos* taking over public offices. Most Jews fled from Spain.

Review Questions

Check your understanding of this chapter by answering the following questions.

  1. What new social class developed in twelfth-century Italy? How did this social class affect the movement toward republican government?

2. What five powers dominated the Italian peninsula in the fifteenth century? How did the Italian city-states contribute to modern diplomacy?

3. How does the concept of individualism help explain the Renaissance?

4. What is humanism? What do humanists emphasize?

5. How did the invention of movable type revolutionize European life?

6. How did the Renaissance in northern Europe differ from that of Italy?

7. Discuss Christian humanism by describing the works and ideas of Thomas More and Desiderius Erasmus.

8. Why did Italy become a battleground for the European superpowers after 1494?

9. What were the obstacles to royal authority faced by the kings of France in the fifteenth century? How did Charles VII and his successors strengthen the French monarchy?

10. What devices did Henry VII of England use to check the power of the aristocracy and strengthen the monarchy?

11. What were the achievements of Ferdinand and Isabella in the areas of national power and national expansion?

12. Why were blacks valued in Renaissance society? What roles did they play in the economic and social life of the times?

13. In what ways did life for upper-class women change during the Renaissance?

14. How was Renaissance art different from medieval art?

15. Who were the New Christians (*conversos*) in Spain and why were they ultimately killed or expelled?

Study-Review Exercises

Define the following key concepts and terms.

Renaissance

oligarchy

signori

communes

popolo

reconquista

humanism

secularism

Spanish conversos

individualism

materialism

hermandades

Machiavellian

Identify and explain the significance of the following people and terms.

English Royal Council and Court of Star Chamber

conquest of Granada

Habsburg-Valois wars

Brunelleschi's Foundling Hospital in Florence

Pico della Mirandola

Desiderius Erasmus

Jan van Eyck

Thomas More

Donatello

Baldassare Castiglione

Niccolò Machiavelli

Johan Gutenberg

Lefèvre d'Etaples

Saint John Chrysostom

Lorenzo Valla

Savonarola

Jerome Bosch

François Rabelais

Explain why each of the following is considered a "new monarch."
Louis XI of France

Henry VII of England

Ferdinand and Isabella of Spain

Charles VII of France

Cesare Borgia

Test your understanding of the chapter by providing the correct answers.

1. The author of a bestselling political critique called *The Prince*. _____

2. Renaissance humanists tended to be *more/less* concerned about religion than about people.

3. In the fifteenth century, infanticide *increased/decreased.*

4. An important English humanist and the author of Utopia. _____

5. Generally, the legal status of upper-class women *improved/declined* during the Renaissance.

6. It *is/is not* clear that the economic growth and the material wealth of the Italian cities were direct causes of the Renaissance.

Major Political Ideas

1. What were the political ideas behind the concept of the "new monarch"?

2. Define "antisemitism" by referring to attitudes and treatment of Jews in Spain.

Issues for Essays and Discussion

The Renaissance was a period during which some people began to think and act in different ways. Sometimes this is referred to as a "self-conscious awareness," a stress on "humanism," and a "secular spirit." What do these terms mean? Answer by making specific reference to developments in literature, political thought, and art.

Was there a "class" dimension to the Renaissance—in other words who benefited the most, the working people, the middle classes, the aristocracy? Was there a gender dimension to the Renaissance as well?

Interpretation of Visual Sources

1. Study the reproduction of the painting entitled *Death and the Miser* by Jerome Bosch. Describe how this painting reflects the religious orientation of the Renaissance in the north of Europe. What is happening in this scene? Account for as many symbolic references as you can. What do you believe to be Bosch's message?

2. Study the reproduction of the painting *Journey of the Magi.* How does this painting reflect corporate patronage of the arts? Is it a religious or a secular painting?

Geography

On Outline Map 13.1 provided, and using Map 13.1 in the textbook as a reference, mark the following: the names of the Italian city-states and their principal cities, underlining the five major powers of Venice, Milan, Florence, the Papal States, and the kingdom of Naples.

Outline Map 13.1

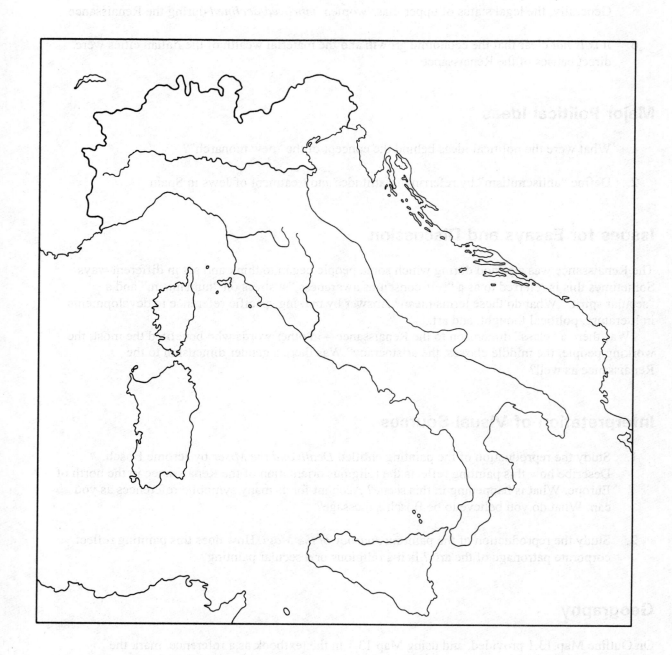

Understanding History Through the Arts

1. What does the music of the Renaissance tell us about the period? The music of the Renaissance is introduced in two recordings, *From the Renaissance* (STL-150) and *From the Renaissance—Concert* (STL-160), in the Time-Life series *The Story of Great Music* (1967), which also includes a book with a good introduction to the period and its musical styles, art, and history. Good written introductions to Renaissance music are H. Brown, *Music in the Renaissance** (1976), and G. Reese, *Music in the Renaissance* (1954).

2. What were the interests and motives of Renaissance artists? A good introduction to Renaissance art and the life of the artist and writer is J. H. Plumb, *The Renaissance* (1961), which includes biographies of Michelangelo, Petrarch, Leonardo, and others and includes hundreds of color plates and a comprehensive history of Renaissance art.

3. How did the art of Rome and Florence differ? What characteristics did they share? Begin your study with R. Goldthwaite, *The Building of Renaissance Florence** (1983); M. Andres et al., *The Art of Florence,* 2 vols. (1989); J. Andreae, *The Art of Rome* (1989); and G. Holmes, ed., *Art and Politics in Renaissance Italy* (1933).

Problems for Further Investigation

1. Was the Renaissance an age of progress and advancement? Urban and rural life, court life, war, and witchcraft are among the many aspects of Renaissance life covered in E. R. Chamberlin, *Everyday Life in Renaissance Times** (1967).

2. What did popular Renaissance writers believe to be important about the age in which they lived? One of the best ways to understand the Renaissance is to read the works of its participants. Three works dealt with in this chapter are Niccolò Machiavelli, *The Prince** (a number of paperback translations are available); Baldassare Castiglione, *The Courtier,** Charles Singleton, trans. (1959); and Thomas More, *Utopia.**

3. How did the Renaissance alter the status of women? Begin your study by reading J. Kelly-Gadol, "Did Women Have a Renaissance?" in R. Bridenthal and C. Koontz, eds., *Becoming Visible: Women in European History* (1977); M. Rose et al., *Women in the Middle Ages and the Renaissance: Literary and Historical Perspectives* (1986); and C. Klapisch-Zuper, ed. *A History of Women*, Vol. III (1994).

4. What were the causes and consequences of the Spanish assault on Spanish Jews? Begin your investigation with J. S. Gerber, *The Jews of Spain* (1992) and H. Kamen, *Inquisition and Society in Spain in the Sixteenth and Seventeenth Centuries* (1985).

---

*Available in paperback.

Self-Test Multiple-Choice Questions

Do not assume that these questions will appear on any examination. It is recommended that you not memorize these questions, but use them only as a self-test. Answers are at the end of this book.

1. Which of the following statements about the earliest printed books is *false*?
   a. They dealt mainly with economic and business subjects.
   b. They encouraged literacy.
   c. Movable type was first developed in Mainz, Germany.
   d. They had an effect on the process of learning.

2. The Renaissance began in
   a. the Low Countries.
   b. Rome.
   c. France.
   d. Florence.

3. The patrons of the Renaissance were mostly
   a. churchmen.
   b. the popes.
   c. the common people.
   d. merchants and bankers.

4. The frail and ugly king who began French economic and political recovery in the early fifteenth century was
   a. Henry Tudor.
   b. Charles VII.
   c. Philip the Fair.
   d. Louis XI.

5. It appears that in Renaissance society blacks were
   a. valued as soldiers.
   b. valued as servants and entertainers.
   c. considered undesirable and not allowed in society.
   d. not much in demand.

6. A major difference between northern and Italian humanism is that northern humanism stressed
   a. economic gain and materialism.
   b. social reform based on Christian ideals.
   c. pagan virtues.
   d. scholastic dogma over reason.

7. Local groups in Spain that were given royal authority to administer justice were the
   a. *conversos.*
   b. liberals.
   c. *hermandades.*
   d. royal tribunal.

8. The court of Star Chamber in England was
   a. a common-law court.
   b. under the control of the barons in the House of Lords.
   c. done away with by the powerful Tudors.
   d. used to check aristocratic power.

9. The superiority of the French monarch over the church was the object of the
   a. Pragmatic Sanction of Bourges.
   b. Habsburg-Valois wars.
   c. Declaration of Calais.
   d. Hundred Years' War.

10. Most of the northern Renaissance thinkers agreed that
    a. democracy, not monarchy, was the only workable political system.
    b. humanity is basically sinful.
    c. Christianity is unacceptable.
    d. society is perfectible.

11. The late-fifteenth-century ruler of England who ended the civil war and strengthened the crown was
    a. John I.
    b. William III.
    c. Henry II.
    d. Henry VII.

12. Which of the following statements about Florence at the time of the Renaissance is *false*?
    a. Its major industry was wool production.
    b. It lost probably half its population to the Black Death.
    c. It was a major banking center.
    d. It was an important Mediterranean port city.

13. The dome of St. Peter's in Rome is considered to be the greatest work of
    a. Brunelleschi.
    b. Donatello.
    c. Michelangelo.
    d. Ghiberti.

14. The term *Renaissance* means
    a. a rise in the average standard of living among the masses.
    b. a resurgence of art and culture in the fourteenth through sixteenth centuries.
    c. an increase in the population after the ravaging effects of the "Four Horsemen of the Apocalypse."
    d. the recovery of the church from economic and moral decline.

15. The financial and military strength of the towns of northern Italy was directly related to
    a. their wealth, which enabled them to hire mercenary soldiers to protect their commercial interests.
    b. their contractual and marital alliances with the rural nobility.
    c. protections provided them by the Holy Roman Emperor.
    d. their alliance with the papacy.

16. The northern Renaissance differed from the Italian Renaissance in that the former was characterized by all of the following *except*
    a. interest in biblical scholarship.
    b. an emphasis on secular and pagan themes in art.
    c. the combination of the best aspects of antiquity and Christianity.
    d. an emphasis on the use of reason.

17. Erasmus advocated
    a. paganism.
    b. Christian education for moral and intellectual improvement.
    c. a monastic life of contemplation and divorce from the material world.
    d. obedience to church doctrine and ritual.

18. The Renaissance artist of talent and ability often lived a life
    a. of economic desperation.
    b. of economic security through patronage.
    c. of luxury, but without social status.
    d. like that of the masses.

19. The most influential book on Renaissance court life and behavior was
    a. Castiglione's *The Courtier*.
    b. Machiavelli's *The Prince*.
    c. Augustine's *City of God*.
    d. Boccaccio's *Decameron*.

20. The best description of Machiavelli's *The Prince* is that it is
    a. a description of how government should be organized and implemented.
    b. a satire on sixteenth-century politics.
    c. a call for Italian nationalism.
    d. an accurate description of politics as practiced in Renaissance Italy.

21. The Wars of the Roses were
    a. civil wars between the English ducal houses of York and Lancaster.
    b. between England and France.
    c. civil wars between the English king, Henry VI, and the aristocracy.
    d. minor disputes among English gentry.

22. Just before the advent of Ferdinand and Isabella, the Iberian Peninsula could best be described as
    a. a homogeneous region sharing a common language and cultural tradition.
    b. a heterogeneous region consisting of several ethnic groups with a diversity of linguistic and cultural characteristics.
    c. tolerant of religious and ethnic traditions different from Christianity.
    d. a region dominated equally by Arabs and Jews.

23. Thomas More's ideas, as best expressed in his book *Utopia,* centered on the belief that
    a. evil exists because men and women are basically corrupt.
    b. political leaders must learn how to manipulate their subjects.
    c. social order is only an unattainable ideal.
    d. corruption and war are due to acquisitiveness and private property.

24. Renaissance men's view of educated women was that they should
    a. be encouraged and given an equal place in society.
    b. have a voice in the affairs of the city.
    c. not be encouraged in any manner.
    d. be allowed to add a social touch to the household, but otherwise remain subservient to men.

25. The culture of the Renaissance
    a. was largely limited to a small mercantile elite.
    b. was widely spread and practiced by a broad middle class.
    c. was confined to the church.
    d. affected all classes, including the peasants.

Studying Effectively—Exercise 3

Learning How to Identify Main Points That Are Effects, Results, Consequences

In the introduction to this *Study Guide* and in the "Studying Effectively" exercises 1 and 2, we noted that learning to underline properly plays an important part in college work. Underlining (or highlighting with a felt-tipped pen) provides a permanent record of what you study and learn. It helps you review, synthesize, and do your best on exams.

We suggested three simple guidelines for effective underlining or highlighting:*

1. Be selective; do not underline or highlight too much.

2. Underline or highlight the main points.

3. Consider numbering the main points.

These guidelines will help you in courses in many different subjects.

Cause and Effect in History

The study of history also requires learning to recognize special kinds of main points. These points are *explanatory* in nature. *They answer why and how questions,* thereby helping you to interpret and make sense of the historical record.

Two particularly important types of why and how questions focus on *cause* and *effect* in history. You are already familiar with questions of this nature, questions that provide much of history's fascination and excitement. "Why did the Roman Empire decline and fall?" That is, what *causes* explain the decline and fall of the Roman Empire? "What were the *effects* of the Black Death?" You should pay particular attention to questions of cause and effect. They give history meaning. They help you increase your ability to think and reason in historical terms.

Two other insights will help you greatly in identifying main points involving cause and effect. First, historians use a number of different words and verbal constructions to express these concepts. Thus "causes" often become "reasons" or "factors," or things that "account for," "contribute to," or "play a role in" a given development. "Effects" often become "results" or "consequences," or are "the product of an impact." In most cases students can consider such expressions as substitutes for cause and effect, although they should be aware that historians are not of one mind on these matters.

---

*The guidelines for underlining are from *RSVP: The College Reading, Study, & Vocabulary Program,* fourth edition, by James F. Shepherd (Houghton Mifflin, 1992). We urge students to consult this very valuable book for additional help in improving their reading and study skills.

Second, cause and effect are constantly interrelated in the historical process. Yesterday's results become today's causes, which will in turn help bring tomorrow's results. To take examples you have studied, the *causes* of the fall of the Roman Empire (such as increasing economic difficulties) brought *results* (such as the self-sufficient agrarian economy) that contributed to—helped cause—the rise of Benedictine monasticism. In short, *a historical development can usually be viewed as a cause or an effect, depending on what question is being answered.*

Exercise A

Read the following passage once as a whole. Read it a second time to underline or highlight it in terms of main points identified as effects or results. Consider numbering the effects in the margin. Then do Exercise B at the end of the passage.

The effects of the invention of movable-type printing were not felt overnight. Nevertheless, within a half-century of the publication of Gutenberg's Bible of 1456, movable type brought about radical changes. Printing transformed both the private and the public lives of Europeans. Governments that "had employed the cumbersome methods of manuscripts to communicate with their subjects switched quickly to print to announce declarations of war, publish battle accounts, promulgate treaties or argue disputed points in pamphlet form. Theirs was an effort 'to win the psychological war.' " Printing made propaganda possible, emphasizing differences between various groups, such as Crown and nobility, church and state. These differences laid the basis for the formation of distinct political parties. Printed materials reached an invisible public, allowing silent individuals to join causes and groups of individuals widely separated by geography to form a common identity; this new group consciousness could compete with older, localized loyalties.

Printing also stimulated the literacy of lay people and eventually came to have a deep effect on their private lives. Although most of the earliest books and pamphlets dealt with religious subjects, students, housewives, businessmen, and upper- and middle-class people sought books on all subjects. Printers responded with moralizing, medical, practical, and travel manuals. Pornography as well as piety assumed new forms. Broadsides and flysheets allowed great public festivals, religious ceremonies, and political events to be experienced vicariously by the stay-at-home. Since books and printed materials were read aloud to the illiterate, print bridged the gap between written and oral cultures.

Exercise B

Study the last paragraph again. Can you see how it is a good example of the historical interaction of cause and effect? Do you see how a given development is an effect or a cause *depending on what historical question is being asked*? Be prepared for such "reversals" in the text, in lecture and class discussion, and on exams.

Hint: In the last paragraph, what is an *effect* of the invention of the printing press? (Ideas could be spread more rapidly.) What "stimulated"—helped *cause*—the spread of literacy? (The invention of the printing press. The authors develop this point further in Chapter 14.)

Chapter 14

Reform and Renewal in the Christian Church

Learning Objectives

After reading and studying this chapter you should be able to:

1. discuss the various religious, social, and political reasons for the Protestant Reformation of the sixteenth century.

2. explain Protestantism's impact on western society.

3. list the theological tenets and the contributions of Luther, Calvin, and Knox.

4. explain how the Catholic church withstood the onslaught of Protestantism.

Chapter Summary

A great religious upheaval called the Protestant Reformation ended the centuries-long religious unity of Europe and resulted in a number of important political changes. In the sixteenth century, cries for reform were nothing new, but this time they resulted in revolution. There were a number of signs of disorder within the church, pointing to the need for moral and administrative reform. For example, it was the granting of indulgences that propelled Martin Luther into the movement for doctrinal change in the church. Luther had come to the conclusion that salvation could not come by good works or indulgences, but only through faith. This was to be one of the fundamental tenets of Protestantism and one of the ideas that pushed Luther and the German nobility to revolt against not only Rome but Rome's secular ally, the Holy Roman Emperor.

It is important to recognize that Luther's challenge to the authority of the church and to Catholic unity in Europe invited and supported an attack on the emperor by the German nobility. The pope and the emperor, as separate powers and allies, represented religious and political unity and conformity in Germany. Thus, the victory of Luther and the nobility was a victory for decentralized authority. It meant the collapse of Germany as a unified power in Europe. This is one reason Catholic France usually supported the German Protestants in their quarrel with Rome.

Outside of Germany the Protestant reformer Calvin had a greater impact on Europe than Luther. Calvin's harsh and dogmatic religion spread from Geneva into northern Europe, England, and Scotland. It was England, in fact, that eventually became the political center of Protestantism. Initiated by Henry VIII, the English Protestant Reformation was at first motivated by the personal

228

and political interests of the king himself. The type of Protestantism eventually adopted by the Church of England was much more moderate—and closer to Catholicism—than that of Scotland.

With the Council of Trent of 1545-1563, the Catholic church, finding the Habsburgs unable to destroy the heretical Protestantism, launched a massive and partly successful Counter Reformation to convince dissidents to return to the church.

All in all, Protestantism developed and spread for economic and political reasons as well as religious ones. In the end, Protestantism meant greater spiritual freedom for some individuals, but spiritual disunity and disorganization for Europe as a whole. In England, Scotland, the Scandinavian countries, and elsewhere, it contributed to the power of the nation and thus meant a further political division of Europe, while in Germany it slowed down the movement toward nationhood.

Study Outline

Use this outline to preview the chapter before you read a particular section in your textbook and then as a self-check to test your reading comprehension after you have read the chapter section.

   I. The condition of the church (ca 1400-1517)
       A. The declining prestige of the church
           1. The Babylonian Captivity and the Great Schism damaged the church's prestige.
           2. Secular humanists satirized and denounced moral corruption within the church.
       B. Signs of disorder in the early sixteenth century
           1. The parish clergy brought spiritual help to the people.
           2. Critics of the church wanted moral and administrative reform in three areas.
               a. Clerical immorality (neglect of celibacy, drunkenness, gambling) created a scandal.
               b. The lack of education of the clergy and law standards of ordination were condemned by Christian humanists.
               c. The absenteeism, pluralism (holding of several benefices, or offices), and wealth of the greater clergy bore little resemblance to Christian gospel.
           3. The prelates and popes of the period, often members of the nobility, lived in splendor and moral corruption.
       C. Signs of vitality in the late fifteenth and early sixteenth centuries
           1. Sixteenth-century Europe remained deeply religious, and calls for reform testify to the spiritual vitality of the church.
           2. New organizations were formed to educate and minister to the poor.
               a. The Brethren of the Common Life in Holland lived simply and sought to make religion a personal, inner experience based on following the scriptures.
               b. The *Imitation of Christ* by Thomas à Kempis urged Christians to seek perfection in a simple way of life.
           3. Pope Julius II summoned an ecumenical council on reform in the church called the Lateran Council (1512-1527).
   II. Martin Luther and the birth of Protestantism
       A. Luther's early years
           1. Luther was a German monk and professor of religion whose search for salvation led him to the letters of St. Paul.
           2. He concluded that faith was central to Christianity and the only means of salvation.

B. Luther's Ninety-five Theses (October 1517)
1. Luther's opposition to the sale of indulgences (remissions of penalties for sin) prompted his fight with Rome.
2. His Ninety-five Theses, or propositions on indulgences, raised many theological issues and initiated a long period of debate in Europe.
   a. Luther rejected the idea that salvation could be achieved by good works, such as indulgences.
   b. An *indulgence* was a release from the penalties to be paid for sin.
   c. He also criticized papal wealth.
3. Luther later denied the authority of the pope and was excommunicated and declared an outlaw by Charles V at Worms in 1521.
4. Meanwhile, Ulrich Zwingli introduced the reformation in Switzerland.
   a. He believed in the supremacy of Scripture, and was opposed to indulgences, the Mass, monasticism, and clerical celibacy.
C. Protestant thought
1. The basic theological tenets of Protestantism were set forth in the Confession of Augsburg, in which Luther provided new answers to four basic theological issues.
   a. He believed that salvation derived through faith alone, not faith and good works.
   b. He stated that religious authority rests with the Bible, not the pope.
   c. He believed that the church consists of the entire community of Christian believers.
   d. And he believed that all work is sacred and everyone should serve God in his or her individual vocation.
   e. In addition, he believed that every believer was his/her own priest.
   f. Catholics believe in *transubstantiation*, Luther in *consubstantiation*, and Zwingli in the Sacrament as a *memorial* only.
2. Protestantism, therefore, was a reformulation of Christian beliefs and practices.
III. The social impact of Luther's beliefs
A. By 1521 Luther's religious ideas had a vast following among all social classes.
1. Luther's ideas were popular because of widespread resentment of clerical privileges and wealth.
2. Luther's ideas attracted many preachers, and they became Protestant leaders.
3. Peasants cited Luther's theology as part of their demands for economic reforms.
   a. Luther did not support the peasants' revolts; he believed in obedience to civil authority.
   b. Widespread peasant revolts in 1525 were brutally crushed, but some land was returned to common use.
4. Luther's greatest weapon was his mastery of the language, and his words were spread by the advent of printing.
   a. Zwingli and Calvin were greatly influenced by his writings.
   b. The publication of Luther's German translation of the New Testament in 1523 democratized religion.
   c. Catechisms and hymns enabled people, especially the young, to remember central points of doctrine.

B. Luther's impact on women
1. Luther gave dignity to domestic work, stressed the idea of marriage and the Christian home, ended confession, and encouraged education for girls.
2. Luther held enlightened views on sex and marriage, although he claimed that women should be no more than efficient wives.

IV. Germany and the Protestant Reformation
A. The Holy Roman Empire in the fourteenth and fifteenth centuries
1. The Golden Bull of 1356 gave each of the seven electors virtual sovereignty.
2. Localism and chronic disorder allowed the nobility to strengthen their territories and reduced the authority of the emperor.
B. The rise of the Habsburg dynasty
1. The Habsburgs gave unity to much of Europe, especially with the marriage of Maximilian I of Austria and Mary of Burgundy in 1477.
2. Charles V, their grandson, inherited much of Europe and was committed to the idea of its religious and political unity.
C. The political impact of Luther's beliefs
1. The Protestant Reformation stirred nationalistic feelings in Germany against the wealthy Italian papacy.
2. Luther's appeal to patriotism earned him the support of the princes, who used religion as a means of gaining more political independence and preventing the flow of German money to Rome.
3. The Protestant movement proved to be a political disaster for Germany.
   a. The dynastic Habsburg-Valois wars advanced the cause of Protestantism and promoted the political fragmentation of Germany.
   b. By the Peace of Augsburg of 1555, Charles recognized Lutheranism as a legal religion and each prince was permitted to determine the religion of his territory.

V. The Growth of the Protestant Reformation
A. Calvinism
1. Calvin believed that God selects certain people to do his work and that he was selected to reform the church.
2. Under John Calvin, Geneva became "a city that was a church" (a theocracy), in which the state was subordinate to the church.
3. Calvin's central ideas, expressed in *The Institutes of Christian Religion,* were his belief in the omnipotence of God, the insignificance of humanity, and predestination.
4. Austere living and intolerance of dissenters characterized Calvin's Geneva.
   a. The Genevan Consistory monitored the private morals of citizens.
   b. Michael Servetus was burned at the stake for denying the Christian dogma of the Trinity and rejecting child baptism.
   c. Calvinists did not view women much differently than Catholics: women were to be obedient to their husbands—and unmarried women were upsetting the natural order.
5. The city of Geneva was the model for international Protestantism, and Calvinism, with its emphasis on the work ethic, became the most dynamic and influential form of Protestantism.
B. The Anabaptists
1. This Protestant sect believed in adult baptism, revelation, religious tolerance, pacifism, and the separation of church and state.

2. Their beliefs and practices were too radical for the times, and they were bitterly persecuted.
   a. Later, the Quakers, the Baptists, and the Congregationalists would trace their origins to the Anabaptists.

C. The English Reformation
   1. The Lollards, although driven underground in the fifteenth century, survived and stressed the idea of a direct relationship between the individual and God.
   2. The English humanist William Tyndale began printing an English translation of the New Testament in 1525.
   3. The wealth and corruption of the clergy, as exemplified by Thomas Wolsey, stirred much resentment.
   4. Henry VIII desired a divorce from his queen, Catherine, daughter of Ferdinand and Isabella of Spain, so he could marry Anne Boleyn.
   5. Pope Clement VII (who did not wish to admit papal error) refused to annul Henry's marriage to Catherine.
   6. Archbishop Cranmer, however, engineered the divorce.
   7. The result was the nationalization of the English church and a break with Rome as Henry used Parliament to legalize the Reformation.
      a. Henry needed money so he dissolved the monasteries and confiscated their lands, but this did not lead to more equal land distribution.
      b. Some traditional Catholic practices, such as confession and the doctrine of transubstantiation, were maintained.
      c. Nationalization of the church led to changes in governmental administration, resulting in greater efficiency and economy.
   8. Under Edward VI, Henry's heir, England shifted closer to Protestantism.
   9. Mary Tudor attempted to bring Catholicism back to England.
   10. Under Elizabeth I a religious settlement requiring outward conformity to the Church of England was made.

D. The establishment of the Church of Scotland
   1. Scotland was an extreme case of clerical abuse and corruption.
   2. John Knox brought Calvinism to Scotland from Geneva.
   3. The Presbyterian church became the national church of Scotland.

E. Protestantism in Ireland
   1. The English ruling class in Ireland adopted the new faith.
   2. Most of the Irish people defiantly remained Catholic.

F. Lutheranism in Sweden, Norway, and Denmark
   1. In Sweden, Norway, and Denmark the monarchy led the religious reformation.
   2. The result was Lutheran state churches.

VI. The Catholic and the Counter-Reformations
A. There were two types of reform within the Catholic church in the sixteenth and seventeenth centuries.
   1. The Catholic Reformation sought to stimulate a new religious fervor.
   2. The Counter-Reformation started in the 1540s as a reaction to Protestantism and progressed simultaneously with the Catholic Reformation.

B. The slowness of institutional reform
   1. Too often the popes were preoccupied with politics or sensual pleasures.
   2. Popes resisted calls for the formation of a general council because it would limit their authority.
C. The Council of Trent
   1. Pope Paul III called the Council of Trent (1545-1563).
      a. An attempt to reconcile with the Protestants failed.
      b. International politics hindered the theological debates.
   2. Nonetheless, the principle of papal authority was maintained, considerable reform was undertaken, and the spiritual renewal of the church was begun.
      a. Tridentine decrees forbade the sale of indulgences and outlawed pluralism and simony.
      b. Attempts were made to curb clerical immorality and to encourage education.
      c. Great emphasis was placed on preaching.
D. New religious orders
   1. The Ursuline order of nuns gained enormous prestige for the education of women.
      a. The Ursulines sought to re-Christianize society by training future wives and mothers.
      b. The Ursulines spread to France and North America.
   2. The Society of Jesus played a strong international role in resisting Protestantism.
      a. Obedience was the foundation of the Jesuit tradition.
      b. With their schools, political influence, and missionary work, they brought many people into the Catholic fold.
E. The Sacred Congregation of the Holy Office
   1. This group, established by Pope Paul III in 1542, carried out the Roman Inquisition as a way to combat heresy.
   2. It had the power to arrest, imprison, and execute, but its influence was confined to papal territories.

Review Questions

Check your understanding of this chapter by answering the following questions.

1. What were some of the signs of disorder within the early sixteenth-century church? What impact did church wealth have on the condition of the church?

2. What were some of the signs of religious vitality in fifteenth- and early-sixteenth-century society?

3. What circumstances prompted Luther to post his Ninety-five Theses?

4. Describe the practice of indulgence selling. What authority did Luther question and on what argument did he base his position?

5. What were Luther's answers, as delineated in the Confession of Augsburg, to the four basic theological issues?

6. What effect did Luther's concept of state authority over church authority have on German society and German history?

7. Why was the condemnation of Luther in 1521 at Worms not enforced by the German nobility? What was the result?

8. Why was Calvin's Geneva called "the city that was a church"? What is a theocracy?

9. In what ways were the Anabaptists radical for their time? Why did many of their beliefs cause them to be bitterly persecuted?

10. What were the causes and results of the English Reformation?

11. What was the Elizabethan Settlement?

12. Charles V has been considered a medieval emperor. In what respects is this true? What were the origins of his empire?

13. What were the goals and methods of the Ursuline order and the Society of Jesus?

14. What were the achievements of the Council of Trent?

15. What was the Inquisition? How extensive was its power?

Study-Review Exercises

Identify and explain the significance of the following people and terms.

Brethren of the Common Life

John Knox

Pope Paul III

Ulrich Zwingli

Archbishop Cranmer

John Tetzel

Martin Luther

transubstantiation/consubstantiation

Angela Merici

Henry VIII

Charles V

Mary Tudor

Pope Alexander VI

Council of Trent

Counter-Reformation

Elizabethan Settlement

Act of Restraint of Appeals

pluralism

benefices

Peace of Augsburg

Ninety-five Theses

preacherships

Explain the subject matter and historical significance of the following works.
The Imitation of Christ

Appeal to the Christian Nobility of the German Nation

The Institutes of the Christian Religion

Define the basic beliefs of the following Christian religions and churches.
Roman Catholicism

Lutheranism

Calvinism

Anabaptism

Church of England

Presbyterian Church of Scotland

Test your understanding of the chapter by providing the correct answers.

1. The Council of Trent *did/did not* reaffirm the seven sacraments, the validity of tradition, and transubstantiation.

2. The English Supremacy Act of 1534 declared the _____ to be the Supreme Head of the Church of England.

3. For the most part, the English Reformation under Henry VIII dealt with *political/theological* issues.

4. He wrote: "How comes it that we Germans must put up with such robbery and such extortion of our property at the hands of the pope?" _____

5. This pope's name became a synonym for moral corruption. _____

6. Mary Tudor, the English queen and daughter of Henry VIII, *was/was not* interested in the restoration of Catholicism in England.

7. In general, Protestantism tended to *strengthen/weaken* Germany as a political unit.

8. During the reign of Elizabeth, the English church moved in a moderately *Protestant/Catholic* direction.

Major Political Ideas

1. In what ways was Protestantism a political idea? Did it help or hinder the development of the nation-state? Compare and contrast the religious settlements made in the German states, England, Scotland, and Ireland. Why was Protestantism on the one hand a source of national strength and on the other a source of national weakness?

2. What was the political message behind Luther's 1520 book, *Appeal to the Christian Nobility of the German Nation*?

Issues for Essays and Discussion

Agree or disagree: Late medieval religious developments paved the way for the adoption and spread of Protestant thought. The Protestant Reformation was inevitable.

Was the Reformation a blessing or a disaster for the people of Europe? Support your argument by making specific reference to Germany, England, and Scotland. What impact did the Reformation have on the power of the monarchs, the well-being of the common man and woman, and the overall balance of European power?

Interpretation of Visual Sources

Study the sixteenth-century woodcut titled *The Folly of Indulgences*. Describe the participants and the event. What is the message? What image of the church does this woodcut present to the popular mind? How important do you believe such prints were in forming public opinion?

View the reproduction of the painting *Calvinist Worship*. What does the arrangement of the church tell us about Calvinist (Reformed) beliefs? Why is the pulpit the central feature? Describe the various seating arrangements and the sort of people who used them.

Geography

On Outline Map 14.1 and using Map 14.1 and Map 14.2 in the textbook as a reference, mark the following: the boundary of the Holy Roman Empire, the territory under the control of Charles V.

Study Map 14.2 in your textbook. Describe the geographic distribution of Lutheran, Calvinist (Reformed), Church of England, and Roman Catholic influence. Why is the city of Geneva so important? Why do you think Protestantism was so dominant in the north of Europe?

Outline Map 14.1

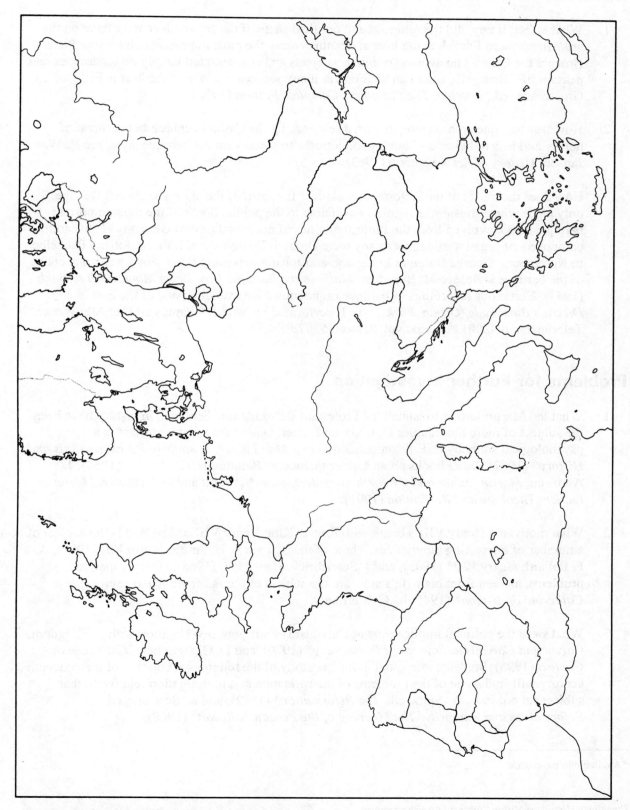

Understanding History Through the Arts

1. What effect, if any, did the religious and political strife of the sixteenth century have on the arts? In northern Europe in the later sixteenth century the most important painter was Pieter Bruegel the Elder, who avoided religious subjects and concentrated largely on landscapes and peasant life. Bruegel's work can be found in many sources, but one of the best is F. Grossmann, ed., *Bruegel, The Paintings: Complete Edition* (1956).

2. How was baroque architecture, in part, a response by the Catholic church to the threat of heresy and loss of believers? For a good introductory essay on the baroque style, see H. W. Janson, *History of Art,* Chapter 6 (1963).

3. How does the music of the Reformation express the spirit of the age? The church was the only place where music was regularly available to the public. Some of the most important baroque music evolved from the Protestant cities of north and central Germany. The leading composers of organ music in Germany were Dietrich Buxtehude in Lübeck, Johann Pachelbel in Nuremberg, George Bohm in Luneburg, and Johann Sebastian Bach. For a written account of the baroque style, see M. Bukofzer, *Music in the Baroque Era: From Monteverdi to Bach* (1947). Numerous recordings of baroque organ music are available; one of the best is *Dietrich Buxtehude, Organ Works,* vol. 1, performed by Michel Chapuis on Das Alte Werke, Telefunken, 6.42001.AF., and vol. 2. as 6.35307.EK.

Problems for Further Investigation

1. What led Martin Luther to launch the Protestant Reformation? Few men in history have been the subject of more biographies than Martin Luther. One of the most important is a psychological study by E. Erikson entitled *Young Man Luther: A Study in Psychoanalysis and History** (1962). Other books about Luther include R. Bainton, *Here I Stand** (1950); J. Atkinson, *Martin Luther and the Birth of Protestantism** (1968); and G. Brendler, *Martin Luther: Theology and Revolution* (1991).

2. What motivated Henry VIII's break with Rome? King Henry VIII of England is the subject of a number of interesting biographies. Three of the best are L. B. Smith, *Henry VIII* (1971); A. F. Pollard, *Henry VIII** (1905); and J. Scarisbrick, *Henry VIII* (1968). Henry's marital problems, as seen from his wife's side, are the subject of the fascinating and exciting *Catherine of Aragon** (1941) by G. Mattingly.

3. What were the political implications of Calvinism? Start your investigation with R. Kingdom, *Calvin and Calvinism: Sources of Democracy** (1970), and D. C. Steinmetz, *Calvinism in Context* (1995). Students interested in further study of the religious revolution of the sixteenth century will find some of the problems of interpretation and investigation relative to that subject set out in L. W. Spitz, ed., *The Reformation** (1972), and K. Sessions, ed., *Reformation and Authority: The Meaning of the Peasant's Revolt** (1968).

---

*Available in paperback.

4. How successful was the Counter-Reformation? Students interested in the Counter-Reformation should begin with E. M. Bums, *The Counter Reformation** (1964).

Self-Test Multiple-Choice Questions

<u>Do</u> <u>not</u> assume that these questions will appear on any examination. It is recommended that you <u>not</u> memorize these questions, but use them only as a self-test. Answers are at the end of this book.

1. Under the Presbyterian form of church government, the church is governed by
    a. bishops.
    b. the king of Scotland.
    c. ministers.
    d. the people.

2. Which one of the following did *not* come from the Anabaptist tradition?
    a. Congregationalists
    b. Puritans
    c. Quakers
    d. Jesuits

3. According to Luther, salvation comes through
    a. good works.
    b. faith.
    c. indulgences.
    d. a saintly life.

4. The cornerstone of Calvin's theology was his belief in
    a. predestination.
    b. indulgences.
    c. the basic goodness of man.
    d. religious tolerance and freedom.

5. John Knox and the Reformation movement in Scotland were most influenced by which of the following?
    a. Catholicism
    b. Calvinism
    c. Lutheranism
    d. The Church of England

---

*Available in paperback.

6. Which of the following is *not* identified with corrupt practices in the early-sixteenth-century church?
    a. Pluralism
    b. The Brethren of the Common Life
    c. Pope Alexander VI
    d. Absenteeism

7. Which of the following clearly did *not* support Luther?
    a. The German peasants
    b. The German nobility
    c. Charles V
    d. Ulrich Zwingli

8. Overall, Henry VIII's religious reformation in England occurred
    a. strictly for economic reasons.
    b. for religious reasons.
    c. mostly for political reasons.
    d. mostly for diplomatic reasons.

9. The Reformation in Germany resulted in
    a. a politically weaker Germany.
    b. a politically stronger Germany.
    c. no political changes of importance.
    d. a victory for imperial centralization.

10. The great Christian humanists of the fifteenth and sixteenth centuries believed that reform could be achieved through
    a. the use of violent revolution.
    b. education and social change.
    c. mass support of the church hierarchy.
    d. the election of a new pope.

11. Luther tacked his Ninety-five Theses to the door in Wittenberg as a response to
    a. the sale of indulgences and papal wealth.
    b. a revelation he experienced instructing him to start a new church.
    c. the illiteracy of the clergy.
    d. the oppressive rule of Frederick of Saxony.

12. The peasants who revolted in 1525 wanted all of the following *except*
    a. the abolition of serfdom.
    b. the reform of the clergy.
    c. the suppression of Luther's movement.
    d. an end to taxes and tithes.

13. Luther's success was a result of all of the following *except*
    a. his appointment by the pope to a church position.
    b. the development of the printing press.
    c. his appeal to the nobility and the middle classes.
    d. a strong command of language.

14. The Holy Roman Emperor who tried to suppress the Lutheran revolt was
    a. Christian III.
    b. Charles V.
    c. Adrian VI.
    d. Henry VII.

15. By 1555 the Protestant Reformation had spread to all but
    a. England.
    b. Scandinavia.
    c. Spain.
    d. Scotland.

16. The chief center of the Protestant reformers in the sixteenth century was
    a. Paris.
    b. Geneva.
    c. Zurich.
    d. Cologne.

17. The Anabaptists appealed to
    a. the nobility.
    b. the poor, uneducated, and unemployed.
    c. the intellectuals.
    d. the merchant classes.

18. Henry VIII dissolved the monasteries largely because
    a. he wanted to distribute the land more equitably.
    b. they were symbolic of papal authority.
    c. he needed the wealth they would bring.
    d. they were a burden on the state.

19. The Scandinavian countries were most influenced by the religious beliefs of
    a. Martin Luther.
    b. John Knox.
    c. Olaus Petri.
    d. the Jesuits.

20. A vow of the Jesuit order making it uniquely different from others was
    a. poverty.
    b. chastity.
    c. obedience to the pope.
    d. pacifism.

21. Luther's German translation of the New Testament
    a. proved that the state was supreme over the church.
    b. convinced women that they had no constructive role in life.
    c. democratized religion.
    d. turned the common people away from the church.

22. The marriage of Maxmilian of Habsburg and Mary of Burgundy in 1477 was a decisive event in early modern history in that
    a. Austria became an international power.
    b. France emerged as the leading continental power.
    c. England became tied to Spain.
    d. German principalities became tied to Austria.

23. The man who wrote *The Institutes of the Christian Religion* and did the most to internationalize Protestantism was
    a. John Knox.
    b. Martin Luther.
    c. Ulrich Zwingli.
    d. John Calvin.

24. Henry VIII of England's divorce from his wife Catherine was complicated by the fact that Catherine's nephew was
    a. the pope.
    b. the emperor, Charles V.
    c. the king of France.
    d. the leader of the English Parliament.

25. The *Index of Prohibited Books* was published by
    a. the Calvinist government of Geneva.
    b. the princes who supported Luther.
    c. the Sacred Congregation of the Holy Office of the pope.
    d. the Anabaptists.

Chapter 15

The Age of European Expansion and Religious Wars

Learning Objectives

After reading and studying this chapter you should be able to:

1. explain the causes and consequences of the religious wars in France, the Netherlands, and Germany.

2. discuss factors that led to the European discovery and conquest of other lands.

3. explain how Europeans influenced the peoples of other continents and how having overseas possessions affected Europe.

4. explain these topics: Portugal's role in the Age of Exploration and Discovery, the significance of advanced technology in Europe's expansion, and the consequences of the Habsburg-Valois and Thirty Years' Wars.

Chapter Summary

This chapter is about war, powerful kings, and European territorial expansion. The growth of royal power and the consolidation of the state in Spain, France, and England accompanied and supported world exploration and a long period of European war.

The Portuguese were the first to push out into the Atlantic, but it was Spain, following close behind, that built a New World empire that provided the economic basis for a period of Spanish supremacy in European affairs. In the short run, Spanish gold and silver from the New World made the Spanish Netherlands the financial and manufacturing center of Europe, and Spain became Europe's greatest military power. In the long run, however, overseas expansion ruined the Spanish economy, created massive European inflation, and brought the end of Spain's empire in Europe.

The attempts by Catholic monarchs to re-establish European religious unity and by both Catholic and Protestant monarchs to establish strong centralized states led to many wars among the European states. Spain's attempt to keep religious and political unity within her empire led to a long war in the Netherlands—a war that pulled England over to the side of the Protestant Dutch. There was bitter civil war in France, which finally came to an end with the reign of Henry of Navarre and the Edict of Nantes in 1598. The Thirty Years' War in Germany (1618 to 1648) had both religious and political roots, and left that area a political and economic shambles.

245

The sixteenth century also saw a vast increase in witch-hunting and the emergence of modern racism, sexism, and skepticism. Generally, the power and status of women in this period did not change. Protestantism meant a more positive attitude toward marriage, but the revival of the idea that women were the source of evil and the end of the religious orders for women caused them to become increasingly powerless in society. North American slavery and racism had their origins in the labor problems in America and in Christian and Muslim racial attitudes. Skepticism was an intellectual reaction to the fanaticism of both Protestants and Catholics and a sign of things to come, while the Renaissance tradition was carried on by Shakespeare's work in early-sixteenth-century England.

Study Outline

Use this outline to preview the chapter before you read a particular section in your textbook and then as a self-check to test your reading comprehension after you have read the chapter section.

    I. Politics, religion, and war
      A. The Spanish-French wars ended in 1559 with a Spanish victory, leading to a variety of wars centering on religious and national issues.
          1. These wars used bigger armies and gunpowder, and led to the need for administrative reorganization.
          2. Governments had to use various propaganda devices, including the printing press, to arouse public opinion.
          3. The Peace of Westphalia (1648) ended religious wars but also ended the idea of a unified Christian society.
      B. The origins of difficulties in France (1515-1559)
          1. By 1500, France was recovering from plague and disorder, and the nobility began to lose power.
          2. The French kings, such as Francis I and Henry II, continued the policies of centralization and were great patrons of Renaissance art but spent more money than they raised.
          3. The wars between France and Emperor Charles V—the Habsburg-Valois wars—were also costly.
          4. To raise money, Francis sold public offices and signed the Concordat of Bologna (1516), in which he recognized the supremacy of the papacy in return for the right to appoint French bishops.
            a. This settlement established Catholicism as the state religion in France.
            b. It also perpetuated corruption within the French church.
            c. The corruption made Calvinism attractive to Christians eager for reform: some clergy and members of the middle and artisan classes.
      C. Religious riots and civil war in France (1559-1589)
          1. The French nobility, many of them Calvinist, attempted to regain power over a series of weak monarchs.
          2. Frequent religious riots symbolized the struggle for power in the upper classes and serious religious concerns among the lower classes.
          3. The Saint Bartholomew's Day massacre of Calvinists in 1572 led to the War of the Three Henrys, a damaging conflict for secular power.

4. King Henry IV's Edict of Nantes (1598) saved France from further civil war by allowing Protestants to worship.

D. The Netherlands under Charles V
   1. The Low Countries were part of the Habsburg empire and enjoyed commercial success and relative autonomy.
   2. In 1556 Charles V abdicated and divided his empire between his brother, Ferdinand, and his son, King Philip of Spain.

E. The revolt of the Netherlands (1556-1587)
   1. Calvinism took deep root among the merchants and financiers.
   2. Regent Margaret attempted to destroy Protestantism by establishing the Inquisition in the Netherlands.
   3. She also raised taxes, causing those who opposed the repression of Calvinism to unite with those who opposed the taxes.
   4. Popular support for Protestantism led to the destruction of many Catholic churches.
   5. The duke of Alva and his Spanish troops were sent by Philip II to crush the disturbances in the Low Countries.
   6. Alva's brutal actions only inflamed the religious war, which raged from 1568 to 1578.
   7. The Low Countries were finally split into the Spanish Netherlands in the south, under the control of the Spanish Habsburgs, and the independent United Provinces of the Netherlands in the north.
      a. The north was Protestant and ruled by the commercial aristocracy.
      b. The south was Catholic and ruled by the landed nobility.
   8. Elizabeth I of England supported the northern, or Protestant, cause as a safeguard against Spain attacking England.
      a. The wars in the Low Countries had badly hurt the English economy.
      b. She had her rival Mary, Queen of Scots, beheaded.

F. Philip II and the Spanish Armada
   1. Philip II of Spain lived at a monastery called the Escorial; here he had a palace but he spent much time in prayer.
   2. Philip II sought pleasure in his youth but in older age sought prayer—but he did not believe that the state should dictate morals.
      a. Like his times, he did not believe in religious toleration.
   3. Phillip II supported Mary Queen of Scotland's plot to kill Elizabeth of England so he planned an invasion of England.
      a. He wanted to keep England in the Catholic fold.
      b. He believed he would never conquer the Dutch unless he defeated England first.
   4. His plan was hurt by his ill health and fear of Turkish attack.
   5. The destruction of the Spanish Armada of 1588 did not mean the end of the war, but it did prevent Philip from forcibly unifying western Europe.
   6. In 1609, Philip III agreed to a truce, recognizing the independence of the United Provinces.

G. The Thirty Years' War (1618-1648)
   1. Protestant Bohemian revolt over religious freedom led to war in Germany.

2. The Bohemian phase (1618-1625) was characterized by civil war in Bohemia between the Catholic League and the Protestant Union.
    a. The Bohemians fought for religious liberty and independence from Habsburg rule.
    b. Ferdinand II wiped out Protestantism in Bohemia.
3. The Danish phase of the war (1625-1629) led to further Catholic victory.
4. The Swedish phase of the war (1630-1635) ended the Habsburg plan to unite Germany.
5. The French phase (1635-1648) ended with a destroyed Germany and an independent Netherlands.
    a. The "Peace of Westphalia" recognized the independent authority of the German princes.
    b. The treaties allowed France to intervene at will in German affairs.
    c. They also denied the pope the right to participate in German religious affairs.

H. Germany after the Thirty Years' War
1. The war was economically disastrous for Germany.
2. The war led to agricultural depression in Germany, which in turn encouraged a return to serfdom for many peasants.

II. Discovery, reconnaissance, and expansion (1450-1650)
A. Overseas exploration and conquest
1. The outward expansion of Europe began with the Viking voyages, and then the Crusades, but the presence of the Ottoman Turks in the East frightened the Europeans and forced their attention westward.
2. Political centralization in Spain, France, and England prepared the way for expansion.
3. The Portuguese, under the leadership of Prince Henry the Navigator, pushed south from North Africa.
    a. By 1500 Portugal controlled the flow of gold to Europe.
    b. Diaz, da Gama, and Cabral established trading routes to India.
    c. The Portuguese gained control of the Indian trade by overpowering Muslim forts in India.

B. Technological stimuli to exploration
1. The development of the cannon aided European expansion.
2. New sailing and navigational developments, such as the caravel ship, the magnetic compass, and the astrolabe, also aided the expansion.

C. The explorers' motives
1. The desire to Christianize the Muslims and pagan peoples played a central role in European expansion.
2. Limited economic and political opportunity for upper-class men in Spain led to emigration.
3. Government encouragement was also important.
4. Renaissance curiosity caused people to seek out new worlds.
5. Spices were another important incentive.
6. The economic motive—the quest for material profit—was the basic reason for European exploration and expansion.

D. The problem of Christopher Columbus
1. Until recently most historians agreed with Morison that Columbus was a great hero who carried Christian civilization to the new world.
2. Now historians note that he enslaved and killed Indians and that he did not discover a new continent; others claim that he destroyed an earthly paradise.
3. In reality, Columbus was a deeply religious man; he saw a link between the expulsion of the Moors and his task as Christian missionary.
   a. But his principal object was to find a direct route to Asia.
   b. When it was clear that he had not found great new spice markets, he turned to setting up a government in the islands.
   c. Thus he paved the way for Spanish imperial administration.

III. Later explorers
A. The people of Columbus's era believed that he had discovered a "New World."
1. Spanish exploitation in the Caribbean led to the destruction of the Indian population.
   a. The population of Hispaniola declined from 100,000 to 300; Indians and black Africans were imported to continue the mining.
2. In 1519 Magellan sailed southwest across the Atlantic for Charles V of Spain; he claimed the "Western Isles" for Spain, and proved the earth was round and larger than Columbus had estimated.
3. Cortez conquered the Aztec Empire and founded Mexico City as the capital of New Spain.
4. Pizarro crushed the Inca empire in Peru and opened the Potosí mines, which became the richest silver mines in the New World.
5. The Low Countries, particularly the cities of Antwerp and Amsterdam, had been since medieval times the center of European trade.
   a. The Dutch East India Company became the major organ of Dutch imperialism.
   b. The Dutch West India Company gained control of much of the African and American trade.
6. France and England made sporadic efforts at exploration and settlement.
B. The economic effects of Spain's discoveries in the New World
1. Enormous amounts of American gold and silver poured into Spain in the sixteenth century.
2. It is probable that population growth and not the flood of American bullion caused inflation in Spain.
3. European inflation hurt the poor the most.
C. Colonial administration
1. The Spanish monarch divided his new world into four viceroyalties, each with a viceroy and *audiencia,* or board of judges, that served as an advisory council and judicial body.
2. The *intendants* were royal officials responsible directly to the monarch.
3. The Spanish acted on the mercantilist principle that the colonies existed for the financial benefit of the mother country.
   a. The Crown claimed the *quinto,* one-fifth of all precious metals mined in South America.
   b. The development of native industries was discouraged.

4. Portuguese administration in Brazil was similar to Spain's.
    a. The crown of Portugal and Spain became one in 1580, and Spanish administrative forms were introduced.
    b. Portugal's mercantilist policies constrained Brazil's growth—but black slave labor led to much cultivation of coffee, cotton, and sugar.
    c. One unique feature of colonial Brazil was the thorough mixture of the races.

IV. Changing attitudes
  A. The wars of religion had bred confusion, uncertainty, and insecurity; it was an age in which sexism, racism, and skepticism began to take on modern forms.
  B. The status of women declined.
    1. Literature on women and marriage called for a subservient wife, whose household was her first priority, and a protective, firm-ruling, and loyal husband.
        a. Catholic marriages could not be dissolved, while Protestants held that divorce and remarriage were possible.
        b. Women did not lose their identity or meaningful work, but their subordinate status did not change.
        c. Elizabeth Hardwick's success in real estate illustrates that some women became rich and powerful.
    2. Prostitution was common, and brothels were licensed.
    3. Protestant reformers believed that convents were antifeminist and that women would find freedom in marriage and sex.
    4. With the closing of convents, marriage became virtually the only occupation for upper-class Protestant women.
  C. The great European witch hunt
    1. Growth in religion and the advent of religious struggle led to a rise in the belief in the evil power of witches.
    2. The thousands of people executed as witches represent society's drift toward social and intellectual conformity.
    3. Witch-hunting reflects widespread misogyny and a misunderstanding of women.
  D. European slavery and the origins of American racism
    1. Black slavery originated with the end of white slavery (1453) and the widespread need for labor, particularly in the new sugar-producing settlements.
    2. Beginning in 1518 Africans were brought to America to replace Indian slavery; this was promoted by the missionary las Casas who wished to protect Indians.
    3. African kings and dealers sold black slaves to European merchants; the first slaves were brought to Brazil.
    4. Settlers brought to the Americas the racial attitudes they had absorbed in Europe from Christianity and Islam, which by and large depicted blacks as primitive and inferior.

V. Literature and art
  A. Religious war and overseas expansion is mirrored in an explosion of intellectual and artistic activity.
  B. The origins of modern skepticism is found in the essays of Montaigne.
    1. Skeptics doubt whether definitive knowledge is ever attainable.

2. Montaigne is the best representative of early modern skepticism and a forerunner of modern attitudes.
   a. In the *Essays* he advocated open-mindedness, tolerance, and rejection of dogmatism.
   b. He rejected the claim that one culture may be superior to another, and he inaugurated an era of doubt.
C. Elizabethan and Jacobean literature
   1. Shakespeare's understanding of human psychology was rooted in his appreciation of classical culture, individualism, and humanism.
      a. His "history plays" were very popular.
      b. His tragedies—Hamlet, Othello, and Macbeth—explore human problems such as ambition, sin, and revenge.
   2. The *Authorized Bible* of King James I *(King James Bible)* is a masterpiece of English vernacular writing.
D. Baroque art and music
   1. In the late sixteenth century, the papacy and the Jesuits encouraged the growth of an emotional, exuberant art intended to appeal to the senses and kindle the faith of ordinary churchgoers.
   2. The baroque style took definite shape in Italy after 1600 and developed with exceptional vigor in Catholic countries.
      a. Rubens developed a sensuous, colorful style of painting characterized by animated figures and monumental size.
      b. In music the baroque style reached its culmination with Bach.

Review Questions

Check your understanding of this chapter by answering the following questions.

1. Describe the Portuguese explorations. Who were the participants and what were their motives?

2. What role did Antwerp and Amsterdam play in international commerce?

3. Why was there such severe inflation in the sixteenth century?

4. What role did technology play in European expansion?

5. What were the major reasons for European expansion in the fifteenth and sixteenth centuries?

6. What were the causes and consequences of the French civil war of 1559 to 1589? Was the war chiefly a religious or a political event?

7. What were the origins and the outcome of the war between the Netherlands and Spain in the late sixteenth and early seventeenth centuries?

8. What were the circumstances surrounding Elizabeth's decision to aid the United Provinces in their war against Spain? What was the Spanish reaction?

9. Why did Catholic France side with the Protestants in the Thirty Years' War?

10. What were the political, religious, and economic consequences of the Thirty Years' War in Europe?

11. What was the social status of women between 1560 and 1648?

12. What do the witch hunts tell us about social attitudes toward women?

13. What were the origins of North American racism?

14. What is skepticism? Why did faith and religious certainty begin to come to an end in the first part of the seventeenth century?

15. What were the major literary masterpieces of this age? What were the themes of Shakespeare's plays?

16. Describe the baroque style.

Study-Review Exercises

Define the following key concepts and terms.

mercantilism

inflation

sexism

racism

skepticism

misogyny

baroque

Identify and explain the significance of the following people and terms.
politiques

Elizabeth I of England

Huguenots

Philip II of Spain

Prince Henry the Navigator

Michel de Montaigne

Christopher Columbus

Bartholomew Diaz

Hernando Cortez

Habsburg-Valois wars

quinto

audiencia

corregidores

Thirty Years' War

defeat of the Spanish Armada

Concordat of Bologna

Peace of Westphalia

Saint Bartholomew's Day massacre

War of the Three Henrys

Edict of Nantes

Test your understanding of the chapter by providing the correct answers.

1. The war that brought destruction and political fragmentation to Germany. _____

2. The Spanish explorer who conquered the Aztecs. _____

3. The law of 1598 that granted religious freedom to French Protestants. _____

4. Spain's golden century. _____

5. The king of Sweden who intervened in the Thirty Years' War. _____

6. After 1551, the seven northern provinces of the Netherlands were called _____

7. The city that became the financial capital of Europe by 1600. _____

8. The monarch of Britain at the time of the Spanish Armada. _____

9. The idea that nothing is completely knowable. _____

10. The emperor who divided the Habsburg empire into two parts. _____

11. The 1516 compromise between church and state in France. _____

12. The first European country to establish sea routes to the east. _____

Major Political Ideas

1. Much of this chapter is about "expansionism" or what came to be called "imperialism." What was the cause of this European movement westward? Were the causes largely political, religious, or economic—or something else? Use Columbus as an example.

2. *Misogyny* and *racism* are "political" terms in that they help to explain the distribution of power within society. Discuss each of these terms in the context of the sixteenth and seventeenth centuries.

3. It is suggested in this chapter that Calvinism contributed to Dutch ideas of national independence. Explain the connection. Do you agree?

Issues for Essays and Discussion

The age of European expansion and religious wars was a period of both the breakdown and reconstruction of society. Describe this process of breakdown and reconstruction by discussing civil war, international war, and overseas expansion from about 1450 to about 1560. What were the causes of these events? What country (or countries) emerged from this era as the most powerful?

Interpretation of Visual Sources

Study the sixteenth-century print *To Purify the Church*. Describe the scene by identifying the precise actions of the participants. What specific types of offensive references are being destroyed? What are the ideas behind this "purification"?

Geography

1. On Outline Map 15.1 provided, and using Map 15.1 and Map 15.2 in the textbook as a reference, mark the following: the exploration routes of da Gama, Columbus, and Magellan, Cueta, the Cape of Good Hope, Amsterdam, Guinea, Calicut, Cape Horn, London, Lisbon, Goa, Antwerp, Mexico City, Moluccas.

2. Using Map 15.4 in the textbook as a reference, identify the areas that were the main sources of African slaves and the main areas of slave importation into the New World. Do the latter areas illustrate the economic origins of the slave trade?

3. On Outline Map 15.3 provided, and using Map 15.3 in the textbook as a reference, mark the following: the areas under Spanish Habsburg control, the areas under Austrian Habsburg control, Prussian lands, the United Netherlands, the German states, the boundary of the old Holy Roman Empire, Swedish possessions, Madrid, Lisbon, Vienna, Amsterdam.

Outline Map 15.1

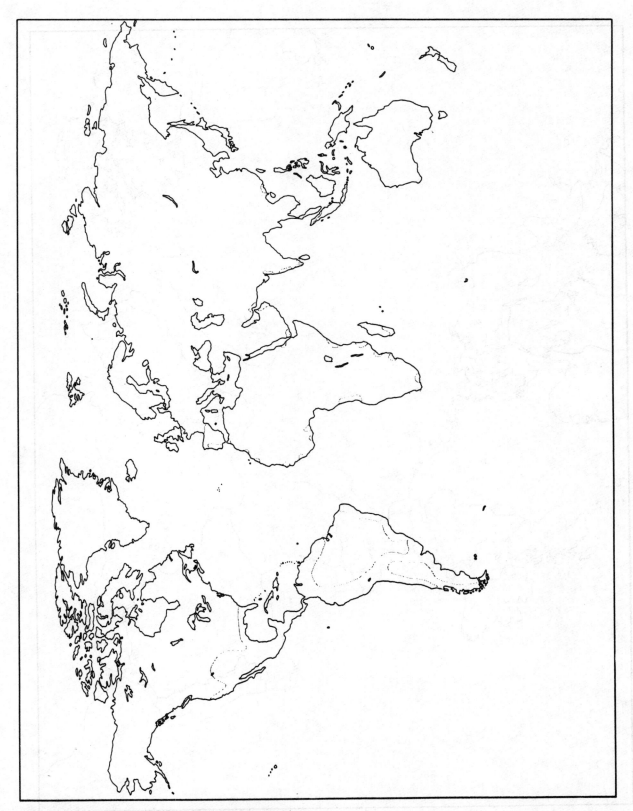

Outline Map 15.3

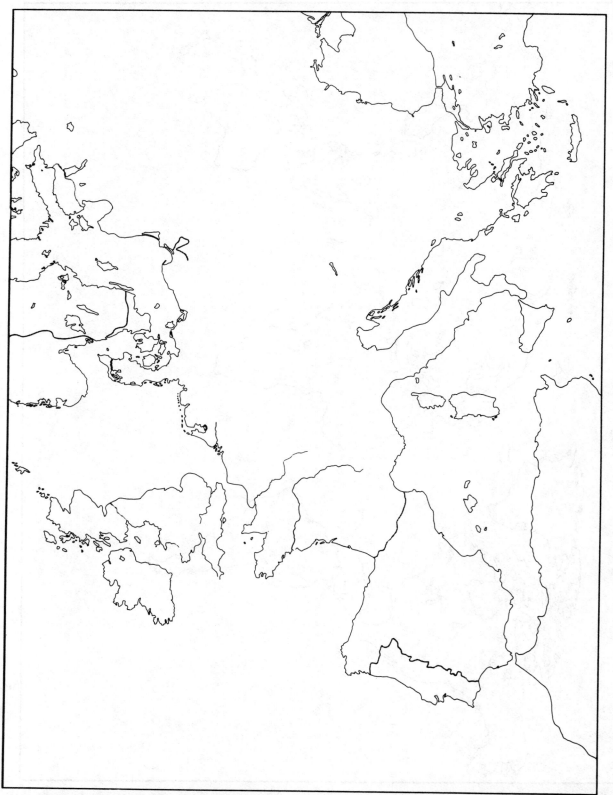

Understanding History Through the Arts

1. What did the Low Countries contribute to the arts? To investigate this subject, start with W. Gaunt, *Flemish Cities, Their History and Art* (1969), and O. Benesch, *The Art of the Renaissance in Northern Europe* (1945). See also E. Cammaerts, *The Treasure-House of Belgium* (1924).

2. What was the art of the New World like? For the arts of America prior to the European discoveries, see S. K. Lothorp et al., *Pre-Columbian Art* (1957), and J. E. Thompson, *The Rise and Fall of Maya Civilization* (1954).

Problems for Further Investigation

1. Was Christopher Columbus a Christian idealist or a Western exploiter? Begin your investigation with the pamphlet by A. W. Crosby, *The Columbian Voyages, the Columbian Exchange, and Their Historians* (1990).

2. Who were the important women of this period? There were a number of extremely important and powerful sixteenth-century women whose biographies make for fascinating reading: R. Roeder, *Catherine de Medici and the Lost Revolution** (1937); J. E. Neal, *Queen Elizabeth I** (1934, 1966); and A. Fraser, *Mary Queen of Scots** (1969). An interesting seventeenth-century woman is Gustavus Adolphus's daughter, whose life is told in G. Masson, *Queen Christina* (1968). N. Harvey, *The Rose and the Thorn* (1977) is an account of the lives and times of Mary and Margaret Tudor.

3. To examine the sources of racism, see D. B. Davis, *Slavery and Human Progress* (1984), and J. L. Watson, ed., *Asian and African Systems of Slavery* (1980) and G. M. Frederickson, *The Arrogance of Race* (1988).

4. Why were such severe religious wars fought in this era? Some of the problems faced in studying the religious conflict in France are discussed in J. H. M. Sahnon, *The French Wars of Religion** (1967). Anyone interested in research on the Thirty Years' War should begin with S. H. Steinberg, *The Thirty Years' War and the Conflict for European Hegemony, 1600-1660** (1966), and R. G. Asch, *The Thirty Years' War: The Holy Roman Empire and Europe* (1997).

---

*Available in paperback.

Self-Test Multiple-Choice Questions

<u>Do</u> <u>not</u> assume that these questions will appear on any examination. It is recommended that you <u>not</u> memorize these questions, but use them only as a self-test. Answers are at the end of this book.

1. Which of the following was a motive for Portuguese exploration in the late fifteenth and sixteenth centuries?
   a. The search for gold
   b. The conversion of peoples to the Islamic religion
   c. The discovery of sea routes to North America
   d. The conquest of Constantinople

2. Beginning in 1581, the northern Netherlands revolted against their political overlord, which was
   a. France.
   b. Spain.
   c. Elizabeth I of England.
   d. Florence.

3. North American racist attitudes toward African blacks originated in
   a. South America.
   b. Spain.
   c. France.
   d. England.

4. In the Thirty Years' War, France supported
   a. the German Catholics.
   b. the Holy Roman Emperor.
   c. Spain.
   d. the German Protestants.

5. Which of the following statements about the Spanish Armada of 1588 is *false*?
   a. It was the beginning of a long war with England.
   b. It failed in its objective.
   c. It prevented Phillip II from reimposing unity on western Europe by force.
   d. It made possible Spanish conquest of the Netherlands.

6. The nation that considered itself the international defender of Catholicism was
   a. France.
   b. Spain.
   c. Italy.
   d. England.

7. Columbus, like many of his fellow explorers, was principally motivated by
   a. a desire to discover India.
   b. a desire to Christianize the Americans.
   c. the desire of Spain to control the New World.
   d. the Spanish need to control the Mediterranean.

8. The earliest known explorers of North America were
   a. the Spanish.
   b. the Vikings.
   c. the Italians.
   d. the English.

9. Which of the following statements describes a feature of Spanish colonial policy?
   a. The New World was divided into four viceroyalties.
   b. Native industries were established.
   c. Each territory had local officials, or *corregidores,* who held judicial and military powers.
   d. The Spanish crown had only indirect and limited control over colonies.

10. To gain control of the spice trade of the Indian Ocean, the Portuguese had to defeat
    a. Spain.
    b. England.
    c. the Muslims.
    d. France.

11. The main contribution of Cortez and Pizarro to Spain was
    a. the tapping of the rich silver resources of Mexico and Peru.
    b. the Christianizing of the New World peoples.
    c. the further exploration of the Pacific Ocean.
    d. the discovery of South Africa.

12. The flow of huge amounts of gold and silver from the New World caused
    a. serious inflation in Spain and the rest of Europe.
    b. the Spanish economy to become dependent on New World gold and silver.
    c. the suffering of the poor because of the dramatic rise in food prices.
    d. Spain's economic strength and dominance in Europe.

13. By which treaty did the king of France, Francis I, recognize the supremacy of the papacy?
    a. The Treaty of Westphalia
    b. The treaty of Cateau-Cambrésis
    c. The Concordat of Bologna
    d. The Edict of Nantes

14. France was saved from religious anarchy when religious principles were set aside for political necessity by King
    a. Henry III.
    b. Francis I.
    c. Henry IV of Navarre.
    d. Charles IX.

15. Calvinism was appealing to the middle classes for each of the following reasons *except*
    a. its heavy moral emphasis.
    b. its stress on leisure and ostentatious living.
    c. its intellectual emphasis.
    d. its approval of any job well done, hard work, and success.

16. The vast palace of the Spanish monarchs, built under the direction of Philip II, was called
    a. Versailles.
    b. the Escorial.
    c. Tournai.
    d. Hampton Court.

17. The Treaty of Westphalia, which ended the Thirty Years' War
    a. further strengthened the Holy Roman Empire.
    b. completely undermined the Holy Roman Empire as a viable state.
    c. maintained that only Catholicism and Lutheranism were legitimate religions.
    d. refused to recognize the independence of the United Provinces of the Netherlands.

18. Who among the following best represents early modern skepticism?
    a. Las Casas
    b. James I
    c. Calvin
    d. Montaigne

19. The Spanish missionary Las Casas convinced Charles V to import Africans to Brazil because of all the following *except*
    a. the enslavement of Africans seemed more acceptable to the church.
    b. he believed they could endure better than the Indians.
    c. the native Indians were not durable enough under such harsh conditions.
    d. the native Indians revolted and refused to work as slave labor.

20. The Portuguese explorer who first reached India was
    a. Bartholomew Diaz.
    b. Prince Henry the Navigator.
    c. Vasco da Gama.
    d. Hernando Cortez.

21. The style of art popular in late-eighteenth-century Europe was called
    a. Elizabethan.
    b. Jacobean.
    c. skepticism.
    d. baroque.

22. The appearance of gunpowder in Europe
    a. made the common soldier inferior to the gentleman soldier.
    b. changed the popular belief that warfare bettered the individual.
    c. eliminated the need for governments to use propaganda to convince their people to support war.
    d. had little effect on the nature of war.

23. The ten southern provinces of the Netherlands, known as the Spanish Netherlands, became the future
    a. Netherlands.
    b. Bohemia.
    c. Belgium.
    d. Schleswig.

24. The Thirty Years' War was fought primarily
    a. on German soil.
    b. in France.
    c. in eastern Europe.
    d. in Spain.

25. The Ottoman capture of Constantinople in 1453 was significant in the history of slavery and racism in that it
    a. introduced the concept of slavery to the Christian European world.
    b. ended the transport of black slaves to Europe.
    c. caused Europeans to turn to sub-Saharan Africa for their slaves.
    d. ushered in a flow of slaves from the Indies.

Chapter 16

Absolutism and Constitutionalism in Western Europe (ca 1589-1715)

Learning Objectives

After reading and studying this chapter you should be able to:

1. discuss factors that led to the transition from feudalism to absolutism in western Europe in the sixteenth and seventeenth centuries.

2. distinguish between absolutism in England and France in the sixteenth and seventeenth centuries.

3. explain how Spain lost its relatively short-lived European hegemony.

4. describe how and why the seventeenth century is considered the "golden age of the Netherlands."

Chapter Summary

The two most important forms of government to evolve in early modern times were the absolute monarchy and the constitutional state. This chapter examines how the political system of absolutism succeeded gloriously in France and faded dismally in England in the seventeenth century. Few kings have been as successful in establishing complete monarchical sovereignty as the great Sun King of France, Louis XIV. Louis gave Europe a masterful lesson on how to collaborate with the nobility to strengthen the monarchy and to reinforce the ancient aristocracy. He was a superb actor and propagandist, who built on the earlier achievements of Henry IV and Richelieu and used his magnificent palace of Versailles to imprison the French nobility in a beautiful golden cage. He succeeded in expanding France at the expense of the Habsburgs, and his patronage of the arts helped form the great age of French classicism. However, the economic progress he first made was later checked by his policy of revoking religious toleration.

While the France of Louis was the classic model of absolutism as the last phase of an historic feudal society, Spain was the classic case of imperial decline. By 1600 Spain was in trouble, and by 1700 it was no longer a major European power. Not only did the silver and labor of America run out, but this great American wealth ruined the Spanish economic and social structure. War with the Dutch, the English, and the French also helped turn Spain into a backwater of Europe.

England and the United Provinces of the Netherlands provide a picture of constitutionalism triumphing over absolutism. For England, the seventeenth century was a long period of political conflict, complete with a bitter civil war and a radical experiment with republicanism. The causes of this era of conflict were varied, but it is clear that by 1689 the English army and Parliament had destroyed the Stuart quest for divine-right absolutism. The period that followed witnessed some important changes in the way the state was managed. The Netherlands was important not only because it became the financial and commercial center of Europe, but also because it provided the period's third model of political development—a loosely federated, middle-class constitutional state.

Study Outline

Use this outline to preview the chapter before you read a particular section in the textbook and then as a self-check to test your reading comprehension after you have read the chapter section.

I. Absolutism

    A. Absolutism defined

        1. In the absolutist state, sovereignty resided in kings—not the nobility or the parliament—who considered themselves responsible to God alone.

        2. Absolute kings created new state bureaucracies and standing armies, regulated all the institutions of government, and secured the cooperation of the nobility.

          a. Some historians deny that absolutism was a stage of development that followed feudalism, but, instead, was "administrative monarchy."

        3. The absolutist state foreshadowed the modern totalitarian state but lacked its total control over all aspects of its citizens' lives.

    B. The foundations of French absolutism: Henry IV, Sully, and Richelieu

        1. Henry IV cared for his people, lowered taxes, achieved peace, and curtailed the power of the nobility.

        2. His minister, Sully, brought about financial stability and economic growth.

        3. Cardinal Richelieu, the ruler of France under King Louis XIII, broke the power of the French nobility.

          a. His policy was total subordination of all groups and institutions to the French monarchy.

          b. He changed the royal council, leveled castles, and crushed aristocratic conspiracies.

          c. He established an efficient administrative system using *intendants*, who further weakened the local nobility.

          d. They delivered royal orders, recruited men for the army, collected taxes, and more.

        4. Through the Edict of Nantes, Henry IV and given religious freedom to Protestants (Huguenots) in 150 towns, but Louis XIII decided otherwise.

          a. He defeated the city of La Rochelle in 1628 and re-instituted the catholic mass.

          b. Richelieu and the French kings faced many urban protests over high taxes and food shortages.

          c. Local authorities usually let local riots "burn themselves out."

5. Under Richelieu, France sought to break Habsburg power.
   a. He supported the struggle of the Swedish king, Gustavus Adolphus, against the Habsburgs.
   b. He acquired land and influence in Germany.
6. Richelieu supported the new French Academy, which created a dictionary to standardize the French language.
7. The French government's ability to tax was severely limited by local rights and the tax-exempt status of much of the nobility and the middle class.
8. Mazarin continued Richelieu's centralizing policies, but these policies gave rise to a period of civil wars known as the Fronde.
   a. *Fronde* meant anyone who opposed the policies of the government.
   b. Many people of the aristocracy and the middle classes opposed government centralization and new taxes; rebellion was widespread.
   c. The conflicts hurt the economy and convinced the new king, Louis XIV, that civil war was destructive of social order and that absolute monarchy was the only alternative to anarchy.

II. The absolute monarchy of Louis XIV
   A. Louis XIV, the "Sun King," was a devout Catholic who believed that God had established kings as his rulers on earth.
   B. He feared the nobility and was successful in collaboration with them to enhance both aristocratic prestige and royal power.
   C. He made the court at Versailles a fixed institution and used it as a means of preserving royal power and as the center of French absolutism.
      1. The architecture and art of Versailles were a means of carrying out state policy—a way to overawe his subjects and foreign powers.
      2. The French language and culture became the international style.
      3. The court at Versailles was a device to undermine the power of the aristocracy by separating power from status.
      4. A centralized state, administered by a professional class taken from the bourgeoisie, was formed.
   D. Financial and economic management under Louis XIV: Colbert
      1. Mercantilism is a collection of governmental policies for the regulation of economic activities by and for the state.
      2. Louis XIV's finance minister, Colbert, tried to achieve a favorable balance of trade and make France self-sufficient so the flow of gold to other countries would be halted.
         a. Colbert encouraged French industry, enacted high foreign tariffs, and created a strong merchant marine.
         b. He hoped to make Canada part of a French empire.
         c. Though France's industries grew and the commercial classes prospered, its agricultural economy suffered under the burdens of heavy taxation, population decline, and poor harvests.
   E. The revocation of the Edict of Nantes
      1. In 1685, Louis revoked the Edict of Nantes—then destroyed Protestant churches and schools; many Protestants fled the country.
      2. Why? Because Louis XIV hated division within France—and because most people supported this policy.

III. French classicism in art and literature
   A. French classicism imitated and resembled the arts of the ancients and the Renaissance.
   B. Poussin best illustrates classical idealism in painting.
   C. Louis XIV was a patron of the composers Lully, Couperin, and Charpentier.
   D. The comedies of Molière and the tragedies of Racine best illustrate the classicism in French theater.

IV. Louis XIV's wars
   A. Louis kept France at war for 33 of the 54 years of his personal rule; the Marquis de Louvois created a professional army for Louis.
      1. The French army under Louis XIV was modern because the state, rather than the nobles, employed the soldiers.
         a. Louis himself took personal command of the army.
         b. Martinet created a rigid but effective system of training.
   B. Louis continued Richelieu's expansionist policy.
      1. In 1667, he invaded Flanders and gained twelve towns.
      2. By the treaty of Nijmegen (1678) he gained some Flemish towns and all of Franche-Comté.
      3. Strasbourg was taken in 1681 and Lorraine in 1684, but the limits of his expansion had been met.
      4. Louis fought the new Dutch king of England, William III, and the League of Augsburg in a war.
         a. The Banks of Amsterdam and England financed his enemies.
         b. Louis's heavy taxes fell on the peasants, who revolted.
      5. This led to the War of the Spanish Succession (1701-1713), which was over the issue of the succession to the Spanish throne: Louis claimed Spain but was opposed by the Dutch, English, Austrians, and Prussians.
         a. The war was also an attempt to preserve the balance of power in Europe and to check France's commercial power overseas.
         b. A Grand Alliance of the English, Dutch, Austrians, and Prussians was formed in 1701 to fight the French.
         c. Eugene of Savoy and Churchill of England led the alliance to victory over Louis.
         d. The war was concluded by the Peace of Utrecht in 1713, which forbade the union of France and Spain.
         e. The war ended French expansionism and left France on the brink of bankruptcy, with widespread misery and revolts.

V. The decline of absolutist Spain in the seventeenth century
   A. Spain had developed an absolutist monarchy but by the 1590s it was in decline.
      1. Fiscal disorder, political incompetence, the lack of a strong middle class, population decline, intellectual isolation, and psychological malaise contributed to its decline.
      2. The Dutch and English began to cut into Spain's trade monopolies.
      3. Spain's supply of silver began to decline, leading to de-evaluation and bankruptcy.
         a. Spain had only a tiny middle class—which had to face many obstacles to their businesses.
         b. Aristocrats were extravagant and their high rents drove the peasants from the land.
      4. Spanish kings lacked force of character and could not deal with all these problems.
   B. Philip IV's minister Olivares mistakenly thought that revival of war with the Dutch would solve Spain's problems; war with France followed—all bringing disaster for Spain.

C. The Treaty of the Pyrenees of 1659, which ended the French-Spanish wars, marked the end of Spain as a great power.
    1. Too much of Spain's past had been built on slavery and gold and silver.
    2. Cervantes's novel *Don Quixote* characterizes the impractical dreams of Spain.

VI. Constitutionalism in England and the Netherlands
  A. Constitutionalism defined
    1. It is the limitation of the state by law; under constitutionalism, the state must be governed according to law, not royal decree.
      a. It implies a balance between the power of the government and the rights of the subjects.
      b. A nation's constitution may be written or unwritten, but the government must respect it.
      c. Constitutional governments may be either republics or monarchies.
    2. Constitutional government is not the same as full democracy because not all of the people have the right to participate.
  B. The decline of royal absolutism in England (1603-1649)
    1. The Stuart kings of England lacked the political wisdom of Elizabeth I.
    2. James I was devoted to the ideal of rule by divine right.
    3. His absolutism ran counter to English belief.
    4. The House of Commons wanted a greater say in the government of the state.
      a. Increased wealth had produced a better educated House of Commons.
      b. Between 1603 and 1640, bitter squabbles erupted between the Crown and the Commons.
  C. The Protestant, or capitalist, ethic and the problem of religion in England
    1. Many English people, called Puritans, were attracted by the values of hard work, thrift, and self-denial implied by Calvinism.
    2. The Puritans, who were dissatisfied with the Church of England, saw James I as an enemy.
    3. Charles I and his archbishop, Laud, appeared to be pro-Catholic.
  D. The English Civil War (1642-1649)
    1. Charles I had ruled without Parliament for eleven years.
    2. A revolt in Scotland over the religious issue forced him to call a new Parliament into session to finance an army.
      a. The Commons passed an act compelling the king to summon Parliament every three years.
      b. It also impeached Archbishop Laud and abolished the House of Lords.
      c. Religious differences in Ireland led to a revolt there, but Parliament would not trust Charles with an army.
    3. Charles initiated military action against Parliament.
      a. The civil war (1642-1649) revolved around the issue of whether sovereignty should reside in the king or in Parliament.
      b. The problem was not resolved, but Charles was beheaded in 1649.
  E. Puritanical absolutism in England: Cromwell and the Protectorate
    1. With the execution of Charles I, kingship was abolished in 1649 and a commonwealth proclaimed.
      a. A commonwealth is a government without a king whose power rests in Parliament and a council of state.

   b. In fact, the army controlled the government; it wrote a constitution called the Instrument of Government which gave power to Cromwell.

  2. Oliver Cromwell, leader of the "New Model Army" that defeated the royalists, came from the gentry class that dominated the House of Commons.

  3. Cromwell's Protectorate became a military dictatorship, absolutist and puritanical.

   a. Cromwell allowed religious toleration for all Christians, except Roman Catholics, and savagely crushed the revolt in Ireland.

   b. He censored the press and closed the theaters.

   c. He regulated the economy according to mercantilist principles.

   d. The mercantilist navigation act that required English goods to be transported on English ships was a boon to the economy and led to a commercial war with the Dutch.

F. The restoration of the English monarchy

  1. The restoration of the Stuart kings in 1660 failed to solve the problems of religion and the relationship between King and Parliament.

   a. According to the Test Act of 1673, those who refused to join the Church of England could not vote, hold office, preach, teach, attend the universities, or assemble, but these restrictions could not be upheld.

   b. Charles II appointed a council of five men (the "Cabal") to serve as both his major advisers and as members of Parliament.

   c. The Cabal was the forerunner of the cabinet system, and it helped create good relations with the Parliament.

  2. Charles's pro-French policies led to a Catholic scare.

  3. James II, an avowed Catholic, violated the Test Act by appointing Catholics to government and university positions.

  4. Fear of a Catholic monarchy led to the expulsion of James II and the Glorious Revolution.

G. Cabinet government

  1. The "Glorious Revolution" that expelled James II and installed William and Mary on the throne ended the idea of divine-right monarchy.

   a. It was "glorious" in that there was no bloodshed.

   b. It established the principal that power was divided between king and Parliament.

  2. The Bill of Rights of 1689 established the principal that law was to be made in Parliament, that Parliament had to be called at least every three years, and that elections were to be free of Crown interference and the judiciary was to be independent of the Crown.

   a. The political philosophy of the Revolution was found in John Locke's work; Locke maintained that people set up government to protect life, liberty, and property.

   b. Locke's ideas that there are natural, or universal, rights played a strong role in eighteenth-century Enlightenment thought.

  3. In the cabinet system, which developed in the eighteenth century, both legislative and executive power are held by the leading ministers, who form the government.

H. The Dutch republic in the seventeenth century

  1. The Dutch republic, known as the United Provinces of the Netherlands, won its independence from Spain—as confirmed by the Peace of Westphalia in 1848.

   a. Dutch achievements in science, art, and literature were exceptional—a "golden age."

2. Power in the republic resided in the local Estates.
   a. The republic was a confederation: a weak union of strong provinces.
   b. The republic was based on values of thrift, frugality, and religious toleration, including that for Jews.
   c. Religious toleration fostered economic growth.
3. The fishing industry was the cornerstone of the Dutch economy—stimulating shipbuilding, a huge merchant marine, and other industries.
4. The Dutch East India Company was formed in 1602; it cut heavily into Portuguese trading in East Asia.
   a. The Dutch West India Company, founded in 1621, traded extensively in Latin America and Africa.
   b. Wages were high for all and most people ate well.
5. War with France and England in the 1670s hurt the United Provinces.

Review Questions

Check your understanding of this chapter by answering the following questions.

1. In what way does the French minister Richelieu symbolize absolutism? What were his achievements?

2. Why can it be said that the palace of Versailles was used as a device to ruin the nobility of France? Was Versailles a palace or a prison?

3. Define mercantilism. What were the mercantilist policies of the French minister Colbert?

4. Was the revocation of the Edict of Nantes an error on the part of Louis XIV?

5. What were the reasons for the fall of the Spanish Empire?

6. Discuss the foreign policy goals of Louis XIV. Was he successful?

7. Define absolutism. How does it differ from totalitarianism?

8. What was the impact of Louis XIV's wars on the French economy and French society?

9. What were the causes of the War of the Spanish Succession? What impact did William III of England have on European events after about 1689?

10. What is constitutionalism? How does it differ from a democratic form of government? From absolutism?

11. What were the attitudes and policies of James I that made him so unpopular with his subjects?

12. Who were the Puritans? Why did they come into conflict with James I?

13. What were the immediate and the long-range causes of the English Civil War of 1642-1649? What were the results?

14. Why did James II flee from England in 1688? What happened to the kingship at this point?

15. Were the events of 1688-1689 a victory for English democracy? Explain.

16. Why is it said that Locke was the spokesman for the liberal English Revolution of 1689 and for representative government?

17. Describe the Dutch system of government. How was it different from that of other western European states? What was unusual about the Dutch attitudes toward religious beliefs?

Study-Review Exercises

Define the following key concepts and terms.

sovereign

totalitarianism

absolutism

mercantilism

republicanism

constitutionalism

cabinet government

French classicism

quixotic

commonwealth

Identify and explain the significance of each of the following people and terms.

The French *intendants*

Sully

paulette

Fronde

Cardinal Richelieu

Richelieu's *généralités*

The French Academy

Louis XIV of France

Versailles

Molière

Racine

Poussin

Count-Duke of Olivares

Dutch Estates General

Dutch East India Company

Peace of Utrecht

Cabal of Charles II

Instrument of Government

Puritans

Oliver Cromwell

James II of England

English Bill of Rights

John Churchill

Philip II of Spain

Explain what each of these men believed about the placement of authority within society.
Cardinal Richelieu

James I of England

Thomas Hobbes

Louis XIV of France

John Locke

Sully

Explain what the following events were and why they were important.
revocation of the Edict of Nantes

Scottish revolt of 1640

War of the Spanish Succession

Glorious Revolution

English Civil War of 1642-1649

Test your understanding of the chapter by providing the correct answers.

1. The highest executive office of the Dutch republic. _____

2. Louis XIV's able minister of finance. _____

3. During the age of economic growth in Spain, a vast number of Spaniards *entered/left* religious orders.

4. For Louis XIV of France the War of the Spanish Succession was a *success/disaster*.

5. The Englishman who inflicted defeat on Louis XIV at Blenheim. _____

6. The archbishop whose goal was to enforce Anglican unity in England and Scotland. _____

7. He made the statement "From where do the merchant's profits come except from his own diligence and industry." _____

Major Political Ideas

1. What are the major characteristics of absolutism and how does it, as a political system, differ from totalitarianism?

2. What is constitutionalism? What is the source of power within a constitutional state? How does constitutionalism differ from absolutism?

3. In 1649 England declared itself a commonwealth, or republican form of government. What is a republican state? Where does power reside in such a state?

Issues for Essays and Discussion

1. The seventeenth century saw great political instability and change, during which some modern forms of political organization emerged. Why did political turmoil exist, what new concepts of politics and power emerged, who were the most important participants in this process, and how was stability achieved?

2. Compare and contrast the political development of France, the Netherlands, and England in the seventeenth century. Of these three states, which is the most "modern"?

Interpretation of Visual Sources

Study the reproduction of the woodcut entitled *The Spider and the Fly*. What is the message the author of this illustration seeks to convey? Does it make a political statement? In your opinion, is there any historical evidence set forth in this chapter to suggest that this print represents historical truth?

Geography

1. Study Map 16.3, "Seventeenth Century Dutch Commerce," in your textbook. Use the space below to describe and define the Dutch empire in terms of area-ports involved and products. Are there any geographical explanations for this mighty empire?

2. On Outline Map 16.1 provided, and using Map 16.1 in the textbook as a reference, mark the territory added to France as a result of the wars and foreign policy of King Louis XIV.
   a. Explain how each of the territories was acquired and from whom.
   b. What changes in the balance of power occurred as a result of the Treaty of Utrecht in 1713?

Outline Map 16.1

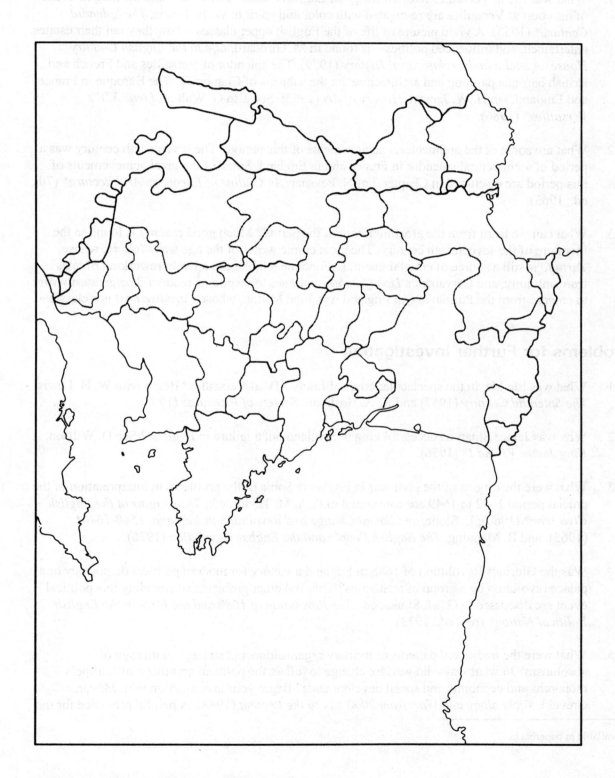

Understanding History Through the Arts

1. What was life at Versailles like? At the great English estates? Louis XIV and the magnificence of his court at Versailles are re-created with color and spirit in W. H. Lewis, *The Splendid Century** (1953). A vivid picture of life of the English upper classes—how they ran their estates, entertained, and influenced politics—is found in M. Girouard, *Life in the English Country House: A Social and Architectural History* (1979). The splendor of Versailles and French and British baroque painting and architecture are the subjects of Chapter 7, "The Baroque in France and England," in H. W. Janson, *History of Art* (1962). See also G. Walton, *Louis XIV's Versailles** (1986).

2. What are some of the architectural achievements of this period? The seventeenth century was a period of architectural splendor in France and in England. Some of the great achievements of this period are discussed in Chapter 7 of N. Pevsner, *An Outline of European Architecture** (7th ed., 1963).

3. What can we learn from the great literature of the period? Much good reading is found in the literature of the seventeenth century. The great comic writer of the age was Molière, whose *Tartuffe* is still a source of entertainment. LaFontaine's fables are a lively reworking of tales from antiquity, and Cervantes's *Don Quixote* continues to inspire its readers. The greatest writer to emerge from the Puritan age in England was John Milton, whose *Paradise Lost* is a classic.

Problems for Further Investigation

1. What was life like in the spectacular court of Louis XIV at Versailles? Begin with W. H. Lewis, *The Splendid Century* (1957) and K. A. Hoffman, *Society of Pleasures* (1997).

2. Why was James Stuart a successful king in Scotland but a failure in England? See D. Willson, *King James VI and I** (1956).

3. What were the origins of the civil war in England? Some of the problems in interpretation of the crucial period 1642 to 1649 are considered in P. A. M. Taylor, ed., *The Origins of the English Civil War** (1960); L. Stone, ed., *Social Change and Revolution in England, 1540-1640** (1965); and B. Manning, *The English People and the English Revolution* (1976).

4. Was the Glorious Revolution of 1688 in England a victory for modern political democracy or a palace revolution by a group of aristocrats? This and other problems surrounding this political event are discussed in G. M. Straka, ed., *The Revolution of 1688 and the Birth of the English Political Nation** (rev. ed., 1973).

5. What were the traditional patterns of military organization and strategy in this age of absolutism? In what ways did warfare change to reflect the political ambitions of Europe's monarchs and economic and social developments? Begin your investigation with M. van Creveld, *Technology and War, from 2000 B.C. to the Present* (1988). A helpful reference for the

---

*Available in paperback.

scholar of military history is R. Dupuy and T. Dupuy, *The Encyclopedia of Military History, from 3500 B.C. to the Present* (1982, 1990).

Self-Test Multiple-Choice Questions

<u>Do</u> <u>not</u> assume that these questions will appear on any examination. It is recommended that you <u>not</u> memorize these questions, but use them only as a self-test. Answers are at the end of this book.

1. Mercantilism
   a. was a military system.
   b. insisted on a favorable balance of trade.
   c. was adopted in England but not in France.
   d. claimed that state power was based on land armies.

2. French Protestants tended to be
   a. poor peasants.
   b. the power behind the throne of Louis XIV.
   c. a financial burden for France.
   d. clever business people.

3. The War of the Spanish Succession began when Charles II of Spain left his territories to
   a. the French heir.
   b. the Spanish heir.
   c. Eugene of Savoy.
   d. the archduke of Austria.

4. Which of the following cities was the commercial and financial capital of Europe in the seventeenth century?
   a. London
   b. Hamburg
   c. Paris
   d. Amsterdam

5. Of the following, the country most centered on middle-class interests was
   a. England.
   b. Spain.
   c. France.
   d. the Netherlands.

6. Which of the following Englishmen was a Catholic?
   a. James II
   b. Oliver Cromwell
   c. Archbishop Laud
   d. William III

7. Which of the following is a characteristic of an absolute state?

    a. Sovereignty embodied in the representative assembly
    b. Bureaucracies solely accountable to the middle classes
    c. A strong voice expressed by the nobility
    d. Permanent standing armies

8.   Cardinal Richelieu's most notable accomplishment was
    a. the creation of a strong financial system for France.
    b. the creation of a highly effective administrative system.
    c. winning the total support of the Huguenots.
    d. allying the Catholic church with the government.

9.   The statement "There are no privileges and immunities which can stand against a divinely appointed king" forms the basis of the
    a. Stuart notion of absolutism.
    b. Stuart notion of constitutionalism.
    c. English Parliament's notion of democracy.
    d. English Parliament's notion of constitutionalism.

10   The English Long Parliament
    a. enacted legislation supporting absolutism.
    b. supported the Catholic tendencies of Charles I.
    c. supported Charles I as a military leader.
    d. enacted legislation against absolutism.

11.   Cromwell's government is best described as a
    a. constitutional state.
    b. democratic state.
    c. military dictatorship.
    d. monarchy.

12.   Absolute monarchs secured mastery over the nobility by all of the following *except*
    a. the creation of a standing army.
    b. the creation of a state bureaucracy.
    c. coercive actions.
    d. regulating religious groups.

13.   Cardinal Richelieu consolidated the power of the French monarchy by doing all of the following *except*
    a. destroying the castles of the nobility.
    b. ruthlessly treating conspirators who threatened the monarchy.
    c. keeping nobles from gaining high government offices.
    d. eliminating the *intendant* system of local government.

14. One way in which Louis XIV controlled the French nobility was by
    a. maintaining standing armies in the countryside to crush noble uprisings.
    b. requiring the presence of the major noble families at Versailles for at least part of the year.
    c. periodically visiting the nobility in order to check on their activities.
    d. forcing them to participate in a parliamentary assembly.

15. The French army under Louis XIV
    a. had no standardized uniforms and weapons.
    b. lived off the countryside.
    c. had an ambulance corps to care for the troops.
    d. had no system for recruitment, training, or promotion.

16. The Peace of Utrecht in 1713
    a. shrunk the size of the British Empire significantly.
    b. represented the balance-of-power principle in action.
    c. enhanced Spain's position as a major power in Europe.
    d. marked the beginning of French expansionist policy.

17. The downfall of Spain in the seventeenth century can be blamed on
    a. weak and ineffective monarchs.
    b. an overexpansion of industry and trade.
    c. the growth of slave labor in America.
    d. the rise of a large middle class.

18. When Archbishop Laud tried to make the Presbyterian Scots accept the Anglican *Book of Common Prayer*, the Scots
    a. revolted.
    b. reluctantly accepted the archbishop's directive.
    c. ignored the directive.
    d. heartily adopted the new prayerbook.

19. Who among the following was a proponent of the idea that the purpose of government is to protect life, liberty, and property?
    a. Thomas Hobbes
    b. William of Orange
    c. John Locke
    d. Edmund Burke

20. After the United Provinces of the Netherlands won independence from Spain, their government could best be described as
    a. a strong monarchy.
    b. a centralized parliamentary system.
    c. a weak union of strong provinces.
    d. a democracy.

21. The Dutch economy was based on
    a. fishing, world trade, and banking.
    b. silver mining in Peru.
    c. export of textiles.
    d. a moral and religious disdain of wealth.

22. Dutch economic decline began with
    a. the end of the War of the Spanish Succession.
    b. the formation of the Dutch East India Company.
    c. its practice of religious toleration.
    d. the adoption of the ideas of John Calvin.

23. During the administration of Robert Walpole in Britain, the idea developed that
    a. the monarch was absolute.
    b. the cabinet should be replaced by a legislative parliament.
    c. the king's chief minister be known as the *stadholder*.
    d. the cabinet be responsible to the House of Commons.

24. The Amstel River was the major link between which of the following cities and its world trading system?
    a. London
    b. Amsterdam
    c. Paris
    d. Amiens

25. Which of the following is a book by Cervantes that has as its hero an idealistic but impractical soldier?
    a. *Don Quixote*
    b. *Tartuffe*
    c. *Te Deum*
    d. *Phèdre*

Chapter 17

Absolutism in Eastern Europe to 1740

Learning Objectives

After reading and studying this chapter you should be able to:

1. describe how "eastern absolutism" worked and why it came about.

2. explain who ruled the absolutist states in Austria, Brandenburg-Prussia, and Russia—and how they maintained power.

3. discuss the significance of the Turkish invasion of eastern Europe and the world of peasants in eastern Europe.

Chapter Summary

This chapter explains why monarchical absolutism developed with greater lasting strength in eastern Europe than in western Europe. In Russia, Prussia, and Austria monarchs became more powerful as the peasants were pushed back into serfdom. That is, peasants gradually lost the personal and economic freedoms they had built up over several hundred years during the Middle Ages. At the same time that eastern nobles gained greater social and economic control over the enserfed peasants, they lost political power to the rising absolute monarchs. Although there were some economic reasons for the re-emergence of serfdom in the east, it was essentially for political reasons that this strong authoritarian tradition emerged. As opposed to western Europe, it was the common people—the peasants—who were the great losers in the power struggle between nobility and monarchy. Absolutism in Russia, Austria, and Prussia emerged because of war, foreign invasion, and internal struggle. For example, the Austrian monarchs solved the problems arising from external conflicts and a multicultural state by building a strong, centralized military state. Prussian absolutism—intended to check the power of the nobility—was achieved by the Hohenzollern monarchs, while Russian absolutism was largely the outgrowth of the Mongol conquest and internal power struggles.

Some of the absolute monarchs were enlightened reformers, but their good intentions were often thwarted by internal problems. However, if reform from above was not very effective, the absolute monarchs' use of architecture and urban planning—much of it in the baroque style—to enhance their images was a noteworthy success. They created buildings and cities that reflected their growing power, and they hired baroque painters and musicians to glorify them and to fill their palaces with paintings and music.

Study Outline

Use this outline to preview the chapter before you read a particular section in your textbook and then as a self-check to test your reading comprehension after you have read the chapter section.

I. Lords and peasants in eastern Europe
   A. Overall, between 1400 and 1650 the princes and landed nobility of eastern Europe rolled back the gains made earlier by the peasantry; serfdom was reimposed.
   B. The medieval background (1400-1650)
      1. Personal and economic freedom for peasants increased between 1050 and 1300.
         a. Serfdom nearly disappeared.
         b. Peasants bargained freely with their landlords and moved about as they pleased.
      2. After 1300, powerful lords in eastern Europe revived serfdom to combat their economic problems.
         a. Laws that restricted the peasants' right of free movement were passed.
         b. Lords took more and more of the peasants' land and imposed heavier labor obligations.
   C. The consolidation of serfdom
      1. The re-establishment of hereditary serfdom took place in Poland, Prussia, and Russia between 1500 and 1650.
      2. The consolidation of serfdom was accompanied by the growth of estate agriculture.
         a. Lords seized peasant land for their own estates.
         b. They then demanded unpaid serf labor on those estates.
      3. Political reasons for changes in serfdom in eastern Europe were the most important.
         a. Serfdom increased because of political, not economic, reasons.
         b. Weak monarchs could not resist the demands of the powerful noble landlords.
         c. The absence of the western concept of sovereignty meant that the king did not think in terms of protecting the people of the nation.
         d. Overall, the peasants had less political power in eastern Europe and less solidarity.
         e. The landlords systematically undermined the medieval privileges of the towns.
            1) The lords sold directly to foreign capitalists instead of to local merchants.
            2) Eastern towns lost their medieval right of refuge.
II. The rise of Austria and Prussia
   A. Austria and the Ottoman Turks
      1. After the Thirty Years' War, the Austrian Habsburgs turned inward and eastward to unify their holdings.
         a. The Habsburgs replaced the Bohemian Czech (Protestant) nobility with their own warriors.
         b. Serfdom increased, Protestantism was wiped out, and absolutism was achieved.
         c. Ferdinand III created a standing army, centralized the government in Austria, and turned toward Hungary for land.
      2. This eastward turn led Austria to became absorbed in a war against the Turks over Hungary and Transylvania.
      3. Under Suleiman the Magnificent the Ottoman-Turks built the most powerful empire in the world, which included part of central Europe.
         a. The Turkish sultan was the absolute head of the state.
         b. There was little private property, and a bureaucracy staffed by slaves.

4. The Ottoman attack on Austria in 1683 was turned back, and the Habsburgs conquered all of Hungary and Transylvania by 1699.
   a. The defeat of the Ottomans had support from Protestant nobles in Hungary and Louis XIV of France.
5. The Habsburg possessions consisted of Austria, Bohemia, and Hungary, which were joined in a fragile union.
   a. The Pragmatic Sanction (1713) stated that the possessions should never be divided.
   b. The Hungarian nobility thwarted the full development of Habsburg absolutism, and Charles VI had to restore many of their traditional privileges after the rebellion led by Rákóczy in 1703.

B. Prussia in the seventeenth century
1. The Hohenzollern family ruled the electorate of Brandenburg but had little real power.
2. The Thirty Years' War weakened the representative assemblies of the realm and allowed the Hohenzollerns to consolidate their absolutist rule.
3. Frederick William (the Great Elector) used military force and taxation to unify his Rhine holdings, Prussia, and Brandenburg into a strong state.
   a. The traditional parliaments, or Estates, which were controlled by the Junkers (the nobles and the landowners), were weakened.
   b. War strengthened the elector, as did the Junkers' unwillingness to join with the towns to block absolutism.

C. The consolidation of Prussian absolutism
1. Frederick William I encouraged Prussian militarism and created the best army in Europe plus an efficient bureaucracy.
2. The Junker class became the military elite and Prussia a militarist state.

III. The development of Russia
A. Between the mid-thirteenth century and 1700 Russia and the West became strikingly different; after 1700 Russia's development was closer to that of the West.

B. The Mongol yoke and the rise of Moscow
1. The Mongols conquered the Kievan state in the thirteenth century and unified it under their harsh rule.
2. The Mongols used Russian aristocrats as their servants and tax collectors.
   a. The princes of Moscow served the Mongols well and became the hereditary great princes.
   b. Ivan I served the Mongols while using his wealth and power to strengthen the principality of Moscow.
   c. Ivan III acquired territory around Moscow—including the rich republic of Novgorod.
   d. Ivan III stopped acknowledging the Mongol khan as the supreme ruler and assumed the headship of Orthodox Christianity.

C. Tsar and people to 1689
1. By 1505, the prince of Moscow—the tsar—had emerged as the single hereditary ruler of the eastern Slavs.
2. The tsars and the boyars struggled over who would rule the state; the tsars won and created a new "service nobility," who held the tsar's land on the condition that they serve in his army.

3. Ivan the Terrible was an autocratic tsar who expanded Muscovy and further reduced the power of the boyars.
   a. He murdered leading boyars and confiscated their estates.
   b. Many peasants fled his rule to the newly conquered territories, forming groups called Cossacks.
   c. Businessmen and artisans were bound to their towns and jobs; the middle class did not develop.
4. The Time of Troubles (1598-1613) was a period characterized by internal struggles and invasions.
   a. There was no heir, and relatives of the tsar fought against each other.
   b. Swedish and Polish armies invaded.
   c. Cossack bands, led by Ivan Bolotnikov, slaughtered many nobles and officials.
5. Michael Romanov was elected tsar by the nobles in 1613, and he re-established tsarist autocracy.
6. The Romanovs brought about the total enserfment of the people, while the military obligations on the nobility were relaxed considerably.
7. A split in the church over religious reforms led to mass protests by the peasants, and the church became dependent on the state for its authority.

D. The reforms of Peter the Great
1. Peter faced a Russian army based on cavalry and not the sort of professional armies being formed in Europe.
2. He conquered Azov, then went on a long tour of inspection of western Europe.
   a. He went to war against the absolutist king of Sweden (Charles XII)—eventually winning the Great Northern War.
   b. He reformed the army and forced the nobility to serve in his bureaucracy.
   c. His new (mainly peasant) army numbered 200,000 plus another 100,000 special troops.
   d. He created schools to train technicians for his army.
3. Army and government became more efficient and powerful as an interlocking military-civilian bureaucracy was created and staffed by talented people.
4. Russian peasant life under Peter became more harsh.
   a. People replaced land as the primary unit of taxation.
   b. Serfs were arbitrarily assigned to work in the factories and mines.
5. Modest territorial expansion took place under Peter, and Russia became a European Great Power.
   a. Russia defeated Sweden in 1709 at Poltava to gain control of the Baltic Sea.
   b. Peter borrowed many Western ideas.

IV. Absolutism and the baroque
A. Palaces and power
1. Baroque culture and art grew out of an effort by the Catholic church to attract followers.
2. Architecture played an important role in politics because it was used by kings to enhance their image and awe their subjects.
3. The royal palace was the favorite architectural expression of absolutist power.
4. The dominant artistic style of the age of absolutism was baroque—a dramatic and emotional style.

    B. Royal cities and urban planning
       1. Karlsruhe is a good example of how cities were rebuilt along orderly lines, and with great avenues and imposing public buildings.
       2. The new avenues brought speed to the city—as elegant carriages raced down the new broad and straight streets.
    C. The growth of St. Petersburg
       1. The new St. Petersburg is an excellent example of the tie among architecture, politics, and urban development.
          a. Peter the Great wanted to create a modern, baroque city from which to rule Russia.
          b. The city became a showplace for the tsar paid for by the Russian nobility and built by peasants.
       2. During the eighteenth century, St. Petersburg became one of the world's largest and most influential cities.
       3. The new city was Western and baroque in its layout and design.
          a. It had broad, straight avenues.
          b. Houses were built in a uniform line.
          c. There were parks, canals, and streetlights.
          d. Each social group was to live in a specific section.
       4. All social groups, especially the peasants, bore heavy burdens to construct the city.
       5. Tsarina Elizabeth and the architect Rastrelli crowned the city with great palaces.

Review Questions

Check your understanding of this chapter by answering the following questions.

1. What were the reasons for the re-emergence of serfdom in eastern Europe in the early modern period?

2. In western Europe the conflict between the king and his vassals resulted in gains for the common man. Why did this not happen in eastern Europe?

3. Why would the reign of the Great Elector be regarded as "the most crucial constitutional struggle in Prussian history for hundreds of years"? What did he do to increase royal authority? Who were the losers?

4. Prussia has traditionally been considered one of the most militaristic states in Europe. How do you explain this development? Who or what was responsible?

5. How did the Thirty Years' War and invasion by the Ottoman Turks help the Habsburgs consolidate power?

6. What was the Pragmatic Sanction and why were the Hungarian and Bohemian princes opposed to it?

7. What role, if any, did war play in the evolution of absolutism in eastern Europe?

8. What was the relationship between baroque architecture and European absolutism? Give examples.

9. It has been said that the common man benefited from the magnificent medieval cathedrals as much as the princes. Can the same be said about the common man and the building projects of the absolute kings and princes? Explain.

10. How did the Vikings influence Russian history?

11. How did the Mongols unify the eastern Slavs?

12. What role did Ivan the Terrible play in the rise of absolutism? Peter the Great?

13. Describe why "baroque" art and architecture came about and give examples of how it was used.

Study-Review Exercises

Define the following key concepts and terms.

absolutism

baroque

Prussian Junkers

Hohenzollern

kholops

Romanov

boyar

autocracy

Vikings

Habsburgs

Mongols

Pragmatic Sanction

Identify and explain the significance of the following people.
Suleiman the Magnificent

Frederick the Great

Charles VI of Austria

Prince Francis Rákóczy

Jenghiz Khan

Ivan the Terrible

Frederick William the Great Elector

Frederick William I

Great Prince Iaroslav the Wise

Ivan III

Peter the Great

Ivan Bolotnikov

Prince Eugene of Savoy

Bartolomeo Rastrelli

Explain what the following events were, who participated in them, and why they were important.
building of the Winter Palace of St. Petersburg

siege of Vienna, 1683

War of the Austrian Succession

Time of Troubles

Battle of Poltava

Test your understanding of the chapter by providing the correct answers.

1. The founder of the new Russian city on the coast of the Baltic Sea. _____

2. After 1500, serfdom in eastern Europe *increased/decreased.*

3. The Ottoman Turkish leader who captured Vienna in 1529. _____

4. In the struggle between the Hungarian aristocrats and the Austrian Habsburgs, the Hungarian aristocrats *maintained/lost* their traditional privileges.

5. This Prussian monarch doubled the size of Prussia in 1740 by taking Silesia from Austria.
   _____

6. The monarchs of eastern Europe were generally *stronger/weaker* than the kings of western Europe in the sixteenth and seventeenth centuries.

Place the following events in correct chronological order.

Election of the first Romanov tsar
Establishment of the Kievan state
Time of Troubles
Invasion by the Mongols
Building of St. Petersburg
Battle of Poltava

1.

2.

3.

4.

5.

6.

Major Political Ideas

1. What is a "service nobility" in Russia?

2. Compare and contrast the power of the nobility and the middle class in Russia with that of the nobility and the middle class in western Europe.

Issues for Essays and Discussion

1. Why did royal absolutism take such strong root in eastern Europe? Why was constitutionalism, such as in England and the Netherlands, not undertaken? Was economics or geography the key difference—or was it something else?

2. Trace the fortunes and political power of the noble classes in Russia, Austria, and Prussia from about 1300 to about the middle of the 1700s. How did the monarchs gain the upper hand?

3. Peter the Great of Russia and Frederick William the Great Elector of Prussia are often viewed as heroes and reformers in the histories of their own countries. How valid is this assessment?

Interpretation of Visual Sources

Study the print entitled *Molding the Prussian Spirit*. Describe the scene. Why would this print have been included in a book for children? What were the reasons for Prussia's "obsessive bent for military organization and military scales of value"?

Geography

1. Study Map 17.1, "The Ottoman Empire at Its Height, 1566," in your textbook. Is this essentially a European or Near Eastern empire? What were the main ethnic groups making up the empire? What held it together? By studying this map can you predict what would eventually tear it apart?

2. On Outline Map 17.3 provided, and using Map 17.3 in the textbook for reference, mark the following: the area covered by the principality of Moscow in 1300, the territories acquired by the principality of Moscow from 1300 to 1689, the acquisitions of Peter the Great.

3. Looking at Map 17.2 in the textbook, identify the three territorial parts of the Habsburg (Austrian) state and explain how they came to be united.

Outline Map 17.3

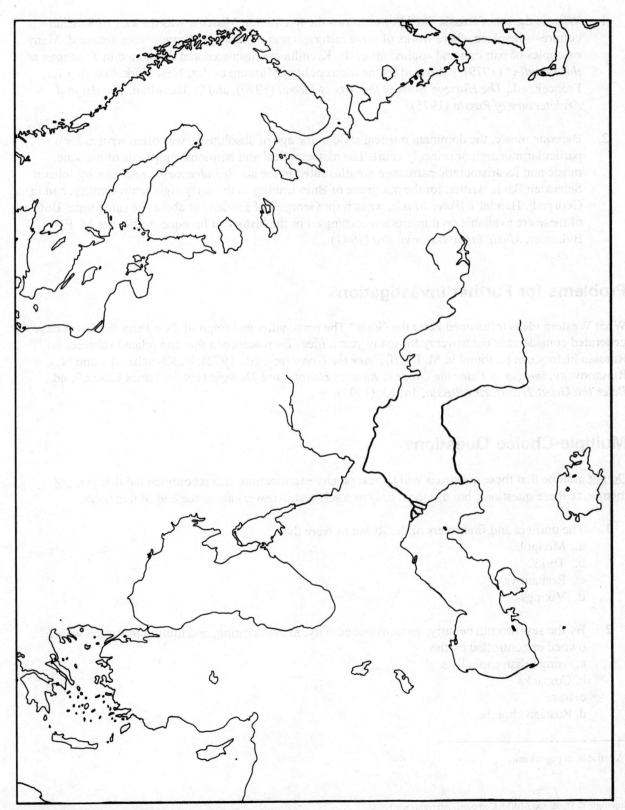

Understanding History Through the Arts

1. What is the art of Russia like? For centuries the Kremlin in Moscow was the axis of Russian culture—the place where works of great historical and artistic significance were amassed. Many examples of painting and applied art of the Kremlin are discussed and illustrated in *Treasures of the Kremlin** (1979), published by the Metropolitan Museum of Art, New York. See also T. Froncek, ed., *The Horizon Book of the Arts of Russia* (1970), and G. Hamilton, *The Art and Architecture of Russia* (1975).

2. Baroque music, the dominant musical style in the age of absolutism, was often written for a particular monarch or princely court. The mathematical and harmonic emphasis of baroque music and its aristocratic patronage are illustrated in the six *Brandenburg Concertos* by Johann Sebastian Bach, written for the margrave of Brandenburg in the early eighteenth century, and in George F. Handel's *Water Music*, written for George I of England at about the same time. Both of these are available on numerous recordings. For the history of baroque music, see M. F. Bukofzer, *Music in the Baroque Era* (1947).

Problems for Further Investigation

What Western ideas influenced Peter the Great? The personality and reign of Tsar Peter the Great have generated considerable controversy for many years. Ideas for research in this and related subjects in Russian history can be found in M. Raeff, *Peter the Great* (rev. ed., 1972); V. Klyuchevsky and N. Riasanovsky, *Images of Peter the Great in Russian History and Thought* (1985); James Cracraft, ed., *Peter the Great Transforms Russia*, 3rd ed. (1991).

Multiple-Choice Questions

Do not assume that these questions will appear on any examination. It is recommended that you not memorize these questions, but use them only as a self-test. Answers are at the end of this book.

1. The unifiers and first rulers of the Russians were the
    a. Mongols.
    b. Turks.
    c. Romanovs.
    d. Vikings.

2. By the seventeenth century, commercial activity, manufacturing, and mining in Russia were owned or controlled by the
    a. rising urban capitalists.
    b. Cossacks.
    c. tsar.
    d. Russian church.

---

*Available in paperback.

3. In eastern Europe the courts were largely controlled by
   a. the peasants.
   b. the monarchs.
   c. the church.
   d. the landlords.

4. The principality called the "sandbox of the Holy Roman Empire" was
   a. Brandenburg-Prussia.
   b. Hungary.
   c. Sweden.
   d. Austria.

5. Ivan the Terrible
   a. failed to conquer the khan.
   b. was afraid to call himself tsar.
   c. monopolized most mining and business activity.
   d. abolished the system of compulsory service for noble landlords.

6. Peter the Great's reforms included
   a. compulsory education away from home for the higher classes.
   b. a lessening of the burdens of serfdom for Russian peasants.
   c. an elimination of the merit-system bureaucracy.
   d. the creation of an independent parliament.

7. The dominant artistic style of the seventeenth and early eighteenth centuries was
   a. Gothic.
   b. romantic.
   c. impressionistic.
   d. baroque.

8. The noble landowners of Prussia were known as
   a. boyars.
   b. Junkers.
   c. Vikings.
   d. Electors.

9. Apparently the most important reason for the return to serfdom in eastern Europe from about 1500 to 1650 was
   a political.
   b. economic.
   c. military.
   d. religious.

10. The Russian Cossacks were
   a. nobles created by Peter the Great.
   b. free groups and outlaw armies.
   c. private armies of the landlords.
   d. Turkish troops who settled in the Black Sea area.

11. After the disastrous defeat of the Czech nobility by the Habsburgs at the battle of White Mountain in 1618, the
   a. old Czech nobility accepted Catholicism in great numbers.
   b. majority of the Czech nobles' land was given to soldiers who had fought for the Habsburgs.
   c. conditions of the enserfed peasantry improved.
   d. Czech nobles continued their struggle effectively for many years.

12. After the Thirty Years' War and the creation of a large standing army, Austria turned its attention to control of
   a. northern Italy.
   b. Prussia.
   c. Hungary.
   d. Poland.

13. The result of the struggle of the Hungarian nobles against Habsburg oppression was that
   a. they suffered a fate similar to the Czech nobility.
   b. they gained a great deal of autonomy compared with the Austrian and Bohemian nobility.
   c. they won their independence.
   d. their efforts were inconclusive.

14. The monarch who established Prussian absolutism and who was named "the Soldiers' King" was
   a. Peter the Great.
   b. Frederick William.
   c. Ivan IV.
   d. Elector Frederick III.

15. The Muscovite princes gained their initial power through
   a. services rendered to the Vikings.
   b. strategic marriages.
   c. services rendered to the Mongols.
   d. defeat of the rival branches of the house of Ruiruk.

16. The rise of the Russian monarchy was largely a response to the external threat of the
   a. French monarchy.
   b. Asiatic Mongols.
   c. Prussian monarchy.
   d. English monarchy.

17. The Time of Troubles was caused by
    a. a dispute in the line of succession.
    b. Turkish invasions.
    c. Mongol invasions.
    d. severe crop failures resulting in starvation and disease.

18. In order to strengthen the Russian military, Peter the Great
    a. made the nobility serve in the civil administration or army for life.
    b. established a navy in the Atlantic.
    c. excluded foreigners from his service.
    d. turned over political power to the military.

19. The real losers in the growth of eastern Europe absolutism were the
    a. peasants.
    b. peasants and middle classes.
    c. nobility.
    d. nobility and the clergy.

20. The Siege of Vienna of 1683 was undertaken by
    a. the Hungarians under Prince Rákóczy.
    b. the Russians.
    c. the Turks.
    d. Frederick William of Prussia.

21. The Battle of Poltava marks a Russian victory over
    a. Sweden.
    b. Turkey.
    c. Prussia.
    d. Austria.

22. All of the following reflected the power and magnificence of royal absolutism *except*
    a. soaring Gothic cathedrals.
    b. baroque palaces.
    c. royal cities.
    d. broad, urban avenues.

23. The result of the Czech noble revolt of 1618 was
    a. their replacement by Habsburg loyalists.
    b. Czech independence.
    c. Czech autonomy within the Habsburg state.
    d. the rise of Protestantism in Bohemia.

24. The Habsburg state was made up of
    a. Austria, Bohemia, and Hungary.
    b. Austria, Prussia, and Hungary.
    c. Hungary, Brandenburg, and Silesia.
    d. Silesia, Bohemia, and Austria.

Chapter 18

Toward a New World-View

Learning Objectives

After reading and studying this chapter you should be able to:

1. define and describe the scientific revolution.

2. explain how the Newtonian world-view differed from the medieval world-view.

3. define and describe the Enlightenment and its ideas about society, religion, the economy, and politics.

Chapter Summary

In the seventeenth and eighteenth centuries the educated classes of Europe changed from a world-view that was basically religious to one that was primarily secular. The development of scientific knowledge was the key cause of this intellectual change. Until about 1500, scientific thought reflected the Aristotelian-medieval world-view, which taught that a motionless earth was at the center of a universe made up of planets and stars in ten crystal spheres. These and many other beliefs showed that science was primarily a branch of religion. Beginning with Copernicus, who taught that the earth revolved around the sun, Europeans slowly began to reject Aristotelian-medieval scientific thought. They developed a new conception of a universe based on natural laws, not on a personal God. Isaac Newton formulated the great scientific synthesis: the law of universal gravitation. This was the high point of the scientific revolution.

   The scientific revolution was more important for intellectual development than for economic activity or everyday life, for above all it promoted critical thinking. Nothing was to be accepted on faith; everything was to be submitted to the rational, scientific way of thinking. This critical examination of everything, from religion and education to war and politics, was the key to the Enlightenment and the work of the philosophes, a group of thinkers who propagandized the new world-view across Europe and the North American colonies. These writers and thinkers, among them Voltaire, Montesquieu, and Diderot, produced books and articles that influenced all classes and whose primary intent was teaching people how to think critically and objectively about all matters.

   The philosophes were reformers, not revolutionaries. Their "enlightened" ideas were adopted by a number of monarchs who sought to promote the advancement of knowledge and improve the lives of their subjects. Most important in this group were Frederick II of Prussia and Catherine II of Russia and the Habsburgs, Maria Theresa and Joseph II. Despite some reforms, particularly in the area of law, Frederick and Catherine's role in the Enlightenment was in the abstract rather than the practical. The

Habsburgs were more successful in legal and tax reform, control of the church, and improvement of the lot of the serfs, although much of Joseph's spectacular peasant reform was later undone. Yet reform of society from the top down, that is, by the absolute monarchs through "enlightened absolutism," proved to be impossible because the enlightened monarchs could not ignore the demands of their conservative nobilities. In the end, it was revolution, not enlightened absolutism, that changed and reformed society.

The chapter closes with a discussion of how the middle class of France used the Parlement of Paris and its judgeships as a counterweight to absolutism and the revival of aristocratic power. This opposition was crushed by Louis XV's chancellor Maupeou, only to reappear with the new King Louis XVI.

Study Outline

Use this outline to preview the chapter before you read a particular section and then as a self-check to test your reading comprehension after you have read the chapter section.

I. The scientific revolution
   A. The scientific revolution of the seventeenth century was the major cause of the change in world-view and one of the key developments in the evolution of Western society.
      1. Only the West developed modern science; historians disagree as to how important to its rise were the nonscientific economic, religious, and social factors.
   B. Scientific thought in the early 1500s
      1. European ideas about the universe were based on Aristotelian-medieval ideas.
         a. Central to this view was the belief in a motionless earth fixed at the center of the universe.
         b. Around the earth moved ten crystal spheres, and beyond the spheres was heaven.
      2. Aristotle's scheme suited Christianity because it positioned human beings at the center of the universe and established a home for God.
      3. Science in this period was primarily a branch of theology.
   C. The Copernican hypothesis
      1. Copernicus, a Polish clergyman and astronomer, claimed that the earth revolved around the sun and that the sun was the center of the universe.
      2. This heliocentric theory was a departure from medieval thought and created doubts about traditional Christianity.
   D. From Brahe to Galileo
      1. Brahe set the stage for the modern study of astronomy by building an observatory and collecting data.
      2. His assistant, Kepler, formulated three laws of planetary motion that proved the precise relationships among planets in a sun-centered universe.
      3. Galileo discovered the laws of motion using the experimental method—the cornerstone of modern science.
         a. He also applied the experimental method to astronomy, using the newly invented telescope.
         b. Galileo was tried by the Inquisition for heresy in 1633 and forced to recant his views.

E. Newton's synthesis
1. In his famous book, *Principia* (1687), Newton integrated the astronomy of Copernicus and Kepler with the physics of Galileo.
   a. He formulated a set of mathematical laws to explain motion and mechanics.
   b. The key feature in his synthesis was the law of universal gravitation.
2. Henceforth, the universe could be explained through mathematics.

F. Causes of the scientific revolution
1. Medieval universities provided the framework for the new science.
2. The Renaissance stimulated science by rediscovering ancient mathematics and supporting scientific investigations.
3. The navigational problems of sea voyages generated scientific research and new instruments.
4. Better ways of obtaining knowledge about the world improved scientific methods.
   a. Bacon advocated empirical, experimental research.
   b. Descartes stressed mathematics and deductive reasoning.
   c. The modern scientific method is based on a synthesis of Bacon's inductive experimentalism and Descartes's deductive mathematical rationalism.
5. After about 1630 (the Counter-Reformation) the Catholic church discouraged science while Protestantism tended to be "pro-science."

G. Some consequences of the scientific revolution
1. A scientific community emerged whose primary goal was the expansion of knowledge.
2. A modern scientific method arose that was both theoretical and experimental and refused to base its conclusions on tradition and established sources.
3. Because the link between pure science and applied technology was weak, the scientific revolution had little effect on daily life before the nineteenth century.

II. The Enlightenment
A. The Enlightenment was an intellectual and cultural movement that tied together certain key ideas and was the link between the scientific revolution and a new world-view; these ideas were:
1. Natural science and reason can explain all aspects of life.
2. The scientific method can explain the laws of human society.
3. Progress—the creation of better societies and better people—is possible.

B. The emergence of the Enlightenment
1. Many writers made scientific thought understandable to a large nonscientific audience.
   a. Fontenelle stressed the idea of progress.
   b. He was also cynical about organized religion and absolute religious truth.
2. Skeptics such as Bayle concluded that nothing can be known beyond all doubt and stressed open-mindedness.
3. The growth of world travel led Europeans to look at truth and morality in relative, not absolute, terms.
4. In his *Essay Concerning Human Understanding*, Locke insisted that all ideas are derived from experience—the human mind at birth is like a blank tablet *(tabula rasa)*.

C. The philosophes and the public
1. The philosophes brought Enlightenment ideas to the ignorant people and brought the Enlightenment to its highest stage of development in France.
   a. The French language was the international language of the educated classes of Europe, and France was Europe's wealthiest state.
   b. Intellectual freedom was possible in France, in contrast to eastern Europe.

        c.   The philosophes were committed to bringing new thinking to the public, but not necessarily the masses.

        d.   In their plays, histories, novels, dictionaries, and encyclopedias, they used satire and double meanings to spread their messages to the public.

   2.   Montesquieu's theory of the separation of powers was extremely influential.

   3.   Voltaire challenged traditional Catholic theology and exhibited a characteristic philosophe belief in a distant God who let human affairs take their own course.

        a.   He opposed legal injustice and unequal treatment before the law.

        b.   He was influenced by his long-time companion, Madame du Chatelet, who was a scientist but who was discriminated against because of her sex.

        c.   He was skeptical of social and economic equality; he hated religious intolerance.

   4.   Diderot and d'Alembert edited the *Encyclopedia*, which examined all of human knowledge and attempted to teach people how to think critically and rationally.

   5.   The later Enlightenment writers built rigid and dogmatic systems.

        a.   D'Holbach argued that humans were completely controlled by outside forces.

        b.   Hume argued that the mind is nothing but a bundle of impressions that originate in sense experiences.

        c.   Rousseau attacked rationalism and civilization; he claimed that children must develop naturally and spontaneously, and in *The Social Contract* argued that the general will of the people is sacred and absolute.

  D.   Urban culture and public opinion

   1.   The cultural transformation brought on by the Enlightenment was related to a growth in the market for books.

        a.   Most of the new buyers of books came from the middle classes, the clergy, and the aristocracy; a tenfold increase in books resulted.

        b.   Publishing in the fields of art and science grew the most; a majority of the new books came from publishers outside of France, largely the Netherlands and Switzerland.

        c.   Underground literature in pornography was of concern to the state because much of it centered on aristocratic immorality.

        d.   All of this resulted in a new emphasis on individual and private reading (a "reading revolution"); some, like Kant, argued that freedom of the press would bring an enlightened age.

   2.   Enlightenment ideas—including new ideas about women's rights—were spread in the salons of upper-class women.

        a.   The salons were often presided over by women.

        b.   Madame Geoffrin's salon was famous; she was the unofficial godmother of the *Encyclopedia*.

        c.   These salons seemed to have functioned as informal "schools" for women.

III. The enlightenment and absolutism

  A.   Many philosophes believed that "enlightened" reform would come by way of "enlightened" monarchs.

   1.   The philosophes believed that a benevolent absolutism offered the best chance for improving society.

   2.   The rulers seemed to seek the philosophes' advice.

   3.   The philosophes distrusted the masses and felt that change had to come from above.

IV. Absolutism in central and eastern Europe
    A. The most influential of the new-style monarchs were in Prussia, Russia, and Austria.
    B. Frederick the Great of Prussia
        1. Frederick II used the War of the Austrian Succession (1740-1748) to expand Prussia into a great power by seizing Silesia.
        2. The Seven Years' War (1756-1763) saw an attempt by Maria Theresa, with the help of France and Russia, to regain Silesia, but it failed.
        3. Frederick allowed religious freedom and promoted education, legal reform, and economic growth but allowed the Junker nobility to keep the middle-class from power in government.
            a. Frederick allowed the repression of Prussian Jews—who were confined to overcrowded ghettos.
    C. Catherine the Great of Russia
        1. Catherine II imported Western culture to Russia, supported the philosophes, and began a program of domestic reform.
        2. The Pugachev uprising in 1773 led her to reverse the trend toward reform of serfdom and give nobles absolute control of their serfs.
        3. She engaged in a policy of territorial expansion and, with Prussia and Austria, carved up Poland.
    D. The Austrian Habsburgs
        1. Maria Theresa of Austria introduced reforms that limited church power, revised the tax system and the bureaucracy, and reduced the power of the lords over the serfs.
        2. Her successor, Joseph II, was a dedicated reformer who abolished serfdom, taxed all equally, and granted religious freedom.
        3. Because of opposition from both the nobles and the peasants, Joseph's reforms were short-lived.
    E. Absolutism in France
        1. Some philosophes, such as Voltaire, believed that the monarchy was the best system, while some of the aristocracy sought to limit the king's power.
        2. Favored by the duke of Orléans, who governed as a regent until 1723, the French nobility regained much of the power it had lost under Louis XIV.
            a. The Parlement of Paris won two decisive victories against taxation.
            b. It then asserted that the king could not levy taxes without its consent.
        3. Under Louis XV the French minister Maupeou began the restoration of royal absolutism by abolishing the Parlement of Paris.
        4. Louis XVI reinstated the old Parlement and the country drifted toward renewed financial and political crises.
    F. The overall influence of the Enlightenment
        1. In France, the rise of judicial and aristocratic opposition combined with liberalism put absolutism on the defensive.
        2. In eastern Europe the results of enlightened absolutism were modest and absolutism remained strong.
        3. By combining state building with the culture and critical thinking of the Enlightenment, absolute monarchs succeeded in expanding the role of the state in the life of society.

Review Questions

Check your understanding of this chapter by answering the following questions.

1. Contrast the old Aristotelian-medieval world-view with that of the sixteenth and seventeenth centuries. What were the contributions of Copernicus, Brahe, Kepler, Galileo, and Newton? What is meant by Newton's "synthesis"?

2. How did the new scientific theory and discoveries alter the concept of God and religion? Did science, in fact, come to dictate humanity's concept of God?

3. What were the scientific and religious implications of Copernicus's theory?

4. Discuss the origins and the momentum of the scientific revolution in terms of (a) its own "internal logic" and (b) external and nonscientific causes.

5. How did Bacon and Descartes contribute to the development of the modern scientific method?

6. Did the Catholic and Protestant churches retard or foster scientific investigation? Explain.

7. What were the consequences of the rise of modern science?

8. What were the central concepts of the Enlightenment?

9. Who were the philosophes and what did they believe?

10. In what ways were Frederick of Prussia and Catherine of Russia enlightened monarchs?

11. Describe the goals and accomplishments of Frederick the Great.

12. What was the effect of Catherine's reign on (a) the Russian nobility, (b) the Russian serfs, and (c) the position of Russia in the European balance of power?

13. What was the cause of the power struggle between the aristocrats and Louis XV of France?

14. Describe the interests and actions of Madame du Chatelet and Madame Geoffrin.

Study-Review Exercises

Define the following key concepts and terms.

Aristotelian world-view

empirical method

Copernican hypothesis

deductive reasoning

rationalism

progress

secular

skepticism

tabula rasa

Parlement of Paris

Enlightenment

enlightened absolutism

philosophes

Gresham College

Identify and explain the significance of each of the following people.

Diderot

Bayle

Kepler

Galileo

Bacon

Descartes

D'Holbach

Newton

Montesquieu

Voltaire

Copernicus

Brahe

Madame du Chatelet

Madame Geoffrin

Catherine the Great

Frederick the Great

Maria Theresa

Louis XV

Joseph II

Explain the new ideas of each the following books. What were some of the consequences of these ideas?
On the Revolutions of the Heavenly Spheres

New Astronomy or Celestial Physics

Two New Sciences

Principia

Conversations on the Plurality of Worlds of 1686

Historical and Critical Dictionary

The Spirit of the Laws

Essay Concerning Human Understanding

Philosophical Dictionary

Encyclopedia: The Rational Dictionary of the Sciences, the Arts, and the Crafts

The Social Contract

Test your understanding of the chapter by providing the correct answers.

1. According to Aristotle, the sublunar world was made up of four elements: air, fire, _____ , and _____ .

2. Copernicus *did/did not* attempt to disprove the existence of God.

3. Galileo claimed that *motion/rest* is the natural state of all objects.

4. The key feature in Newton's synthesis was the law of _____ .

5. In the medieval universities, science emerged as a branch of _____ .

6. The method of finding latitude came out of study and experimentation in the country of _____ .

7. The idea of "progress" *was/was not* widespread in the Middle Ages.

8. In the seventeenth and eighteenth centuries a close link between pure (theoretical) science and applied technology *did/did not* exist.

9. A _____ is one who believes that nothing can ever be known beyond all doubt.

10. Voltaire believed that _____ was history's greatest man because he used his genius to benefit humanity.

11. Overall, Joseph II of Austria *succeeded/failed* as an enlightened monarch.

Place the following ideas in correct chronological order.

Copernicus's idea that the sun is the center of the universe
Montesquieu's theory of the separation of powers
D'Holbach's theory that human beings were machines
Aristotle's view of a motionless earth at the center of the universe
Newton's law of universal gravitation

1.

2.

3.

4.

5.

Major Political Ideas

1. Describe the concept of enlightened absolutism in terms of its political and legal goals. Did it work? What was the response of the aristocracy to this political concept?

2. This chapter emphasizes the difference between a secular and religious view of the world. What is meant by *secular* and what effect did a secular world-view have on political loyalties?

Issues for Essays and Discussion

In the course of the eighteenth century the basic outlook on life and society held by many men and women changed dramatically. In what ways did this transformation affect scientific, political, religious, social, and economic thought? In working out your argument explain how specific new scientific ideas and methods of reasoning led directly to new political and social ideas.

Interpretation of Visual Sources

Study the print of Louis XIV's visit to the Royal Academy in 1671. Write a paragraph on how this print illustrates the relationship between science and politics. Did the scientific revolution have a great effect on how kings ran their states? Why were some monarchs interested in science? Does this print give any clues?

Geography

Why did Poland "disappear" between 1772 and 1795? Compare Map 18.1 to Map 17.2. Describe what the "partition of Poland" was, when it took place, why, and who benefited.

Understanding History Through the Arts

How did the Enlightenment affect the arts? This period is often referred to as the age of the baroque style, and the achievements of its great artists are discussed in M. Kitson, *The Age of the Baroque* (1966). See also Chapter 6 in N. Pevsner, *An Outline of European Architecture* (7th ed., 1963), and E. Kaufmann, *Architecture in the Age of Reason—Baroque and Post-Baroque in England, Italy, and France* (1955,* 1968). On the subject of the Scottish Enlightenment, see T. A. Markus, ed., *Order and Space: Architectural Form and Its Context in the Scottish Enlightenment* (1982). Few artists captured English life as well as the painter Hogarth, whose *Rake's Progress and Harlot's Progress* point to the consequences of moral decay. Hogarth's paintings can be seen and studied in W. Gaunt, *The World of William Hogarth* (1978), and D. Bindman, Hogarth* (1981). For a description of French life by painters of the time, see T. E. Crow, *Painters and Public Life in Eighteenth-Century Paris* (1985).

Problems for Further Investigation

1. Write an essay in which you describe and analyze an important work of the Enlightenment. What were the ideas set forth by the author and how do these ideas reflect or illustrate Enlightenment thought and change? The two greatest philosophes of the age of Enlightenment were Rousseau and Voltaire. Rousseau's ideas on education and natural law are set forth in *Emile,* and Voltaire's most-praised work is *Candide,* a funny and sometimes bawdy parody of eighteenth-century life and thought. Selections from the great Encyclopedia are found in S. Gendzier, ed., *Denis Diderot: The Encyclopedia: Selections* (1967). Much of the fiction of the eighteenth century reflects, often in satire, the spirit of the new world-view—Jonathan Swift, *Gulliver's Travels*; Daniel Defoe, *Moll Flanders*; and Henry Fielding, Tom Jones, are just a few of the many novels of this period. In Germany, the *Sturm und Drang* (storm and stress) movement embraced the ideas of the Enlightenment and romanticism and produced works such as Lessing's *Nathan the Wise*, which stressed a universal religion.

---

*Available in paperback.

2. How have historians interpreted the meaning and impact of the Enlightenment? Students interested in this topic will want to begin with three books that set forth some of the major issues and schools of interpretation on the subject: B. Tierney et al., eds., *Enlightenment—The Age of Reason** (1967), and R. Wines, ed., *Enlightened Despotism** (1967), and A. Farge, *Subversive Worlds: Public Opinion in Eighteenth Century France* (1994).

Self-Test Multiple-Choice Questions

<u>Do</u> <u>not</u> assume that these questions will appear on any examination. It is recommended that you <u>not</u> memorize these questions, but use only as a self-test. Answers are at the end of this book.

1. Catherine the Great accomplished which of the following?
   a. Annexed part of Poland
   b. Freed the Russian serfs
   c. Denied any sort of religious toleration
   d. Persecuted the philosophes of France

2. "Enlightened" monarchs believed in all of the following *except*
   a. reform.
   b. democracy.
   c. cultural values of the Enlightenment.
   d. secularism.

3. Geoffrin and Deffand were
   a. scientific writers.
   b. religious leaders in France.
   c. leaders of the Enlightenment salons.
   d. leaders of the serf uprising in France.

4. The philosophes were
   a. mainly university professors.
   b. generally hostile to monarchical government.
   c. enthusiastic supporters of the Catholic church.
   d. satirists who wished to reform society and humanity.

5. The social setting of the Enlightenment
   a. excluded women.
   b. was characterized by poverty and boredom.
   c. was dominated by government officials.
   d. was characterized by witty and intelligent conversation.

---

*Available in paperback.

6. Catherine the Great
   a. believed the philosophes were dangerous revolutionaries.
   b. freed the serfs to satisfy Diderot.
   c. increased the size of the Russian Empire.
   d. established a strong constitutional monarchy.

7. According to medieval thought, the center of the universe was the
   a. sun.
   b. earth.
   c. moon.
   d. heaven.

8. The Aristotelian world-view placed emphasis on the idea of
   a. the sun as the center of the universe.
   b. the rejection of Christian theology.
   c. an earth that moves in space.
   d. crystal spheres moving around the earth.

9. Copernicus's theory of a sun-centered universe
   a. suggested the universe was small and closed.
   b. questioned the idea that crystal spheres moved the stars around the earth.
   c. suggested that the worlds of heaven and earth were radically different from each other.
   d. suggested an enormous and possibly infinite universe.

10. The first astronomer to prove his theories through the use of mathematical equations was
    a. Galileo.
    b. Kepler.
    c. Brahe.
    d. Newton.

11. D'Holbach, Hume, and Rousseau are examples of the later Enlightenment trend toward
    a. rigid systems.
    b. social satire.
    c. religion.
    d. the idea of absolutism.

12. The French philosopher who rejected his contemporaries and whose writings influenced the romantic movement was
    a. Rousseau.
    b. Voltaire.
    c. Diderot.
    d. Condorcet.

13. The gathering ground for many who wished to discuss the ideas of the French Enlightenment was the
    a. salon.
    b. lecture hall.
    c. palace at Versailles.
    d. University of Paris.

14. Frederick II is considered an enlightened monarch because he
    a. regained Silesia from Prussia.
    b. wrote poetry and improved the legal and bureaucratic systems.
    c. kept the aristocrats in a dominant position socially and politically.
    d. avoided war.

15. Catherine the Great of Russia hardened her position on serfdom after the
    a. Pugachev rebellion.
    b. Moscow rebellion.
    b. Polish rebellion.
    c. "Five Year" rebellion.

16. After Louis XIV's death
    a. the nobility lost considerable power.
    b. the lower classes secured judicial positions in the Parlement.
    c. the French government struggled with severe economic difficulties.
    d. absolutism remained firmly entrenched during the succeeding reign.

17. Which of the following used the War of the Austrian Succession to expand Prussia into a great power?
    a. Joseph II
    b. Frederick II
    c. Frederick William I
    d. Louis XIV

18. The aggressiveness of Prussia, Austria, and Russia led to the disappearance of which eastern European kingdom from the map after 1795?
    a. Hungary
    b. Sweden
    c. Brandenburg
    d. Poland

19. Francis Bacon's great contribution to scientific methodology was
    a. the geocentric theory.
    b. the notion of logical speculation.
    c. the philosophy of empiricism.
    d. analytic geometry.

20. Which of the following men set the stage for the modern study of astronomy by building an observatory and collecting data?
    a. Darwin
    b. Hume
    c. Newton
    d. Brahe

21. The Parlement of Paris was
    a. a high court dominated by nobles who were formerly middle class.
    b. a center of royal absolutism.
    c. used by Maupeou to strengthen the king's position.
    d. not interested in tax reform or finance.

22. Maria Theresa was a devout Catholic who
    a. sought to limit the church's influence in Austria.
    b. was not interested in the Enlightenment.
    c. did nothing to improve the lot of the agricultural population.
    d. was a weak monarch unable to hold the Austrian Empire together.

23. After 1715 in France, the direction of political change was
    a. toward greater absolutism.
    b. away from Enlightenment political thought.
    c. in favor of opposition forces—largely the nobility and the Parlement of Paris.
    d. toward "enlightened absolutism."

24. Descartes' idea was that the world consists of two fundamental entities or substances, which we can call
    a. the physical and the spiritual.
    b. water and air.
    c. reason and passion.
    d. deduction and induction.

Studying Effectively—Exercise 4

Learning to Classify Information According to Sequence

As you know, a great deal of historical information is classified by sequence, in which things follow each other in time. This kind of *sequential order* is also known as *time order* or *chronological order*.
Attention to time sequence is important in the study of history for at least two reasons.

1. It helps you organize historical information effectively.

2. It promotes historical understanding. If you know the order in which events happen, you can think intelligently about questions of cause and effect. You can begin to evaluate conflicting interpretations.

Since time sequences are essential in historical study, the authors have placed a number of timelines in the text to help you organize the historical information.

Two Fallacies Regarding Time Sequences

One common fallacy is often known by the famous Latin phrase *post hoc, ergo propter hoc*: "after this, therefore because of this." This fallacy assumes that one happening that follows another *must* be caused by the first happening. Obviously, some great development (such as the Protestant Reformation) could come after another (the Italian Renaissance) without being caused by it. *Causal relationships must be demonstrated, not simply assumed on the basis of the "after this, therefore because of this" fallacy.*
A second common, if old-fashioned, fallacy assumes that time sequences are composed only of political facts with precise data. But in considering social, intellectual, and economic developments, historians must often speak with less chronological exactitude—in terms of decades or even centuries, for example. Yet they still use time sequences, and students of history must recognize them. For example, did you realize that the sections on "The Scientific Revolution" and "The Enlightenment" in Chapter 18 are very conscientious about time sequence, even though they do not deal with political facts?

Exercise

Reread the large section in Chapter 18 on "The Scientific Revolution" with an eye for dates and sequential order. Then in the space below and with the book open make a "Timeline for the Scientific Revolution." Pick out at least a dozen important events and put them in the time sequence, with a word or two to explain the significance when possible.

314

Suggestion: Do not confine yourself solely to specific events with specific dates. Also, integrate some items from the subsection on the causes of the scientific revolution into the sequence. You may find that constructing timelines helps you organize your study.

After you have completed your timeline, compare it with the one on the following page, which shows how one of the authors of the text did this assignment.

Timeline for the Scientific Revolution

Date   Event

_____   _____

_____   _____

_____   _____

_____   _____

_____   _____

_____   _____

_____   _____

_____   _____

_____   _____

_____   _____

_____   _____

_____   _____

_____   _____

_____   _____

SAMPLE
Timeline for the Scientific Revolution

Date	*Event*
(1300-1500)	Renaissance stimulates development of mathematics
early 1500s	Aristotle's ideas on movement and universe still dominant
1543	Copernicus publishes *On the Revolution of the Heavenly Spheres*
1572, 1577	New star and comet create more doubts about traditional astronomy
1546-1601	Tycho Brache—famous astronomer, creates mass of observations
1571-1630	Johannes Kepler—his three laws prove Copernican theory and demolish Aristotle's beliefs
1589	Galileo Galilei (1564-1642) named professor of mathematics
1610	Galileo studies moon with telescope and writes of experience
1561-1626	Francis Bacon—English scientific enthusiast, advocates experimental (inductive) method
1596-1650	René Descartes—French philosopher, discovers analytical geometry in 1619 and advocates theoretical (deductive) method
to about 1630	All religious authorities oppose Copernican theory
about 1632	Galileo tried by papal inquisition
1622	Royal Society of London founded—brings scientists and practical men together
1687	Isaac Newton publishes his *Principia*, synthesizing existing knowledge around idea of universal gravitation
	to late 1700s Consequences of scientific revolution primarily intellectual, not economic

Chapter 19

The Expansion of Europe in the Eighteenth Century

Learning Objectives

After reading and studying this chapter you should be able to:

1. compare and contrast farming methods and the supply of food before and after the Agricultural Revolution.

2. account for the dramatic population increase in Europe during the eighteenth century.

3. explain how European nations developed world trade during the eighteenth century.

4. discuss the consequences of European expansion for the common people.

Chapter Summary

How did our "modern" world begin? This chapter discusses the important economic and demographic changes of the eighteenth century, which led up to the Industrial Revolution. It also prepares us for understanding the life of ordinary people in the eighteenth century, which is the subject of the following chapter.

The chapter covers four important and interrelated subjects. First, the centuries-old "open-field" system of agricultural production, a system that was both inefficient and unjust, is described. This system was gradually transformed into a more productive system of capitalistic farming (called the "enclosure" system), first in the Low Countries and then in England. Some English peasants suffered in the process, but on the whole the changes added up to a highly beneficial agricultural revolution. The second topic is the explosive growth of European population in the eighteenth century. This growth, still imperfectly understood, was probably due largely to the disappearance of the plague and to new and better foods, such as the potato. Doctors and organized medicine played a very minor role in the improvements in health. Third, the chapter discusses the movement of manufacturing from urban shops to cottages in the countryside. Rural families worked there as units in the new domestic system, which provided employment for many in the growing population. The domestic system was particularly effective in the textile industry, which this chapter examines in detail.

Finally, the chapter shows how the mercantilist economic philosophy of the time resulted in world wars for trade and colonies. Mercantilism also led to the acquisition of huge markets for British manufactured goods, especially cloth. The demand from these new markets fostered the continued growth of the domestic system and put pressure on it. This eventually led to important inventions and the development of the more efficient factory system. Thus the modern world was born. It is important to look for the interrelatedness of these changes and to keep in mind that it was in only one country, Great Britain, that all of these forces were fully at work.

Study Outline

Use this outline to preview the chapter before you read a particular section in your textbook and then as a self-check to test your reading comprehension after you have read the chapter section.

    I. Agriculture and the land
       A. The hazards of an agrarian economy
          1. The agricultural yields in seventeenth-century Europe were not much higher than in ancient Greece.
          2. Frequent poor harvests and bad weather led to famine and disease.
       B. The open-field system
          1. The open-field system, developed during the Middle Ages, divided the land into a few large fields, which were then cut up into long, narrow strips.
          2. The fields were farmed jointly by the community, but a large portion of the arable land was always left fallow.
          3. Common lands were set aside for community use.
          4. The labor and tax system throughout Europe was unjust, but eastern European peasants suffered the most.
             a. There were few limitations on the amount of forced labor the lord could require.
             b. Serfs could be sold.
          5. By the eighteenth century most peasants in western Europe were free from serfdom, and many owned some land.
       C. The agricultural revolution
          1. It was not possible for the peasants to increase their landholdings by taking land from the rich landowners.
          2. The use of idle fallow land by crop rotation increased cultivation, which meant more food.
             a. The secret was in alternating grain crops with nitrogen-storing crops, such as peas and beans, root crops, and grasses.
             b. This meant more fodder for animals, which meant more meat for the people and more manure for fertilizer.
             c. These improvements necessitated ending the open-field system by "enclosing" the fields.
          3. Enclosure of the open fields also meant the disappearance of common land which hurt the small landholders and village poor.
             a. Many peasants and some noble landowners opposed these changes.
             b. The enclosure process was slow, and enclosed and open fields existed side by side for a long time.
             c. Only in the Low Countries and England was enclosure widespread.

D. The leadership of the Low Countries and England
   1. By the middle of the seventeenth century, the Low Countries led in intensive farming.
       a. This Dutch lead was due largely to the need to feed a growing population.
       b. The growth of the urban population provided good markets for the produce.
   2. Dutch engineers such as Vermuyden helped England drain its marshes to create more arable land.
       a. Townsend was one of the pioneers of English agricultural improvement.
       b. Tull advocated the use of horses for plowing and drilling equipment for sowing seeds.
E. The cost of enclosure
   1. Some historians argue that the English landowners were more efficient than continental owners, and that enclosures were fair.
   2. Others argue that the enclosure acts forced small peasants and landless cottagers off the land.
   3. In reality, the enclosure and the exclusion of cottagers and laborers had begun as early as the sixteenth century.
       a. It was the independent peasant farmers who could not compete, and thus began to disappear.
       b. The tenant farmers, who rented land from the big landlords, benefited from enclosure.
       c. By 1815 a tiny minority of English and Scottish landlords held most of the land—which they rented to tenants, who hired laborers.
   4. The eighteenth-century enclosure movement marked the completion of the rise of market-oriented estate agriculture and the emergence of a landless rural proletariat.
II. The beginning of the population explosion
A. The limitations on population growth
   1. The traditional checks on growth were famine, disease, and war.
   2. These checks kept Europe's population growth rate fairly low.
B. The new pattern of population growth in the eighteenth century
   1. The basic cause of population growth was fewer deaths, partly owing to the disappearance of the plague.
       a. Stricter quarantine measures helped eliminate the plague.
       b. The elimination of the black rat by the brown rat was a key reason for the disappearance of the disease.
   2. Advances in medicine, such as inoculation against smallpox, did little to reduce the death rate in Europe.
   3. Improvements in sanitation promoted better public health.
   4. An increase in the food supply meant fewer famines and epidemics, especially as transportation improved.
   5. The growing population often led to overpopulation and increased rural poverty.
III. The growth of cottage industry
A. Rural industry
   1. The rural poor took in manufacturing work to supplement their income.
   2. By the eighteenth century this cottage industry challenged the monopoly of the urban craft industry.

B. The putting-out system
   1. The putting-out system was based on rural workers producing cloth in their homes for merchant-capitalists, who supplied the raw materials and paid for the finished goods.
   2. This capitalist system reduced the problem of rural unemployment and provided cheap goods.
   3. England led the way in the conversion from urban to rural textile production.
C. The textile industry in England as an example of the putting-out system
   1. The English textile industry was a family industry: the women would spin and the men would weave.
      a. This took place in their tiny cottage.
      b. Each cottage had a loom—e.g., Kay's new "flying shuttle" loom.
   2. A major problem was that there were not enough spinners to make yarn for the weaver.
   3. Strained relations often existed between workers and capitalist employers.
   4. The capitalist found it difficult to control the worker.
IV. Building the Atlantic economy in the eighteenth century
A. Mercantilism and colonial wars
   1. Mercantilism is a system of economic regulations aimed at increasing the power of the state, particularly by creating a favorable balance of trade.
   2. English mercantilism was further characterized by the use of government regulations to serve the interests of private individuals.
   3. The Navigation Acts were a form of economic warfare.
      a. They required that most goods exported to England be carried on British ships.
      b. These acts gave England a virtual trade monopoly with its colonies.
   4. The French quest for power in Europe and North America led to international wars.
      a. The loss of the War of the Spanish Succession forced France to cede parts of Canada to Britain.
      b. Maria Theresa of Austria sought to crush Prussia—this led to the Seven Years' War.
      c. New France under Montcalm was finally defeated by British forces at Quebec in 1759.
      d. The Seven Years' War (1756-1763) was the decisive struggle in the French-British competition for colonial empire; France ended up losing its North American possessions.
B. Land and wealth in North America
   1. Colonies helped relieve European poverty and surplus population as settlers eagerly took up farming on the virtually free land.
      a. The availability of land made labor expensive in the colonies.
      b. Cheap land and scarce labor were critical factors in the growth of slavery.
   2. The Spanish, Portuguese, and the Dutch introduced slavery into the Americas in the sixteenth century.
      a. The Dutch transported thousands of Africans to Brazil and the Caribbean to work on sugar plantations.
      b. British adoption of slavery in North America created a new class of rich plantation owners.

3. The English mercantilist system benefited American colonists.
   a. They exported food to the West Indies to feed the slaves and sugar and tobacco to Britain.
   b. The American shipping industry grew.
4. The population of the North American colonies grew very quickly during the eighteenth century, and the standards of living were fairly high.

C. The growth of foreign trade
1. Trade with the English colonists compensated for a decline in British trade on the Continent.
2. The colonies also encouraged industrial growth in Britain.

D. Revival in colonial Latin America
1. Spain's political revitalization was matched by economic improvement in its colonies.
   a. Silver mining recovered in Mexico and Peru.
   b. Trade grew, though industry remained weak.
2. In much of Latin America, Creole landowners dominated the economy and the Indian population by means of debt peonage.
3. Compared to North America, racial mixing was more frequent in Spanish America.

E. Adam Smith and Economic Liberalism
1. Despite mercantilism's contribution to imperial growth, a reaction to it set in.
2. The Scottish professor Adam Smith founded modern economics through his general idea of freedom of enterprise in foreign trade.
   a. He claimed that mercantilism stifled economic growth.
   b. He advocated free competition; he believed that pursuit of self-interest would lead to harmony and progress, for workers as well as employers.

Review Questions

Check your understanding of the chapter by answering the following questions.

1. How did the open-field system work? Why was much of the land left uncultivated while the people sometimes starved?

2. What changes brought the open-field system to an end?

3. Where did the modern agricultural revolution originate? Why?

4. What is meant by *enclosure*? Was this movement a great swindle of the poor by the rich, as some have claimed?

5. Was the dramatic growth of population in the eighteenth century due to a decreasing death rate or an increasing birthrate? Explain.

6. How was the grip of the deadly bubonic plague finally broken?

7. What improvements in the eighteenth century contributed to the decline of disease and famine?

8. How did the putting-out system work and why did it grow?

9. What were the advantages and disadvantages of the putting-out system for the merchant-capitalist? For the worker?

10. What was mercantilism? How could it have been a cause of war? Of economic growth?

11. The eighteenth century witnessed a large number of expensive and drawn-out wars. Who was attempting to alter the balance of power? Were the causes of these wars economic or political?

12. Did the American colonists and the American colonial economy benefit or suffer from the British mercantilistic colonial system?

13. What role did the Creoles play in colonial Latin America? The *mestizos*? The Indians?

14. What was the general message set forth in Professor Adam Smith's book, *The Wealth of Nations*? How would his ideas impact on government?

Study-Review Exercises

Define the following key concepts and terms.

agrarian economy

famine foods

common land

open-field system

enclosure

mercantilism

cottage industry

putting-out system

fallow fields

agricultural revolution

crop rotation

asiento

mestizos

primogeniture

Creole elite

Identify and explain the significance of each of the following people and terms.
Marquis de Montcalm

Jethro Tull

Charles Townsend

Cornelius Vermuyden

bubonic plague

Asiatic brown rat

British Navigation Acts

Treaty of Paris

Peace of Utrecht

spinning jenny

turnips

potatoes

Explain the following wars in the age of mercantilism by filling in the appropriate information in the table.

Name of War	Dates	Participants	Causes	Outcome
Anglo-Dutch wars				
War of the Spanish Succession				
War of the Austrian Succession				
Seven Years' War				

Fill in the blank with the letter of the correct answer.

1. _____ Its disappearance encouraged population growth.

2. _____ Agricultural land set aside for general village use.

3. _____ The area with the highest average standard of living in the world.

4. _____ After 1763 the major power in India.

5. _____ West African slave trade.

6. _____ Led Europe in agricultural improvement.

7. _____ Offspring of racial intermarriage.

8. _____ The most important new eighteenth-century food.

a. Low Countries
b. *mestizos*
c. commons
d. Thirty Years' War
e. American colonies
f. potato
g. *asiento*
h. France
i. bubonic plague
j. Britain

Major Political Ideas

1. What was agricultural enclosure? A widely believed political ramification of the agricultural revolution was that the rich landowners used their power, including political influence, to swindle the poor cottagers and push farm laborers off the land. Do you agree? What are the arguments on both sides, and which is most convincing?

2. Mercantilism was a form of economic capitalism. Define it in full. What is the impact of mercantilism on political thought and political policy? Did mercantilism lead to war?

Issues for Essays and Discussion

From the late seventeenth century into the eighteenth century, western Europe (particularly the Netherlands and Britain) experienced an agricultural change, population explosion, and a growth of rural industry. Explain these changes. Make reference to specific events. In what way, if any, are these three interrelated?

Interpretation of Visual Sources

Study the photograph entitled *Enclosing the Fields*. What country do you suspect this is? Distinguish the traditional "open field" from the new "enclosed" organization. Identify the old ridges and furrows. Why were fields such as these enclosed?

Geography

1. Study Map 19.1, "Industry and Population in Eighteenth-Century Europe." Where were the five or six principal European centers for textile production? Does there appear to be any relationship between textile production and population density? What questions and observations does this map raise with regard to present and future economic growth?

2. On Outline Map 19.2 provided, and using Map 19.2 in the textbook as reference, mark the colonial holdings of the European countries in North America in 1755. What territorial changes took place in North America after 1763? Which European country gained most territory after 1763? Which country lost the most territory after 1763? Did the largest colonial holdings go to the largest European countries—or was a position on the Atlantic the key factor?

Outline Map 19.3

Understanding History Through the Arts

What influence did the culture of the East have on the imperialist westerners? Begin your inquiry with R. Schwab, *The Oriental Renaissance: Europe's Rediscovery of India and the East, 1680-1880* (1987). Conversely, a study of how the West influenced the architecture of India is found in G. H. R. Tillotson, *The Tradition of Indian Architecture: Continuity, Controversy, and Change Since 1850* (1990), and N. Evenson, *Indian Metropolis: A View Toward the West* (1990).

Problems for Further Investigation

1. What were the motives of those who carved out great new empires in South and North America? Why did the northern Europeans settle in North America and the southern Europeans concentrate on South America? Begin your study with D. K. Fieldhouse, *The Colonial Empires* (1971), and R. Davies, *The Rise of Atlantic Economies* (1973). Students interested in Scottish history will find the subject of how Scotland came to dominate the North American tobacco trade covered in T. Devine, *The Tobacco Lords: A Study of the Tobacco Merchants of Glasgow and Their Trading Activities, 1740-1850* (1975).

2. What were the new patterns of urbanization in this age of population growth and agricultural change? An important work on this subject that shows where urbanization took place over a 350-year period is J. De Vries, *European Urbanisation, 1500-1800* (1987).

3. Why did the agricultural revolution take place? How did agricultural change and rural life differ from place to place within Europe? For more on agricultural life in Britain, start with M. Overton, *Agricultural Revolution in England* (1996) and for the Netherlands, see J. de Vries, *The Dutch Rural Economy in the Golden Age, 1500-1700* (1974). On the subject of soil, climate, land tenure, and the routine of peasant life in Russia before 1917, turn to R. Pipes, *Russia Under the Old Regime** (1974, 1982). For Europe in general, F. Huggett, *The Land Question and European Society Since 1650** (1975), presents a picture of how agricultural changes affected the development of European society.

4. Was enclosure a blessing or a great swindle for the British farmer? This question has been debated by historians and social commentators since the movement toward business agriculture began in sixteenth-century England. The general argument against enclosure was first set out in the sixteenth century by Sir Thomas More, who claimed (in his book *Utopia*) that it resulted in rural unemployment and rural crime. It is the enclosures between 1750 and 1850, however, that are the most controversial. The best contemporary coverage of the debate is G. E. Mingay, *Enclosure and the Small Farmer in the Age of the Industrial Revolution** (1968), which also contains a useful bibliography.

---

*Available in paperback.

Self-Test Multiple-Choice Questions

<u>Do</u> <u>not</u> assume that these questions will appear on any examination. It is recommended that you <u>not</u> memorize these questions, but use them only as a self-test. Answers are at the end of this book.

1. Dutch agricultural innovation in the eighteenth century was due to
   a. the movement of people from cities to rural areas.
   b. British examples.
   c. population growth and extensive urbanization.
   d. the discovery of the open-field system.

2. Which of the following was a weakness of the cottage textile industry?
   a. An imbalance between spinning and weaving
   b. Shortage of labor
   c. Rigid control of the quality of the product
   d. Not enough demand for the product

3. Which of the following is a characteristic of eighteenth-century economic change?
   a. Decreased world trade
   b. The decline of the cottage system of textile production
   c. The creation of more common lands and open fields for production
   d. The increase in both population and food supply

4. The English enclosure movement ultimately resulted in
   a. more land for a greater number of farmers.
   b. fewer opportunities for the well-off tenant farmers.
   c. the concentration of landowning in the hands of a tiny minority.
   d. opportunity for the landless laborer to purchase small farms.

5. The agricultural improvements of the mid-eighteenth century were based on the elimination of
   a. livestock farming.
   b. the open-field system.
   c. rotation of fields.
   d. nitrogen-producing plants, such as peas and beans.

6. Which of the following prevented eighteenth-century peasants from earning a profit on their land?
   a. The combination of oppressive landlords and poor harvests
   b. The plague
   c. The relatively light taxes imposed on them by landlords
   d. Their reliance on crop rotation

7. The mercantilist attitude toward the state was that
   a. the government should regulate the economy.
   b. governmental power should be increased at the expense of private profit.
   c. using governmental economic power to help private interests is unethical.
   d. the economy should be left to operate according to its natural laws.

8.   The new farming system consisting of crop rotation and the use of nitrogen-fixing crops caught on quickly in
     a.   the Low Countries and England.
     b.   Russia.
     c.   eastern Europe as a whole.
     d.   Scandinavia.

9.   The rapid development of Dutch farming was the result of all of the following *except*
     a.   the increasing number of cities and towns.
     b.   Dutch reluctance to accept agricultural innovations.
     c.   an unencumbered political and economic system.
     d.   a dense population.

10. A fair description of the European population before 1700 would be that it
     a.   was remarkably uniform in its growth.
     b.   increased steadily on account of very young marriages and large families.
     c.   decreased slightly on account of war, famine, and disease.
     d.   grew slowly and erratically.

11. After 1720, the plague did not reappear because of all of the following *except*
     a.   the development of an effective vaccination against the disease in 1718.
     b.   the practice of isolating carriers of the dread disease.
     c.   the invasion of the Asiatic brown rat.
     d.   quarantine in Mediterranean ports.

12. In the mid-seventeenth century, England's major maritime competitor was
     a.   France.
     b.   the Netherlands.
     c.   Spain.
     d.   Denmark.

13. The Seven Years' War between France and Britain resulted in
     a.   British dominance in North America and India.
     b.   French dominance in North America and India.
     c.   a stalemate.
     d.   British dominance only in North America.

14. The slow growth of industry in North America during the colonial period was caused by
     a.   the availability of land and the high cost of labor.
     b.   a lack of capital for investment.
     c.   a scorn for industry.
     d.   British settlers in America having no use for manufactured goods.

15. The black-to-white ratio in America by 1774 was
    a. one to four.
    b. one to eight.
    c. one to ten.
    d. one to two.

16. The abundance of land in the American colonies encouraged all of the following *except*
    a. increased population through natural increase and immigration.
    b. a higher standard of living.
    c. the growth of slavery in the southern colonies.
    d. economic inequality.

17. Which of the following resulted from British mercantilist policies?
    a. A reduction of exports to the Continent
    b. A serious decline of Dutch shipping and commerce
    c. British colonists no longer purchasing all of their goods from Britain
    d. A decline of trade with colonial plantation owners

18. The group that used the new farming methods to the fullest in England was
    a. independent farmers.
    b. well-financed, profit-minded tenant farmers.
    c. large landowners.
    d. small landowning wage laborers.

19. The group who formed the aristocratic elite in Spanish America was the
    a. Creoles.
    b. Indians.
    c. *mestizos*.
    d. Habsburgs.

20. The landowners who dominated the economy and the Indian population of Spain's Latin American empire are known as
    a *mestizos*.
    b. Creoles.
    c. mercantilists.
    d. warlords.

21. Vermuyden's famous "Dutch river" canal was located in
    a. Cambridgeshire, England.
    b. the swampland south of Amsterdam.
    c. the province of Groningen in the Netherlands.
    d. eastern Germany.

22. The initial target of the English Navigation Acts was
    a. France.
    b. Spain.
    c. the American colonists.
    d. the Dutch.

23. As a result of British victory in the War of the Spanish Succession, Spain was forced to give up the *asiento*, meaning
    a. the Isthmus of Panama.
    b. Nova Scotian fishing rights.
    c. Mexico.
    d. the West African slave trade.

24. The Seven Years' War, which ended in 1763, was a victory for
    a. France, who received Louisiana.
    b. Spain, who won the *asiento* back.
    c. Britain, who won territory in North America and India.
    d. the colonists in America, who won free trade rights.

25. British men and women, by the workings of the mercantilist system, were able to purchase goods such as sugar, tobacco, and dried fish
    a. only from plantations within the empire, such as America.
    b. from any country in the world.
    c. from the Continent, largely the Dutch, because of cheapness.
    d. from the Spanish merchants of Central and South America.

Chapter 20

The Changing Life of the People

Learning Objectives

After reading and studying this chapter you should be able to:

1. describe the living conditions of the people, and the changing attitudes about marriage, pregnancy, women, and children.

2. describe in what ways and why diet and medical care changed for the masses.

3. describe the influence of religion and the church in everyday life—and the mixing of religion and leisure.

Chapter Summary

This chapter is about how men and women lived in preindustrial society. The aspects of everyday life, such as family relations, sex, marriage, health, and religion, took a secondary place in history. As a result, much of our understanding of these subjects is often based on myth rather than on solid historical research and interpretations. This chapter corrects some of the long-standing myths and provides a close look at the life of the people.

Contrary to early belief, for example, it appears that in western Europe the nuclear rather than the extended family was very common among preindustrial people. Furthermore, preindustrial people did not marry in their early teens, and illegitimacy was not as common as usually thought, and certainly less so than today. The concept of childhood as we know it hardly existed. The author also shows that when the poor got enough to eat their diet was probably almost as nutritionally sound as that of rich people. As for medical science, it probably did more harm than good in the eighteenth century. Also explained in this chapter are the reasons for a kind of "sexual revolution," particularly for women, beginning in the mid-eighteenth century, when young people began engaging in sex at an earlier age and illegitimacy began to rise. These changes accompanied new patterns of marriage and work—much of which were connected to the growth of new economic opportunities for men and women.

Education and literacy improved significantly, particularly in countries such as Prussia and Scotland. In the area of religion the eighteenth century witnessed a tug of war between the Enlightenment's attempt to demystify Christianity and place it on a more rational basis and a popular movement to retain traditional ritual, superstition, and religious mysteries. In Protestant and Catholic countries alike, rulers and religious leaders sought to purify religion by eliminating many ritualistic practices. The response to this reform by the common people in Catholic countries was a resurgence of religious ritual and mysticism, while in Protestant Germany and England there occurred a popular religious revival based on piety and emotional conversion. Meanwhile, most of Europe—Catholic and Protestant—saw the state increase its control over the church.

Study Outline

Use this outline to preview the chapter before you read a particular section in your textbook and then as a self-check to test your reading comprehension after you have read the chapter section.

I. Marriage and the family
  A. Extended and nuclear families
    1. The nuclear family, not the extended family, was most common in preindustrial western and central Europe.
      a. This conclusion is based on new studies of "parish registers."
    2. Early marriage was not common prior to 1750, and many women (perhaps as much as half) never married at all.
      a In a typical English village, women and men married at twenty-seven.
    3. Marriage was commonly delayed because of poverty and/or local law and tradition.
  B. Work away from home
    1. Many boys left home to work as craftsmen or laborers.
    2. Girls left to work as servants—where they often were physically and sexually mistreated.
  C. Premarital sex and community controls
    1. Illegitimate children were not common in preindustrial society; premarital sex was common, but marriage usually followed.
      a. The traditional (open-field) village system was a check upon both illegitimacy and early marriage.
      b. Public action against domestic disputes and marital scandals was frequent—often taking the form of degrading public rituals.
    2. Birth control methods were primitive and undependable.
      a. Coitus interruptus was the most common form of birth control.
  D. New patterns of marriage and illegitimacy
    1. Between about 1750 and 1850 the number of illegitimate births soared—in some places from 2 to 25 percent of all births.
      a. Fewer young women were abstaining from premarital intercourse and fewer young men were marrying the women they got pregnant.
    2. One cause for this was that the growth of cottage industry (and later, the factory) resulted in people marrying earlier and for love.
    3. Another cause was that more young villagers were moving to towns and cities where they were no longer subject to village controls.
      a. Low wages, inequality, and changing economic and social conditions made it difficult for women to acquire a marriage based on romance.
II. Children and Education
  A. Childhood was dangerous because of adult indifference, neglect, and even abuse.
  B. Child care and nursing
    1. Infant mortality was very high.

2. Breast-feeding of children was common among poor women.
   a. Breast-fed infants were more likely to survive than the infant who was fed artificial foods.
3. Middle- and upper-class women hired wet nurses.
4. The occupation of wet-nursing was often exploitative of lower-class women.

C. Foundlings and infanticide
1. "Killing nurses" and infanticide were forms of population control.
2. Foundling hospitals were established but could not care for all the abandoned babies.
   a. Some had as many as 25,000 children.
   b. In reality, many were simply a form of legalized infanticide.

D. Attitudes toward children
1. Attitudes toward children were different from those of today, partly because of the frequency of death.
   a. Parents and doctors were generally indifferent to children.
   b. Children were often neglected or treated brutally.
2. The Enlightenment brought about more humane treatment of children.
   a. Critics like Rousseau (see Listening to the Past) called for more love and understanding of children.
   b. The practice of swaddling was discouraged.

E. Schools and popular literature
1. Formal education outside the home became more important for the upper classes in the sixteenth century.
   a. But education for common people did not begin until the seventeenth and eighteenth centuries.
2. Both Catholic and Protestant reformers encouraged popular education.
   a. Protestant Prussia led the way in universal education.
   b. Education was important in Presbyterian Scotland and elsewhere.
3. Literacy increased, especially in France and Scotland, between 1700 and 1800.
   a. The Bible was still the favorite book, but new pamphlets called chapbooks became popular.
   b. Another form was popular literature, such as fairy tales, romances, and fictionalized history.
   c. Some popular literature dealt with practical arts; most new literature did not challenge the political and social system.

III. Food and medical practice
A. The life span of Europeans increased from twenty-five years to thirty-five years between 1700 and 1800, partly because diet improved and plagues disappeared.
B. Diet and nutrition
1. The diet of ordinary people depended on grain.
   a. Peasants and poor people ate mainly grains and vegetables.
2. Most people believed in the "just price," whereby fair prices would be upheld by the government if needed.
   a. This view eventually clashed with the view of a free-market economy; food riots were often the result.
3. Vegetables were important in the diet of the poor; milk and meat were rarely eaten.
   a. Only in Britain and the Low Countries did people eat more meat.

      4.   Rich people ate quite differently from the poor.
         a.   Their diet was rich in meat and wine.
         b.   They spurned fruits and vegetables.

C. The impact of diet on health
    1.   There were nutritional advantages and disadvantages to the diet of the poor.
       a.   Their breads were very nutritious; the basic bread-and-vegetables diet was adequate.
       b.   The key dietary problem was getting enough green vegetables and milk.
    2.   The rich often ate too much rich food.

D. New foods, such as the potato, and new methods of farming brought on new patterns of food consumption.
    1.   The potato substantially improved the diet of the poor.
       a.   For some poor people, particularly in Ireland, the potato replaced grain as the primary food in the eighteenth century.
       b.   Elsewhere in Europe, the potato took hold more slowly, but became a staple by the end of the century.
    2.   There was a growth in market gardening and an improvement in food variety in the eighteenth century.
    3.   There was some improvement in knowledge about diet, and Galen's influence declined.
    4.   Greater affluence caused many to turn to less nutritious food such as white bread and sugar.

E. The medical practitioners
    1.   The Enlightenment led to research and experimentation in medicine and a rise in the number of practitioners.
       a.   The demonic view of disease was common.
       b.   Women were increasingly excluded from the medical professions.
       c.   Faith healers were used to exorcise the demons.
    2.   Apothecaries (pharmacists) sold drugs that were often harmful to their patients; some drugs worked but too much reliance was placed on purging the bowels.
    3.   Physicians frequently bled or purged people to death.
    4.   Surgeons made progress in treating wounds but they often operated without anesthetics and in the midst of dirt.
    5.   Midwives were medical practitioners who treated various female needs—such as delivery of babies.
       a.   For economic reasons, male surgeons discredited women midwives.

F. Hospitals and medical experiments
    1.   Patients were crowded together, often several to a bed.
    2.   There was no fresh air or hygiene.
    3.   Hospital reform, partly due to Diderot's writings, began in the late eighteenth century.
    4.   Mental illness was misunderstood and treated inhumanely.
    5.   Some attempts at reform occurred in the late eighteenth century.

G. Medical experimentation intensified after 1750.
    1.   Some medical experimentation was creative quackery.

2. The conquest of smallpox was the greatest medical triumph of the eighteenth century; 80 percent of the population was stricken at some point in life.
    a. Montague's and Jenner's work on inoculation was the beginning of a significant decline in smallpox.
    b. Jenner's work laid the foundation for the science of immunology in the nineteenth century.

IV. Religion and popular culture
   A. The institutional church
      1. Despite the critical spirit of the Enlightenment, the local parish church remained important in daily life, and the priest or pastor was the link between the people and the church hierarchy.
      2. The Protestant belief in individualism in religion was tempered by increased state control over the church and religious life.
      3. Catholic monarchs also increased state control over the church, making it less subject to papal influence.
         a. Spain took control of ecclesiastical appointments and the Inquisition and, with France, pressured Rome to dissolve the Jesuits.
         b. In Austria, Maria Theresa and Joseph II greatly reduced the size and influence of the monasteries and convents.
   B. Protestant revival
      1. The complacency of earlier Protestantism ended with the advent of "Pietism," which stressed religious enthusiasm, popular education, and individual religious development.
      2. In England, Wesley was troubled by religious corruption, decline, and uncertainty.
         a. His Methodist movement rejected the Calvinist idea of predestination and stressed salvation through faith.
         b. Wesley's ministry brought on a religious awakening, particularly among the lower classes.
   C. Catholic piety
      1. In Catholic countries the old religious culture of ritual and superstition remained popular.
      2. Catholic clergy reluctantly allowed traditional religion to survive.
   D. Leisure and religion
      1. Carnival time saw a combination of religious celebration and popular recreation, often giving common people a chance to release their frustrations and aggressions.
      2. Common culture was oral, and participation tended to be by way of the group, not the individual activity.
      3. In the eighteenth century leisure tended to become more commercialized, including profit-oriented spectator sports.
         a. Blood sports, such as bullbaiting, were popular.
      4. The educated elites and the clergy led an attack on popular entertainment—hence a wedge was driven between common people and the educated public.

Review Questions

Check your understanding of this chapter by answering the following questions.

1. Did the typical preindustrial family consist of an extended or a nuclear family? What evidence can you cite to support your answer?

2. When did the custom of late marriage begin to change? Why?

3. Did preindustrial men and women practice birth control? What methods existed?

4. How do you explain that prior to 1750 there were few illegitimate children but that there was a growth of illegitimacy thereafter?

5. How and why did life expectancy improve in the eighteenth century?

6. What were the differences in the diets of the rich and the poor in the eighteenth century? What nutritional deficiencies existed?

7. How important was the potato in the eighteenth century?

8. How important were the eighteenth-century advances in medical science in extending the life span?

9. What was the demonic view of disease?

10. It is said that when it came to medical care, the poor were better off than the rich because they could not afford doctors or hospitals. Why might this have been true?

11. Why was there so much controversy over the smallpox inoculation? Was it safe?

12. How was mental illness regarded and treated in the eighteenth century?

13. Describe the forms in which popular religious culture remained in Catholic Europe.

14. Define pietism and describe how it is reflected in the work and life of John Wesley.

15. Describe the various forms popular leisure took in the eighteenth century and describe how and why changes were under way.

Study-Review Exercises

Define the following key concepts and terms.

extended family

demonic view of disease

nuclear family

preindustrial childhood

illegitimacy explosion

Methodists

coitus interruptus

purging

"killing nurses"

Jesuits

Identify and explain the significance of each of the following people.
Lady Mary Montague

Edward Jenner

James Graham

Joseph II

John Wesley

Test your understanding of the chapter by providing the correct answers.

1. It is apparent that the practice of breast-feeding *increased/limited* the fertility of lower-class women.

2. The teenage bride *was/was not* the general rule in preindustrial Europe.

3. Prior to about 1750, premarital sex usually *did/did not* lead to marriage.

4. In the eighteenth century, the _____ was the primary new food in Europe.

5. People lived *longer/shorter* lives as the eighteenth century progressed.

6. The key to Jenner's discovery was the connection between immunity from smallpox and _____, a mild and noncontagious disease.

7. In Catholic countries it was largely *the clergy/the common people* who wished to hold on to traditional religious rituals and superstitions.

8. The Englishman who brought religious "enthusiasm" to the common folk of England. _____

Major Political Ideas

1. Do you believe that the material circumstances of preindustrial life had any affect on the way people thought and acted politically?

2. Does this chapter suggest that there was a cultural or economic division of society?

3. Was society more or less divided in terms of gender roles? In terms of class?

Issues for Essays and Discussion

1. Did the common people of preindustrial Europe enjoy a life of simple comfort and natural experiences? Or was theirs a life of brutal and cruel exploitation? Discuss this in terms of the nature of family life, childhood, diet and health, and education and religion.

2. In general, was life, by the late eighteenth century, getting better or worse?

Interpretation of Visual Sources

1. Study the reproduction of the print entitled *The Five Senses*. What is the theme of this print? What does it tell us about the treatment of children? Is this typical of how society treated children? How does the illustration mirror some of the ideas of the Enlightenment? (Refer to Chapter 18.)

2. Study the reproduction of the print *Hospital Life*. How many characteristics of eighteenth-century medical practice can you identify by viewing this scene?

Geography

View Map 20.1, "Literacy in France on the Eve of the French Revolution" in your textbook.
    What factor is used to measure "literacy?" What are the regional differences? Why do you suppose such differences existed? Perhaps there is a clue in Map 19.1.

Understanding History Through the Arts

1. What can art tell us about childhood in the preindustrial era? Painting is one of the major sources of information for the history of childhood. Preindustrial childhood is the subject of *Children's Games* by Pieter Brueghel the Elder, a lively, action-packed painting of over two hundred children engaged in more than seventy different games. The painting is the subject of an interesting article by A. Eliot, "Games Children Play," *Sports Illustrated* (January 11, 1971): 48-56.

2. How is preindustrial life portrayed in literature and film? Samuel Richardson wrote a novel about the life of a household servant who became the prey of the lecherous son of her master, *Pamela, or Virtue Rewarded** (1740). Tom Jones, eighteenth-century England's most famous foundling, was the fictional hero of Henry Fielding's *Tom Jones* and the subject and title of director Tony Richardson's highly acclaimed, award-winning film version of Fielding's novel. Starring Albert Finney, Susannah York, and Dame Edith Evans, the film re-creates, in amusing and satirical fashion, eighteenth-century English life. A more recent film adaptation is Richardson's *Joseph Andrews*, based on another Fielding novel.

---

*Available in paperback.

3. Was urban life more comfortable than rural life? What was the great attraction of the city? London was the fastest-growing city in the eighteenth century. How people lived in London is the subject of two highly readable and interesting books: M. D. George, *London Life in the Eighteenth Century** (3rd ed., 1951), and R. J. Mitchell and M. D. R. Leys, *A History of London Life** (1963).

Problems for Further Investigation

1. What was daily life like for poor men and women in this period? Few men in preindustrial society earned enough to support a family. This, in part, explains why and when men and women married, and why most people worked. See A. Imhof, *Lost Worlds: How Our European Ancestors Coped with Everyday Life and Why life Is So Hard Today* (1996). The subject of women and the family economy in eighteenth-century France is discussed by O. Hufton in *The Poor of Eighteenth-Century France* (1974).

2. Until about twenty years ago, it was fashionable to believe that the population explosion was due to improvements made by medical science. Although this theory is generally disclaimed today, it appears to be enjoying a slight revival. For both sides of the argument, begin your study with M. Anderson, *Population Change in North-Western Europe, 1750-1850** (1988), and then read the following journal articles (which also have bibliographies): T. McKeown and R. G. Brown, "Medical Evidence Related to English Population Change," *Population Studies* 9 (1955); T. McKeown and R. G. Record, "Reasons for the Decline in Mortality in England and Wales During the Nineteenth Century," *Population Studies* 16 (1962); and P. Razzell, "Population Change in Eighteenth-Century England: A Reinterpretation," *Economic History Review*, 2nd series, 18-2 (1965). For the history of disease, see D. Hopkins, *Princes and Peasants: Smallpox in History* (1977).

Self-Test Multiple-Choice Questions

<u>Do</u> <u>not</u> assume that these questions will appear on any examination. It is recommended that you <u>not</u> memorize these questions, but use them only as a self-test. Answers are at the end of this book.

1. One of the chief deficiencies of the diet of both rich and poor Europeans was the absence of sufficient
    a. meat.
    b. fruit and vegetables.
    c. white bread.
    d. wine.

---

*Available in paperback.

2. A family in which three or four generations live under the same roof under the direction of a patriarch is known as a(n)
   a. nuclear family.
   b. conjugal family.
   c. industrial household.
   d. extended family.

3. Prior to about 1750, marriage between two persons was more often than not
   a. undertaken freely by the couple.
   b. controlled by law and parents.
   c. based on romantic love.
   d. undertaken without economic considerations.

4. The establishment of foundling hospitals in the eighteenth century was an attempt to
   a. prevent the spread of the bubonic plague.
   b. isolate children from smallpox.
   c. prevent willful destruction and abandonment of newborn children.
   d. provide adequate childbirth facilities for rich women.

5. All but which of the following sentences about preindustrial society's attitudes toward children is true?
   a. Parents often treated their children with indifference and brutality.
   b. Poor children were often forced to work in the early factories.
   c. Doctors were the only people interested in the children's welfare.
   d. Killing of children by parents or nurses was common.

6. It appears that the role of doctors and hospital care in bringing about improvement in health in the eighteenth century was
   a. very significant.
   b. minor.
   c. helpful only in the area of surgery.
   d. helpful only in the area of preventive medicine.

7. In the seventeenth and early eighteenth centuries people usually married
   a. surprisingly late.
   b. surprisingly early.
   c. almost never.
   d. and divorced frequently.

8. Which of the following was *not* a general characteristic of the European family of the eighteenth century?
   a. The nuclear family
   b. Late marriages
   c. Many unmarried relatives
   d. The extended family

9. The overwhelming reason for postponement of marriage was
   a. that people didn't like the institution of marriage.
   b. lack of economic independence.
   c. the stipulation of a legal age.
   d. that young men and women valued the independence of a working life.

10. In the second half of the eighteenth century, the earlier pattern of marriage and family life began to break down. Which of the following was *not* a result of this change?
    a. A greater number of illegitimate births
    b. Earlier marriages
    c. Marriages exclusively for economic reasons
    d. Marriages for love

11. The "illegitimacy explosion" of the late eighteenth century was encouraged by all but which one of the following?
    a. The laws, especially in Germany, concerning the right of the poor to marry
    b. The mobility of young people needing to work off the farm
    c. The influence of the French Revolution, which repressed freedom in sexual and marital behavior
    d. The decreasing influence of parental pressure and village tradition

12. Which of the following statements best describes the attitude toward children in the first part of the eighteenth century?
    a. They were protected and cherished.
    b. They were never disciplined.
    c. They were treated as they were—children living in a child's world.
    d. They were ignored, often brutalized, and often unloved.

13. Most of the popular education in Europe of the eighteenth century was sponsored by
    a. the church.
    b. the state.
    c. private individuals.
    d. parents, in the home.

14. Which of the following would most likely be found in an eighteenth-century hospital?
    a. Isolation of patients
    b. Sanitary conditions
    c. Uncrowded conditions
    d. Uneducated nurses and poor nursing practices

15. The greatest medical triumph of the eighteenth century was the conquest of
    a. starvation.
    b. smallpox.
    c. scurvy.
    d. cholera.

16. The practice of sending one's newborn baby to be suckled by a poor woman in the countryside was known as
    a. the cottage system.
    b. infanticide.
    c. wet-nursing.
    d. overlaying.

17. Which of the following was *not* a common food for the European poor?
    a. Vegetables
    b. Beer
    c. Dark bread
    d. Milk

18. It appears that the chief dietary problem of European society was the lack of an adequate supply of
    a. vitamins A and C.
    b. vitamin B complex.
    c. meat.
    d. sugar.

19. Probably the best thing an eighteenth-century sick person could do with regard to hospitals would be to
    a. enter only if an operation was suggested by a doctor.
    b. enter only if in need of drugs.
    c. enter only a hospital operating under Galenic theory.
    d. stay away.

20. The country that led the way in the development of universal education was
    a. Britain.
    b. Prussia.
    c. France.
    d. Austria.

21. In which of the following countries did a religious conviction that the path to salvation lay in careful study of the Scriptures lead to an effective network of schools and a very high literacy rate by 1800?
    a. Austria
    b. England
    c. France
    d. Scotland

22. The desire for "bread as white as snow" led to
    a. a decline in bacterial diseases.
    b. a significant nutritional advance.
    c. an increase in the supply of bread.
    d. a nutritional decline.

23. The general eighteenth-century attitude toward masturbation was that it
    a. was harmless and perhaps healthy.
    b. unacceptable for women but okay for men.
    c. caused insanity and thereby must be prevented.
    d. did not exist.

24. The general trend in Catholic countries was for monarchs to follow the Protestant lead in
    a. limiting the power and influence of the church.
    b. adopting the idea of predestination.
    c. casting off all allegiance to the papacy.
    d. protecting the poor.

25. During the eighteenth century the Society of Jesus
    a. found its power and position in Europe rise.
    b. gained considerable land in Portugal and France.
    c. was ordered out of France and Spain.
    d. avoided politics and property accumulation altogether.

Chapter 21

The Revolution in Politics, 1775-1815

Learning Objectives

After reading and studying this chapter you should be able to:

1. distinguish between the causes of the American and French revolutions.

2. explain the effect of these revolutions on the people.

3. discuss the impact of the French Revolution on the status of men and women of the middle and lower classes.

Chapter Summary

The French and American revolutions were two of the most important political events of all times. They were also a dramatic conclusion to the Enlightenment, and both revolutions, taken together, form a major turning point in human history. This chapter explains what these great revolutions were all about.

The chapter begins by describing classical liberalism, the fundamental ideology of the revolution in politics. Liberalism, which had deep roots, called for freedom and equality at a time when monarchs and aristocrats took their great privileges for granted. The immediate cause of the American Revolution, the British effort to solve the problem of war debts, was turned into a political struggle by the American colonists, who already had achieved considerable economic and personal freedom. The American Revolution stimulated reform efforts throughout Europe.

It was in France that the ideas of the Enlightenment and liberalism were put to their fullest test. The bankruptcy of the state gave the French aristocracy the chance to grab power from a weak king. This move backfired, however, because the middle class grabbed even harder. It is significant that the revolutionary desires of the middle class depended on the firm support and violent action of aroused peasants and poor urban workers. It was this action of the common people that gave the revolution its driving force.

In the first two years of the French Revolution, the middle class, with its allies from the peasantry and urban poor, achieved unprecedented reforms. The outbreak of an all-European war against France in 1792 then resulted in a reign of terror and a dictatorship by radical moralists, of whom Robespierre was the greatest. By 1795, this radical patriotism wore itself out. The revolutionary momentum slowed, and the Revolution deteriorated into a military dictatorship under the opportunist Napoleon. Yet, until

1815 the history of France was that of war, and that war spread liberalism to the rest of Europe. French conquests also stimulated nationalism. The world of politics was turned upside down.

Study Outline

Use this outline to preview the chapter before you read a particular section in your textbook and then as a self-check to test your reading comprehension after you have read the chapter section.

    I. Liberty and equality
       A. In the eighteenth century, liberty meant human rights and freedoms and the sovereignty of the people.
          1. Liberals demanded that citizens' rights had no limits except those that assure rights to others.
          2. Revolutionary liberals believed that the people were sovereign.
       B. Equality meant equal rights and equality of opportunity.
          1. But most liberals did not extend such rights to women.
          2. "Equality" pertained to equality of opportunity and legal equality, not economic equality.
       C. The roots of liberalism
          1. The Judeo-Christian tradition of individualism, reinforced by the Reformation, supported liberalism.
          2. Liberalism's modern roots are found in the Enlightenment's concern for freedom and legal equality, as best expressed by Locke and Montesquieu.
       D. The attraction of liberalism
          1. Liberalism was attractive to the prosperous, well-educated elites.
          2. It lacked popular support because common people were more interested in economic issues and the protection of traditional practices and institutions.
   II. The American Revolution (1775-1789)
       A. Some argue that the American Revolution was not a revolution at all but merely a war for independence.
       B. The origins of the Revolution
          1. The British wanted the Americans to pay their share of imperial expenses.
            a. Americans paid very low taxes.
            b. Parliament passed the Stamp Act (1765) to raise revenue.
            c. Vigorous protest from the colonies forced its repeal (1766).
          2. Although no less represented than Englishmen themselves, many Americans believed they had the right to make their own laws.
            a. Americans have long exercised a great deal of independence.
            b. Their greater political equality was matched by greater social and economic equality—there was no hereditary noble or serf class.
          3. The issue of taxation and representation ultimately led to the outbreak of fighting.
       C. The independence movement was encouraged by several factors.
          1. The British refused to compromise, thus losing the support of many colonists.
          2. The radical ideas of Thomas Paine, expressed in the best-selling *Common Sense*, greatly influenced public opinion in favor of independence.

3. The Declaration of Independence, written by Thomas Jefferson and passed by the Second Continental Congress (1776), further increased the desire of the colonists for independence.

4. Although many Americans remained loyal to Britain, the independence movement had wide-based support from all sections of society.

5. European aid, especially from the French government and from French volunteers, contributed greatly to the American victory in 1783.

D. Framing the Constitution and the Bill of Rights

1. The federal, or central, government was given important powers—the right to tax, the means to enforce its laws, and the regulation of trade—but the states had important powers too.

2. The executive, legislative, and judicial branches of the government were designed to balance one another.

3. The Anti-Federalists feared that the central government had too much power; to placate them, the Federalists wrote the Bill of Rights, which spells out the rights of the individual.

    a. Liberty did not, however, necessarily mean democracy.

    b. Equality meant equality before the law, not equality of political participation or economic well-being.

E. The American Revolution reinforced the Enlightenment idea that a better world was possible, and Europeans watched the new country with fascination.

III. The French Revolution (1789-1791)

A. The influence of the American Revolution

1. Many French soldiers, such as Lafayette, served in America and were impressed by the ideals of the Revolution.

2. The American Revolution influenced the French Revolution, but the latter was more violent and more influential; it opened the era of modern politics.

B. The breakdown of the old order

1. By the 1780s, the government was nearly bankrupt.

2. The French banking system could not cope with the fiscal problems, leaving the monarchy with no choice but to increase taxes.

C. Legal orders and social realities: the three estates

1. The first estate, the clergy, had many privileges and much wealth, and it levied an oppressive tax (the tithe) on landowners.

2. The second estate, the nobility, also had great privileges, wealth, and power, and it taxed the peasantry for its own profit.

3. The third estate, the commoners, was a mixture of a few rich members of the middle class, urban workers, and the mass of peasants.

D. Revisionist historians challenge the traditional interpretation of the origins of the French Revolution.

1. They argue that the bourgeoisie was not locked in conflict with the nobility, that both groups were highly fragmented.

    a. The nobility remained fluid and relatively open.

    b. Key sections of the nobility were liberal.

    c. The nobility and the bourgeoisie were not economic rivals.

2. Nevertheless, the old interpretation, that a new social order was challenging the old, is still convincing and valid.

E. The formation of the National Assembly of 1789
1. Louis XVI's plan to tax landed property was opposed by the Assembly of Notables and the Parlement of Paris.
2. Louis then gave in and called for a meeting of the Estates General, the representative body of the three estates.
   a. Two-thirds of the delegates from the clergy were parish priests.
   b. A majority of the noble representatives were conservative, but fully a third were liberals committed to major change.
   c. The third estate representatives were largely lawyers and government officials.
   d. The third estate wanted the three estates to meet together to ensure the passage of fundamental reforms.
   e. According to Sieyès in *What Is the Third Estate?*, the third estate constituted the true strength of the French nation.
3. The dispute over voting in the Estates General led the third estate to break away and form the National Assembly, which pledged, in the Oath of the Tennis Court, not to disband until they had written a new constitution.
4. Louis tried to reassert his monarchical authority and assembled an army.
F. The revolt of the poor and the oppressed
1. Rising bread prices in 1788-1789 stirred the people to action.
2. Fearing attack by the king's army, angry Parisians stormed the Bastille on July 14, 1789.
   a. The people took the Bastille, and the king was forced to recall his troops.
   b. This uprising of the masses saved the National Assembly.
   c. All across France peasants began to rise up against their lords.
   d. The Great Fear seized the countryside.
3. The peasant revolt forced the National Assembly to abolish feudal obligations.
G. A limited monarchy established by the bourgeoisie
1. The National Assembly's Declaration of the Rights of Man (1789) proclaimed the rights of all citizens and guaranteed equality before the law and a representative government.
2. Meanwhile, the poor women of Paris marched on Versailles and forced the royal family and the government to move to Paris.
3. The National Assembly established a constitutional monarchy and passed major reforms.
   a. The nobility was abolished as a separate legal order.
   b. All lawmaking power was placed in the hands of the National Assembly.
   c. The jumble of provinces was replaced by 83 departments.
   d. The metric system was introduced.
   e. Economic freedom was promoted.
4. The National Assembly granted religious freedom to Jews and Protestants, nationalized the property of the church, and abolished the monasteries.
5. This attack on the church turned many people against the Revolution.
IV. World war and republican France (1791-1799)
A. Foreign reactions and the beginning of war
1. Outside France, liberals and radicals hoped that the revolution would lead to a reordering of society everywhere, but conservatives such as Burke (in *Reflections on the Revolution in France*) predicted it would lead to chaos and tyranny.

2. Wollstonecraft challenged Burke (in *A Vindication of the Rights of Woman*), arguing that it was time for women to demand equal rights.
3. Fear among European kings and nobility that the revolution would spread resulted in the Declaration of Pillnitz (1791), which threatened the invasion of France by Austria and Prussia.
4. In retaliation, the patriotic French deputies, most of them Jacobins, declared war on Austria in 1792.
   a. But France was soon retreating before the armies of the First Coalition.
   b. A war of patriotic fervor swept France.
5. In August of 1792 a revolutionary crowd attacked the royal place and the Legislative Assembly imprisoned the king.

B. The "second revolution" and rapid radicalization in France
1. The National Convention proclaimed France a republic in 1792.
2. However, the convention was split between the Girondists and the Mountain, led by Robespierre and Danton.
3. Louis XVI was tried and convicted of treason by the National Convention and guillotined in early 1793.
4. French armies continued the "war against tyranny" by declaring war on nearly all of Europe.
5. In Paris, the struggle between the Girondists and the Mountain for political power led to the political rise of the laboring poor.
6. The sans-culottes—the laboring poor—allied with the Mountain and helped Robespierre and the Committee of Public Safety gain power.

C. Total war and the Terror
1. Robespierre established a planned economy to wage total war and aid the poor.
   a. The government fixed prices on key products and instituted rationing.
   b. Workshops were nationalized to produce goods for the war effort, and raw materials were requisitioned.
2. The Reign of Terror was instituted to eliminate opposition to the Revolution, and many people were jailed or executed.
3. The war became a national mission against evil within and outside of France, and not a class war.
   a. Ideas of common tradition and democracy combined with the danger of foreign and internal foes to encourage nationalism.
   b. A huge army of patriots was led by young generals who relied on mass attack to overwhelm the enemy.

D. The Thermidorian reaction and the Directory (1794-1799)
1. Fear of the Reign of Terror led to the execution of its leader, Robespierre.
2. The period of the Thermidorian reaction following Robespierre's death was marked by a return to bourgeois liberalism.
   a. Economic controls were abolished; the poor lost their fervor for revolution.
   b. Riots by the poor were put down and rural women brought back the Catholic church and worship.
   c. The middle class wrote another constitution to protect their power; the Directory, a five-man executive body, was established.
3. A military dictatorship, under Bonaparte, was established in order to prevent a return to peace and monarchy.

V. The Napoleonic era (1799-1815)
  A. Napoleon's rule
    1. Napoleon appealed to many, like Abbé Sieyès, who looked for a strong military leader to end the country's upheaval.
    2. Napoleon was named first consul of the republic in 1799.
    3. He maintained order and worked out important compromises.
        a. His Civil Code of 1804 granted the middle class equality under the law and safeguarded their right to own property.
        b. He confirmed the gains of the peasants.
        c. He centralized the government, strengthened the bureaucracy, and granted amnesty to nobles.
        d. He signed the Concordat of 1801, which guaranteed freedom of worship for Catholics.
    4. Napoleon brought order and stability to France but betrayed the ideals of the Revolution by violating the rights of free speech and press and free elections.
        a. Women had no political rights; they lost many gains they had made, and the Napoleonic Code re-established the power of the male in the family.
        b. There were harsh penalties for political offenses.
  B. Napoleon's wars and foreign policy
    1. He defeated Austria (1801) and made peace with Britain (1802), the two remaining members of the Second Coalition.
    2. Another war (against the Third Coalition—Austria, Russia, Sweden, and Britain) resulted in British naval dominance at the Battle of Trafalgar (1805).
    3. Napoleon used the fear of a conspiracy to return the Bourbons to power to get himself proclaimed emperor in 1804.
    4. The Third Coalition collapsed at Austerlitz (1805), and Napoleon reorganized the German states into the Confederation of the Rhine.
    5. In 1806, Napoleon defeated the Prussians at Jena and Auerstädt.
        a. In the Treaty of Tilsit (1807), Prussia lost half its population, while Russia accepted Napoleon's reorganization of western and central Europe.
        b. Russia also joined with France in a blockade against British goods.
    6. Napoleon's Grand Empire in Europe meant French control of continental Europe.
        a. Napoleon introduced many French laws, abolishing feudal dues and serfdom in the process.
        b. However, he also levied heavy taxes.
    7. The beginning of the end for Napoleon came with the Spanish revolt (1808) and the British blockade.
    8. The French invasion of Russia in 1812 was a disaster for Napoleon—over 500,000 died or were taken prisoner.
    9. Napoleon was defeated by the Fourth Coalition (Austria, Prussia, Russia, and Great Britain) and abdicated his throne in 1814, only to be defeated again at Waterloo in 1815.
    10. The Bourbon dynasty was restored in France under Louis XVIII.
VI. Summary
  A. The French revolution left a range of political options and alternative visions of the future—including liberalism, assertive nationalism, radical democratic republicanism, embryonic socialism, and self-conscious conservatism.

Review Questions

Check your understanding of the chapter by answering the following questions.

1. The ideas of liberty and equality were the central ideas of classical liberalism. Define these ideas. Are they the same as democracy?

2. According to Locke, what is the function of government?

3. Did the Americans or the British have the better argument with regard to the taxation problem?

4. Why is the Declaration of Independence sometimes called the world's greatest political editorial?

5. What role did the European powers play in the American victory? Did they gain anything?

6. Describe the three estates of France. Who paid the taxes? Who held the wealth and power in France?

7. With the calling of the Estates General, "the nobility of France expected that history would repeat itself." Did it? What actually did happen?

8. What were the reforms of the National Assembly?

9. What were the cause and the outcome of the peasants' uprising of 1789?

10. What role did the poor women of Paris play in the Revolution?

11. Why did the Revolution turn into war in 1792?

12. Who were the sans-culottes? Why were they important to radical leaders such as Robespierre? What role did the common people play in the Revolution?

13. Why did the Committee of Public Safety need to institute a Reign of Terror?

14. Describe the Grand Empire of Napoleon in terms of its three parts. Was Napoleon a liberator or a tyrant?

15. What caused Napoleon's downfall? Was it inevitable?

Study-Review Exercises

Define the following key concepts and terms.

liberalism

liberty and equality

checks and balances

natural or universal rights

republican

popular sovereignty

tithe

Identify and explain the significance of each of the following people and terms.

Stamp Act

Battle of Trafalgar

American Bill of Rights

Loyalists

Constitutional Convention of 1787

Jacobins

Girondists

Mountain

Reign of Terror

National Assembly

Declaration of the Rights of Woman

Bastille

sans-culottes

Girondists

"the baker, the baker's wife, and the baker's boy"

Lord Nelson

Mary Wollstonecraft

Edmund Burke

Marie Antoinette

Marquis de Lafayette

Thomas Jefferson

Robespierre

John Locke

Abbé Sieyès

Test your understanding of the chapter by providing the correct answers.

1. Napoleon's plan to invade England was made impossible by the defeat of the French and Spanish navies in the Battle of _____ in 1805.

2. Overall, the common people of Paris played *a minor/an important* role in the French Revolution.

3. The author of the best-selling radical book *Common Sense*. _____

4. Prior to the crisis of the 1760s, American colonists had exercised *little/a great deal of* political and economic independence from Britain.

5. The peasant uprising of 1789 in France ended in *victory/defeat* for the peasant class.

6. By the 1790s, people like Sieyès were increasingly looking to *the people/a military ruler* to bring order to France.

Major Political Ideas

1. Define liberalism. What did it mean to be a liberal in the eighteenth and nineteenth century sense? How does this liberalism compare to twentieth-century liberalism? To democracy? What is the relationship between liberalism and the Enlightenment idea of natural law?

2. How did Americans interpret the term *equality* in 1789? Has it changed since then? Are the definitions of *liberalism* and *equality* unchangeable, or do they undergo periodic redefinition?

Issues for Essays and Discussion

1. What were the causes, both immediate and long term, of the French Revolution? Was it basically an economic event? A social or political struggle? Support your argument by making reference to specific events and ideas.

2. Why did the French Revolution become violent? Is it inevitable that all revolutions turn into violence and dictatorship?

3. Was the American Revolution a true revolution or a war of independence? Support your argument with reference to specific events and ideas.

Interpretation of Visual Sources

Study the reproduction of the print *To Versailles*. Who are the participants and what are their motives? Is a recognizable social class represented here? Did demonstrations such as this have any impact on the course of the Revolution?

Geography

1. On Outline Map 21.1 provided, and using Map 21.1 in the textbook as a reference, mark the following: the boundaries of France before the outbreak of war in 1792, and the areas acquired by France by 1810.

2. Look closely at Map 21.1 in the text. Can you find the four small British outposts scattered throughout Europe? How were these outposts necessary to and a reflection of Britain's military power? What did these outposts mean for smugglers and Napoleon's efforts to stop British trade with continental countries?

Outline Map 21.1

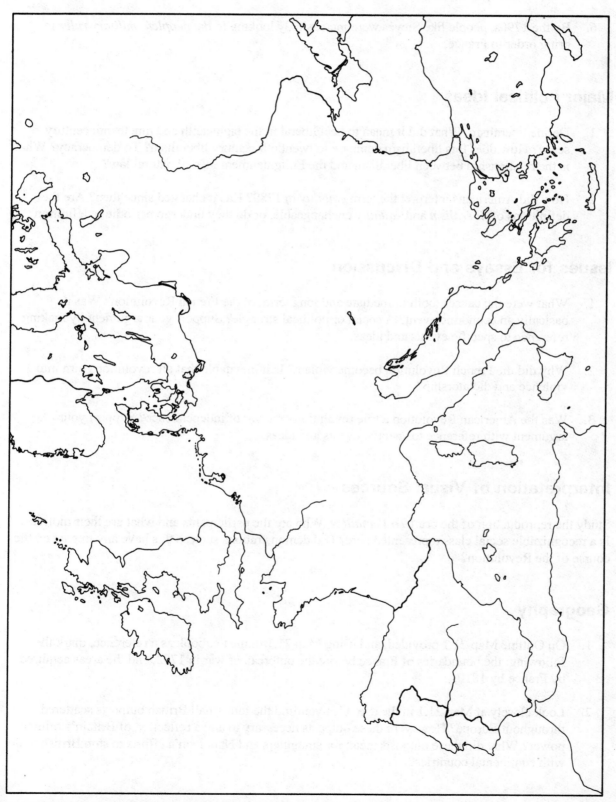

Understanding History Through the Arts

1. How did the era of revolution affect architecture? Out of the Enlightenment and the upheaval of the Revolution, and in response to the desire to create a new social order based on principles of natural law, French architects took traditional classical and baroque features and merged them with an interest in natural geometrical shapes. The result was an original architecture of bold and gigantic buildings. The leading architects in this movement were Etienne-Louis Boullée and Claude-Nicolas Ledoux. Their work can be found in most general histories of architecture, but the student may wish to begin with E. Kaufmann, *Architecture in the Age of Reason** (1954), and A. Vidler, *Claude-Nicolas Ledoux: Architecture and Social Reform at the End of the Ancien Régime* (1990).

2. What was the impact of the French Revolution on art? The Revolution in France forced art to become a statement of politics and political ideals. The style was a "new classicism" based on simplicity and rationality, with references to Roman civic virtue. This new style, whose goal was to inspire patriotism, was made popular by Jacques Louis David. David, a member of the National Convention, painted a number of emotional masterpieces that glorified first the Revolution—such as *Oath in the Tennis Court* and *The Death of Marat*—and later the patriotic aims of Napoleon. For a view of David and other revolutionary artists of the late eighteenth century, see E. Kennedy, *A Cultural History of the French Revolution* (1989), and R. Paulson, *Representations of Revolution, 1789-1820** (1987).

Problems for Further Investigation

1. Do individuals determine history, or is history the product of the economic-social-political environment? The various arguments of scholars over the motives and contributions of Napoleon are brought together in D. H. Pinkney, ed., *Napoleon: Historical Enigma** (1969). The story of Admiral Lord Nelson, Britain's hero and victor of great sea battles, is interestingly told in R. Hough, *Nelson, A Biography* (1980).

2. King George III of Britain has often been viewed, in American history, as the archenemy of liberty and constitutionalism. Is this a fair assessment? The debate over his role has gone on for a number of years and is the subject of a book of collected opinions, *George III: Tyrant or Constitutional Monarch?** (1964), edited by E. A. Reitan.

3. How important were common men and women in the French Revolution? Did the people of Paris play a role in determining the Revolution's political ideas? Group action in a revolution makes for an interesting study. The role of women in the Revolution in France (and in other times) is well handled in E. Boulding, *The Underside of History: A View of Women Through Time* (1976). The Paris "mob" that participated in the Revolution in France is the subject of the interesting study by George Rude, *The Crowd in the French Revolution** (1959). See also D. Levy and H. Applewhite, eds., *Women and Politics in the Age of Democratic Revolution* (1990).

---

*Available in paperback.

4. How did the French Revolution start? Students interested in the origins of the French Revolution will want to check R. W. Greenlaw, ed., *The Economic Origins of the French Revolution** (1958), and those interested in political theory may want to consider a study of liberalism, beginning with H. Schultz, ed., *English Liberalism and the State: Individualism or Collectivism** (1972).

Self-Test Multiple-Choice Questions

<u>Do</u> <u>not</u> assume that these questions will appear on any examination. It is recommended that you <u>not</u> memorize these questions, but use them only as a self-test. Answers are at the end of this book.

1. Eighteenth-century liberals stressed
   a. economic equality.
   b. equality in property holding.
   c. equality of opportunity
   d. racial and sexual equality.

2. Which came first?
   a. Formation of the French National Assembly
   b. Execution of King Louis XVI
   c. American Bill of Rights
   d. Seven Years' War

3. The French Jacobins were
   a. aristocrats who fled France.
   b. monarchists.
   c. priests who supported the Revolution.
   d. revolutionary radicals.

4. The French National Assembly was established by
   a. the middle class of the Third Estate.
   b. King Louis XVI.
   c. the aristocracy.
   d. the sans-culottes.

5. The National Assembly did all but which of the following?
   a. Nationalized church land
   b. Issued the Declaration of the Rights of Man
   c. Established the metric system of weights and measures
   d. Brought about the Reign of Terror

---

*Available in paperback.

6. In 1789 the influential Abbé Sieyès wrote a pamphlet in which he argued that France should be ruled by the
   a. nobility.
   b. clergy.
   c. people.
   d. king.

7. In 1799 Sieyès argued that authority in society should come from
   a. the people.
   b. the leaders of the Third Estate.
   c. a strong military leader.
   d. the Directory.

8. In the first stage of the Revolution the French established
   a. a constitutional monarchy.
   b. an absolutist monarchy.
   c. a republic.
   d. a military dictatorship.

9. Edmund Burke's *Reflections on the Revolution in France* is a defense of
   a. the Catholic church.
   b. Robespierre and the Terror.
   c. the working classes of France.
   d. the English monarchy and aristocracy.

10. Generally, the people who did not support eighteenth-century liberalism were the
    a. elite.
    b. members of the middle class.
    c. masses.
    d. intellectuals.

11. Most eighteenth-century demands for liberty centered on
    a. the equalization of wealth.
    b. a classless society.
    c. better welfare systems.
    d. equality of opportunity.

12. Americans objected to the Stamp Act because the tax it proposed
    a. was exorbitant.
    b. was not required of people in Britain.
    c. would have required great expense to collect.
    d. was imposed without their consent.

13. The American Revolution
    a. had very little impact on Europe.
    b. was supported by the French monarchy.
    c. was not influenced by Locke or Montesquieu.
    d. was supported by almost everyone living in the United States.

14. Which of the following was a cause of the outbreak of revolution in France in 1789?
    a. Peasant revolt in the countryside
    b. The death of Louis XVI
    c. The demand of the nobility for greater power and influence
    d. The invasion of France by foreign armies

15. The first successful revolt against Napoleon began in 1808 in
    a. Spain.
    b. Russia.
    c. Germany.
    d. Italy.

16. Prior to about 1765, the American people were
    a. fairly independent of the British government.
    b. subject to heavy and punitive British controls.
    c. paying a majority share of British military costs.
    d. under the direct control of the East India Company.

17. The major share of the tax burden in France was carried by the
    a. peasants.
    b. bourgeoisie.
    c. clergy.
    d. nobility.

18. The participation of the common people of Paris in the revolution was initially attributable to
    a. their desire to be represented in the Estates General.
    b. the soaring price of food.
    c. the murder of Marat.
    d. the large number of people imprisoned by the king.

19. For the French peasants, the Revolution of 1789 meant
    a. a general movement from the countryside to urban areas.
    b. greater landownership.
    c. significant political power.
    d. few, if any, gains.

20. The group that announced that it was going to cut off Marie Antoinette's head, "tear out her heart, and fry her liver" was the
    a. National Guard.
    b. Robespierre radicals.
    c. revolutionary committee.
    d. women of Paris.

21. The group that had the task of ridding France of any internal opposition to the revolutionary cause was the
    a. Revolutionary Army.
    b. secret police.
    c. republican mob of Paris.
    d. Committee of Public Safety.

22. In her writings, Mary Wollstonecraft argues that
    a. the liberating promise of the French Revolution must be extended to women.
    b. British life is threatened by the revolutionary chaos in France.
    c. Burke is correct in his defense of inherited privilege.
    d. women should devote themselves to education, not politics.

23. Some historians have questioned the traditional interpretation of the French Revolution by arguing that
    a. the Revolution was solely the result of a clash of economic classes.
    b. the key to the Revolution was the social and economic isolation of the nobility.
    c. fundamental to the Revolution was the clash between the bourgeois and noble classes.
    d. the nobility and the bourgeois had common political and economic interests.

24. The abolition of many tiny German states and the old Holy Roman Empire and the reorganization of fifteen German states into a Confederation of the Rhine was the work of
    a. the Congress of Vienna.
    b. Frederick William III of Prussia.
    c. the Continental system.
    d. Napoleon.

25. Napoleon's plan to invade Britain was scrapped as a result of
    a. the Treaty of Amiens.
    b. the Battle of Trafalgar.
    c. the fall of the Third Coalition.
    d. economic restraints in France.

Answers to Self-Test Multiple Choice Questions

Chapter 1

1. a. No. Urban life would not arise until the development of settled agriculture, in the Neolithic Age. Paleolithic society had not yet developed either the social or technological expertise for urban life. (See page 7.)
   b. Correct. The social organization of Paleolithic tribes was quite conducive to successful hunting while primitive art either depicted scenes from the hunt in hopes of good luck or magical mastery over the animals. (See pages 6-7.)
   c. No. The development of written language would have to wait until the Neolithic Era. The needs of Paleolithic society did not call for a written language. (See pages 6-7, 8.)
   d. No. Systematic agriculture did not develop until the Neolithic Era, after the last Ice Age around 7000 B. C., but hunters and gatherers had apparently supplemented their food supply with some farming. (see pages 6-7.)

2. a. No. Egyptian culture, despite its longevity and advanced state was rather insulated from the rest of the Ancient Near East, a result of the geographical factors of Egyptian history. (See page 20.)
   b. Correct. Mesopotamia was the cradle of civilizations; with the frequency of war and migrations in this area after the rise of the Mesopotamian culture it continued to influence subsequent cultures. (See pages 15-6.)
   c. No. The Assyrian culture was not very influential, indeed their only claim to fame was their military organization; in fact the Assyrians assimilated the native Mesopotamian culture after they had conquered the area. (See pages 47-51 in chapter 2.)
   d. No. Hittite culture arose after the Mesopotamian civilization and was influenced by the Mesopotamian culture. (See pages 30-1.)

3. a. No. The Egyptian god of the dead was not Amon-Re, but Osirus. (See page 22.)
   b. No. Osiris, who later became the god of the dead, not Amon-Re, was the Egyptian god of fertility. (See page 22.)
   c. Correct. Originally, Amon and Re had been two distinct sun gods, but the Egyptians had merged them and worshiped Amon-Re as the king of the gods. (See pages 22.)
   d. No. Frequently agricultural gods and fertility gods share the same functions. Further, given the regularity and fertility of Egyptian agriculture, Osiris, as the goddess of fertility seems to have been sufficient. (See page 22.)

4. a. No. The Hittites, who assimilated Mesopotamian culture developed a strong relationship with the Egyptians, but did not really adapt to their culture. This failure had nothing to do with Hittite military success. (See pages 30-1.)
   b. No. Having fought the Egyptian army of Ramses II to stalemate, the Hittites and Egyptians formed a very solid alliance which eventually included the Babylonians. (See page 31.)
   c. Correct. Hittite military success in their conquest of Mesopotamia and against the Egyptians resulted from the technological advance of iron weapons, which were much superior to the bronze weapons then used by the Egyptians. (See page 31.)
   d. No. The Hittites, like most other newcomers to Mesopotamia, quickly assimilated the more advanced Mesopotamian culture. (See pages 30-1.)

5. a. No. Hammurabi's code, which was quite harsh by our standards, did not often call for the incarceration of people convicted of crimes, attempting instead to make the punishment match the crime. (See pages 17-9.)
    b. No. Under Hammurabi's code, a person was sold into slavery for bad debts, usually. In addition, the code attempted to match crime with punishment. (See pages 17-9.)
    c. Correct. This punishment, drowning, is emblematic of the code's attempt to make the punishment match the crime, thus watering down drinks was punished by "watering down" the tavern-keeper. (See pages 17-9.)
    d. No. Although Hammurabi's code was quite harsh, this punishment does not fit the crime committed, one of the key features of the code. (See pages 17-9.)

6. a. Correct. The discovery of the Ebla Tablets in Syria in 1975 demonstrated that the Eblaites had learned the art of writing from the Mesopotamians. (See page 16.)
    b. No. Actually the Bible has many parallels to Mesopotamian religious beliefs and stories. The Eblaites had helped to spread these stories and ideas to other Semitic peoples. (See pages 13-4, 16.)
    c. No. Mesopotamian influence was widespread in the Ancient Near East, a fact which is supported by the discovery of the Ebla Tablets. (See page 16.)
    d. No. Many Mesopotamian ideas and stories can be found in the Old Testament, such as the Great Flood, the Creation of the world, etc. (See pages 13-4, 16.)

7. a. No. Actually, Hammurabi combined the concept of tribal kingship with the Mesopotamian concept of urban kingship. (See pages 16-7.)
    b. Correct. This was perhaps Hammurabi's primary political goal, to affect the political unification of Mesopotamia under the control of Babylon. (See pages 16-7.)
    c. No. Hammurabi actually fostered the worship of Marduk in order to enhance his own political power. (See pages 16-7.)
    d. No. Although Hammurabi was not as barbaric as the Assyrians, he was not averse to conquering neighboring peoples to bring them under his control. (See pages 16-7.)

8. a. No. Hammurabi was not a Semitic but an Amorite chieftain. (See page 16.)
    b. No. Marduk was the chief Babylonian god, not a Semitic chieftain. (See pages 16-7.)
    c. No. Osiris was the Egyptian goddess of fertility not a Semitic chieftain. (See pages 16, 22.)
    d. Correct. Sargon, the first "world conqueror" established a short-lived empire in Sumer which helped the spread of Mesopotamian culture throughout the Fertile Crescent. (See page 16.)

9. a. Correct. Given the importance of agriculture and the absolute necessity of irrigation, it should not be surprising that Hammurabi's code devoted a great deal of attention to laws concerning agriculture and irrigation. (See page 18.)
    b. No. One of the key features of Hammurabi's code was the harshness of the punishments, usually set to match the crime, handed down. (See pages 17-9.)
    c. No. One of the key features of Hammurabi's code was the different levels of crimes and punishments based on social status. (See pages 17-9.)
    d. No. Actually, consumer protection was a feature of Hammurabi's code. For instance tavern-keepers who watered down drinks were drowned. (See pages 17-9.)

10. a. Correct. With the regularity of the floods of the Nile, irrigation was as not essential for Egypt. (See pages 10, 20.)
    b. No. Anatolia, one of the disparate centers of early agricultural development is also an arid area that would call for irrigation. (See pages 10, 20.)
    c. No. Syria, within Mesopotamia an arid region, also needed irrigation. (See pages 10, 20.)

d.   No. Assyria, also within arid Mesopotamia, would have required irrigated agriculture. (See pages 10, 20.)

11.   a.   No. The geography of Mesopotamia, with its harsh climate, mountains, and violent rivers, greatly impeded communication. (See page 11.)
b.   Correct. The forbidding geography of Mesopotamia - harsh climate, mountains, violent rivers - greatly impeded communication within Sumerian society. (See page 11.)
c.   No. Although the inhabitants of Sumer were able to grow crops, fish in the rivers and obtain many other valuable commodities from their immediate surroundings, they were forced to import stone and metals. (See page 11.)
d.   No. Despite the abundance of many things in Sumer, the Sumerians were forced to import such items as metals. (See page 11.)

12.   a.   No. Quite the contrary, the rivers (and other geographical factors) encouraged the disunity of Mesopotamian society. (See pages 10-1.)
b.   No. The rivers of Mesopotamia were quite unpredictable; only with the advent of irrigation (which was also used to drain off flood waters) were the Mesopotamians able to deal with excess water. (See pages 10-1.)
c.   No. Although the rivers did impede the political unity of Mesopotamia, they did not prevent invasion. (See pages 10-1.)
d.   Correct The presence of the rivers, with their supply of water, allowed the Mesopotamians to develop irrigation. (See page 10-1.)

13.   a.   No. One of the salient features of Mesopotamian history is the political disunity, usually attributed to geographical factors. (See pages 11, 13-4.)
b.   Correct. The harsh environment of Mesopotamia fostered a rather grim and pessimistic view of life, which was reflected in Mesopotamian religious beliefs. (See pages 13-4.)
c.   No. The Mesopotamians attempted to control floods, by irrigation and appeasement of the gods; they did not appreciate the value of the floods which could destroy a city. (See pages 13-4.)
d.   No. The Mesopotamians, far from "appreciating" nature, attempted to explain their harsh and unpredictable environment by attributing natural catastrophes to the capricious gods. (See pages 13-4.)

14.   a.   No. Semitic peoples already inhabited the region which Hammurabi would himself conquer. (See pages 16, 19.)
b.   Correct. The Kassites conquered Hammurabi's empire, with assistance from the Hittites. Their three-hundred year reign was crucial for the preservation and spread of Mesopotamian culture. (See pages 19-20.)
c.   No. While the Egyptians at various times in their history were imperialistic, they never conquered Babylon; indeed, they formed an alliance with the Babylonians. (See pages 19, 31.)
d.   No. The Sumerians were one of the original peoples of the area subsequently conquered by Hammurabi himself. (See pages 15-6, 19.)

15.   a.   Correct. The *lugal* was the king (secular leader) in Sumerian cities, who rose to power as a war leader, elected by the citizenry; with the frequency of warfare in Mesopotamia this person soon became the supreme figure in the city. (See page 16.)
b.   No. The *lugal* was the secular leader not the religious leader of a Sumerian city. (See page 16.)
c.   No. The *lugal* was the king of a Sumerian city; indeed councils of elders had no place in the governance of these political entities. (See page 16.)
d.   No. The *lugal* was the king of a Sumerian city, not a slave-owner. (See page 17.)

16.   a.   No. The Sumerian cities all had their own respective gods; Marduk was not a Sumerian deity. (See pages 13-4, 16-7.)

b.   No. The chief god of the Egyptians was Amon-Re, not Marduk. (See pages 16-7, 22-3.)

c.   Correct. Marduk was the chief god of the Amorites, a Semitic peoples. (See pages 16-7.)

d.   No. The Hittites adopted much of the Mesopotamian culture, which they had conquered, including several native deities. (See pages 16-7, 31.)

17. a.   No. Even though the common people of Egypt were at the bottom of the social and economic scale, they did have the right to appeal to the pharaoh. (See page 23.)

b.   Correct. As in most societies, the common people of Egypt were at the bottom of the socio-economic ladder. (See page 23.)

c.   No. Like most of the civilizations of the Ancient Near East, socio-economic status was not determined by a person's color or race. (See page 23.)

d.   No. The Egyptians were not related to the Mesopotamians, a fact underscored by the relative isolation of Egypt. (See page 23.)

18. a.   No. Enlil was a very important deity of the Sumerians, but not the hero of the epic poem. (See pages 14-5.)

b.   No. Osiris was an Egyptian god. (See pages 14, 22.)

c.   Correct. The wanderings of Gilgamesh represent the Sumerians attempt to answer the enduring questions of life and death. (See page 14.)

d.   No. Khunanup was the hero of an Egyptian story about dishonest officials. (See page 14.)

19. a.   No. The Hittites belonged to the same language group as the Persians, but were not Persians. (See pages 27-9, 51-3 in chapter 2.)

b.   No. The Hittites came from a different region and belonged to a different language group than the Semites. (see pages 15-6, 27-9.)

c.   No. Akkad was the homeland of the Semitic peoples. (See pages 16, 27-9.)

d.   Correct. The Hittites belonged to the peoples who shared a common language group which historians have identified as Indo-European. (See pages 27-9.)

20. a.   Correct. Osiris was resuscitated each year by the goddess Isis, with help from Anubis. (See page 22.)

b.   No. Aton was the monotheistic sun-god foisted on the Egyptians by the Pharaoh Akhenaten. (See pages 22, 26.)

c.   No. Amon-Re was the traditional chief god of the Egyptians. (See page 22.)

d.   No. Serapis was one of the gods worshiped by the so-called mystery religions in the era following the conquest of Alexander the Great. (See chapter 4.)

21. a.   No. Akhenaten, although a member of the imperialistic Eighteenth Dynasty, was more interested in religion than conquest. (See page 26.)

b.   Correct. Akhenaten and his wife Nefertiti attempted to supplant the traditional Egyptian religion with the worship of the monotheistic Aton. (See page 26.)

c.   No. Akhenaten was too involved in the implementation of the worship of Aton to concern himself with agricultural improvements, particularly given the efficacy of Egyptian agriculture. (See pages 20, 26.)

d.   No. Indeed, Akhenaten waged wholesale war on the traditions of Egypt. (See page 26.)

22. a.   No. Although the discovery of iron was quite important, it did not result in a massive restructuring of human society. (See pages 7-10.)

b.   No. There is a very fine line between religion and mythology, neither of which caused a fundamental change in the way people went about their daily lives, in search of sustenance. (See pages 7-10.)

c.   Correct. With the development of systematic agriculture, the ways in which people lived their lives was fundamentally altered: family, food source, religion, settlements, life-span, everything. (See pages 7-10.)

    d.   No. Citizenship in Sumer, according to recent research, had always been free; such a development would not have affected how people fed themselves or how long they lived and the like. (See pages 7-10, 14.)

23.   a.   No. Hammurabi's code was concerned with the establishment and maintenance of order and stability in Babylon, not with such philosophical questions. (See pages 17-9.)

    b.   Correct. The Mesopotamian myths, including one about a primeval sea which produced heaven and earth, were the earliest attempts to answer such questions. (See pages 13-4.)

    c.   No. Egyptian religion, as a result of the favorable nature of their climate and geography, seemed to more concerned with the cyclical pattern of their existence. (See pages 21-22.)

    d.   No. Akhenaten's religious beliefs are debatable, but there is no evidence that he attempted to answer such questions; further Akhenaten came along long after earlier myths had already attempted to resolve these questions. (See page 26.)

24.   a.   No. The common people, even though they did have the right to appeal, were subject to the pharaoh's taxes (which were sometimes as high as 20%). (See page 23.)

    b.   No. The common people, peasants, were subject to forced labor on such projects as the pyramids and canals. (See page 23.)

    c.   No. Young men were drafted into the pharaoh's army, which served as both a fighting force and as a labor corps. (See page 23.)

    d.   Correct. Despite the frequent harshness of both the tax liability and the tax collection methods, Egyptian peasants could appeal to the pharaoh. (See page 00.)

25.   a.   Correct. Egypt was nearly self-sufficient: the fertility of its soil, the regular floods of the Nile, enormous quantities of stone, clay, precious metals. Copper and timber were available from Sinai and Lebanon which were close at hand. (See page 20.)

    b.   No. What Egypt lacked in raw materials (which was very little) was obtained from areas west of Egypt, not south. (See page 20.)

    c.   No. Egypt did not need to resort to conquest as it was almost self-sufficient; not until the Eighteenth Dynasty did the pharaohs become imperialistic. (See page 20, 25-6.)

    d.   No. Egypt was certainly self-sufficient in food-stuffs; the materials they did import were not necessities. (See page 20.)

1. a. Correct. As Hebrew society evolved, women enjoyed much less freedom, especially in religion. Previously, many women had served as priestesses to Yahweh, but over time the worship of Yahweh became more male-oriented and male-dominated. (See page 46.)
    b. No. Aspects of women's biology, especially menstruation and childbirth, were seen as impure. (See page 46.)
    c. No. As in most traditional societies, Hebrew women did have responsibility for the early education of the children. Fathers, however, instructed sons in religious matters, history, and a craft or trade. (Seepage 46.)
    d. No. With the evolution of Hebrew society the worship of Yahweh became more male-oriented and male-dominated. (See page 46.)

2. a. No. During Solomon's reign, he brought Israel into the commercial mainstream of the region and applied his energies to creating a nation out of the collection of Hebrew tribes. (See page 42.)
    b. No. Actually it was just the opposite; he did his best to create a unified kingdom out of the Twelve Tribes. (See page 42.)
    c. No. Solomon, on the contrary, is famous for the construction of the temple to house the Ark of the Covenant. (See page 42.)
    d. Correct. Solomon, in order to finance the construction his famous Temple of the Ark of the Covenant, levied the highest taxes to date on the Hebrew people. (See page 42.)

3. a. No. The Persians, who created one of the largest empires of all time, were remarkable for their toleration and enlightened rule. (See pages 47-8, 51.)
    b. Correct. The Assyrians, who were the rulers of a vast empire, were only able to keep it together by their very brutal and militaristic practices. (See pages 47-8.)
    c. No. The Phoenicians are remembered for their contributions in the realm of commercial activities and the development of a phonetic alphabet and were not militaristic people. (See pages 38, 47-8.)
    d. No. While certainly taking part in war, the Hebrews were in no way the most brutal. (See pages 41, 47-8.)

4. a. No. Actually this is just the opposite of Cyrus's policies. (See pages 53-5.)
    b. Correct. Indeed, the hallmark of the Persian Empire was their enlightened toleration of non-Persian cultures. (See pages 53-5.)
    c. No. Although some Persian rulers adopted Zoroastrianism, they did not attempt to impose it on their subjects. (See pages 53-5.)
    d. No. Cyrus was far removed from the traditional warrior-king, with a very advanced notion of kingship. (See pages 53-5.)

5. a. No. On the contrary, Zoroaster stressed the individual's responsibility to choose between good and evil. (See pages 55-6.)
    b. Correct. Indeed, central to the Zoroastrian religion is the constant battle between good (Ahuramazda) and evil (Ahriman), the earliest example of such a concept. (See pages 55-6.)
    c. No. According to Zoroaster, there was a divine kingdom after death for those who had lived according to good and truth. (See pages 55-6.)
    d. No. Zoroaster promised that there would eventually be a triumph of good over evil, i.e. a Last Judgment, at which Ahuramazda would decide each person's eternal fate. (See pages 55-6.)

6. a. No. While Egypt was reunited by another kingdom, it was the "Kingdom of the Nile". (See page 38.)
    b. No. The Phoenicians were a commercial, sea-faring peoples who were not interested in political conquests. (See pages 38-9.)

c.   Correct. The Sudanese Kingdom of Kush, under their king Piankhy, did reunite Egypt. These people had already adopted much of Egyptian culture. (See page 38.)

d.   No. Although Ethiopia, far to the south of Egypt, had been influenced by Egyptian religion it had nothing to do with the reunification of Egypt. (See page 38.)

7.   a.   No. Despite the collapse of their empire, Egyptian culture continued to be a powerful influence on other peoples. (See pages 38-9.)

b.   No. Although Solomon was able to unite the Hebrew tribes, they were never more than a small kingdom. (See pages 38-9, 42.)

c.   Correct. The disappearance of these two large empires did allow for less powerful peoples to develop their own cultures. (See pages 38-9.)

d.   No. Actually, the disappearance of the Hittite and Egyptian empires allowed for a rather vigorous period of economic, social and political development. (See pages 38-9.)

8.   a.   Correct. As in most societies that move from nomadic to settled life style, the nuclear family became much more important to Hebrew society as the extended family became less important. (See page 46.)

b.   No. Normally when a society moves from a nomadic to a settled life style, the nuclear family pattern eclipses the extended family pattern of organization, which is what happened in the Hebrew society. (See page 46.)

c.   No. Although polygamy was allowed in the new settled society of the Hebrews, monogamy was still much more prevalent than polygamy because the common man could only afford one wife. (See page 46.)

d.   No. It is true that the status of women was lessened by the development of a settled life style, but Hebrew society had never been a matriarchy. (See page 46.)

9.   a.   No. Paradoxically, the peace and prosperity enjoyed by the Israeli kingdom did not result in a era of prosperity for small farmers. (See page 46.)

b.   No. During the time of peace and prosperity enjoyed by the Hebrew kingdom, large estates came to dominate agricultural production. (See page 46.)

c.   No. The increase in the number of large estates was accompanied by an increase in the number of slaves, who were employed extensively on these large estates. (See page 46.)

d.   Correct. With the peace and prosperity enjoyed by the Kingdom of Israel, some Hebrews began to amass larger holdings by buying out small farmers, greatly contributing to the decline of the small family farm. (See page 46.)

10. a.   No. The early Hebrews were unusual in their fierce loyalty to Yahweh and their resistance to other religions. (See pages 45-9, 55-6.)

b.   No. The Egyptians were relatively isolated from the influence of outside elements like Zoroastrianism, a fact which was reinforced by the stability of Egyptian life and religion. (See pages 53-6.)

c.   Correct. The Persian king Darius did adopt Zoroastrianism, but true to the Persian concept of toleration did not impose this religion on his subjects. (See pages 55-6.)

d.   No. Tradition has it that Zoroaster's teachings met with opposition and coldness, but his thought was very influential in Iran and continued to influence religious thought for centuries. (See pages 55-6.)

11. a.   No. Cyrus's successors were able to maintain the greatness of the Persian Empire by avoiding such a tripartite dismembering. (See pages 56-7.)

b.   Correct. The division of the Persian Empire into twenty *satrapies* was part of the bureaucratic organization of the Persian Empire that exemplified the astute governance of the Persians. (See pages 56-7.)

c.   No. The Persian Empire was not divided into two separate parts like this, but was subdivided into bureaucratic regions that were incorporated into the central government. (See pages 56-7.)
d.   No. The military districts of the Persian Empire corresponded to the political subdivisions of the empire. (See pages 56-7.)

12.   a.   No. King Darius was a later ruler of the Persian Empire, who adopted Zoroastrianism. (See pages 53-4, 56.)
b.   No. Zoroaster was not a political ruler but the founder of a religion. (See pages 53-5.)
c.   Correct. The creation of the Persian Empire was the work of Cyrus the Great who had an unprecedented concept of empire. (See pages 53-4.)
d.   No. Siyalk was the site on an archeological excavation near modern-day Tehran, Iran from which we have learned a great deal about the Iranians and the previous inhabitants. (See pages 53-4.)

13.   a.   No. Divorce was available only to men, a function of the low status of women in Hebrew society. (See page 46.)
b.   No. As in most agricultural societies marriage was most often arranged for family and economic reasons. (See page 46.)
c.   No. The Hebrews imposed restrictions against mixed marriages to forestall any inroads of alien religions into Hebrew society. (See page 46.)
d.   Correct. Actually, children were so important that polygamy was allowed; another indication of the importance of children was the custom of a brother having to marry his brother's widow if no children had been produced. (See page 46.)

14.   a.   Correct. The central plateau is the predominant geographical feature of Iran, which helped explain its crucial role in the migrations of many peoples. (See pages 51-2.)
b.   No. Although there are mountains on the periphery of Iran they are not the primary geographic feature. (See pages 51-2.)
c.   No. Dense tropical coastal areas are not to be found in Iran. (See pages 51-2.)
d.   No. This is not a geographical feature, but a historical construct. (See pages 51-2, chap. 1.)

15.   a.   Incorrect. By the seventh century B.C., iron production had increased, giving rise to greater agricultural productivity. (See page 53.)
b.   Incorrect. Horse breeding and overland trade worked to stimulate each other and add to the wealth of the Iranians. (See page 53.)
c.   Incorrect. Small-farm agriculture was the basis of the Iranian society and was enhanced by the other aspects of the Iranian economy. (See page 53.)
d.   Correct. The mining and trade of gold was not a feature of the Iranian economy, which did boast iron production, horse trading and small-farm agriculture. (See page 53.)

16.   a.   No. The Hebrews, who were conquered by the Persians, did not really possess the bureaucratic and military organization necessary to the Persian Empire. (See page 51.)
b.   No. Although the Sumerians were very influential to the development of other cultures in the Ancient Near East, the Persians did not derive their military or political organizational practices from the Sumerians. (See page 51, chap. 1.)
c.   Correct. Although the Persians were wiser than the Assyrians, they did adopt some of the bureaucratic and military organizational practices from the Assyrians. (See page 51.)
d.   No. The Philistines, an agricultural society, did not possess the military, political or organizational practices necessary for an empire. (See page 51.)

17.   a.   Correct. Based on Cyrus's vision of empire, the Persians relied on good relations with conquered peoples to govern their empire. (See pages 51, 54.)
b.   No. While the Assyrians were brutal, the Persians chose not to emulate this type of governance.

(See pages 51, 54.)

c. No. Actually, the Persians allowed subjugated peoples to retain their own customs. (See pages 51, 54.)

d. No. While relying on good relations, the Persians were not democrats. (See pages 51, 54.)

18. a. No. The Phoenicians were best known for their commercial not military activities. (See pages 38-40.)

b. Correct. The Phoenicians were the preeminent merchants and traders of the ancient world. (See pages 38-40.)

c. No. The Phoenicians were not known for their religious innovations, but the development of a phonetic alphabet and their commercial activities. (See pages 38-40.)

d. No. The Phoenicians were a small kingdom, more concerned with commercial activity than political conquest. (See pages 38-40.)

19. a. No. Although the collapse of the Egyptian empire allowed for the development of the Phoenician society, the Phoenicians were not responsible for this collapse. (See pages 38-40.)

b. No. The Phoenicians were not farmers; their economy was based on urban and overseas trade. (See pages 38-40.)

c. No. The Phoenicians were not a warlike people, unlike the Philistines who did wage almost constant war against the Hebrews. (See pages 38-40.)

d. Correct. The Phoenicians were a renowned trading and seafaring people, founding cities such as Carthage. (See pages 38-40.)

20. a. No. The Hebrews never acquired an empire, even their kingdom was fraught with divisiveness and was eventually conquered. (See pages 42-4, 57.)

b. No. The Hittite Empire was restricted to Mesopotamia and was not large compared to the first world empire which came later. (See page 57, chap. 1.)

c. No. The Egyptian Empire was limited to regions close to the Egyptian homeland of the Nile delta and thus not the largest. (See page 57, chap 1.)

d. Correct. The Persian Empire founded by Cyrus the Great, the first "world empire," stretched from Europe to India and the Black Sea to Arabia, clearly the largest of the ancient world and one of the largest of all time. (See page 57.)

21. a. Correct. The Magi were the early priestly class of the Iranians. (See page 55.)

b. No. *Satrapies* were the political subdivisions of the Persian Empire. (See pages 55, 57.)

c. No. The Medes were a branch of the Iranian peoples that were eventually conquered by Cyrus the Great. (See pages 53-5.)

d. No. Scribes are generally considered to be literate officials of the governments. (See page 55, chap. 1)

22. a. No. Monotheism is a much broader term and does not refer to any specific body of belief. (See pages 44-5.)

b. No. The worship of nature is known as pantheism. (See pages 44-5.)

c. No. Monotheism has nothing to do with whom one marries, but refers to a form of religious belief. (See pages 44-5.)

d. Correct. Monotheism, as one can see from its component parts - mono (one) and theism (religion) - does refer to the worship of a single deity. (See pages 44-5.)

23. a. No. Ahuramazda was a Persian deity. (See pages 55-6.)

b. No. Mithra was a Persian deity. (See pages 55-6.)

c. Correct. Zarathustra (Zoroaster) was the religious thinker who introduced such concepts as good versus evil into Persian religion. (See pages 55-6.)

    d.   No. Ahriman was a Persian deity. (See pages 55-6.)

24.   a.   No. Moses was the (perhaps) legendary Hebrew leader credited with leading the Jews out of Egypt and the creation of Mosaic Law. (See page 44.)

    b.   No. Solomon was the king of Israel who contributed greatly the creation of a united Jewish kingdom. (See pages 42, 44.)

    c.   Correct. Yahweh was the name of the Hebrew god. (See page 44.)

    d.   No. Zoroaster, a Persian, developed his own advanced religion. (See pages 44, 55.)

25.   a.   No. Actually Iran developed and maintained close links with its neighbors. (See pages 51-2.)

    b.   Correct. Iran's geographical position and topography help explain its traditional role as the highway between East and West. (See pages 51-2.)

    c.   No. Urban places had developed in Iran even before the Persians and Medeans moved into the area as shown by the excavations at Siyalk. (See pages 51-2.)

    d.   No. The very fact that the Iranians migrated into Iran argues against this response; in addition, this area attracted many migrating peoples, but the harshness of the climate and topography of the area surrounding the central plateau caused them to move on. (See pages 51-2.)

Chapter 3

1.　a.　No. Homer and Hesoid were not historians but authors of epic and religious works. (See pages 68, 83.)
　　b.　Correct. Herodotus, the "father of History," and Thucydides, writing on the Persian wars and the Peloponnesian War respectively, were the main historians of ancient Greece. (See page 83.)
　　c.　No. Sophocles and Aristotle were not historians; Sophocles was a dramatist and Aristotle a philosopher. (See pages 83, 85-6.)
　　d.　No. Plato and Socrates were not historians but famous philosophers. (See pages 83, 85-6.)

2.　a.　No. There is no archeological evidence to indicate the presence of an invading people destroying the Mycenean world. (See pages 66-7.)
　　b.　No. Historians have determined that human beings, not natural disaster, such as a famine, were responsible for the collapse of the Mycenean civilization. (See pages 66-7.)
　　c.　Correct. With the lack of "hard" evidence to the contrary, historians have accepted the Greek legends which told of grim wars between the Myceneans themselves as the cause of the disappearance of the Mycenean civilization. (See pages 66-7.)
　　d.　No. There is no evidence to support such an hypothesis; many historians believe that human factors, not natural disaster, destroyed this civilization. (See pages 66-7.)

3.　a.　No. Actually Sparta was an enemy of the Delian League for their imperialistic and oppressive policies. (See pages 81-3.)
　　b.　No. Although Thebes was involved in the Delian League and the Peloponnesian War, it was not the leader of the League. (See pages 81-3.)
　　c.　Correct. Athens, emboldened by the success of the Delian League against the Persians, turned the League into an imperialistic device for the creation of an "Athenian lake" out of the Aegean Sea. (See pages 81-3.)
　　d.　No. Delos was the city-state where the league was founded, but it was not the dominant city-state in the League. (See pages 81-3.)

4.　a.　No. The Greeks emerged after the Egyptians (see Chapter 1); by 1650 B.C., Greek-speaking peoples had established themselves at Mycenea in the Peloponnesus. (See pages 64-5.)
　　b.　No. The political unit of the Myceneans was the kingdom not the polis, a political unit which would arise during the "Dark Ages" of Greek history. (See page 65.)
　　c.　No. Actually Mycenean society was marked by social distinctions and slavery, indicated by the existence of an extensive division of labor. (See page 65.)
　　d.　Correct. Not only was the royal palace the seat of political power, the economy was also tightly controlled from the palace; craftsmen labored within the walls to produce the goods desired by the king and his retainers. (See page 65.)

5.　a.　No. These two works were written by Hesiod, not Homer. (See page 69.)
　　b.　Correct. These works by Homer are epic poems which provide much information about the Dark Ages. (See page 69.)
　　c.　No. This was written by Herodotus, not Homer. (See pages 69, 83.)
　　d.　No. These were two plays written by Aeschylus. (See pages 69, 85.)

6.　a.　No. The public square or marketplace, the *agora*, evolved from the place where the warrior assembly met to become the political and economic center of the polis. (See pages 69-72.)
　　b.　No. As the polis evolved during the "Dark Ages" most poleis featured a place of refuge, usually elevated, known as the acropolis. (See pages 69-72.)
　　c.　No. Since agriculture was the base of most Greek poleis' economies, their territory included the land, both fields and pastures, around the polis. (See pages 69-72.)
　　d.　Correct. Since poleis could be governed in a number of different ways, from monarchy to tyranny, not all poleis had a king. Further, the priesthood in Greek city-states was not very institutionalized (as in the Ancient Near East) and did not own much land. (See pages 69-72.)

A12

7. a. Correct. Even though many inhabitants of Greek city-states did not have political rights (women, aliens, slaves) everyone else in the polis was involved in the political affairs of the polis. (See pages 69-70.)
    b. No. The Greek city-states rarely were religious communities, being much more secular in nature. (See pages 69-70.)
    c. No. Most Greek city-states involved all of its citizens, not just merchants, in the affairs of the polis. (See pages 69-70.)
    d. No. Most Greek city-states involved all of its citizens, not just the warriors (who were usually citizen-warriors,) in the affairs of the polis. (See pages 69-70.)

8. a. No. While Solon was an important reformer of Athenian politics, he had nothing to do with these buildings. (See pages 78, 83-5.)
    b. Correct. The Age of Pericles was noted for its artistic achievements; these buildings represent that achievement. They were built with funds coerced from the Delian League and through conquest. (See pages 83-5.)
    c. No. Alcibiades was an Athenian general who deserted to the Spartans during the Peloponnesian War. (See pages 83-5.)
    d. No. Aristophanes did live during this age, but was a satirist and had little to do with these buildings. (See pages 83-5, 87.)

9. a. No. The Greeks did not compile collections of sacred writings, save for Hesiod's _Theogony_. (See page 68.)
    b. No. Each city-state's customs provided the laws for the individual city-state. (See page 68.)
    c. No. Although historians have learned a great deal about ancient Greece from the _Iliad_ and the _Odyssey_, they are not historical records but epic legends. (See page 68.)
    d. Correct. These two works were epic poems by the legendary Homer about the Trojan War and the return home of the hero Ulysses. (See page 68.)

10. a. No. Tyrtaeus was a Spartan poet who described the ferocity of the Second Messenian War. (See page 76.)
    b. No. Archilochus was a colonist and poet, but not remembered for his erotic poetry. (See pages 75-6.)
    c. No. Lesbos was the island home of the poet Sappho. (See page 76.)
    d. Correct. Sappho's bisexuality was frankly expressed in her erotic poetry. (See page 76.)

11. a. No. Actually Solon, an Athenian reformer, refused to become a tyrant even at the urging of his fellow citizens. (See page 78.)
    b. Correct. Solon was the Athenian reformer who effectively solved the social problems brought on by increasing indebtedness and the subsequent slavery of many small farmers; he is responsible for the admission of commoners into the assembly. (See pages 78-9.)
    c. No. Although some city-states were ruled by kings, Athens was not one of them. (See pages 78-9.)
    d. No. Priests were only employed to care for the upkeep on temples and perform the rituals; thus these people are mostly unknown to historians. (See pages 78-9.)

12. a. Correct. One of the forms by which a polis could be governed was _tyranny_, in which one man seized power by unconstitutional means. (See page 72.)
    b. No. Although this is the modern connotation, some tyrants achieved power by appealing to the poor. (See page 72.)
    c. No. A tyrant could arise with support from any group within society; generally he would be opposed by well-to-do people. (See page 72.)
    d. No. This seems a reasonable conclusion but the example of the Athenian tyrant Pisistratus, whose

reign actually promoted the growth of democracy, argues against this response. (See pages 72, 79.)

13.   a.   No. Athens' status as a commercial center was due to its geographical position, not the work of one politician. (See page 79.)

        b.   No. Actually Cleisthenes was able to prevail in the political struggle following the downfall of Pisistratus' excessively harsh son Hippias by garnering support of the common people. (See page 79.)

        c.   No. Although he was a very successful politician and seems to have come to power as a tyrant, he faithfully followed the forms of the Athenian constitution. (See page 79.)

        d.   Correct. Cleisthenes used his power to reform the political system of Athens extensively. His innovations, such as the *deme*, resulted in the creation of Athenian democracy. (See page 79.)

14.   a.   No. Leagues such as the Delian League were not the vehicles of colonization, which was usually carried out by individual cities. (See page 81.)

        b.   Correct. The original purpose of the Delian League was to fight the Persians and liberate Greek cities under Persian rule. (See page 81.)

        c.   No. Mediterranean trade was rather vigorous already and did not need to be promoted. (See page 81.)

        d.   No. The Greeks of this period do not seem to have been cultural imperialists. (See page 81.)

15.   a.   Correct. Believing that the Peloponnesian War would be the greatest in Greek history, Thucydides, an Athenian general who had been exiled for a defeat in the early stages of the war, attempted to analyze this deadly conflict. (See page 83.)

        b.   No. Thucydides did not describe the Athenian democracy; as an historian, he attempted to analyze other aspects of Greek history. (See page 83.)

        c.   No. The events of the Persian wars were chronicled by the Father of History, Herodotus, not Thucydides. (See page 83.)

        d.   No. Thucydides was not an apologist for Athenian policy; as an historian, he attempted to analyze other aspects of Greek history. (See page 83.)

16.   a.   No. *The Oresteia* expressed the agony of the individual through the themes of betrayal, murder and reconciliation. (See pages 85-6.)

        b.   No. The last play of the trilogy, *The Eumenides*, urged the use of reason and justice to reconcile fundamental conflicts. (See pages 85-6.)

        c.   No. Aeschylus, in the last play of the trilogy, concludes with a prayer that civil dissension not be allowed to destroy the city-state. (See pages 85-6.)

        d.   Correct. The trilogy does concern itself with the sexual taboo of incest, which is dealt with in the Theban plays, specifically *Oedipus the King*, of Sophocles. (See pages 85-6.)

17.   a.   No. One of the greatest tributes to the Athenians is that they did not attempt to censure their playwrights even when they attacked the policies of Athens. (See pages 85-7.)

        b.   No. Aristophanes' plays were frequently bawdy and coarse, lampooning everything in sight. (See pages 86-7.)

        c.   No. Quite the contrary, Aristophanes railed against the Peloponnesian War. (See pages 86-7.)

        d.   Correct. As most other comic playwrights, Aristophanes was a merciless critic of political and social affairs in Athens, frequently criticizing Pericles and other leaders. (See pages 86-7.)

18.   a.   No. Although many Greeks did fish, this was not the main activity of most Greeks. (See page 88.)

        b.   No. Despite the commercial activities of many Greeks, this was not the main activity of most Greeks. (See page 88.)

        c.   No. Most Greeks were only part-time warriors, coming to the defense of the polis when needed. (See page 88.)

        d.   Correct. Even though Greece was not the most agriculturally productive land in the world, most

Greeks supported themselves (and their polis) by farming. (See page 88.)

19. a.   No. Although women did not enjoy the status of male citizens, their status was not as low as that of slaves. (See pages 88-9.)
b.   No. Women in Athens, and Greece in general, did not enjoy the status of citizenship, but did have an important unofficial role. (See pages 88-9.)
c.   Correct. The status of women was strictly protected by law, even if this protection was more to protect the husband's interests. (See pages 88-9.)
d.   No. Despite the unofficial role of women in Athenian society, they did not enjoy greater rights than did men. (Indeed this has *rarely* been the case.) (See pages 88-9.)

20. a.   No. Actually homosexuality was much more prevalent among the upper classes than the lower classes, probably because the lower classes were too busy providing for their material existence. (See page 91.)
b.   No. Most Greeks believed that homosexuality posed no threat to any institutions, including the family. (See page 91.)
c.   No. Given the rather tolerant nature of Greek religion and society in general, it would be unlikely that homosexuality would be considered an insult to the Greek religion, especially in light of the licentiousness of the Greek gods. (See page 91.)
d.   Correct. Indeed, many Greeks accepted homosexuality as a normal part of life; historians have been unable to explain this satisfactorily. (See page 91.)

21. a.   No. The economic and trade center of Athens, like most other city-states, was the *agora* not the acropolis. (See pages 84-5.)
b.   Correct. Pericles had appropriated Delian League funds to construct a series of buildings to honor Athena, the patron goddess of Athens. (See pages 84-5.)
c.   No. The Athenian Acropolis, like those of other poleis, was located on the highest point in Athens and thus not really near the harbor. (See pages 84-5.)
d.   No. As in the other Greek poleis, the center of political (and economic) activity was the *agora*, not the acropolis; this response also implies the unity of Greece , which was not forthcoming until the Macedonians conquered them. (See pages 84-5.)

22. a.   No. Thucydides firmly rejected the notion that the fate of human beings was decided by the gods. (See page 86.)
b.   Correct. Thucydides did believe that human beings decided their own fate as a result of their own desires and actions. (See page 87.)
c.   No. Neither nature nor the gods but humans themselves determined their own fate. (See page 87.)
d.   No. Thucydides believed that the fate of human beings was determined by and could be understood through the desires and actions of individuals. (See page 87-88.)

23. a.   No. Actually women played a vital, if unofficial, role in Greek society. (See page 89.)
b.   No. Greek women did not have citizenship status and thus could not hold any political office. (See page 89.)
c.   Correct. Anthropologists use the term *liminal* to describe the very real, but unofficial, influence wielded by women; it was certainly applicable to Greek women. (See page 89.)
d.   No. The death of a husband did not change the status of a woman. (See page 89.)

24. a.   No. Alexander the Great was the son of the Macedonian king who conquered Greece. (See pages 98-9 and Chapter 4.)
b.   Correct. Philip II copied the military innovations of the Theban Epameinodas and took advantage of the bitter internecine warfare among the Greeks to conquer them. (See pages 98-9.)
c.   No. Cleon was an Athenian leader during the Peloponnesian War, not a ruler of Macedonia. (See

pages 82-3, 98-9.)

   d.   No. Cleisthenes was the Athenian reformer who was perhaps most responsible for the establishment of Athenian democracy. (See pages 79, 98-9.)

1. a. No. Epicureans were taught to ignore politics, which would disturb the soul. (See pages 125-6.)
    b. No. Indeed, Epicurus, the founder of Epicureanism, taught that pain was to be avoided. (See pages 125-6.)
    c. Correct. Epicureanism taught that happiness could be found by ignoring the outside world and examining one's personal feelings and reactions. (See pages 125-6.)
    d. No. Although Epicurus, the founder of Epicureanism, did not deny the existence of gods, he taught that they had no effect on human life. (See pages 125-6.)

2. a. No. Actually the Stoics taught that people should participate in politics and worldly affairs. (See page 126.)
    b. No. The Cult of Isis was a mystery religion, based on Egyptian beliefs, and not a school of philosophy. (See pages 124, 126.)
    c. No. Alexander was educated by the philosopher Aristotle and not the Stoics. (See pages 105, 126.)
    d. Correct. The Stoics reasoned that since all men were brothers and were in harmony with the universe, one law - part of the natural order of life - governed them all. (See page 126.)

3. a. No. Actually the reverse is true; Easterners only adopted a veneer of Hellenism. (See pages 110-112, 117.)
    b. Correct. Hellenized Easterners, in order to prosper under Hellenistic regimes, adopted much of Greek culture, but retained the essentials of their own culture. (See pages 110-112, 117.)
    c. No. Rarely were Easterners fully assimilated into Greek culture. (See pages 110-112, 117.)
    d. No. Actually, the culture of the Easterners was quite advanced and the intermingling of Greek and Eastern culture resulted in the uniqueness of Hellenistic culture. (See pages 110-112 and Chapters 1 and 2.)

4. a. No. Within the Hellenistic world, while some Greeks were middle-class traders, this social group also included many who were not Greek and in the Hellenistic cities where the population was not predominantly Greek, most traders would not have been Greeks. (See page 111.)
    b. Correct. As a result of the need of the Hellenistic monarchs for loyal government officials, they actively recruited Greeks to serve them and these Greeks thus become the favored class. (See page 111.)
    c. No. Although slavery was widespread, the Greeks were *not* slaves. (See page 111.)
    d. No. Greek religion was not very popular amongst the Easterners, who retained their own native, priestly class. (See page 111.)

5. a. No. Persia was the first of Alexander's conquest; after subduing the Persians, the young conqueror pushed further east. (See pages 105-6.)
    b. Correct. Alexander's troops, after crossing the Indus River and experiencing more hard fighting and other hardships, refused to cross the Hyphasis River in India, effectively halting the conquest of Alexander. (See pages 105-6.)
    c. No. Bactria was part of the Persian empire; it took Alexander an additional four years to conquer it. (See pages 105-6.)
    d. No. Even Alexander the Great was unable to extend his sway as far as China. (See pages 105-6.)

6. a. No. Actually the Greeks had little to do with the native populations. (See pages 107-9.)
    b. No. As Alexander was unable to conquer India and the Greek religion did not have an established church, he did not establish the Greek church in India. (See pages 106, 108-9, and Chapter 3.)
    c. Correct. The founding of colonies throughout the East had a profound effect on the cultures of Greece and the East, producing the unique Hellenistic culture. (See pages 108-9.)

d.   No. Alexander, even though he sometimes respected other people's customs, did not impose them on the Greeks. (See pages 108-9.)

7.   a.   No. The Greeks had never believed that women were equal (see Chapter 3) and this did not change in the Hellenistic Age. (See pages 111, 115.)
     b.   No. Women did participate in politics on a limited basis and some received honorary citizenship, but women were not given full citizenship. (See page 111, 115.)
     c.   Correct. The increased participation of women in economic affairs resulted in the improved status of women. (See pages 111, 115.)
     d.   No. Although many women, especially those from royal families, did perform many noble and self-sacrificing deeds, this does not explain the general improvement in the status of women. (See pages 111, 115.)

8.   a.   Correct. While all of the Hellenistic kings paid special attention to agriculture as it was the basis of much of their revenue, the Ptolemies in Egypt were able to build on the centralized authority of the Pharaohs to control and improve Egyptian agriculture. (See page 122.)
     b.   No. Even though all the Hellenistic monarchs were concerned with agriculture -- it was the basis of much of their revenue -- the Macedonians were not the most successful in this area. (See page 122.)
     c.   No. The Seleucids, like the other Hellenistic monarchs, were very concerned with agriculture as it provided much of their revenues but they were not the most successful in this area. (See page 122.)
     d.   No. The Athenians did make great strides in agricultural improvements; this would be the accomplishment of one of the successor dynasties of Alexander's empire. (See page 122.)

9.   a.   No. *Tyche* refers to a rather pessimistic world view of many Greeks, not a revelation in the religious sense of the word. (See page 122.)
     b.   No. *Tyche* refers to a rather pessimistic world view of many Greeks, not trait such as honor. (See page 122.)
     c.   No. *Tyche* refers to the rather pessimistic world view of many Greeks, not a character or physical trait such as strength. (See page 122.)
     d.   Correct. In the Hellenistic world many people sought solace in religions and philosophy, others simply believed that *Tyche,* or fate, ruled their lives. (See page 122.)

10. a.   Correct. Euclid, the Greek mathematician, compiled the existing knowledge on geometry into his still influential book *The Elements of Geometry*. (See page 127.)
     b.   No. Archimedes was perhaps the greatest thinker of the Hellenistic period, but the compilation known as *The Elements of Geometry* was not his work. (See pages 127.)
     c.   No. Aristarchus of Samos put forth the theory of a heliocentric universe, a view that would not be accepted until the work of Nicolas Copernicus in 1542; he was not responsible for *The Elements of Geometry*. (See pages 126-7.)
     d.   No. Eratosthenes was a philosopher, mathematician and geographer, the last being the area of his greatest contributions, not the compilation of *The Elements of Geography*. (See pages 127-8.)

11. a.   No. The Seleucid dynasty, which ruled Asia Minor, was founded by one of Alexander's generals. (See page 108.)
     b.   No. The Ptolemaic dynasty, which ruled Egypt, was founded by one of Alexander's generals. (See page 108.)
     c.   No. The Antigonid dynasty, which ruled Macedonia, was founded by one of Alexander's generals. (See page 108.)
     d.   No. Athens, like Sparta, sank to the level of a third-rate power and did not produce a royal dynasty. (See page 108.)

12. a.   No. During the Hellenic period (before Alexander's conquests) philosophy had been exclusive

province of the rich, but not during the Hellenistic period. (See page 124.)

b.   No. During the Hellenistic period, as people searched for something permanent, many people turned to philosophy. (See page 124.)

c.   No. The Successor Kingdoms were not interested in propaganda tools; rather philosophy interested many people as they searched for meaning in their lives. (See page 124.)

d.   Correct. With the decline in traditional religion and the polis, enhanced by the increase in migration, many common people sought answers to the meaning of life in philosophy. (See page 124.)

13.   a.   No. The Cynics taught that people should forego luxury and the like, but not that they should avoid pain, which is an Epicurean concept. (See pages 124-5.)

b.   Correct. The Cynics urged a return to nature; by living simply and rejecting material things, nature would provide all necessities. (See pages 124-5.)

c.   No. Actually, the Cynics advised people to discard traditions and customs. (See pages 124-5.)

d.   No. The Cynics urged people to discard all luxuries and live naturally. (See pages 124-5.)

14.   a.   No. Actually, Epicureans were taught to ignore politics, which disturbed the soul. (See pages 125-6.)

b.   Correct. Epicurus, who believed that any violent emotion is undesirable, advocated mild self-discipline. (See pages 125-6.)

c.   No. Although Epicurus did not deny the existence of the gods, he believed that they had no effect on human existence. (See pages 125-6.)

d.   No. For Epicureans pleasure was defined as the absence of pain; they did not advocate a life devoted to the pursuit of pleasure. (See pages 125-6.)

15.   a.   No. The Stoics advocated a universal state which was ethical and virtuous, clearly opposed to the concept of "might makes right". (See page 126.)

b.   No. The Stoics were concerned with living virtuous lives; they did not evolve the concept of pain over pleasure. (See page 126.)

c.   Correct. The Stoics stressed the unity of man and the universe, stating that all men were brothers and that they should live in accordance with nature. (See page 126.)

d.   No. Although the Stoics advocated political involvement, they were indifferent to specific political forms. (See page 126.)

16.   a.   No. Aristotle, not Aristarchus, had originally put forth the idea that the sun revolved around the earth, which was adopted by the second century Egyptian astronomer Claudius Ptolemy, and would be the basis of astronomy until challenged by Copernicus in the sixteenth century. (See page 126, and Chapter 18.)

b.   No. The relative position (and orbit) of the moon and the earth was not much considered; more important was the relative position of the sun and the earth. (See page 126.)

c.   Correct. Aristarchus of Samos concluded that the sun was much larger than the earth and that the earth and the planets revolved around the sun, a view that would not be accepted until the work of Nicolas Copernicus in the sixteenth century. (See page 126, and Chapter 18.)

d.   No. The idea that the heavenly bodies were fixed (usually in crystal spheres) did have many proponents such as Ptolemy, but Aristarchus of Samos was not among them. (See page 126.)

17.   a.   No. Although the ancient world was aware of the importance of economics, this field would have to wait until a more recent era to become a science. (See page 128.)

b.   No. Physics, as a science, had its origins in the Hellenic period, not the Hellenistic period. (See page 128, and Chapter 3.)

c.   Correct. The scientific study of botany, begun by Aristotle's pupil Theophrastus, did have its origins in the Hellenistic period. (See page 128.)

d.   No. Geology as a science would have to wait for a more recent period to become a science. (See page 128.)

18. a.   Correct. Herophilus, building on the work of Hippocrates, discovered the nervous system. (See page 129.)
b.   No. Erasistratus conducted research on the brain and nervous system, but did not discover the nervous system. (See page 129.)
c.   No. Heraclides was a member of the Empirical school of medicine and discovered the medicinal benefits of opium and other drugs, not the nervous system. (See page 129.)
d.   No. Serapion, along with Philinius, founded the Empirical school of medicine which emphasized the use of drugs and medicine to treat illnesses. (See page 129.)

19. a.   No. The study of anatomy was stressed by the Dogmatic school; the Empirical school had been founded because the Empiricists believed that the Dogmatics had become too speculative. (See page 129.)
b.   No. The study of physiology was stressed by the Dogmatic school, which the Empiricists opposed as being too speculative. (See page 129.)
c.   No. Vivisection was the technique by which the Dogmatic school conducted its research on anatomy and physiology, which the Empiricists criticized as too speculative. (See page 129.)
d.   Correct. The Empiricists used observation and the use of medicines and drugs to treat illnesses. (See page 129.)

20. a.   No. Despite the existence of many such designs, labor-saving devices were rarely utilized during the Hellenistic period. (See page 120.)
b.   No. There were no new techniques of production introduced during the Hellenistic period. (See page 120.)
c.   No. The use of animal power was not a feature of Hellenistic industry. (See page 120.)
d.   Correct. During the Hellenistic period human labor was so cheap and plentiful that it was relied on almost exclusively. (See page 120.)

21. a.   No. Actually the polis was not abandoned totally, but was retained in form but not spirit. (See page 111.)
b.   No. In the Hellenistic east, the polis was introduced but without key features, which deprived the polis of its fundamental characteristics, leaving it a mere facade. (See page 111.)
c.   No. Under the Hellenistic monarchies, the poleis lost all claims to independence and were a mere facade of the Hellenic poleis. (See page 111.)
d.   Correct. The Hellenistic poleis were mere reflections of the Hellenic city-states; the new poleis lacked the independence and civic pride of the older city-states. (See page 111.)

22. a.   Correct. Jews in Hellenistic cities adopted much of Greek culture (language, political ideas, business organization, etc.) but remained Jews at heart. (See page 117.)
b.   No. Actually they adopted enough of Greek culture (language, political forms, trade associations, etc.) to be successful, economically. (See page 117.)
c.   No. Actually, the Jews adopted many aspects of Greek culture, but not Greek religion. (See page 117.)
d.   No. Despite the fact that some Jews in Asia Minor and Syria incorporated Greek (or local Eastern) cults into their worship, and some did adopt Stoic philosophy, Jews for the most part remained bound to their religion. (See page 117.)

23. a.   No. With the abundance of cheap human labor, there was nothing resembling an industrial revolution. (See pages 118-120.)
b.   No. The material demands of the Hellenistic period were unchanged from before; most trade was in essentials like grain. (See pages 118-120.)
c.   No. Actually the increased geographical knowledge resulting from Alexander's conquest and his

empire greatly facilitated trade between the East and the Mediterranean world. (See pages 118-120.)

d. Correct. The spread of Greeks throughout the East created new markets and stimulated trade, increased geographical knowledge and the Alexandrian cities had regularized the trade routes; both of these contributed to a broad commercial network linking East and West. (See pages 118-120.)

24. a. No. As a result of the establishment of the Alexandrian cities, trade between east and west was strong, with luxury goods moving along the caravan routes. (See pages 119-120.)

b. No. The slave trade flourished in this era; by the numerous wars provided a ready source of slaves. (See pages 119-120.)

c. No. In this period, all types of bulk commodities were traded throughout the region. (See pages 119-120.)

d. Correct. Manufactured goods remained tied to local markets in this era and thus not a part of the expanding trade network. (See pages 119-120.)

25. a. No. Actually the demand for goods increased in the Hellenistic period, with no increase in unemployment. (See page 120.)

b. No. Actually it was just the opposite, human labor was abundant and thus cheap, rendering technological innovation superfluous. (See page 120.)

c. No. The abundance of labor actually worked to retard any technological advances. (See page 120.)

d. Correct. With the abundance of cheap human labor (enhanced by burgeoning slavery) technological advances were rendered unnecessary. (See page 120.)

Chapter 5

1.   a.   No. Actually the *paterfamilias* was the eldest male of the family. (See page 147.)

      b.   No. In theory, the *paterfamilias* could legally kill his wife for adultery. (See page 147.)

      c.   Correct. Until his death, the sons could not own property; after the death of the *paterfamilias*, the wife and children inherited the property. (See page 147.)

      d.   No. Despite his immense power, the *paterfamilias* usually called a council of the adult males of the family to discuss important family matters. (See page 147.)

2.   a.   No. The wars of conquest had actually left Roman agriculture in a shambles; Rome resorted to importing grain. (See page 152.)

      b.   Correct. As a result of their extended absence (and the ravages of Hannibal) the Roman farmers returned to find their farms in ruins. (See page 152.)

      c.   No. Actually, the political strength of the small farmers declined from the early Republic era as a result of their impoverished state. (See page 152.)

      d.   No. Actually, the veterans who returned from the wars of conquest were forced to sell off their farms and moved to the cities to find work, which was often not to be had. (See page 152.)

3.   a.   Correct. The ability of the Romans not only to conquer but to incorporated other peoples into their state was their greatest accomplishment. (See pages 135-42.)

      b.   No. The Romans added little in the way of agricultural or commercial innovations; politics was their specialty. (See pages 135-42.)

      c.   No. In matters of art the Romans learned from the Greeks. (See pages 135-42.)

      d.   No. In matters of literature, as in art and philosophy, the Romans learned from the Greeks. (See pages 135-42.)

4.   a.   No. It is true that the Romans conquered other peoples, but rather than let them govern themselves, Romans incorporated conquered peoples into the Roman system. (See page 140.)

      b.   No. Given the warlike and imperialistic nature of the Romans, it would have been unlikely that they would live peacefully with their neighbors. (See page 140.)

      c.   No. Although the Romans preferred to incorporate other peoples peacefully, the Romans were not averse to using force to accomplish this incorporation. (See page 140.)

      d.   Correct. The true genius of the Romans lay in their ability not only to conquer other peoples (which has been done since the dawn of time) but to incorporate them into the Roman system. (See page 140.)

5.   a.   Correct. The office of emperor, which was created in essence by Augustus Caesar, was part of the Roman Empire not Republic. (See page 141, and Chapter 6.)

      b.   No. During the Republic, *quaestors* assisted consuls in their duties, particularly overseeing the public treasury and the prosecution of criminals. (See page 141.)

      c.   No. During the Republic, *praetors* handled the duties of the consuls when they were away, and dealt primarily with the administration of justice. (See page 141.)

      d.   No. During the Republic, *consuls* were the chief magistrates of the state, with very broad duties. (See page 141.)

6.   a.   No. The Struggle of the Orders did result in the creation of the office of tribune, charged with protecting the plebeians from the arbitrary conduct of the patricians. (See pages 142-3.)

      b.   Correct. Actually the Struggle of the Orders resulted in increased power for the plebeians, not the patricians. (See pages 142-3.)

      c.   No. The Law of the Twelve Tables was a product of the Struggle of the Orders; this allowed all citizens to know the law. (See pages 142-3.)

      d.   No. The Struggle of the Orders, which could have caused anarchy and violent class warfare, actually created a stronger, more unified Rome. (See pages 142-3.)

7.
a. No. Actually the reforming Gracchi brothers hoped to improve the situation for the urban poor and peasant farmers. (See page 154.)
b. No. The Gracchi brothers were members of the patrician class. (See page 154.)
c. Correct. The reforming Gracchi brothers hoped to alleviate the severe social and economic problems facing the Republic by alleviating the problems of the urban poor and peasant farmers. (See page 154.)
d. No. Actually Gaius Gracchus proposed extending full Roman citizenship to all Italians. (See page 154.)

8.
a. No. Unlike Greece, the Italian typography was hospitable with a pleasant climate, thus conducive to both strong agriculture and political unity. (See page 135.)
b. Correct. Actually the Apennines run north-south not east and west. (See page 135.)
c. No. Of the Italian rivers only the Arno is navigable. (See page 135.)
d. No. The southward course of the Apennines creates two broad plains, the Latium and the Campania. (See page 135.)

9.
a. No. While the Greeks did establish many colonies in the Mediterranean world, Rome was not one of them. (See page 139.)
b. No. The tribe of Autun is not mentioned by Roman legend. (See page 139.)
c. No. Livy was a Roman historian who lived at time of Jesus; he did write about the founding of Rome. (See page 139.)
d. Correct. According to legend the brothers Romulus and Remus, twins who had escaped the destruction of Troy and were raised by wolves, founded Rome in 753 B.C. (See page 139.)

10.
a. No. Tarquin the Proud was a king of the Etruscans, not a Roman. (See page 139.)
b. Correct. The story of Cincinnatus exemplifies the solid, down-to-earth nature of the Romans, as both farmers, soldiers and citizens. (See pages 000.)
c. No. Servius Tulluis, according to Roman tradition, had organized the state into the *centuries* for military purposes and created the *comitia centuriata* to decide policy. (See pages 140-1.)
d. No. Pyrrhus was king of Epirus whose costly victories against the Romans gave us the phrase "Pyrrhic victory". (See page 145.)

11.
a. Correct. The consuls of the Republic had many duties, including administration of the state and command of the army, and were the chief magistrates of republican Rome. (See page 141.)
b. No. *Quaestors* were originally appointed by the consuls to assist them and were principally concerned with the public treasury and the prosecution of criminals. (See page 141.)
c. No. *Praetors* were inaugurated in 366 B.C., and dealt primarily with the administration of justice and were important in the development of Roman jurisprudence. (See page 141.)
d. No. Senators were members of the patrician assembly which had consultative powers; it was an important institution because of its stability and continuity. (see pages 140-1.)

12.
a. No. The text makes no reference to Philip of Carthage. (See pages 145-6.)
b. Correct. Hannibal, son of Hamilcar, invaded Italy in 218 B.C., crossing the Alps with his famous elephants and laying waste to much of the countryside but was unable to crush Rome's "iron circle" of central Italy. (See pages 145-6.)
c. No. Alexander had made his conquests long before the rise of Rome and his efforts had been directed eastward and southward from his native Macedonia. (See pages 145-6 and Chapter 4.)
d. No. Menenius Agrippa, which is a Roman name, was not a Cathaginian leader. (See pages 145-6.)

13.   a.   No. Actually Roman women had a position of authority and respect in the family. (See page 147.)

b.   No. Roman women had a vast array of household duties to perform and was not constrained to the performance of religious rituals. (See page 147.)

c.   Correct. Roman women, within the family, enjoyed a position of authority and respect, and were responsible for running the family household. (See page 147.)

d.   No. Although the mother was responsible for the early education of her children, at the age of seven male children began to undertake more formal education. (See page 147.)

14.   a.   No. Although slaves were prevalent in Roman society, they were not considered inferior human beings, merely the victims of unfortunate circumstances. (See pages 148-9.)

b.   No. As in the ancient world, slavery was not based on racial terms but was considered a misfortune that befell some people. (See pages 148-9.)

c.   No. Recruitment into the Roman army, until the Empire, was limited to citizens. (See pages 148-9.)

d.   Correct. The practice of freeing slaves, manumission, was available and indeed became so common that it had to be limited by law. (See pages 148-9.)

15.   a.   No. Gaius Marius was a Roman general who played a key role in the upheavals at the end of the republican era. (See pages 150, 154.)

b.   Correct. Ennius, influenced by Greek philosophy and drama, was the father of Latin poetry. (See page 150.)

c.   No. Scipio Aemilianus was a prime example of the influence of Greek culture on the Romans, but he was not the father of Latin poetry. (See page 150.)

d.   No. Cato represented the traditional Roman, unlikely to become a poet. (See pages 147-8, 150.)

16.   a.   No. Roman conservatives considered the baths to be a great waste of time. (See page 150.)

b.   No. Most Roman conservatives decried the influence of Greek culture on the traditions of the Romans, including the baths. (See page 150.)

c.   Correct. Roman conservatives, who decried increasing Greek influence, felt the baths encouraged idleness. (See page 150.)

d.   No. Although political discussions did take place in the baths, conservatives felt that the baths were nothing more than a waste of time. (See page 150.)

17.   a.   No. Actually the wars of Republican Rome left Roman agriculture in a shambles. (See pages 151-2, 154.)

b.   Correct. The ravages of Hannibal and the extended absence of many farmer-soldiers left Roman agriculture in a state of decay. (See pages 151-2, 154.)

c.   No. The development of *latifundia* provided Rome with the needed food supplies, at least into the imperial era. (See pages 151-2.)

d.   No. Actually the development of *latifundia* led to a centralization and consolidation of land ownership in the later years of the Republic. (See pages 151-2.)

18.   a.   No. Sulla was a military leader who opposed Marius during the civil wars at the end of the Republic and was not a land reformer. (See pages 154-7.)

b.   Correct. Tiberius Gracchus was the elder Gracchi brother who realized the social problems of the Republic and tried to correct them by land reform, for which he was murdered, leading to an era of political violence. (See page 154.)

c.   No. Cato was a statesman and lawyer of the earlier years of the Republic and was not a land reformer. (See pages 147-8, 154.)

d.   No. Caesar, although he did propose some reforms, did not advocate giving public land to the poor. (See pages 154, 157-8.)

19.   a.   No. Cincinnatus was the exemplar of the citizen-soldier, but did not introduce any reforms in the

army. (See pages 154-7.)

b.   No. Tiberius was one of the Gracchi brothers that proposed reforms to help the poor of Rome but
c.   No. Sulla was a military man and was involved in the civil wars but did not reform the army. (See pages 154-7.)
d.   Correct. Marius, a general in the Roman army, was responsible for reforming the army and greatly enhancing its political power and thus further undermining the Republican constitution. (See pages 154-7.)

20.   a.   No. Although many plebeians sold their farms and moved to the cities to find work, they found little work. (See page 152.)
b.   Correct. When the plebeian soldiers sold their farms and moved to the cities they found that the majority of the job were in the hands of slaves. (See page 152.)
c.   No. Christians were too few at this time to be an important factor in the labor pool of the Republic. (See page 152 and Chapter 6.)
d.   No. The army was too involved with military matters to allow the soldiers to dominate the labor market. (See page 152.)

21.   a.   No. The Etruscan economy was based on trade, not conquest. (See page 136.)
b.   No. Rome was never the center of the Etruscans community. (See page 136.)
c.   No. The Etruscans were an urban people and thus agriculture and rural life was not the basis of their wealth. (See page 136.)
d.   Correct. The Etruscans, an urban people, were skillful metal workers and were able to amass their wealth by trading manufactured products in Italy and beyond. (See page 136.)

22.   a.   No. This term refers to a form of citizenship granted to non-Romans, not slavery. (See page 140.)
b.   No. *Civitas sine suffragio* refers to a form of limited citizenship granted to non-Romans. (See page 140.)
c.   Correct. This is the form of limited citizenship granted to Rome's Italian allies; it did not include the right to vote or hold office. (See page 140.)
d.   No. This term refers to a type of citizenship, not military service. (See page 140.)

23.   a.   No. Western Greece was too far removed from both Rome and Carthage to be a battleground between the two. (See page 145.)
b.   No. Gaul was too far north to become the battleground between Rome and Carthage. (See page 145.)
c.   No. Northern Africa was the location of Carthage and although the Romans would eventually invade the area and destroy Carthage, it was not the "wrestling ground" between the two. (See page 145.)
d.   Correct. Sicily, located between Rome and Carthage, provided the "wrestling ground". (See page 145.)

24.   a.   No. Actually manumission became so frequent that it had to be limited by law. (See pages 148-9.)
b.   No. Although manumission was limited by law, it remained legal. (See pages 148-9.)
c.   No. Romans had always held out the hope of manumission; it was not common only among Christians, who did not question the practice of slavery. (See pages 148-9.)
d.   Correct. In fact, manumission, which had always been an option, became so common that it had to be limited by law. (See pages 148-9.)

25.   a.   Correct. *Latifundia* developed as a result of the wealth garnered by some individuals during the wars of conquest; these rich men invested in land by buying up the small farms of returning soldiers and creating huge estates. (See page 152.)

b. No. *Latifundia* denotes a form of land tenureship in Rome after the wars of conquest, not a client-kingdom. (See page 152.)

c. No. *Latifundia* refers to a form of land tenureship which arose in Rome following the wars of conquest; patricians and plebeians, despite the reforms of the Struggle of the Orders, were never really considered equals. (See page 152.)

d. No. *Latifundia* refers to a form of land tenureship, not a form of citizenship. (See page 152.)

1. a.   No. Jesus, a Jew, was born in Bethlehem and raised in Galilee, not Persia. (See pages 172-5.)
    b.   No. Jesus taught a message of peace and that the Jews should "render unto Caesar the things that are Caesar's;" he wanted to establish a spiritual, not earthly, kingdom. (See pages 172-5.)
    c.   No. As Jesus repeatedly told his disciples, his was a kingdom "not of this world" and was not interested in the creation of an earthly kingdom. (See pages 172-5.)
    d.   Correct. Jesus' teachings were orthodox Judaism, except that he insisted that he taught in his own name, not in the name of Yahweh. (See pages 172-5.)

2. a.   No. Trajan was certainly one of the "good emperors" but he did not introduce this reform; he did play an important role in the career of the emperor who did, however. (See pages 177-8.)
    b.   No. Diocletian was in important reforming emperor, but he was not responsible for this reform. (See pages 177-8, 186-9.)
    c.   No. Pontius Pilate was a hard-bitten Roman soldier and provincial administrator, but never attained the office of emperor. (See pages 173-4, 177-8.)
    d.   Correct. Hadrian, the hand-picked successor of Trajan and experienced at defending the frontiers of Rome, separated civil from military service, improving the efficiency of the imperial bureaucracy and enabling those with little taste for the military to serve the empire. (See pages 177-8.)

3. a.   Augustus, who could have declared himself dictator, found this idea repugnant and attempted rather to restore the Republic with himself as the most powerful individual in the government. (See pages 163-4.)
    b.   Correct. Augustus held tremendous, monarchical power, but cloaked it in the constitutional forms of the Republic. (See pages 163-4.)
    c.   No. Although Augustus retained the forms of the Republic, the concentration of power in his hands clearly rendered the Rome of Augustus anything but a republic. (See pages 163-4.)
    d.   No. Rome had never been a democracy and the Augustan settlement did not create such a form of government. (See pages 163-4.)

4. a.   No. The emperor Diocletian, although a reformer, did not help spread Christianity; in fact, during his reign Christians were persecuted. (See pages 172-5, 186-9.)
    b.   No. St. Peter, like Jesus, was born in the Jewish culture and did not attempt to spread the message to Gentiles. (See pages 172-5.)
    c.   No. Livy was a Roman historian who lived at the time of Christ but was not a Christian. (See pages 169-70, 172-5.)
    d.   Correct. Paul of Tarsus, a Hellenized Jew influenced by Stoic philosophy, made a significant break with Christianity's parent religion Judaism and was most influential in spreading the religion to non-Jews. (See pages 172-5.)

5. a.   No. Actually crime increased, with both lawless soldiers and barbarians roaming the countryside. (See pages 185-6.)
    b.   Correct. Indeed for many ordinary people during this era of turmoil, official corruption was the most pressing problem they faced. (See pages 185-6.)
    c.   No. Actually, the importance of the villas, being self-sufficient and capable of self-defense, increased. (See pages 185-6.)
    d.   No. Many small farmers, beset by both the increased crime and increased official corruption, turned to large landowners for protection in return for their freedom and land. (See pages 185-6.)

6. a.   No. The *Res Gestae* was a history of Augustus's reign. (See page 164.)
    b.   No. The *Sanhedrin* was the Jewish council of elders. (See pages 164, 171.)

c. No. *Dominus* is a generic term meaning "lord." (See page 164.)

d. Correct. His official title was *princeps civitatus* (he had many others as well); his power came from his personal control of the army. (See page 164.)

7. a. No. Augustus, realizing the importance of the provinces, improved provincial administration and encouraged self-government and urbanism. (See pages 164-5.)

b. No. Augustus did not oppress the provinces, instead he encouraged self-government and better administration. (See pages 164-5.)

c. No. Augustus fully realized the importance of the provinces and the people who inhabited them; prejudice against minorities was not an aspect of his governance. (See pages 164-5.)

d. Correct. Augustus encouraged the development of self-government in the provinces and respected (and ordered his governors to respect) local customs. (See pages 164-5.)

8. a. Correct. The Zealots were one of two Jewish movements responding to Roman rule; the Zealots were extremists who worked and fought to rid Judea of the Romans. (See pages 171-2.)

b. No. Baruch was indicative of the militant apocalyptic sentiment prevalent in Judea, which foretold the destruction of the Roman Empire and the coming of the Messiah, but was not openly antagonistic towards the Romans. (See pages 171-2.)

c. No. The Essenes were an ascetic sect that believed that the coming of the Messiah was at hand; their social organization closely resembled that of the early Christians. (See pages 171-2.)

d. No. The Hittites were an ancient people who had created an empire in the Ancient Near East. (See pages 171-2 and Chapter 1.)

9. a. Correct. This openness to both sexes and all classes of people attracted many people to Christianity. (See pages 174-5.)

b. No. Actually Christianity and the mystery religions shared a number of features, such as baptism. (See pages 174-5.)

c. No. Actually Christianity gave many people a cause, stressing the ideal of striving for a goal. (See pages 174-5.)

d. No. Jesus' message of forgiveness and acceptance of sinners was integral aspect of the Christian message and important in its spread. (See pages 174-5.)

10. a. No. Augustus and his successors actually encouraged the rise of free farmers and slavery declined. (See page 183.)

b. No. Although trade increased and tons of Egyptian wheat went to feed the populace of Rome, the small free farmer was the backbone of agriculture. (See page 185.)

c. No. Under Augustus and his successors, slavery had declined and instead small free farmers became once again the backbone of agriculture. (See page 185.)

d. Correct. Augustus and his successors encouraged the rise of small free farmers. (See page 186.)

11. a. No. The Romans did not demand that the Christians worship the Roman gods (polytheism is by nature tolerant of new gods) only that they observe the rituals. (See pages 189-90.)

b. Correct. The Romans did not demand that the Christians believe in the Roman gods only that they observe the rituals, an act of importance given the identification of the state with the gods. (See pages 189-90.)

c. No. The Romans, like other peoples with polytheistic beliefs, did not demand that the Christians renounce Jesus. (See pages 189-90.)

d. No. Actually the Jews were no more favored among Romans than were the Christians, so it would have been unlikely that the Romans would have made such a demand. (See pages 189-90.)

12. a. No. Kiev was founded by the Varangians in the Ukraine and would serve as the capital of their state. (See page 190 and Chapter 8.)

b.   Correct. The city which bears Constantine's name, Constantinople, sitting on Hellespont dividing Europe from Asia, was the new capital of the Empire. (See page 190.)

c.   No. Alexandria had been founded by Alexander the Great (indeed there were several cities bearing variations of this name) and was not the new capital of the Roman Empire. (See page 190 and Chapter 4.)

d.   No. Athens, the ancient Greek city-state, was not the new capital of the Roman Empire. (See page 190 and Chapter 3.)

13.   a.   No. Even though Constantine was a remarkable man, he was not a historian and died before the "fall" of Rome. (See pages 176, 186-90.)

b.   No. The Roman historian Livy was rather prolific but he lived before the "fall" of Rome. (See pages 168, 176.)

c.   Correct. The Englishman Edward Gibbon in 1776 published his impressive *History of the Decline and Fall of the Roman Empire*. (See page 176.)

d.   No. Paul of Tarsus was the man responsible for the spread of Christianity to Gentiles; he lived before the "fall" of Rome. (See pages 174, 176.)

14.   a.   No. Judea had been conquered before Augustus's reign. (See pages 165-6.)

b.   Correct. Augustus pushed the Roman frontier into the region of modern Germany. (See pages 165-6.)

c.   No. Britain had been conquered before Augustus's reign. (See pages 165-6 and Chapter 5.)

d.   No. This region had been conquered earlier. (See pages 165-6 and Chapter 5.)

15.   a.   No. Virgil's masterpiece the *Aeneid* was written before the birth of Christ. (See pages 168-9.)

b.   No. Actually Virgil was an ardent Roman patriot and believed the imperialistic expansion of Rome to have been very positive. (See pages 168-9.)

c.   Correct. Virgil was an ardent Roman patriot and believed Rome to be the protector of good against the forces of darkness. (See pages 168-9.)

d.   No. Virgil identified Aeneas as a Trojan hero who escaped the destruction of Troy; the *Aeneid* was thus not a history of the fall of Athens but of the mythic origins of Rome. (See pages 168-9.)

16.   a.   Correct. Augustus did appoint Herod; his fellow Jews hated Herod's acceptance of Greek culture. (See page 171.)

b.   No. Jesus was considered a revolutionary trouble-maker by the Roman authorities and was never considered a candidate for such a position. (See page 171-2.)

c.   No. Philip Augustus was a king of France during the High Middle Ages. (See page 171 and Chapter 9.)

d.   No. Cato was a lawyer and politician of the Roman Republic. (See page 171 and Chapter 5.)

17.   a.   No. The third century was characterized by civil wars, a result of the political power of the army and ambitions of Roman generals. (See pages 185-6.)

b.   No. The disastrous civil wars of the third century allowed the migrating barbarian tribes to enter the empire. (See pages 185-6.)

c.   No. The twin factors of civil war and barbarian invasion brought on serious economic problems for the empire. (See pages 185-6.)

d.   Correct. With the problems of civil war, barbarian invasion and economic decline, the empire was too distracted to contemplate imperial expansion. (See pages 185-6.)

18.   a.   No. *Villa* was not a term used to refer to Jewish military districts. (See page 189.)

b.   No. *Villa* was not a term used to refer to the embryonic banking system of Rome. (See page 189.)

c.   No. Roman civil service districts were referred to as *dioceses*, not *villas*. (See page 189.)

d.   Correct. A *villa* was a large, self-sufficient estate, capable of defending itself, that arose in response to the turmoil of the third century; this was the precursor of the medieval manor. (See page 189.)

19.   a.   No. Horace was a fine poet and a great admirer of Augustus but is not considered the greatest poet of Rome. (See pages 168-70.)

     b.   No. Livy was an historian not a poet. (See pages 168-9.)

     c.   No. Caligula was not a poet but a corrupt and brutal emperor. (See pages 168-9, 171.)

     d.   Correct. Virgil, with such works as *Georgics* and the *Aeneid*, is considered Rome's greatest poet. (See pages 168-9.)

20.   a.   No. Although Diocletian made many reforms in the territorial administration, he did not grant independence to the frontiers. (See pages 186-7.)

     b.   No. While reforms of local administration were made, there was no tripling of the number of local rulers. (See pages 186-7.)

     c.   No. While there was a degree of delegation of authority and Diocletian did establish the Tetrarchy, with the empire divided into four administrative units, he did not appoint four emperors. (See pages 186-7.)

     d.   Correct. To solve the problems of the empire, Diocletian divided the empire into a western and eastern half, with the western half being ruled by a colleague entitled *augustus*; these two divisions were further subdivided into two parts, creating the Tetrarchy. (See pages 186-7.)

21.   a.   Correct. The worst defect of the Augustan settlement was the army's ability to interfere in politics, especially the Praetorian Guard, which was very prevalent in the Flavian period. (See page 176.)

     b.   No. The Flavians were not reformers and did not interfere in the banking system; an attempt at reform of banking was made by Constantine and Diocletian. (See pages 176, 186-7.)

     c.   No. The Flavian period was ushered in by defeat at the hands of the Goths; this would not happen for another 200 years. (See pages 176, 183.)

     d.   No. The rebellion in Judea occurred before the Flavians appeared. (See pages 171-2, 176.)

22.   a.   No. Actually when Decius invaded Rome in 249, he left a huge gap in the frontier defenses along the Danube. (See pages 185-6.)

     b.   No. This period of civil war and subsequent barbarian invasion precluded imperial expansion. (See pages 185-6.)

     c.   No. Actually it was just the opposite; the political aspirations of Roman generals greatly detracted from the defense of the frontiers. (See pages 185-6.)

     d.   Correct. When Decius marched on Rome, he left a gap along the Danubian frontier through which the Goths poured. (See pages 185-6.)

23.   a.   No. Allowing a free market in such indispensable commodities as food and wine would have resulted in speculation and higher prices and, thus, more rioting. (See page 179.)

     b.   No. The government wisely realized that suppression would not have solved the problems facing the poor masses of Romans. (See page 179.)

     c.   No. Land reform was not the solution tried by the government; such a course of action would have taken to long to have been effective. (See page 179.)

     d.   Correct. The government, by maintaining the grain supply and distributing it freely (along with other critical commodities such as wine,) attempted to keep the favor of the Roman population. (See page 179.)

24.   a.   No. Actually Hadrian introduced reforms which separated civil from military service. (See page 178.)

     b.   Correct. As the imperial bureaucracy had grown tremendously since the reforms of Claudius,

Hadrian reformed this system by separating civil and military service and putting the bureaucracy on an organized, official basis. (See page 178.)

c.   No. Actually, Augustus is credited with the creation of the constitutional monarchy. (See pages 178, 163-4.)

d.   No. The conquest of Gaul had already been accomplished by Julius Caesar and Augustus Caesar. (See page 178 and Chapter 5.)

25.   a.   No. Actually Greek colonies were independent of their founding cities. (See pages 164-7 and Chapter 3.)

b.   No. Actually the Roman colonies developed a symbiotic relationship with the native cultures and created a cultural fusion. (See pages 164-7.)

c.   No. The Roman colonies were linked tightly to the economic system of the Empire. (See pages 164-7.)

d.   Correct. Roman colonies were tightly integrated into the political, social, and economic network of the Empire. (See pages 164-7.)

Chapter 7

1. a. No. The Council of Nicaea condemned the Arianian heresy. (See pages 200-1.)
    b. No. Actually, the council had been called by the Emperor Constantine, thus providing precedence for secular rulers to interfere in church affairs. (See pages 200-1.)
    c. Correct. The Nicene Creed defined the orthodox position on the subject: Christ and God were of the same substance. (See pages 200-1.)
    d. No. Actually, this was the position of Arius, whose viewpoint was condemned as heresy by the council. (See pages 200-1.)

2. a. No. Even though the writers of the penitentials were attempting to strengthen faith in God, they seem to have been most concerned with particular aspects of individual behavior. (See page 207.)
    b. No. The penitentials were more concerned with matters of faith and sin among the newly converted, not with their allegiance to Rome. (See page 207.)
    c. No. Although baptism and violence were concerns, the penitentials were not as concerned with these issues as they were with other aspects of individual behavior of the newly converted. (See page 207.)
    d. Correct. The penitentials were more concerned with the sexual activities of the newly converted. (See page 207.)

3. a. No. Actually one of the main reasons for its success was its applicability to both men and women. (See pages 212-4.)
    b. Correct. The greatness of the *Rule*, in many respects, comes from its flexibility, applying to men and women, of various social classes, regions and historical eras. (See pages 212-4.)
    c. No. The Benedictine vows are designed to efface self-love. (See pages 212-4.)
    d. No. Although intellectual labor was considered important, the *Rule* also emphasized the usefulness of spiritual and physical labor. (See pages 212-4.)

4. a. No. Despite the achievements of Muslim literature, this was not the greatest contribution to the West. (See pages 234-5.)
    b. Correct. Muslim scholars such as Al-Khwarizmi did much too preserve, transmit and enhance classical mathematics, while al-Razi and other physicians did the same for medical knowledge. (See pages 234-5.)
    c. No. Roman law profoundly influenced the development of European law. (See pages 234-5.)
    d. No. While troubadour music would be greatly influenced by the Moors in Spain, this was not the greatest Islamic contribution to the West. (See pages 234-5 and Chapter 12.)

5. a. Correct. Under pressure from the Danish invasions, the Anglo-Saxon kingdoms were united by Alfred. (See page 223.)
    b. No. Christianity had been accepted in Britain before the immigration of the Angles and Saxons. (See pages 201-2, 223.)
    c. No. The last Roman emperor in the West had fallen 400 hundred years before Alfred lived and the last Roman emperor in East fell some 600 years after Alfred. (See page 223 and Chapters 6 and 17.)
    d. No. Remarkable though Alfred was, he did create a new law code. (See page 223.)

6. a. No. Like Christianity and Judaism, Islam worships one god (monotheism.) (See pages 231-3.)
    b. Correct. There are many similarities among Islam, Christianity and Judaism; according to Islam, Muhammed is the successor (and last) of earlier prophets such as Abraham and Jesus. (See pages 231-3.)
    c. No. Islamic belief, like Christianity, features a Day of Judgment. (See pages 231-3.)
    d. No. According to Islamic belief, no amount of good behavior can insure salvation; salvation is the

gift of Allah. (See pages 231-3.)

7. a.   No. This connotation would be that of the Christian church hierarchy on the eve of the Reformation, but was not how Paul used the term. (See pages 199-200 and Chapter 14.)
    b.   Correct. Paul was referring to the local community of believers; later he would use it to refer to the entire community of Christians. (See pages 199-200.)
    c.   No. During Paul's time, there was no pope. (See pages 199-200.)
    d.   No. Although Paul would later use this term to refer to the entire community of Christians, this was not the original usage. (See pages 199-200.)

8. a.   No. The theory of papal supremacy is usually attributed to Bishop Ambrose, although Augustine did play a role in the debate over secular and religious authority. (See pages 200, 209-11.)
    b.   No. The New Testament had long existed before Augustine was born. (See pages 209-11 and Chapter 6.)
    c.   Correct. In his writings, Augustine was able to reconcile Christian theology with pagan knowledge, allowing a synthesis which provide a great deal of the cultural and intellectual foundation of European civilization. (See pages 209-11.)
    d.   No. Augustine was never bishop of Rome. (See pages 209-11.)

9. a.   No. By the time of the appearance of the *Rule*, Germany had been almost completely converted. (See pages 204-5, 212-5.)
    b.   Correct. The vows contained in the *Rule*, as well as the monastic organizational framework supplied, were designed to lessen one's love of self and concentrate on love of God and other humans. (pages 212-5.)
    c.   No. New economic ventures was not part of the design of the *Rule*, but many Benedictine monasteries did indeed become very wealthy. (See pages 212-5.)
    d.   No. The *Rule* was not designed to prepare individuals to become government officials, although many clerics (including monks) did indeed serve secular rulers. (See pages 212-5.)

10. a.   Correct. The *Qur'an* is the collected wisdom of Muhammed and the basis of the Islamic faith. (See pages 231-3.)
    b.   No. The *Qur'an* has nothing to do with any aspect of Germanic society, including infanticide. (See pages 231-3.)
    c.   No. While Mecca is an important religious center for Muslims, the site of, among other shrines, the Kaaba, and the destination of Muslims on pilgrimage, the *Qur'an* is not part of this religious center. (See pages 231-3.)
    d.   No. The *Qur'an* is not a Muslim official; the leading Muslim official at that time was the caliph. (See pages 231-3.)

11. a.   No. Sexual behavior would become an issue only when the Germans had been converted to Christianity. (See pages 219-22.)
    b.   No. The concept of civil rights had not yet evolved in early German legal thought. (See pages 219-22.)
    c.   No. In early Germanic society, being nomadic, property rights had not yet developed. (See pages 219-22.)
    d.   Correct. Given the violent nature of early Germanic society, the early law codes tended to be lists of fines for criminal offenses, designed to control societal violence. (See pages 219-22.)

12. a.   No. The *laeti* were non-Roman refugees from barbarian invasions who sought protection inside the Empire, not the basic social unit of Germanic society. (See page 219 and Chapter 6.)
    b.   No. The *comitatus* was the warrior band found in Germanic groups, but was not the basic unit of Germanic society. (See page 219.)

c.   No. *Foederati* were Germanic tribes allied with the Roman empire and not the basic unit of Germanic society. (See page 219 and Chapter 6.)

d.   Correct. The basic social unit of Germanic society was the *folk*, or the tribe, which was believed united by ties of blood. (See page 219.)

13.   a.   No. Arius was the originator of a heresy on the substance of God and Christ and not the author of a statement on church-state relations. (See pages 200-1.)

b.   No. Emperor Theodosius's interference in church affairs would actually lead to the statement. (See pages 200-1.)

c.   No. Diocletian, as a very powerful Roman emperor, had interfered in many areas of life, but he did not issue an ecclesiastical statement (he was not a member of the Christian clergy) on church-state relations. (See pages 200-1 and Chapter 6.)

d.   No. As a response to the interference of Theodosius in church affairs, Bishop Ambrose issued this statement, affirming the independence, even superiority, of the church. (See pages 200-1.)

14.   a.   Correct. Gaiseric was the Vandal leader who sacked Rome. (See pages 201-2.)

b.   No. St. Paul was instrumental in the establishment of the Christian church. (See pages 201-2 and Chapter 6.)

c.   No. Leo I, in the absence of secular authority in Rome, met the invading Attila the Hun and persuaded him to spare Rome. (See pages 201-2.)

d.   No. Gregory I, in the absence of secular authority in Rome, served to provide inspired leadership in a serious time of disease and famine. (See pages 201-2.)

15.   a.   No. Although baptism was an aspect of the conversion experience and one of the sacraments, conversion was so much more than merely being baptized. (See page 204.)

b.   Correct. In religious terms, conversion means a complete turning toward God. (See page 204.)

c.   No. Although confession was an aspect of the conversion experience and one of the sacraments, conversion was so much more than merely confessing. (See page 204.)

d.   No. Although confirmation was an aspect of the conversion experience and one of the sacraments, conversion was so much more than merely undergoing confirmation. (See page 204.)

16.   a.   No. Preaching was one of the key techniques used to convert the pagans. (See page 205.)

b.   No. Edification, through stories of Christ and lives of the saints, would appeal to semi-literate pagan peoples and was one of the key techniques. (See page 205.)

c.   No. The adaptation of the pagan places and practices was crucial in smoothing the transition from pagan to Christian beliefs. (See page 205.)

d.   Correct. While religious and public life had been and continued to be intertwined, group penitentials and group baptisms were not typical techniques. (See page 205.)

17.   a.   No. On the continent, including Germany, church organization and monastic life were separate. (See page 203.)

b.   No. While Irish monks did found a monastery at Iona for the conversion of Scotland, ecclesiastical organization maintained separation between parish and monastic organizations in Scotland. (See pages 203.)

c.   Correct. Local churches and monastic life were interdependent in Ireland, resulting from the organization set up by St. Patrick. (See page 203.)

d.   No. On the continent, including Italy, church organization and monastic life were separate. (See page 203.)

18.   a.   No. Cassiodorus, being from an elite Roman family, did not found his monastery to pursue nothing other than mortification and prayer. (See page 212.)

b.   Correct. In his Vivarium, Cassiodorus provided an atmosphere that was conducive to study and other scholarly pursuits. (See page 212.)

c.   No. Cassiodorus, being from an elite Roman family, was not overly found of manual labor. (See page 212.)

d.   No. Cassiodorus, being from an elite Roman family, was founded his monastery as a place to retire from the cares of society. (See page 212.)

19.   a.   No. These are famous monastic vows, but are not those of the *Rule*. (See page 212.)

b.   No. Certainly, Benedictine monks and nuns carry out the work of God, but that is not the vow. (See page 212.)

c.   Correct. These three vows are designed to wean the monk or nun from love of self and direct them to love of God. (See page 212.)

d.   No. Benedictine monasticism was not aimed at missionary activity. (See page 212.)

20.   a.   Correct. The flexibility and applicability of the *Rule* made Benedictine monasticism the dominant order for many centuries and is still today a very influential force in the Catholic church. (See pages 212-3.)

b.   No. When the Benedictine order established itself, there were no emperors in the West. (See pages 212-3, 201 and Chapter 6.)

c.   No. While many Benedictines were very clever, this does not explain the success of the *Rule*. (See pages 212-3.)

d.   No. Eremitical monasticism was most prevalent in the milder climate of the Mediterranean world; Europe was too cold and dangerous for eremitical monasticism. Moreover, the church hierarchy in the West frowned on it. (See pages 210-3.)

21.   a.   No. Although conversion of the Slavic peoples would occur through Byzantine efforts, Justinian did not conquer them or the Turks (who would not appear for several centuries.) (See page 226 and Chapters 8 and 17.)

b.   Correct. Justinian's greatest accomplishment was in the compilation of the *Code* and the various other publications on jurisprudence. (See page 226.)

c.   No. While Justinian's marriage to Theodora no doubt provided much personal satisfaction, it was not his greatest achievement. (See pages 226, 228.)

d.   No. The Cyrillic alphabet has been attributed to Orthodox missionaries, Cyril and Methodius, in a much later period than Justinian's. (See page 226 and Chapter 8.)

22.   a.   No. The *corpus* was a very influential publication of much greater significance than the mere snippets from these authors. (See page 226.)

b.   No. The *corpus* did not include contributions from Russian or Greek laws. (See page 226.)

c.   No. The *corpus* did not include Greek legal practices. (See page 226.)

d.   Correct. The *corpus* was the distilled legal genius of the Romans. (See page 226.)

23.   a.   No. This is not literal translation of *Islam*, but Islamic religion does feature a Judgment Day. (See page 232.)

b.   Correct. *Islam* means literally "submission to the word of God"; from this meaning one can infer the relationship between the individual and Allah. (See page 232.)

c.   No. While the *Qu'ran* is the sacred book of Islam, this is not the literal meaning of the term *Islam*. (See page 232.)

d.   While this is certainly one of the pillars of Islam, this is not the literal meaning of the term *Islam*. (See page 232.)

24.   a.   Correct. Despite the omniscient nature of God, according to all three, humans do have free will; in Islam, no amount of good works can insure salvation; according to Muhammed, predestination gave

the believer the will to do achieve the impossible. (See page 233.)

b.   No. Since Muhammed was believed to be the successor to Abraham and Jesus, their followers (Jews and Christians) are also included in the Qur'an. (See page 233.)

c.   No. All three religions are monotheistic. (See page 233.)

d.   No. Indeed, all three religions are monotheistic, and, according to scholars, worship the same God. (See page 233.)

25.   a.   No. Mecca is one of the holiest places for Muslims, but it is located in Arabia, not Spain. (See pages 232, 234.)

b.   No. While Madrid is located in Spain, during this period it was of little importance. (See page 234.)

c.   No. Iona is not located in Spain; the name refers both to an island group off of Greece and a monastery in Scotland. (See pages 234, 204.)

d.   Correct. Toledo was the leading center of learning in Spain, an example of the richness of Islamic urban life in this period. (See page 234.)

1. a. No. Actually the rise of the Carolingian dynasty rested partly on the support of the Christian leadership, which is underscored by the support given to Charles Martel and his son Pippin III by missionaries like St. Boniface. (See pages 245-6.)

   b. No. St. Boniface established many monasteries (and reformed many others) based on and according to *The Rule of St. Benedict*. (See pages 245-6.)

   c. Correct. St. Boniface preached against such Germanic practices as divorce, polygamy, and incest; he was supported by the Carolingian rulers. (See pages 245-6.)

   d. No. St. Boniface had too many other things to attack to be concerned with Roman ideas and traditions. (See pages 245-6.)

2. a. No. Although Western society received much from Muslim society, it did not have a significant impact on the Northumbrian (and later Carolingian) cultural revival. (See page 251.)

   b. No. Then, and later, Jews were ostracized from Western society. (See page 251.)

   c. Correct. Irish-Celtic culture permeated the church in Northumbria and resulted in a flowering of artistic and scholarly activity. (See page 251.)

   d. No. Actually Frankish society, through the efforts of the Northumbrian scholar Alcuin (recruited by Charlemagne,) was influenced by the Irish-Celtic society. (See pages 251, 255.)

3. a. No. Missionaries were typically called missionaries, *missi dominici* does not refer to them. (See page 249.)

   b. No. Peasant farmers were frequently referred to as *villeins* or serfs, not *missi dominici*. (See pages 244-5.)

   c. Correct. *Missi dominici* served as a link between local authorities and the central government of Charlemagne and were responsible for a variety of duties. (See page 249.)

   d. No. Military outposts were frequently referred to as *marches*, not *missi dominici*. (See page 249.)

4. a. No. There is a great deal of controversy surrounding the coronation of Charlemagne as emperor; it seems unlikely that Charlemagne himself placed the crown on his head. (See page 247.)

   b. No. Charlemagne's father Pippin had been dead some time before Charlemagne's coronation as emperor. (See pages 245, 247.)

   c. Correct. There is some controversy over who actually initiated the imperial coronation of Charlemagne, himself of the papacy, but it seems likely that he was invested with the imperial office by Pope Leo III. (See page 247.)

   d. No. The Frankish council had little to do with the imperial coronation; there is a great deal of controversy over whether the imperial coronation was initiated by Charlemagne of the pope. (See page 247.)

5. a. No. The Vikings were part of the invasions of the ninth century; from Scandinavia, the Vikings were superb seamen who ravaged the coasts and inland waterways of Europe. (See pages 262-5.)

   b. Correct. The Franks were a Germanic tribe that had moved into the Roman Empire in the third century, establishing themselves in Gaul. (see pages 262-5 and Chapter 6.)

   c. No. The Magyar tribes were fierce horsemen who crossed the Danube about 890 (people thought they were returning Huns, thus the territory they eventually settled in became known as Hungary) and subdued northern Italy and forced Bavaria and Saxony to pay tribute. (See pages 262-5.)

   d. No. The Muslims exploded onto the world scene, successfully conquering (and converting) the peoples of north Africa, moving into Spain; in the east, Muslim invasions (of the Islamic Turks) conquered much of the territory of the Byzantine Empire and the Ancient Near East. (See pages 262-5.)

6. a.   No. The *missi dominici* were royal officials who provided the link between local authorities and Charlemagne's central government. (See page 249.)
b.   No. On the violent frontiers, Charlemagne established fortified regions, known as *marches*, to prevent the depredations of raiders such as the Vikings. (See page 249.)
c.   No. Part of the Carolingian renaissance included the encouragement of art and literature by Charlemagne, exemplified by his recruitment and support of Alcuin and the Palace School. (See pages 249, 254-6.)
d.   Correct. Actually the Carolingians, Charlemagne included, owed much of their success to the support of the papacy. (See pages 247, 249.)

7. a.   No.   Although Charlemagne would recruit one of the greatest minds of the Northumbrian culture, Charlemagne's court was not the center of this activity. (See pages 251, 253-4.)
b.   Correct. The Northumbrian monasteries, located in northern-most Britain, were the centers of this period of creativity. (See pages 251, 253-4.)
c.   No. Although later some feudal lords would give support to the intellectual and artistic pursuits of scholars, this was not the center of Northumbrian creativity. (See pages 251, 253-4.)
d.   No. Northumbrian creativity was centered in the Northumbrian monasteries, which were not located Lombardy. (See pages 251, 253-4.)

8. a.   Correct. After years of fighting between the three sons of Louis the Pious and much intrigue and feudal violence among the nobles of the empire, the Treaty of Verdun in 843, formally divided Charlemagne's empire into three parts. (See pages 258-9.)
b.   No. Charles Martel was a predecessor of Charlemagne and Louis the Pious and thus could not have kept the empire together after the death of Louis. (See pages 245, 258-9.)
c.   No. Although English kings would rule parts of modern-day France later (see Chapter 12), this was not the case in the ninth century. (See pages 258-9.)
d.   No. Actually, before his death Louis the Pious made several divisions of his empire; with the succession in question and intrigue and violence rampant among the Frankish nobility, the remnants of Charlemagne's empire was indeed weak, but hardly unified. (See pages 258-9.)

9. a.   No. Louis the German was one of the heirs of Louis the Pious to Charlemagne's empire and not a monk. (See pages 251, 253-4, 258-9.)
b.   No. Pippin III was the Carolingian ruler who secured the title of king, based on the concept of he who holds the actual power should have the title of king; he was not a monk. (See pages 245, 251, 253-4.)
c.   Correct. Bede, usually referred to as the Venerable Bede, was the finest representative of Northumbrian scholarship and has been praised by modern scholars for his *Ecclesiastical History of the English Nation*. (See pages 251, 253-4.)
d.   No. Augustine, the bishop of Hippo, was justly famous for his writings which reconciled Christianity with the Classical world, but he did not write the *Ecclesiastical History of the English Nation*. (See pages 251, 253-4 and Chapter 7.)

10. a.   No. Actually the Battle of Tours halted the advance of the Muslim invaders into Europe; the spread of Christianity in the Frankish kingdom was the work of missionaries. (See page 255.)
b.   Correct. Frankish troops, under the Carolingian Charles Martel, defeated the Muslims at Tours, effectively halting their advance into Europe. (See page 256.)
c.   No. Although Pippin II did obtain the title of mayor of the palace, it was his son Charles Martel that defeated the Muslims at the Battle of Tours. (See page 257.)
d.   No. The Vikings would not appear on the scene until the ninth century and did not often fight battles but were raiders. (See pages 258, 262-5.)

11. a.   No. The biographer of Charlemagne was Einhard the Saxon, not St. Boniface. (See pages 245-6.)

b.   No. Although *Beowulf* may have indeed been written by a monk, St. Boniface is unlikely to have been the author. (See pages 245-6, 253.)

c.   Correct. St. Boniface was instrumental in the conversion of the Germanic peoples to Christianity, for which he is known as the Apostle of Germany. (See pages 245-6.)

d.   No. There were some medical treatises produced in medieval Europe, but St. Boniface was not responsible for any of these. (See pages 245-6, 256-8.)

12.   a.   No. *Beowulf* is a fine representation of Anglo-Saxon society and ideals; it does not provide any information on early Germanic marriage laws. (See page 258.)

b.   No. Although *Beowulf* was probably composed by a monk, it represents military and aristocratic lifestyles. (See page 258.)

c.   No. *Beowulf* is permeated with classical, Germanic and Christian elements and although the story is rather fantastic it is not an example of a German fairy tale. (See page 258.)

d.   Correct. Historians have considered *Beowulf* a fine source for information about Anglo-Saxon (and indeed European) culture and society. (See page 258.)

13.   a.   Correct. The sheer size of the empire, underscored by the lack of an effective bureaucracy and the power of local lords spelled the doom of the Carolingian empire. (See pages 258-9.)

b.   No. Actually the Arabs had been halted by Charlemagne's grandfather, Charles Martel at the Battle of Tours, and the Arabs were being held at bay by the Byzantines. (See pages 258-9.)

c.   No. The collapse of the empire actually began during the reign of Charlemagne's son Louis the Pious; the grandsons were unable to prevent it, indeed their violent squabbles over their shares did not help the situation, nor did the violent intrigues of the empire's nobility. (See pages 258-9.)

d.   No. Actually Charlemagne's son Louis the Pious had been crowned emperor before Charlemagne died, thus the immediate succession following Charlemagne's death was not a problem. (See pages 258-9.)

14.   a.   No. Aix-la-Chapelle was the seat of Charlemagne's government, not a medical center. (See pages 257-8.)

b.   No. Although Bologna was later the site of a university, it was associated with the study of law not medicine. (See pages 257-8 and Chapter 9.)

c.   Correct. The school at Salerno attracted Arabic, Greek and Jewish physicians, making it the first medical center in Europe. (See pages 258-9.)

d.   No. Strasbourg was the seat of the Archbishop of Strasbourg but not a medical center. (See pages 257-8.)

15.   a.   No. Hospitals were not yet part of the medical establishment, with most medical care being provided by monasteries and convents. (See page 257.)

b.   No. The female physician Tortula was an expert in gynecological medicine, not Constantine the African. (See page 257.)

c.   No. The medicinal properties of heroin had been discovered during the Hellenistic age (by Heraclides of Tarentum). (See page 257 and Chapter 4.)

d.   Correct. Because of his thorough knowledge of oriental languages, Constantine the African served as an important transmitter of Arabic medical knowledge. (See page 257.)

16.   a.   No. If anything overpopulation, not under population, stimulated the Viking raids, but historians are still debating this topic. (See pages 262-4.)

b.   No. Living in Scandinavia, it seems unlikely that the Vikings were looking for a colder climate in which to live. (See pages 262-4.)

c.   Correct. Although historians are still debating the motivation for the Viking expansion, the most plausible explanation seems to have been the search for trade; overpopulation and climatic changes may also have prompted the Viking expansion. (See pages 262-4.)

d.   No. Actually the Vikings' shipbuilding technology was vastly superior to that of the Carolingians who were basically "land lubbers". (See pages 262-4.)

17.   a.   No. Although the church did exercise much power and would be incorporated into the feudal system, in general, feudalism did not regulate the church. (See pages 259-61.)
b.   No. Feudalism regulated the political structure of Europe; manorialism was concerned with the lives of the peasants. (See pages 259-61.)
c.   Correct. Feudalism was a system the regulated the relations among the military elite of Europe, between nobles of varying degrees and the monarchs, providing the political structure for society. (See pages 259-61.)
d.   No. Absolute monarchs would not arise for another 700 years and when they did, they would attempt to dismantle the vestiges of feudalism. (See pages 259-61 and Chapter 16.)

18.   a.   No. At the local level, feudal lords had full judicial power, serving as police, judge, jury, and executioner; this was a function of the evolution of the feudal and manorial systems. (See pages 259-62.)
b.   Correct. Theoretically, religious affairs were controlled by the church and its hierarchy; given the close relationship between nobility and upper clergy and the establishment and maintenance of parish churches on their manors (which included often paying for the education of the parish priests,) feudal lords may have also played a significant role in the religious life of his peasants. (See pages 259-62.)
c.   No. At the local level, feudal lords had full political power; indeed political power became a private, inheritable right. (See pages 259-62.)
d.   No. As a result of the evolution of the manorial system, which was intertwined with the feudal system, the lord owned most of the land and the peasants of the manor were forced to work his lands, pay rents and other fees and obligations, in return for protection.(See pages 259-62.)

19.   a.   Queen Brunhilda was the wife of King Sigebert and actually ruled the East Frankish kingdom and Burgundy and was noted for her ruthless, murderous tactics; she did not rule the monastery of Whitby. (See pages 244, 251.)
b.   No. The monastery of Whitby was not ruled by Martha of Aachen. (See page 251.)
c.   Correct. The double monastery of Whitby was ruled by the remarkable noblewoman St. Hilda who was known for her intellectual achievements and administrative ability. (See page 251.)
d.   No. The Abbess Marie was not the first female ruler of Whitby. (See page 251.)

20.   a.   Correct. Perhaps Charlemagne's most enduring legacies, the Carolingian Renaissance has been justly praised for its preservation of classical culture. (See pages 254-6.)
b.   No. Feudalism refers to the system of obligations amongst the military elite of Europe. (See pages 254-6, 259-62.)
c.   No. Danelaw refers to the Danish law that was imposed on England after the Danes conquered England. (See pages 254-6, 265.)
d.   No. This term refers to the special relationship between the Frankish kings and the papacy, meaning "king and priest"; their kingship thus had spiritual and moral character. (See pages 247, 254-6.)

21.   a.   No. *Missi* were generally agents of some institution; Charlemagne used the *Missi dominici* as links between local authorities and the central government. (See pages 248-9.)
b.   No. *Villas* were the self-sufficient estates that emerged in the third century and were the precursors of medieval manors. (See pages 248-9 and Chapter 6.)
c.   No. Courts generally refer to the households of lords and monarchs. (See page 248.)
d.   Correct. Indeed the fortified areas in northwestern Spain (and elsewhere on the fringes of Charlemagne's empire) were known as *marches*. (See page 248.)

22.   a.   Correct. The events depicted in *The Song of Roland* refer to the defeat of Count Roland's forces by the Basques on the retreat of Charlemagne's expedition to Spain. (See page 249.)

       b.   No. Although Charlemagne conducted many campaigns, he did not venture as far as Greece. (See page 249.)

       c.   No. Charlemagne never lead a "crusade" to England. (See page 249.)

       d.   No. Charlemagne conducted many campaigns in Germany but never suffered a defeat there. (See page 249.)

23.   a.   No. Although there would later be emperors named Leopold, this quote refers to the imperial coronation of Charlemagne. (See page 247.)

       b.   Correct. Even though there is some controversy over who instigated the imperial coronation, there is no doubt that this quote refers to the imperial coronation of Charlemagne. (See page 247.)

       c.   No. Charles Martel, a predecessor of Charlemagne, despite his obvious political power was never crowned. (See pages 245, 247.)

       d.   No. Boniface was a Christian missionary responsible for much of the conversion of the Germanic peoples; he was not a secular ruler. (See pages 245-7.)

24.   a.   No. Scholars believe that *vik* is an old Norse word, but it does not mean boat. (See page 262.)

       b.   No. The word *vik* has nothing to do with feudalism; it is an old Norse word . (See page 262.)

       c.   Correct. Some scholars believe *vik* to be an old Norse word meaning *creek*; thus Vikings were pirates who waited in creeks (or bays) for passing vessels. (See page 262.)

       d.   No. Some scholars believe *vik* to be an old Norse word, but it does not mean "red". (See page 262.)

25.   a.   Correct. Manorialism is the economic organization, which parallels the political and military organization known as feudalism, of medieval Europe. (See pages 261-2.)

       b.   No. Feudalism was the system by which military society was organized; manorialism evolved alongside this political and military system. (See pages 259-62.)

       c.   No. The spread of ancient texts is associated with the Carolingian renaissance and has little to do with manorialism. (See pages 254-6, 261-2.)

       d.   No. Manors were not converted to learning centers; intellectual activities and education took place in monasteries and cathedral schools. (See pages 254-6, 261-2.)

Chapter 9

1.   a.   No. Although the curia does refer to an institution of the Church, it was not the headquarters of the Italian bishops whose official headquarters would typically be their respective bishoprics. (See page 282.)

      b.   No. While the papal financial office was one division of the curia, the curia was so much more than merely the papal financial office. (See page 282.)

      c.   No. The curia was an institution of the Church, not the imperial court. (See page 282.)

      d.   Correct. The curia is the term used to refer to the papal bureaucracy and court of law. (See page 282.)

2.   a.   No. Although vast amounts of wealth were extracted from Germany by the Church, Pope Gregory VII did not have designs on the secular throne of Henry IV's German empire. (See pages 280-2.)

      b.   No. The position of pope, like all other powerful positions in Europe, was the exclusive domain of aristocrats; peasants had no opportunity to rise so high. (See pages 280-2.)

      c.   Correct. The conflict between Henry IV and Gregory VII was over the issue of lay investiture; Henry wanted to control the appointment of church officials and use them in his bureaucracy, a position which conflicted with Gregory's desire to establish the independence of the church. (See pages 280-2.)

      d.   No. While Henry IV and many other German emperors became embroiled in the political affairs of Italy, the conflict between he and Gregory VII was not over the territorial spoils of Italy. (See pages 280-2.)

3.   a.   Correct. The battle of Edington, won by Alfred, king of the West Saxons, and signaled a great political revival which resulted in the unification of the Anglo-Saxon kingdoms. (See page 274.)

      b.   No. The rise of Normandy was the work of Duke Rollo and his descendant Duke William I, and had nothing to do with the battle of Edington. (See pages 273-4.)

      c.   No. Although the Danes exerted sway over most of northern Europe, this was not the result of the battle of Edington, which was actually a defeat for the Danes. (See page 274.)

      d.   No. Actually the victory of the battle of Edington prevented the fall of Anglo-Saxon law and culture in England. (See page 274.)

4.   a.   No. Lay investiture, although a problem, was not the selling of offices, but the appointment of religious officials by secular rulers. (See pages 278, 280-2.)

      b.   No. The chancery was part of the papal bureaucracy. (See pages 278, 282.)

      c.   No. Excommunication, expulsion from the church, was a form of religious censure, not the selling of church offices. (See page 278.)

      d.   Correct. Simony, a widespread abuse in this era, was the selling of any, including the highest, position in the church. (See page 278.)

5.   a.   Correct. As the defeat in the lay investiture controversy had deprived the emperors of an efficient bureaucracy, they were unable to control their nobility, who entrenched their local power. (See pages 280-2.)

      b.   No. Even though the papacy had technically won, the prestige of the papacy had been damaged and no tangible positive results were forthcoming. (See pages 280-2.)

      c.   No. Deprived of their only source of loyal and trained officials, the German emperors were unable to centralize their domains, resulting in a weak, decentralized state. (See pages 280-2.)

      d.   No. The college of cardinals was little affected by the lay investiture controversy. (See pages 280-2.)

6.   a.   No. Nicolaites were priests who married, a practice reformers hoped to eliminate. (See pages 278-9.)

b.   Correct. The Cistercians, a new order founded at the monastery of Citeaux, sought to remove themselves from corrupting secular influence and thus renounced any gifts from rich patrons; their piety was very influential as was their work at opening new lands to agriculture. (See pages 273, 278.)

c.   No. Cardinals are the highest officials within the church hierarchy, not a monastic order. (See pages 278, 280.)

d.   No. The curia is the term used to refer to the papal bureaucracy and court of law. (See pages 278, 282.)

7.   a.   No. It was not the coronation of William which marked the revival of the Holy Roman Empire; the William mentioned in this chapter was responsible for the emergence of Normandy as a powerful feudal state. (See pages 273-5.)

b.   Correct. In 962 the coronation of Otto revived the Holy Roman Empire. (See pages 274-5.)

c.   No. The coronation of Gregory did not mark the revival of the Holy Roman Empire; the Gregory referred to in this chapter was the pope who became embroiled in the lay investiture controversy with Emperor Henry IV. (See pages 274-5, 280-2.)

d.   No. Charles V would be one of the most powerful of all Holy Roman Emperors but he would not come to power until 1519. (See pages 274-5 and Chapter 15.)

8.   a.   No. Otto forced religious officials to pay him feudal homage, thus binding them to him. (See page 274.)

b.   No. Otto used the feudal relationship with powerful ecclesiastical officials, who had military forces, to augment his military power. (See page 274.)

c.   Correct. Otto was not a priest and, thus, not eligible to become pope. (See page 274.)

d.   No. Otto used higher clergy exclusively in his administration which was the backbone of his state. (See page 274.)

9.   a.   Correct. The Burgundian abbey of Cluny became synonymous with monastic reform and religious revival, supplying many of the reformist Church leaders. (See pages 277-8.)

b.   No. Canossa was the monastery at which Henry IV appealed to Gregory VII to hear his confession during the lay investiture controversy. (See pages 277-8, 281.)

c.   No. Flanders is a geo-political region located in present-day Belgium, not a High Middle Ages' monastery . (See pages 277-8.)

d.   No. Worms was the site of the imperial diet where the lay investiture controversy was finally resolved. (See pages 277-8, 282.)

10.   a.   No. The emperor did not receive the power to choose the pope, a position which the church would never have allowed. (See page 280.)

b.   Correct. As a result of the reforms of the eleventh century, the college of cardinals, then numbering about 25 and dominated by Italians, would choose the new pope. (See page 280.)

c.   No. Townspeople were sometimes able to choose their own municipal leaders but were not given the power to choose the pope. (See page 280.)

d.   No. Although the Roman population could influence the choice of pope, they were not officially mandated to choose the pope. (See page 280.)

11.   a.   No. Actually Duke William I strictly controlled the currency himself and supervised the church by participating the selection of bishops and abbots. (See pages 273-4.)

b.   Correct. As part of his policy to make the practice of feudalism effective, William I forbade the construction of private castles, a symbol of aristocratic independence, and executed vassals who defaulted on their feudal obligations. (See pages 273-4.)

c.   No. Actually William I executed vassals who defaulted on their feudal obligations; it was the strict observance of feudal obligations which many historians ascribe as the primary reason for William's success. (See pages 273-4.)

d. No. In reality, William I supervised the church by participating in the selection of high church officials such as bishops and abbots. (See pages 273-4.)

12. a. No. Otto and William I of Normandy were not contemporaries and, thus, could not have concluded an alliance with each other. (See pages 273-5.)

b. No. Commerce, during the time of Otto, underwent a strong resurgence which was not hampered by heavy taxation. (See pages 274-5.)

c. No. Although Otto was crowned by the pope, the German emperor's policy would eventually lead to the lay investiture controversy between Pope Gregory VII and Henry IV. Moreover, popes and emperors often found themselves opposing each other in the struggle to dominate northern Italy. (See pages 274-5.)

d. Correct. Otto made extensive use of the ecclesiastical officials in Germany, critical for controlling the power of the local nobility and establishing a strong bureaucracy. (See pages 274-5.)

13. a. No. The new monastic orders founded at Cluny, Gorze and Citeaux were prominent in the reform movement. (See pages 277-8.)

b. Correct. Lay investiture was one of the abuses which Gregory VII strongly attacked, resulting in the debilitating controversy with Henry IV of Germany. (See pages 277-82.)

c. No. This refers to removing the influence of secular rulers and individuals over the church in many different areas and was one of Gregory VII's primary goals. (See pages 277-82.)

d. No. The papacy provided little leadership in the tenth century, was riddled with corruption and licentiousness; many called for its reform. (See pages 282-3.)

14. a. No. Actually Nicolaism was one of the abuses which reformers hoped to correct. (See page 279.)

b. Correct. The elimination of Nicolaites, married priests, was one of the reforms sponsored by the reformers of the eleventh century. (See page 279.)

c. No. This response refers to the practice of *simony*, which was also a target of reformers, as was Nicolaism. (See pages 278-9.)

d. No. Nicolaites were married priests, one of the many practices which the reformers of the eleventh century worked to correct. (See page 279.)

15. a. Correct. The Crusades grew out of the long conflict in Spain, known as the *reconquista*, between the Christians and the Muslims. (See page 283.)

b. No. Although the schism between the Catholic and Orthodox branches of Christianity and the Turkish control of the Holy Land encouraged the Crusades, this was not the origins of the Crusades. (See page 283.)

c. No. Christian influence never declined in Italy. Indeed the Catholic Church still exerts tremendous influence in Italy today. (See page 283.)

d. No. Although the Crusades were good for business, southern Italy did not share in this; the increased trade was with the East, but was not a causative factor in the Crusades. (See page 283.)

16. a. No. Philip I's adulterous marriage was resolved by Pope Innocent III, in the twelfth century; such an issue would not have merited a reform movement itself. (See pages 280-2.)

b. No. The practice of simony, selling of church offices, was an abuse that the monastic reformers of Cluny had attacked before Gregory VII became pope. (See pages 280-2.)

c. Correct. Gregory VII was not interested in merely the moral reform of the clergy but wanted to centralize church organization under the control of the pope; central to this effort was the concept of "freedom of the church," directed primarily against lay investiture. (See pages 280-2.)

d. No. William of Normandy's excommunication was not the goal of Gregory's reform movement,

A44

even though his policies could have led to his excommunication. (See pages 280-2.)

17. a. No. Even though Gregory VII was renowned for his inflexibility, Henry challenged him over a substantive issue. (See pages 280-2.)
   b. No. The pope, like all high officials in medieval Europe, was a position which peasants were very unlikely to obtain. (See pages 280-2.)
   c. No. Gregory no doubt wanted Henry's complete obedience in all things, but the conflict was over a more substantive issue than this. (See pages 280-2.)
   d. Correct. Henry IV, following the precedent set by Otto I, was dependent upon ecclesiastical officials for his bureaucracy; Gregory's reform movement, which attacked the practice of lay investiture, seriously undermined the position of the Holy Roman Emperor. (See pages 280-2.)

18. a. No. The Crusades were launched by Pope Urban II not Innocent III. (See pages 283-4.)
   b. No. Although Innocent III was a canon lawyer, like many other popes, this was not the reason his pontificate represents the high point of papal authority. (See page 283.)
   c. Correct. Innocent III's pontificate is considered the high point of papal authority because of the influence he exerted: adjudicating rival claims to the imperial crown, compelling Philip of France to take back his wife, forcing King John of England to accept an archbishop he did not want. (See page 283.)
   d. No. The issue of clerical marriage, Nicolaism, had already been dealt with before Innocent's pontificate. (See pages 280, 283.)

19. a. No. The papal bureaucracy and court, known as the curia, became the symbol of papal authority and power, exemplified by Innocent III. (See pages 282-3.)
   b. No. The papal curia, with its chancery, financial office, court and bureaucracy, served as the first strong monarchial bureaucracy. (See pages 282-3.)
   c. No. Slowly but surely the papal curia evolved into the final court of appeals for all of Christian Europe. (See pages 282-3.)
   d. Correct. All of these responses are correct. The papal curia was a symbol of papal power and authority, served as the model for monarchial bureaucracies and became the final court of appeal for all of Christian Europe. (See pages 282-3.)

20. a. Correct. As a result of careless preparation, inadequate financing, and the greed of the Venetian leadership, the Crusaders were landed by the Venetian contractors at Constantinople, where the Crusaders sacked the city. (See pages 283-9.)
   b. No. The Second Crusade did not sack Constantinople, but did indeed reach the Holy Land and battled the Muslim rulers of that region for its control. (See pages 283-9.)
   c. No. Almost all of the Crusades were "eastern" (save for those launched against European heretics, Jews in the Rhineland, and the emperor Frederick II); there was no crusade designated "Eastern." (See pages 283-9.)
   d. No. The First Crusade was perhaps the most successful, eventually capturing Jerusalem from the "infidels." (See pages 283-9.)

21. a. No. Mining continued to be performed as it had for centuries. (See page 276.)
   b. No. The innovations in energy use did not derive from building dams. (See page 276.)
   c. No. The development of the steam engine would have to wait for a few more centuries. (See page 276 and Chapter 22.)
   d. Correct. The increase in the number of watermills and windmills was remarkable, greatly increasing the productivity of European agriculture and having the greatest impact of any developments of the era on most Europeans. (See page 276.)

22. a. No. Actually at this time the monasteries were fabulously wealthy which might have resulted in

the decline in spiritual fervor. (See page 278.)

b.   No. Actually at this time, violence, especially in the form of war, declined. (See page 278.)

c.   Correct. The opulence and wealth of many monasteries resulted in a decline of monastic observance and spiritual fervor. (See page 278.)

d.   No. The development of the Cistercian monastic movement arose in response to the decline of monastic observance and spiritual fervor caused by the luxurious lifestyle of the rich monasteries. (See page 278.)

23.   a.   Correct. Lay investiture hit Germany hardest because the Holy Roman Empire was most dependent upon ecclesiastical officials, the pope invested the emperor, and both claimed Italy; the papacy, further, did not want to create too many enemies at once. The papal victory essentially arrested efforts at creating a strong state in Germany. (See pages 280-2.)

b.   No. France was guilty of the practice of lay investiture but Gregory VII did not wish to fight too many battles at once, thus France was spared the controversy. (See pages 280-2.)

c.   No. English kings were guilty of the practice of lay investiture but Gregory VII did not wish to fight too many battles at once, thus England was spared the controversy (See pages 280-2.)

d.   No. Italy was not the focus of the lay investiture controversy as there was no centralizing monarchical power there, except the German emperor who claimed control of Italy. (See pages 280-2.)

24.   a.   No. Actually, the Capetian kings of France, who only controlled the tiny area known as the Île-de-France were much poorer and weaker than the dukes of Normandy and Aquitaine. (See page 274.)

b.   No. The Capetian kings did lay the foundations for later political unification and stability, but such unity and stability would not arise until much later. (See page 274.)

c.   Correct. Controlling only the tiny Île-de-France, the Capetian kings were much poorer and weaker than the dukes of Normandy and Aquitaine. (See page 274.)

d.   No. The Capetian kings were much weaker militarily than the dukes of Normandy and Aquitaine; despite being elected to the kingship, however, Hugh Capet and his descendants would rule France until the end of the monarchy in the early nineteenth century. (See page 274.)

25.   a.   No. Actually some women did go on Crusades, such as Eleanor of Aquitaine, but since the chroniclers were aristocratically biased and the Crusades were military in nature, usually a male arena, we have little information about middle-class and peasant women participating in the Crusades. (See page 288.)

b.   No. Actually, as men, noble and otherwise, went off to the Holy Land, their wives were forced to take charge of the manor, business or farm, greatly increasing their independence vis-à-vis men. (See page 288.)

c.   No. Historians are not really able to gauge the impact on birth rates, but this does not seem to have been affected. (See page 288.)

d.   Correct. As men left for the Holy Land, women were forced to take responsibility for the manor, business, or farm; further, prostitution offered many new business opportunities. (See page 288.)

1. a.   No. The village church was the center of community life; virtually every form of activity, religious, cultural, social, political, and economic, took place there. (See page 312.)
    b.   No. Mystery plays, based on biblical stories, were performed in the sanctuary, porch or in the village square, which was often in front of the church. (See page 312.)
    c.   No. The plays, sermons, and even the stained glass windows and statues all served to educate the people of the village. (See page 312.)
    d.   Correct. As the church was the center of the village life, for all the people of the parish, it could not have been open only to aristocrats. (See page 312.)

2. a.   No. Actually the problems of the twelfth century were not the result of an inability to recruit monks; indeed, noble families continued the practice of child-oblation. (See pages 327-9.)
    b.   No. Although some peasants refused to pay their levies, this was not the real problem facing most monasteries. (See pages 327-9.)
    c.   Correct. In the twelfth century, older monastic houses experienced increasing expenses, especially for expensive additions to the liturgical vestments, which led to a steadily worsening economic situation, as at Cluny. (See pages 327-9.)
    d.   No. Although wives increasingly managed the estates in the husbands' absence on Crusade, placing the administration of one's estate under the control of a monastery had not been a very common practice and was not the real problem facing the monasteries. (See pages 327-9 and Chapter 9.)

3. a.   No. Although all knights were not noble, all nobles were knights. (See pages 315-6.)
    b.   No. The medieval nobility's primary function was to serve as the local political authority and provide for the military needs of the region. (See pages 315-6 and Chapter 8.)
    c.   Correct. Father-son relations tended to be characterized by a great deal of tension, a function of the inheritance and property laws of the time. (See page 320.)
    d.   No. Indeed, the castle was the primary aristocratic symbol, and was enhanced by the lavishness of his dress, number of retainers and even the beauty of his wife. (See page 316.)

4. a.   No. Up until the thirteen century, monasteries did not recruit from the middle classes; with the emergence of new orders and increased competition from the new orders for members, more monks were recruited from the middle classes. (See pages 318, 323.)
    b.   Correct. Up until the thirteenth century, the vast majority of those entering monasteries were from the aristocracy, usually having been given as child oblates, a function of both inheritance laws and social mores; after this monasteries would begin to recruit members from the middle classes. (See pages 318, 323.)
    c.   No. Peasants were rarely recruited into monasteries. (See pages 318, 323.)
    d.   No. The village schools were not really a factor in the recruitment of monks; this was much more a function of social class. (See pages 318, 323.)

5. a.   No. Even though being knighted was an important event in a young man's life, it did not automatically infer adulthood. (See page 320.)
    b.   No. There was no simple legal age as this response implies. (See page 320.)
    c.   Correct. The acquisition of property, through inheritance, purchase or marriage, conveyed adult status to a young man. (See page 320.)
    d.   No. The demonstration of military prowess, which was usually culminated by knighthood, although important did not infer adult status on a young man. (See page 320.)

6. a.   No. Actually it is the other way around, a free person could move as he pleased while a serf was

bound to the land. (See pages 302-5.)

　　b.　No. The only obligation a free person owed to the landlord was to pay the rent while a serf had many obligations of diverse kinds. (See pages 302-5.)

　　c.　No. Both paid rent on the land each farmed; the serf also had to pay a variety of other fees and perform a variety of services. (See pages 302-5.)

　　d.　Correct. The free person could live as he pleased and where he pleased, as long as he paid his rent. The serf, however, owed a variety of payments and labor obligations to his lord. (See pages 302-5.)

7.　　a.　Correct. In order to equalize the land of each peasant, the land of the manor was divided into strips scattered over the manor and was redivided every year. (See pages 305-7.)

　　b.　No. Actually medieval farmers were not ignorant of the value of fertilizer, employing animal manure in this capacity. (See pages 305-7.)

　　c.　No. In the early twelfth century the use of iron implements increased; even though the wooden plow continued to be the basic instrument, it was usually shod with iron. In the fourteenth century other iron implements were introduced. (See pages 305-7.)

　　d.　No. Actually there was a good deal of improvement; from the ninth to the thirteenth century cereal yields doubled. (See pages 305-7.)

8.　　a.　No. The horizons of medieval peasants was rather limited; most people rarely traveled more than twenty-five miles beyond their villages. (See page 307.)

　　b.　Correct. The close-knit nature of the village and the family gave the medieval peasant a strong sense of community and pride of place, which was reflected in the adornment of the village church. (See page 308.)

　　c.　No. The dull, even crushing sense of frustration drove many peasants to escape through the use of alcoholic beverages, a fact attested to by the extraordinary number of accidental deaths. (See page 308.)

　　d.　No. Although women managed the house, they also shared in the back-breaking labor of the fields. (See page 308.)

9.　　a.　No. Actually vegetables, especially cabbage which grew everywhere, was a staple of the peasant diet; every house had a small garden. (See pages 308-10.)

　　b.　Correct. Meat was a very expensive commodity and was likely to make an appearance on the peasant's table only on high feast days. (See page 309.)

　　c.　No. The mainstay of the diet of peasants (and indeed all Europeans) all over Europe was bread. (See page 309.)

　　d.　No. Beer was the universal drink of common people all over Europe and vast quantities of it were consumed. (See page 309.)

10.　　a.　No. Actually the rate of infant mortality was staggering, given existing birthing practices, childhood diseases, and inadequate diet. (See page 317.)

　　b.　No. Although infanticide had been fairly common in the ancient world, ecclesiastical pressure had resulted in a decline of this practice. (See page 317.)

　　c.　No. Neither the church nor the state legislated against the selling of children. (See page 317.)

　　d.　Correct. As the church had eliminated the practice of infanticide, this was no longer an option for parents unable or unwilling to raise their children; oblation increased and so did simple abandonment. (See pages 317-8.)

11.　　a.　No. Most noblewomen married when they were in their teens, usually to a man in his thirties. (See page 320.)

　　b.　No. Within the nobility, the importance of inheritance and political considerations usually resulted in arranged marriages. (See page 320.)

c.   Correct. By the twelfth century it had become customary for bride's family to provide a dowry to the husband. (See page 320.)

d.   No. As noblemen tended to prefer younger wives so that they would be blessed with more children, women tended to be in their teens when they married. (See page 320.)

12.   a.   Correct. Although it is difficult to generalize, daily life in most monasteries combined attention to liturgy (prayer, etc,) and manual labor, as most monastic houses were economic units and required such work. (See pages 324-7.)

b.   No. As monasteries were usually self-contained economic units, there was the necessity of manual labor, usually performed by lay brothers, to keep the monastery going. (See pages 324-7.)

c.   No. Although the diversity of monastic existence across Europe does render generalization difficult, historians have determined that life usually featured a combination of attention to the liturgy and manual labor. (See pages 324-7.)

d.   No. Even though some monasteries were justly famous for their achievements in manufacturing and agriculture, religious duties remained primary. (See pages 324-7.)

13.   a.   No. With the increase in land reclamation projects, agricultural labor was in demand and serfs could gain their freedom by migrating to these new areas. (See pages 302-3.)

b.   No. Actually with the advent of a more cash-based economy serfs could buy their freedom, but usually only through a third-party intermediary. (See page 302.)

c.   Correct. Fleeing the manor and residing in a free town for a year and a day was the most prevalent form of a serf obtaining his freedom. (See page 302.)

d.   No. As the example of the serfs of the Abbey of Bourbourg shows, some did obtain their freedom even though they had remained on the manor; as the demand for agricultural labor increased, many lords were forced to reduce the obligations of their serfs. (See pages 303, 305.)

14.   a.   No. The term *chevalier* did not refer to monks, no matter how rich. (See page 316.)

b.   No. The term *chevalier* did not refer to a religious order devoted to agricultural reform; the Cistercian order was concerned with agricultural reform. (See page 316.)

c.   Correct. The term *chevalier*, which is a French word meaning "horseman", was used to refer to knights in France, in the rest of Europe it became a generic term for nobles. (See page 316.)

d.   No. The term *chevalier* did not refer to court painters and architects. (See page 316.)

15.   a.   No. A medieval manor could have any number of villages; there was usually at least one village on a manor. (See page 305.)

b.   No. A plantation, in its modern connotation, is usually worked by slave labor, not tenant farmers or serfs which characterized medieval manors. (See page 305.)

c.   Correct. Although medieval manors varied greatly in size and wealth, they can be characterized as the estate of a lord and his dependent tenants. (See page 305.)

d.   No. A medieval manor could have any number of villages; there was usually at least one village on a manor. (See page 305.)

16.   a.   No. While a yield ratio of six to one would have been greatly appreciated, the level of agricultural technology could not produce such a ratio. (See page 307.)

b.   No. While a yield ratio of ten to one would have been greatly appreciated, the level of agricultural technology could not produce such a ratio. (See page 307.)

c.   Correct. According to the author of a thirteenth-century treatise on land husbandry, Walter of Henley, the land should yield three times its seed, for sheer survival. (See page 307.)

d.   No. While a yield ratio of five to one would have been greatly appreciated, the level of agricultural technology could not produce such a ratio. (See page 307.)

17.   a.   No. No amount of hard work, thrift or sobriety was enough to earn noble status. (See page 316.)

b.   No. No matter how clever a businessman might be, generally this was not enough to earn noble status; in some regions such as Anjou, however, rich men were ennobled. (See page 316.)

c.   Correct. Certainly the European nobility was hereditary; on rare occasion exceptional service to the king could earn noble status. (See page 316.)

d.   No. Only later, during the seventeenth century, was it possible for a person to buy a patent of nobility. (See page 316 and Chapter 16.)

18.   a.   No. Although more nobles were becoming literate by the eleventh and twelfth centuries, this was still a relative rarity and not the basis of education and training. (See pages 319.)

b.   No. Even though more nobles were beginning to read and write some Latin, this was still a relative rarity and not the basis of education and training. (See pages 319.)

c.   No. Only those sons who entered the religious orders had the chance to become canon lawyers. (See pages 319.)

d.   Correct. Although more and more nobles were beginning to read and write some Latin, the arts of war and chivalry remained the basis of training for young aristocrats. (See pages 319.)

19.   a.   Correct. Women played a large role in the functioning of the estate, especially when the husband was away on a Crusade, for instance. (See page 321.)

b.   No. Although the bearing and raising of children was very important, women had other opportunities and responsibilities as well. (See page 321.)

c.   No. Certainly the role of the woman was enhanced when the husband was away, but opportunities and responsibilities existed even when the husband was present. (See page 321.)

d.   No. Actually women played an important role in many areas of family life. (See page 321.)

20.   a.   No. It was not until the fourteenth century, when established monasteries began to face competition for members from newer orders, that the business classes become a target for recruitment. (See pages 322-3.)

b.   No. Peasants have rarely been recruited into monasteries. (See pages 322-3.)

c.   No. Only with increased competition from new orders in the fourteenth century did the petite bourgeoisie begin to be recruited and then relatively rarely. (See pages 322-3.)

d.   Correct. Until the fourteenth century, the vast majority of the monks recruited came from the nobility, usually through child-oblation. (See pages 322-3.)

21.   a.   No. Although the abbot was the head of the monastery and had ultimate responsibility, he generally did not handle the day-to-day management of the monastery. (See pages 324-5.)

b.   No. Novices were new monks who were still being trained and thus would not be in a position of such authority. (See pages 324-5.)

c.   Correct. Although the abbot was the head of the monastery and had ultimate responsibility, the cellarer, or financial manager, was responsible for the management of the monastic estate. (See pages 324-5.)

d.   No. The almoner was responsible for the feeding and care of the poor around the monastery. See pages 324-5.)

22.   a.   No. The Dominicans were not a monastic but a mendicant order, more urban than rural. (See page 326 and Chapter 11.)

b.   No. Although many Benedictine monasteries had strong agricultural traditions and were very rich, they were not especially renowned for employing new agricultural techniques. (See page 326 and Chapter 8.)

c.   No. The Franciscans, like the Dominicans, were not a monastic but mendicant order, and were more urban than rural. (See page 326 and Chapter 11.)

d.   Correct. The Cistercians, whose constitution insisted that they accept land far from human habitation, pioneered in land reclamation and other new techniques. (See pages 324, 326.)

23.　a.　No. Although many monasteries were seats of learning, with strong scholarly traditions, this was not considered to be their primary social function. (See page 324.)

　　b.　No. Monastic houses did provide food and care for the poor, even having an official, the almoner, in charge of this, but this was not their primary social function. (See pages 324-5.)

　　c.　No. Certainly monasteries provided education for the children of the nobility, but this was not their primary social function. (See page 324.)

　　d.　Correct. The monks, and the rest of society, believed that their primary social function was to pray for the rest of society. (See page 324.)

24.　a.　No. Prior to the appearance of the Black Death, perhaps as high as 94% of peasant farmers were married. (See page 308.)

　　b.　No. This is largely a myth for Europe; while peasant families in Asia and elsewhere were often organized around the extended families, European peasant families were not. (See page 308.)

　　c.　Correct. According to recent research, the peasant household consisted of a married couple (or a widow) with a couple of children, not the large extended family so long assumed to be the basic family structure of European peasants. (See page 308.)

　　d.　No. Actually most couples married in their twenties, with the typical number of children being three, not five. (See page 309.)

25.　a.　No. *Ministerials* is the term used to refer to the large class of unfree knights in Germany. (See page 316.)

　　b.　No. *Miles* is the Latin term used in England and France to refer to nobles. (See page 316.)

　　c.　Correct. *Villeins* is the term used to refer to the inhabitants of English villages who were typically enserfed. (See pages 302, 316.)

　　d.　No. *Chevalier*, the French word meaning "horseman," came to be used throughout Europe to refer to knights; non-French people gradually adopted it to refer to the nobility. (See page 316.)

Chapter 11

1. a.   No. Actually it was illegal for Jews to own land in most parts of Europe. (See page 348.)
   b.   No. The nobility, which had no Jewish members, had a near-monopoly on military power. (See page 348.)
   c.   No. As many Jews could read and write, and many others had risen to important positions in local and state hierarchies, Jews generally had the reputation of being learned. (See page 348.)
   d.   Correct. As many Jews could read and write, and many others had risen to important positions in local and state hierarchies, Jews generally had the reputation of being learned. (See page 348.)

2. a.   No. While many burghers were involved in trade, this was not the definition of a burgher. (See page 350.)
   b.   Correct. These words come from the Old English and Old German words for a walled or fortified place. (See page 350.)
   c.   No. People of Hamburg would be considered burghers, but this is not the definition of the words. (See pages 350.)
   d.   No. Hamburgers are a modern, American creation and have absolutely nothing to do with the Middle Ages. (See page 350.)

3. a.   No. Josiah Cox Russell did not develop the theory that towns sprang up when merchants gathered at an attractive spot, such as a fortress. (See page 350.)
   b.   No. Eileen Power did not develop the theory that towns sprang up when merchants gathered at an attractive spot, such as a fortress. (See page 350.)
   c.   Correct. The Belgian historian Henri Pirenne maintained that towns sprang up when merchants gathered at an attractive spot, such as a fortress. (See page 350.)
   d.   No. While Marc Bloch was one of the most influential historians of the twentieth century, he did not develop the theory that towns sprang up when merchants gathered at an attractive spot, such as a fortress. (See page 350.)

4. a.   No. Actually, the towns did not gain political independence despite their alliance with the monarchs. (See pages 351-4.)
   b.   No. Actually religious authority held sway in many towns, such as ecclesiastical cities and in cities such as Geneva. (See pages 351-4.)
   c.   Yes. Cities were allowed to develop and enforce their own law codes, such as law merchant, by the new monarchs. (See pages 351-4.)
   d.   No. Despite being an important source of tax revenues and fortified strongholds for the monarchs, cities had little influence on military affairs. (See pages 351-4.)

5. a.   No. No doubt many artisans and craftspeople would have liked to have courts to deal with these individuals, but such courts were controlled by the merchant guilds. (See page 353.)
   b.   Yes. To control quality and price of goods, labor recruitment, and to offset the power of the merchant guilds, craft guilds were formed by these people. (See page 353.)
   c.   No. Actually merchant guilds were formed by merchants, not artisans. (See page 353.)
   d.   No. The scutage was a feudal tax levied on noble widows and orphans; it had nothing to do with urban craftspeople. (See page 353.)

6. a.   No. Actually, it was just the opposite; the French state featured differentiation and diversity at the local level, while the royal government was very centralized. (See page 338.)
   b.   Yes. The royal government, with its baillis and seneschals, was highly centralized, but as a result of the manner in which territory had been added to the French state, many areas retained their old laws and political practices. (See page 338.)
   c.   No. Despite a great deal of local autonomy, the oversight of the baillis and seneschals prevented

complete local government. (See page 338.)

d. No. France was profoundly different; French royal officials were paid professionals, while in England such individuals were unpaid, local notables. (See pages 338-9.)

7. a. No. France was a strong state at this time and Frederick Barbarossa would not have been able to embroil himself in its affairs. (See pages 340-2.)

b. No. The Holy Roman Empire was composed primarily of German territory; indeed, had Frederick Barbarossa concentrated on German affairs, he might have solved the problems of the Holy Roman Empire. (See pages 340-2.)

c. No. England was a strong, unified state at this time and Frederick Barbarossa could not have become embroiled in its affairs. (See pages 340-2.)

d. Yes. Frederick Barbarossa, like so many other German emperors was lured by the promise of rich rewards in Italy; had he concentrated on Germany, rather than becoming embroiled in Italy, he might have solved the problems of the Holy Roman Empire. (See pages 340-2.)

8. a. No. Actually, democracy was centuries away, and not guaranteed by the Magna Carta. (See page 347.)

b. Yes. Responding to the king's incompetent foreign policy and misuse of feudal taxes, the English nobility, backed by the leading ecclesiastical and lay leaders, forced King John to sign the Magna Carta, a document which established the principle that everyone must obey the law. (See page 347.)

c. No. While certain monarchs in the seventeenth century would make such a claim, the Magna Carta is no way implied such a principle. (See page 347 and Chapter 16.)

d. No. Although this would eventually come to characterize the English form of government, the Magna Carta did not imply such a principle. (See page 347 and Chapters 16, 25.)

9. a. No. The pointed arch was one of the defining characteristics of Gothic cathedral, resulting from improved construction techniques and building materials and giving the sense of light. (See pages 364-5.)

b. No. The ribbed vault was one of the defining characteristics of Gothic cathedral, resulting from improved construction techniques and building materials and giving a sense of light. (See pages 364-5.)

c. Correct. Improved construction techniques and building materials, as well as the decline of barbarian invasions which lessened the need for this type of wall, made thick walls no longer necessary. (See pages 364-5.)

d. No. The flying buttress was one of the defining characteristics of Gothic cathedral, resulting from improved construction techniques and building materials and giving a sense of light. (See pages 364-5.)

10. a. No. Actually architects played a minor role in the construction of these cathedrals; the individual most responsible for the planning and execution of the project was the master mason. (See pages 365-9.)

b. No. Religion continued to be very important to most people, but the construction of these cathedrals was very expensive and could only be undertaken during prosperous times. (See pages 365-9.)

c. No. Despite improved techniques and materials, these cathedrals remained very expensive to build. (See pages 365-9.)

d. Yes. Cathedrals were a symbol of urban wealth and civic pride, and cities competed to outdo each other in the magnificence of their respective cathedrals. (See pages 365-9.)

11. a. No. Although Muslims had been very important in the preservation, transmission and enhancement of classical knowledge, they played little role in the development of the. (See page 360.)

b. Yes. The organization, curriculum, and teaching method of the university was a unique contribution of western Europe. (See page 360.)

c. No. While the Greeks certainly had educational institutions, such as the Academy, they did not develop anything resembling the medieval universities. (See page 360.)

d.   No. While the Romans did educate their children, this tended to be a private undertaking; they did not develop anything like the medieval universities. (See page 360.)

12.   a.   No. Maintenance of law and order was one of the primary functions of the sheriffs. (See page 339.)

b.   No. Collection of taxes was one of the primary functions of the sheriffs. (See page 339.)

c.   No. At the king's request, sheriffs were also responsible for raising infantry troops. (See page 339.)

d.   Correct. The Anglo-Saxon sheriffs were replaced with Norman sheriffs. (See page 339.)

13.   a.   Yes. Probably as a function of contact with other regions, increased wealth and literacy and growing unhappiness with the established hierarchy and theology of the church, heresy tended to flourish in the urban centers. (See page 368.)

b.   No. Rural regions tended to remain true to the faith. (See page 368.)

c.   No. While southern France did experience heretical movements, heresy was not limited to southern France. (See page 368.)

d.   No. The plague had not yet hit Europe too severely and this was an era of urban prosperity in general. (See page 368.)

14.   a.   Correct. England and Sicily, with well-developed state bureaucracies (especially for finances,) had the most efficient bureaucracies. (See pages 339-45.)

b.   No. While England had one of the most efficient bureaucracies, deficiencies in financial administration curtailed the efficiency of the French bureaucracy. (See pages 339-45.)

c.   No. England had one of the most efficient bureaucracies, but Italy at that time was not yet a state and thus did not have an efficient bureaucracy. (See pages 339-45.)

d.   No. While Sicily had one of the most efficient bureaucracies, deficiencies in financial administration curtailed the efficiency of the French bureaucracy. (See pages 339-45.)

15.   a.   No. Although Richard's crusading had been expensive, it was not the immediate cause of the barons' forcing of King John to sign the Magna Carta. (See pages 346-7.)

b.   No. Even though Richard's ransom had been expensive, it was not the immediate cause of the barons' forcing of King John to sign the Magna Carta. (See pages 346-7.)

c.   Yes. With his finances already strained, John's unsuccessful and expensive involvement in France led to the signing of the Magna Carta. (See pages 346-7.)

d.   No. While financial problems would indeed lead to John II's signing of the Magna Carta, an attack on Scotland was not the cause. (See pages 346-7.)

16.   a.   No. Although great universities, such as Cambridge and Oxford, would be established very early in England, it was not the home of the first universities. (See pages 360-1.)

b.   No. Although great universities, such as the University of Paris, would be established very early in France, it was not the home of the first universities. (See pages 360-1.)

c.   Correct. The universities at Bologna and Salerno in Italy were the first universities. (See pages 360-1.)

d.   No. Although great universities would be established very early in Germany, it was not the home of the first universities. (See pages 360-1.)

17.   a.   Correct. Indeed, prior to the systematization of law in the thirteenth century, many prominent individuals had been openly homosexual. (See page 349.)

b.   No. Homosexuality was not outlawed until the systematization of law in the thirteenth century. (See page 349.)

c.   No. While there are no figures on the size of the homosexual population in this era, judging from the existence of publicly known homosexuals as Richard I of England and Archbishop Ralph, it was not an uncommon phenomenon. (See page 349.)

d.   No. There were many well-known homosexual individuals such as Richard I of England and Archbishop Ralph of Tours. (See pages 349.)

18.   a.   No. While manor schools had provided some early educational opportunities, they did not represent the origins of the universities. (See page 360.)

b.   No. Monasteries did perform a significant educational role, but the universities did not originate in them. (See page 360.)

c.   Correct. The cathedral schools, located in major urban areas and thus affected by and responding to the needs of the commercial expansion of the towns, were the origins of the universities. (See page 360.)

d.   No. Public schools did not exist at this time. (See page 360.)

19.   a.   No. *Summas* were vast reference works compiled by scholars, but not really an aspect of the teaching method utilized in the universities. (See pages 362-4.)

b.   No. A *gloss* was the interpretation of a passage of from a biblical or classical source; texts and glosses were sometimes compiled into a textbook, but the gloss was not the standard teaching method. (See pages 362-4.)

c.   No. Books were much too expensive for each student to buy; glosses were often circulated in lieu of books. (See pages 362-4.)

d.   Correct. Typically the professor would read from a text, such as the Bible or the works of Aristotle, and then explain it; this was called the lecture and was the standard method of instruction in the universities. (See pages 362-4.)

20.   a.   No. In England, where common law prevailed, it applied to all classes of individuals. (See page 348.)

b.   No. Actually, Roman law was more permanent and static than common law. (See page 348.)

c.   Yes. Common law relied on a body of precedence, and existing social and cultural values, to adjudicate cases. (See page 348.)

d.   No. Although torture did occur in England, where common law evolved, it was much more likely to be part of Roman legal and evidentiary procedure. (See page 348.)

21.   a.   Correct. The xenophobia associated with the Crusades and governmental and church efforts at social conformity resulted in an era of increasing intolerance towards Jews and other minorities. (See pages 348-9.)

b.   No. The xenophobia associated with the Crusades and governmental and church efforts at social conformity resulted in an era of increasing intolerance towards Jews and other minorities. (See pages 348-9.)

c.   No. The xenophobia associated with the Crusades and governmental and church efforts at social conformity resulted in an era of increasing intolerance towards Jews and other minorities, an unlikely era in which to undergo political emancipation. (See pages 348-9.)

d.   No. The xenophobia associated with the Crusades and governmental and church efforts at social conformity resulted in an era of increasing intolerance towards Jews and other minorities. (See pages 348-9.)

22.   a.   No. While many cities did have a function as an ecclesiastical center, this was not the primary function of urban centers. (See pages 343-60.)

b.   No. While many cities did have a function as a political center (and many did run their own affairs,) this was not the primary function of urban centers. (See pages 343-60.)

c.   No. While many cities did serve as royal strongholds (most were allied with the monarchs,) this was not the primary function of urban centers. (See pages 343-60.)

d.   Yes. For while the cities had many functions, the most important was as a vast marketplace. (See pages 343-60.)

23.   a.   No. John of Salisbury wrote *The Statesman's Book*, not the *Summa Theologica*. (See pages 360, 363.)
b.   No. Peter Abelard was an influential scholar, writing *Sic et Non*, but did not write the *Summa Theologica*. (See pages 361, 363.)
c.   Correct. Thomas Aquinas, one of the most influential scholars of the era, did write the *Summa Theologica*, a vast collection dealing with a number of theological questions. (See page 363.)
d.   No. William of Sens was an architect and did not write the *Summa Theologica*. (See pages 363, 365.)

24.   a.   Correct. The Waldensians are examples of the explosion of heresy in the High Middle Ages; disgusted with traditional church teaching and clerical wealth, they attacked the sacraments and the hierarchy of the church. (See page 369.)
b.   No. The Waldensians were not involved in the power struggles of the Holy Roman Empire. (See pages 369, 339-42.)
c.   No. The Waldensians were not the merchant bankers of Hamburg. (See page 369.)
d.   No. The Waldensians did not build this cathedral, which was erected by order of Abbot Suger of the abbey of Saint Denis, a Clunaic monastery. (See pages 369, 364.)

25.   a.   No. The Albigensians (also known as Cathars) were heretics, not followers of St. Dominic (Domingo de Guzman.). (See page 369.)
b.   No. Although many followers of Saint Dominic were bourgeois, this is a generic term referring to urban dwellers. (See pages 350, 369.)
c.   No. While many of his followers were univérsity graduates, and some would become leaders of universities, they were not referred to as the masters of the Cathedral School at Paris. (See page 369.)
d.   Yes. Because these individuals, organized into the Dominican Order, worked to spread the Gospel to the urban population, rather than remain cloistered in monasteries, they became known as the "Preaching Friars". (See page 369.)

1. a.   No. Actually the conciliar movement was an attack on papal supremacy and was not an effort to give the pope a weapon against heresy. (See pages 393-6.)
    b.   No. The conciliar movement was concerned with reform in the Church and was not connected to any parliamentary movement in France. (See pages 393-6.)
    c.   No. Although new monastic orders had appeared, vowing poverty, they were not the product of the conciliar movement. (See pages 393-6.)
    d.   Correct. The conciliar movement, led by such men as Marsiglio of Padua and John Wyclif, attacked the notion of papal supremacy and argued that the authority of the church was vested in a general council made up of laymen as well as priests. (See page 393-6.)

2. a.   No. Chinese soldiers, no doubt helped spread the plague, but they never made an appearance in Europe. (See pages 380-1.)
    b.   No. Spanish adventurers returned from South America with such gifts as syphilis, but not the plague. (See pages 380-1.)
    c.   No. Both England and France were ravaged by the plague, but it is was not English soldiers who introduced it into Europe. (See pages 380-1.)
    d.   Correct. The expansion of trade, with the opening of the Straits of Gibralter and new ship designs allowed Genoese and Venetian sailors to sail further and further; in 1347 a Genoese ships brought the plague to Messina, from which it spread quickly throughout Europe. (See pages 380-1.)

3. a.   Correct. As a result of the population losses from the plague, farm laborers were in an advantageous position and were able to obtain higher wages. (See pages 384, 402.)
    b.   No. Actually the massive loss of life, paradoxically, resulted in higher standard of living, including more food, for the survivors. (See pages 384, 402.)
    c.   No. Although many city dwellers fled the plague, there was no need for surviving farm laborers to migrate as economic conditions now favored them to a certain extent. (See pages 384, 402.)
    d.   No. The plague, in and of itself, did not result in excommunication; surviving farm laborers did not face such an action. (See pages 384, 402.)

4. a.   No. The urban "mobs" after the Hundred Years' War did not constitute a major new source of criminals, despite the outbreak of several urban revolts, such as the *ciompi* in Florence, which was a social uprising. (See page 400.)
    b.   No. Although there were several peasant uprisings following the Hundred Years' War, these should be seen as social and economic movements, not acts of criminality. (See page 400.)
    c.   Correct. Following the Hundred Years' War, many nobles once again had little to do and were hurt by inflation; these people, the so-called "fur-collar criminals," resorted to extortion and kidnaping. (See page 400.)
    d.   No. The bourgeoisie has traditionally been the most law-abiding of any social grouping. (See page 400.)

5. a.   No. As a result of the Black Death and the Hundred Years' War (and other catastrophes), the population of Europe in the fourteenth century was greatly diminished. (See pages 379-80.)
    b.   Correct. Ironically, the standard of living actually improved, a function of the lower number of people consuming the same resources; this is underscored by the twelfth and thirteenth centuries' population growth and declining standard of living. (See pages 379-80, 400-1.)
    c.   No. As a result of the Babylonian Captivity and other abuses, such as simony, pluralism, absenteeism and clerical extravagance, the church suffered a serious decline in influence. (See pages 392-6.)
    d.   No. Actually England and France were at war so much that the conflict between the two during the fourteenth and fifteenth centuries is known as the Hundred Years' War. (See pages 386-92.)

6. a. Correct. Medieval people had no rational explanation for the plague; most people -- lay, scholarly and medical -- believed that the Black Death was caused by some "vicious property in the air." (See page 383.)
   b. No. Certainly the poor sanitation and cramped housing contributed greatly to the spread of the plague, but very few people made any connection the two. (See page 383.)
   c. No. Nineteenth-century scientists pinpointed the cause as a bacillus, *Pasteurella pestis*, in the blood stream of fleas; fourteenth-century people had no idea about this. (See page 383.)
   d. No. The black rat was preferred by the fleas carrying the deadly bacillus, but fourteenth-century people did not understand or realize this. (See page 383.)

7. a. No. As a result in the grievous decline in population, laborers were in an advantageous position and were able to earn higher wages. (See page 384.)
   b. No. The plague was not discerning about whom it carried off; in an age of mounting criticism of clerical behavior, the German clergy worked to provide what care and solace they could; as a result their mortality rate was phenomenally high. (See page 384.)
   c. Correct. Flagellantism, and other forms of extreme behavior, increased. (See pages 384-5.)
   d. No. Literature and art of the fourteenth century reflected the terribly morbid concern with death, such as the Dance of Death. (See pages 384-6.)

8. a. No. Edward III, the eldest surviving male descendant of Philip the Fair, was the English king who claimed the throne of France in 1337, ostensibly to protect his claim to Aquitaine. (See pages 377-92.)
   b. Correct. Actually the war was brought on by the dynastic conflict between the heirs of Philip the Fair, when Philip's last surviving son, Charles IV, died childless. (See pages 377-92.)
   c. No. Joan of Arc was the French peasant girl who miraculously saved the day for the Dauphin Charles of France. (See pages 377-92.)
   d. No. The Dauphin Charles was the beneficiary of the miraculous succor provided the French monarchy in the relief of Orleans in 1429. (See pages 377-92.)

9. a. No. With the population loss caused by the plague, agricultural wages had gone up; actually the revolt in England was a case of rising expectations. (See pages 400-3.)
   b. Correct. In England, particularly, landlords attempted to legislate lower wages with the Statute of Laborers of 1351, which was unenforceable. (See pages 400-3.)
   c. No. Actually the decline in population had greatly lessened land pressure to the point were this was not a factor in the conflict. (See pages 400-3.)
   d. No. Many peasants had served during the Hundred Years' War, but the basic causes of these conflicts were social and economic. (See pages 400-3.)

10. a. No. Cardinal Robert of Geneva was elected antipope, as Clement VII, and set himself up at Avignon in opposition to the legally elected pope, thus beginning the Great Schism. (See page 393.)
    b. No. Pope Urban V, indeed any pope, would not have been the proponent of conciliar authority, which directly challenged the authority of the pope. (See pages 392-3.)
    c. No. Although John Wyclif was the proponent of radical ideas, especially the idea that each Christian should read the Bible, and challenged the authority of the pope, he was not the author of the *Defensor Pacis*. (See pages 393-4.)
    d. Correct. Marsiglio of Padua, rector of the University of Paris, in his *Defensor Pacis* argued that the church should be subordinate to the state and that the papacy should be subordinate to a general council. (See page 393.)

11. a. No. The huge cost of the war compelled Edward III to summon not only the great barons and bishops, but also the knights and burgesses to raise the funds necessary; the frequency of the sessions further enforced the development of Parliament. (See page 391.)

b.   Correct. In order to finance the war effort, the English government raised taxes on the wool crop until the price was too high for Italian and Flemish buyers. (See pages 390-1.)

c.   No. Actually the man-power drain caused by the war effectively prevented the reclamation of old lands and the opening of new lands. (See pages 390-1.)

d.   No. Actually manpower losses, especially amongst the knights who generally handled the work of government, was a serious consequence. (See pages 390-1.)

12.   a.   No. Although Wyclif is generally considered the precursor of the Reformation, from which we get the term Protestant, but his followers were not referred to as such. (See pages 393-4 and Chapter 14.)

b.   No. No doubt the popes believed Wyclif's followers to be outlaws, but they were not known as "outlaws." (See pages 393-4.)

c.   Correct. Wyclif's followers were called Lollards, which is derived from their criticism of the "mumblers of prayers and psalms," that is, Catholic priests. (See pages 393-4.)

d.   No. Flagellants exhibited extreme behavior, occasioned by the physical and psychological suffering of the Plague. (See pages 384-5, 393-4.)

13.   a.   Correct. Fur-collar crime, from the miniver fur which only nobles could wear, resulted from the restlessness of English nobles following the Hundred Years' War, exacerbated by inflation, was characterized by robbery and extortion committed by nobles against the poor. (See page 400.)

b.   No. Robin Hood represented the resentment of the common people for fur-collar criminals. (See page 400.)

c.   No. Although some churchmen did commit crimes, fur-collar crime was that perpetrated by nobles on the poor. (See pages 400.)

d.   No. Actually fur-collar crime refers to robbery and extortion perpetrated on the poor by English nobles. (See page 400.)

14.   a.   No. The plague made its first appearance in southern Europe and spread north. (See page 380.)

b.   No. The plague, which originated in the east, made its first appearance in southern Europe and spread steadily northward. (See page 380.)

c.   Correct. The plague made its first appearance at Messina, from which it spread across Sicily, then to Italy, and worked its way steadily northward. (See page 380.)

d.   No. The plague made its first appearance in southern Europe and then spread steadily northward. (See page 380.)

15.   a.   No. Although the confiscation of Aquitaine by Philip IV was one of the issues in the conflict between the English and French monarchs, it was not the original cause of the war. (See pages 386-7.)

b.   Correct. Edward III's claim to the French crown, based on being the last male descendant of Philip the Fair, touched off the Hundred Years' War. (See pages 386-7.)

c.   No. Although the rich Flemish wool trade was highly prized, the initial cause of the war was the rival claims to the throne. (See pages 386-7.)

d.   No. There were many causative factors of the Hundred Years' War but religion was not one of them. (See pages 386-7.)

16.   a.   No. Actually the crossbow was greatly outmatched by one of the English innovations, the long bow, which allowed for much more rapid reloading. (See pages 387-9.)

b.   Correct. The firing of cannon at Crécy was probably the first use of artillery in the West; long bows easily outmatched the French crossbows, with their much more rapid reloading. (See pages 387-9.)

c.   No. Actually cavalry was basic to all armies at the time and had been the backbone of Europe's military for centuries. (See pages 387-9 and Chapter 8.)

d.   No. Pikes were a traditional weapon of peasant infantry; the true innovations were the cannon and long bow. (See pages 387-9.)

17. a. No. Even though some marriages did enjoy romantic love, parents still planned their children's marriages with an eye toward economic and social advancement. (See pages 396-8.)

b. No. Prospective brides and grooms or their parents continued to chose partners that would enhance their economic and social standing. (See pages 396-8.)

c. No. Actually divorce did not exist in the Middle Ages. (See pages 396-8.)

d. No. Quite the contrary, many young couples entered into matrimony without the benefit of clergy, believing marriage to be a private contract. (See pages 396-8.)

18. a. Correct. Dante's *Divine Comedy*, an allegorical trilogy describing the realms of Hell, Purgatory and Paradise, was written in Italian, the vernacular language of Italy. (See page 406.)

b. No. Jacques de Vitry was a French preacher of the thirteenth century used to illustrate the recurring nature of peasant revolts in the Middle Ages. (See pages 400, 406.)

c. No. Clement VII's election an antipope triggered the Great Schism; he was not a vernacular writer. (See pages 393, 406.)

d. No. Marsiglio of Padua was the author of *Defensor Pacis* and a proponent of the conciliar movement, not a vernacular writer. (See pages 393, 406.)

19. a. No. The male attire favored by Joan of Arc scandalized the French court, but did not deter her from saving the Valois monarchy. (See pages 389-90.)

b. Correct. The Maid of Orleans saved the French crown for the Valois and was later burned at the stake by the English. (See pages 389-90.)

c. No. The English, having received her from the Burgundians, accused Joan of heresy and burned her at the stake. (See pages 389-90.)

d. No. Joan was the child of well-to-do peasants in the village of Domremy in Champagne. (See pages 389-90.)

20. a. No. Even though the English had reached the walls of Paris by 1419 it was not the relief of Paris that was the decisive turning point in the war. (See pages 389-90.)

b. No. Naval battles did not really have an impact on the war. (See pages 389-90)

c. Correct. The relief of Orleans, led by Joan of Arc, resulted in the withdrawal of the English and the coronation of the Dauphin Charles as King of France. (See page 390.)

d. No. The Battle of Poitiers, like Crécy and Agincourt, were great victories for the English. (See pages 389-90.)

21. a. No. Prostitution, the "oldest profession," has always existed; in the late Middle Ages houses of prostitution were legal. (See page 377.)

b. No. With marriage postponed until the right economic moment, for all classes, men from all social strata visited prostitutes; some prostitutes were able to amass sizable fortunes. (See page 377.)

c. Correct. Prostitution, an urban phenomenon, was legalized and regulated in cities all over Europe; nevertheless, the prostitute was scorned and distrusted, not respected. (See page 377.)

d. No. Prostitution, which needs a large pool of available men accustomed to cash transactions, was an urban not rural phenomenon. (See page 377.)

22. a. No. Actually the opposite is true, as the guilds restricted entry into the ranks of apprentices and journeymen and placed additional hurdles in the way of would-be masters, the relationship began to resemble that of boss and worker. (See pages 398-9.)

b. No. The crafts guilds continued to control tightly the production process; the relationship between master and journeyman deteriorated. (See pages 398-9.)

c. No. Although apprenticeship became more restricted it was not abandoned and remained one of the primary means of maintaining the guild's monopoly through the control of recruitment. (See page 398-9.)

A60

d. Correct. In order to maintain their monopolies, crafts guilds carefully restricted recruitment and advancement, which worsened the master-journeyman relationship. (See pages 398-9.)

23. a. No. *Canterbury Tales* is set in England, not Italy; Boccacio's *Decameron* offered a description of the plague in Italy. (See page 409.)
b. Correct. Chaucer's *Tales* present a rich panorama of English social life and the cultural tensions of the times. (See page 409.)
c. No. The stories presented in Chaucer's *Tales* reflect a variety of worldly interests and social tensions; the pilgrims are ostensibly Christian but many of them are also materialistic, sensual and worldly. (See page 409.)
d. No. Actually the *Tales* seem to suggest that society was ambivalent in its concern for the next world and more interested in enjoying this one. (See page 409.)

24. a. No. Actually England suffered a net loss of cash revenues as a result of the war. (See pages 390-2.)
b. No. Actually the heavy taxation of the wool crop had driven prices too high for Italian and Flemish buyers, greatly damaging the wool trade. (See pages 390-2.)
c. No. Although some English knights did amass fortunes, these were rapidly squandered away. (See pages 390-2.)
d. Correct. Despite the huge ransom collected for King John of France and the indemnities paid by captured towns and castles, England suffered a net loss. (See pages 390-2.)

25. a. Correct. Involving perhaps 100,000 people, the English Peasant Revolt was probably the largest of the Middle Ages. (See pages 401-2.)
b. No. The Peasant Revolt was quite important, effectively wiping out rural serfdom in England. (See pages 401-2.)
c. No. With over 100,000 people involved, on the peasant side, this revolt affected almost the entire population of England. (See pages 401-2.)
d. No. The revolt was a response of the peasants to the years of aristocratic arrogance and abuse and was touched off by efforts to reimpose a head tax on all adult males. (See pages 401-2.)

Chapter 13

1. a.   Correct. Actually most of the earliest printed books and pamphlets dealt with religious subjects, but people did seek books on all subjects: medicine, practical and travel manuals, as well as pornography. (See page 430.)
    b.   No. Certainly the availability of books encouraged literacy as people from all walks of life, if they could afford it, sought books on a variety of subjects. (See page 430.)
    c.   No. Through the efforts of three men -- Johann Gutenburg, Johann Fust and Peter Schoffer -- all working in Mainz, moveable type was developed. (See pages 429-30.)
    d.   No. As printing developed, literacy spread; thus the availability of printed material bridged the gap between written and oral cultures. (See page 430.)

2. a.   No. Although the Low Countries would experience a distinct Renaissance, the so-called Northern Renaissance, the Renaissance did not begin there. (See pages 415-6, 437-40.)
    b.   No. Rome would be the beneficiary of a great deal of Renaissance art, but the Renaissance did not begin there. (See pages 415-6.)
    c.   No. Historians agree that the Renaissance arose from the commercial revival of earlier centuries, led by northern Italian cities; France would become a great patron of Renaissance art but the Renaissance did not begin there. (See pages 415-6.)
    d.   Correct. The first literary and artistic mainfestations of the Renaissance appeared in Florence, which was an enourmously weaalthy city. (See pages 415-6.)

3. a.   No. Certainly churchmen, especially high church officials, were patrons but they did comprise the vast majority of Renaissance patrons. (See pages 423-5.)
    b.   No. The popes, such as Julius II, did patronize Renaissance artists, but the popes were not the most important segment of the art-consuming community. (See pages 423-5.)
    c.   No. Art was too expensive for common people to become patrons; further art was not considered public property. (See pages 423-5.)
    d.   Correct. Increasingly in the fifteenth century, wealthy individuals (merchants and bankers) sponsored Renaissance artists, using the art to glorify themselves and their families. (See pages 423-5.)

4. a.   No. The Tudors were an English dynasty (of Welsh origins) and thus did not begin French economic and political recovery; they did greatly strengthen the English monarchy. (See pages 440-2.)
    b.   Correct. Charles VII reconciled the civil war between Burgundy and Armagnac, reorganized the royal council (using middle-class men) and introduced new taxes to strengthen royal finances. (See pages 440-1.)
    c.   No. Philip the Fair had ruled France before the Hundred Years' War; indeed one of the major causes of this war had been the rival claims of his descendants. (See page 444 and Chapter 12.)
    d.   No. Louis XI, the "Spider King," was the son of Charles VII and carried on the work of his father. (See pages 444-1.)

5. a.   No. In Renaissance society, blacks, like women, were valued as signs of wealth; they served in a variety of functions but not as soldiers. (See pages 435-7.)
    b.   Correct. Blacks performed a variety of functions, but were primarily employed as servants and entertainers. They, like women, were signs of wealth and used for display. (See pages 435-7.)
    c.   No. Although blacks were certainly considered inferior (and the color was associated with evil), they were considered a sign of wealth and used for display. (See pages 435-7.)
    d.   No. Actually, blacks were prized for the unusual appearance, serving many functions at the courts of rich Renaissance princes and businessmen. (See pages 435-7.)

6. a.   No. North of the Alps, humanists had a program for broad social reform based on Christian ideals, with a distinctly religious character. (See pages 437-40.)

b.   Correct. Northern humanists were interested in the development of an ethical way of life, combining the best elements of classical and Christian cultures; they wanted to reform society based on these ideals. (See pages 437-40.)

c.   No. Pagan themes (along with secular themes and Greco-Roman motifs) characterized the Italian Renaissance; in the north the humanists stressed biblical and early Christian themes. (See pages 437-4.0)

d.   No. Actually northern humanists, such as John Colet and Erasmus of Rotterdam, stressed the use of reason as the foundation for an ethical way of life. (See pages 437-40.)

7.   a.   No. *Conversos* were Spanish Jews who had converted to Christianity. (See pages 442, 444.)

b.   No. Liberal, during the Renaissance, referred to the humanists' program of educational and moral behavior, not the local groups given judicial authority in Spain. (See pages 423-6, 442.)

c.   No. In order to curb the rebellious aristocracy, Isabella and Ferdinand revived the old medieval institution, the *hermandades* ("brotherhoods"), giving them police and judicial authority. (See page 442.)

d.   No. A royal tribunal, by definition, would not have been a local group; Ferdinand and Isabella did restructure the royal council, which had full judicial power. (See page 442.)

8.   a.   No. The Star Chamber was a special court, operating under special rules of evidence and procedure, not a common-law court. (See page 442.)

b.   No. Actually the Star Chamber was designed to limit the power and influence of the English barons and was an offshoot of the royal council. (See page 442.)

c.   No. The Tudor monarch Henry VII instituted the Star Chamber to reduce aristocratic trouble-making. (See page 442.)

d.   Correct. Instituted by Henry VII, the Star Chamber was designed to prevent noble interference in the administration of justice and combat fur-collar crime; this measure helped to strengthen the English monarchy. (See page 442.)

9.   a.   Correct. In 1438, Charles VII issued the Pragmatic Sanction of Bourges which asserted the French crown's right to appoint bishops and the supremacy of a general council over the pope; a later compromise confirmed the so-called Gallican liberties. (See pages 440-1.)

b.   No. The Habsburg-Valois wars were fought between the German and French dynasties for control of Italy and other territories. (See pages 4401, 419.)

c.   No. The "Declaration of Calais" did not resolve the issue of French monarchial control over the church, this was dealt with by the Pragmatic Sanction of Bourges in 1438. (See pages 440-1.)

d.   No. The Hundred Years' War was a dynastic and civil struggle and not concerned with the issue of monarchial control of the French church. (See pages 440-1 and Chapter 12.)

10.   a.   No. Democracy, even in as radical a work as Thomas More's *Utopia,* was not considered a viable form of government. (See pages 437-40.)

b.   No. Most northern humanists believed that human nature had been corrupted by sin, but was fundamentally good and capable of improvement. (See pages 437-40.)

c.   No. Northern humanists stressed Christian themes, especially the Christian virtues of love, faith and hope. (See pages 437-40.)

d.   Correct. Most humanists believed that through education and reason, combined with Christian virtues, society could be perfected. (See pages 437-40.)

11.   a.   No. John had actually weakened the crown by signing the Magna Carta. (See pages 441-2 and

b.   No. William III, and his wife Mary, were invited to the throne of England following the Glorious Revolution of 1688, signaling the predominant position of Parliament in the English political system. (See pages 441-2 and Chapter 16.)

c.   No. Henry II had been instrumental in the development of the English judicial system in the twelfth century. (See pages 441-2 and Chapter 11.)

d.   Correct. Henry VII, of the Welsh house of Tudor, ended the civil war, instituted the royal council and Star Chamber to lessen the influence of the English aristocracy thus strengthening the crown. (See pages 441-2.)

12.   a.   No. Indeed the wool industry was the largest source of Florentine wealth. (See pages 415-6.)

b.   No. Florence, as did many other cities, suffered tremendously from the Black Death, losing perhaps half of its population. (See pages 415-6.)

c.   No. By the end of the thirteenth century Florence had acquired control of papal banking, leading to Florentine bankers' domination of European banking. (See pages 415-6.)

d.   Correct. Actually Florence is an inland city, but this did not hamper its economic development. (See pages 415-6.)

13.   a.   No. Brunelleschi constructed the magnificent dome of the Cathedral of Florence and pioneered in perspective. (See pages 422, 426.)

b.   No. Donatello was a famous sculptor, but he is not responsible for the dome of St. Peter's. (See pages 422, 426.)

c.   Correct. The dome of St. Peter's in Rome is considered to be the masterpiece of the Renaissance genius Michelangelo. (See page 422.)

d.   No. Ghiberti was an important Renaissance artist and was selected to design the bronze doors of the Baptistry of the Cathedral of Florence, not St. Peter's dome. (See pages 422, 425.)

14.   a.   No. Although there had been an economic revival which was the basis for the Renaissance, the term Renaissance does not refer to economic growth. (See pages 415, 420.)

b.   Correct. The term Renaissance refers to the resurgence in art and culture characterized by individualism, humanism and a reverence for antiquity. (See pages 415, 420.)

c.   No. Even though the term Renaissance means "rebirth" and there was an increase in population, the term does not refer to population growth. (See pages 415, 420.)

d.   No. Actually the church did not experience a recovery; indeed a spirit of secularism permeated the church and society. (See pages 415, 420.)

15.   a.   No. Certainly the wealth of the various northern Italian cities was a factor in their political strength, but there was not a direct relationship. (See pages 415-7.)

b.   Correct. As the rural nobility realized the wealth of the cities and married into the commercial elites, the financial and military strength of the towns was enhanced. (See pages 415-7.)

c.   No. Actually the Holy Roman Emperor invaded Italy in an attempt to control the rich cities. (See pages 415-7.)

d.   No. The papacy frequently attempted to dominate Italian politics, sometimes through alliances with France, the Holy Roman Emperor or some combination of Italian city-states. (See pages 415-7.)

16.   a.   No. The northern Renaissance did emphasize biblical scholarship, which was eschewed by the Italian Renaissance. (See pages 437-40.)

b.   No. Northern humanists believed that the use of reason could form the foundation for an ethical way of life. (See pages 437-40.)

c.   No. In order to develop an ethical way of life, northern humanists believed that the best elements of classical and Christian culture should be combined. (See pages 437-40.)

d.   Correct. All of these features were aspects of the Northern Renaissance, in the attempt to develop an ethical way of life. (See pages 437-40.)

17.   a.   No. The Dutch humanist Erasmus advocated "the philosophy of Christ," that is, an inner attitude of Christian faith, not paganism. (See pages 437-9.)

b.   Correct. One of the fundamental themes in all of Erasmus' scholarly work was the importance of

Christian education for moral and intellectual development. (See pages 437-9.)

c. No. Erasmus had been forced to enter a monastery as a young orphan and he intensely disliked the monastic life. (See pages 437-9.)

d. No. Erasmus advocated the "philosophy of Christ" which was not the formalism, ceremony or laws of the church, but an inner attitude of the heart. (See pages 437-9.)

18. a. No. Renaissance artists of talent usually worked on commission from a member of the rich elite and achieved economic security. (See pages 425-8.)

b. Correct. Being the beneficiary of upper-class patronage, talented artists achieved economic security and sometimes great wealth. (See pages 425-8.)

c. No. Actually the status of artists had risen and they were considered free intellectual workers; the patronage of wealthy elites usually insured economic security. (See pages 425-8.)

d. No. Not really; talented artists enjoyed economic security (and sometimes great wealth) and, given the importance of art, social status. (See pages 425-8.)

19. a. Correct. Castiglione's *The Courtier* had great influence on court behavior and was widely read, influencing social mores and patterns of conduct of elite groups; the "courtier" became the model for European gentlemen and ladies. (See page 429.)

b. No. Machiavellli's *The Prince* described the politics of Renaissance Italy, not courtly life and behavior. (See page 429.)

c. No. St. Augustine's *City of God* was the expression of Christian historical and religious thought of the third and fourth centuries. (See pages 429 and Chapter 7.)

d. No. Boccacio's *Decameron* is a collection of tales describing a frankly acquisitive, sensual and worldly society, not courtly life and behavior. (See pages 422, 429.)

20. a. Correct. Some political scientists have maintained that Machiavelli was describing the actual competitive framework of the Italian states with which he was familiar. (See page 429.)

b. No. *The Prince* was not a satire; written in exile, some scholars have argued that Machiavelli was attempting to describe the Italian political system accurately. (See page 429.)

c. No. Machiavelli made Cesare Borgio the hero of *The Prince* because of his work in uniting Italy, but the book is much more than just a call for Italian nationalism. (See page 429.)

d. No. This cannot be the correct answer, as Machiavelli did not write a satire, but an accurate description of Italian politics. (See page 429.)

21. a. Correct. The Wars of the Roses, the civil war between the ducal houses of York (the white rose) and Lancaster (the red rose) disrupted trade, agriculture and domestic industry. (See page 441.)

b. No. There have been many wars between England and France over the centuries, but the Wars of the Roses were a series of civil wars between rival noble factions. (See page 441.)

c. No. Henry VI, pious but mentally disturbed, did not challenge the aristocracy and the authority of the monarchy was seriously diminished during his reign. (See page 441.)

d. No. Actually the English gentry supported the efforts of Henry VII (and his predecessors) to suppress the violent aristocracy, exemplified by the Wars of the Roses and the impact on the economy. (See pages 441.)

22. a. No. On the eve of the accession of Ferdinand and Isabella, the Iberian peninsula lacked a common culture, with different languages, laws and religious customs. (See pages 442.)

b. Correct. Prior to the reign of Ferdinand and Isabella the central theme of the Spanish experience was disunity and pluralism, without a common culture; the different languages, laws and religious customs made for a rich diversity. (See page 442.)

c. No. Under the Muslims, the Iberian peninsula was a relatively tolerant area, but in the fourteenth century anti-Semitism was strong; the expulsion of the Muslims is another indication that the Iberian peninsula was not tolerant. (See page 442.)

d.   No. By the middle of the fifteenth century, Spain (with the exception of Granada) had been won for Christianity, eliminating Arab influence; Jews continued to be important economically and culturally but were never dominant in numbers or politically. (See page 442.)

23.   a.   No. The prevailing European view had been that people were basically corrupt; More contended that society's flawed institutions, especially private property, were responsible for corruption. (See page 437.)
b.   No. That political leaders should learn to manipulate their subjects is a concept put forth by Machiavelli not Moore. (See pages 429, 437.)
c.   No. Exemplified by his *Utopia*, More believed that society could be perfected, through the reform of the social institutions that mold the individual. (see page 424.)
d.   Correct. The concept that corruption and war were due to society's flawed institutions, such as private property, and not to the inherently corrupt nature of humanity was extremely radical. (See page 437.)

24.   a.   No. On the contrary, Renaissance men believed that educated women violated nature and thus ceased to be a woman, and threatened male dominance in the intellectual realm. (See pages 432-4.)
b.   No. Whereas education prepared young men to rule and participate in the public affairs of the city, it prepared a woman for the social functions of the home. (See pages 432-4.)
c.   No. Although some men felt education "robbed a woman of her nature," educated women were generally accepted as decorations for the home. (See pages 432-4.)
d.   Correct. During the Renaissance, women did receive a better education, but this education was to be used to adorn the home of the husband, not to challenge men intellectually. (See pages 432-4.)

25.   a.   Correct. Renaissance culture was the exclusive province of the wealthy business elite; it did not affect the broad middle classes, much less the workers and the peasants. (See pages 426-8.)
b.   No. The typical small tradesperson or craftsman could not comprehend the sophisticated essays of Renaissance writers (even if one had the time to read one) and certainly could not afford to patronize an artist. (See pages 426-8.)
c.   No. Although many high church officials patronized Renaissance artists, Renaissance culture was the domain of the business patriarchate. (See pages 426-8.)
d.   No. In reality, the Renaissance continued, even widened, the gulf between the rich elite and the masses; workers and peasants did not have the time or money for artistic concerns. (See pages 426-8.)

1. a. No. Indeed the abuses of the Catholic clergy, including the bishops, was a prime cause for the spread of Protestantism in Scotland. (See page 473.)
   b. No. The king of Scotland James V and his daughter Mary Queen of Scots were both staunch Catholics and opposed any religious reforms. (See page 473.)
   c. Correct The Protestant church in Scotland is called the Presbyterian Church because the *presbyters*, or ministers, govern it. (See page 473.)
   d. No. Although the people were more involved in church affairs, the ministers were in charge of the church. (See page 473.)

2. a. No. The localism and independence of each Anabaptist community found resonance in the democratic church organization of the Congregationalists. (See page 470.)
   b. No. In that neither was Catholic and that both believed that only a few people would receive the "inner light," Puritans and Anabaptists are from the same tradition. (See page 470.)
   c. No. The pacifism of the Anabaptists was later echoed by the Quakers. (See page 470.)
   d. Correct. The Jesuits, a Catholic service order, had been founded to combat the beliefs of people such as the Anabaptists. (See pages 470, 478.)

3. a. No. "Good works" were rejected by Luther as the means by which salvation could be achieved. (See page 458.)
   b. Correct. Luther believed that salvation comes through faith alone; faith is the free and arbitrary gift of God. (See page 458.)
   c. No. Indulgences are a type of "good work" and thus rejected by Luther as the means to salvation; indeed the sale of indulgences prompted the Ninety-five Theses. (See page 458.)
   d. No. Faith alone (the free gift of God) determined salvation; indeed, according to Luther all vocations have equal merit in the eyes of God. (See page 458.)

4. a. Correct. With implacable logic Calvin argued that God, all-knowing and all-powerful, had already determined who would be saved: predestination; this belief undermines totally the concept of free will. (See pages 467-9.)
   b. No. Indulgences were part of the Catholic dogma and generally rejected by Protestant reformers such as Calvin. (See pages 455-6, 467-9.)
   c. No. For Calvin, people were insignificant, whether good or evil; the cornerstone of his belief system was predestination. (See pages 467-9.)
   d. No. Actually Calvin reserved his harshest condemnation for religious dissenters, even burning one, Michael Servetus. (See pages 467-9.)

5. a. No. Knox and his followers were moving away from Catholicism and thus unlikely to be influenced by Catholic dogma. (See page 473.)
   b. Correct. Knox had studied and worked with Calvin in Geneva and brought Calvin's theology to Scotland. (See page 473.)
   c. No. Calvinism, not Lutheranism, had become the compelling force in international Protestantism; Knox had worked and studied with Calvin in Geneva. (See page 473.)
   d. No. The Church of England remained too Catholic; many English Puritans hoped to model the reformed English church on the Calvinistic Scottish church. (See page 473.)

6. a. No. Indeed pluralism -- holding more than one church office -- was rampant in the Catholic Church at the time, especially prevalent was high-ranking Italian clergymen holding benefices throughout Europe. (See page 453.)
   b. Correct. The Brethren of Common Life was a society of pious lay people founded in Holland in the Late fourteenth century which stressed spirituality and simplicity. (See page 453.)

c.   No. Under Pope Alexander VI, a member of the infamous Borgia family, the papal court attained new heights of impropriety, with the pope even acknowledging his mistress and children. (See page 453.)

d.   No. Absenteeism went hand-in-hand with pluralism: high-ranking clergymen collecting revenues but rarely if ever visiting their benefices, paying a poor priest a pittance to fulfill the religious duties. (See page 453.)

7.   a.   No. The German peasantry were attracted to Luther's beliefs, especially the idea that a Christian is a free man and subject to no one. (See pages 459-61.)

b.   No. The German nobility, especially after Luther denounced the Peasant Revolt, supported Lutheranism; they also saw it as a way to enhance their wealth at the expense of the Catholic Church. (See pages 465-6.)

c.   Correct. Charles V, Holy Roman Emperor, had Luther declared an outlaw of the Empire at Charles' first diet at Worms in 1521. (See pages 456, 465-6.)

d.   No. Ulrich Zwingli, a humanist from Zurich, was strongly influenced by Luther and introduced Lutheran reforms in that city. (See pages 456, 459.)

8.   a.   No. Henry's motives combined personal, political, social and economic elements; economic motives, primarily the wealth of the monasteries, was a key factor. (See pages 470-3.)

b.   No. Religious reasons figured very little in Henry's decision; he even retained much of Catholic theology. (See pages 470-3.)

c.   Correct. The problem of producing a male heir and thus sparing England civil war was a key factor in Henry's decision to divorce Catherine of Aragon. (See pages 470-3.)

d.   No. Actually the diplomatic situation called for Henry to remain quiet, as Catherine's nephew was Emperor Charles V. (See pages 470-3.)

9.   a.   Correct. The competition between Catholic Emperor Charles V and the German princes (exacerbated by the Habsburg-Valois wars) added greatly to the political fragmentation of Germany. (See pages 465-6.)

b.   No. Actually the opposite is true; religious conflict added to the tradition of decentralization in Germany. (See pages 465-6.)

c.   No. In reality the conflict over religion resulted in a major division in Germany between Protestant north and Catholic south. (See pages 465-6.)

d.   No. Charles V was unable to defeat the German princes, thus removing any chance of imperial centralization. (See pages 465-6.)

10.   a.   No. The Christian humanists, signs of vitality in the church believed that reform could be achieved through education, piety and social change, not violent revolution. (See pages 453, 470.)

b.   Correct. The Christian humanists, with a long tradition (see Chapter 13,) believed that reform could achieved through education and social change. (See pages 453, 470.)

c.   No. The Christian humanists, with a long tradition (see Chapter 13,) felt that the church hierarchy was one of the main problems and believed that reform could achieved through education and social change. (See pages 453, 470.)

d.   No. The Christian humanists, with a long tradition (see Chapter 13,) felt that the church hierarchy, including the papacy, was one of the main problems and believed that reform could achieved through education and social change. (See pages 453, 470.)

11.   a.   Correct. Luther's Ninety-five Theses was a direct response to a big "indulgence sale" held by Archbishop Albert to pay for his new benefices. (See pages 454-6.)

b.   No. Luther did undergo a revelation concerning faith and salvation, but his Ninety-five Theses was a direct response to a big "indulgence sale" held by Archbishop Albert to pay for his new benefices. (See pages 454-6.)

c.   No. Although clerical illiteracy was a problem, Luther's Ninety-five Theses was a direct response to a big "indulgence sale" held by Archbishop Albert to pay for his new benefices. (See pages 454-6.)

d.   No. Actually Frederick of Saxony was Luther's benefactor and protector. (See pages 454-6.)

12.   a.   No. The peasants believed that Luther's call for religious freedom had a secular and social application as well, and argued for their own freedom from serfdom. (See pages 459-61.)

b.   No. As many of the abuses suffered by the peasantry came at the hands of ecclesiastical lords (such as bishops,) the peasants demanded clerical reform. (See pages 459-61.)

c.   Correct. Actually the peasants based their calls for freedom on Luther's call for religious freedom; Luther condemned the uprisings. (See pages 459-61.)

d.   No. The peasants complained bitterly about excessive taxes and tithes, which had exacerbated agrarian problems. (See pages 459-61.)

13.   a.   Correct. Although Luther had been a member of the Catholic clergy, he was not appointed to any positions by the pope and was excommunicated. (See pages 461-2.)

b.   No. The development of the printing press enabled the rapid and pervasive dissemination of Luther's ideas. (See pages 461-2.)

c.   No. Luther's condemnation of the peasant uprisings and his support of secular authority appealed to the nobility, (support of Luther was also a cloak for political independence) while his idea that all occupations have merit in God's eyes was appealing to the middle class. (See pages 461-2, 465-6.)

d.   No. Luther was a brilliant writer and speaker which helped him spread his ideas; his ability as a writer was greatly enhanced by the printing press. (See pages 461-2.)

14.   a.   No. Charles V had Luther declared an outlaw of the Empire and attempted to maintain the religious uniformity of Europe. (See pages 463-6.)

b.   Correct. Charles V had Luther declared an outlaw of the Empire and attempted to maintain the religious uniformity of Europe. (See pages 463-6.)

c.   No. Charles V had Luther declared an outlaw of the Empire and attempted to maintain the religious uniformity of Europe. (See pages 463-6.)

d.   No. Charles V had Luther declared an outlaw of the Empire and attempted to maintain the religious uniformity of Europe. (See pages 463-6.)

15.   a.   No. By 1555, England, as a result of Henry's actions, had undergone a "Protestant Reformation". (See pages 466, 470-3.)

b.   No. Scandinavia by 1555 had adopted Lutheranism. (See pages 466, 475.)

c.   Correct. Spain, home of Emperor Charles V, was a bastion of Roman Catholicism. (See pages 466, 476.)

d.   No. Scotland, as a result of the work of John Knox, had adopted Calvinism. (See pages 466, 473.)

16.   a.   No. Paris, the capital of Catholic France, was not the center of Protestant reformers. (See pages 467-9.)

b.   Correct. Calvin's Geneva (and his powerful influence) drew religious reformers from all over Europe and was to spark many imitations. (See pages 467-9)

c.   No. Zurich, the home of Zwingli, could not compete with Calvin and Geneva. (See pages 467-9, 456.)

d.   No. Geneva, Calvin's headquarters, was the center of the international Protestant movement. (See pages 467-9.)

17.   a.   No. With the somewhat anti-social beliefs of the Anabaptists, it would have been unlikely that the nobility would be attracted to this religion. (See pages 469-70)

b.   Correct. The Anabaptists, with their message of pacifism and communal living, appealed to the dispossessed: the poor, unemployed, uneducated. (See pages 469-70.)

c.   No. Anabaptists did not appeal to the intellectuals, but to the dispossessed of Europe. (See pages 469-70.)

d.   No. The merchant classes would not have been attracted to Anabaptism because of its anti-acquisitive belief system. (See pages 469-70.)

18. a.   No. Actually Henry needed the wealth of the monasteries; the land was not distributed equitably, but tended to be acquired by the wealthy elite. (See page 471.)

b.   No. It was not for any papal symbolism but the wealth of the monasteries that motivated Henry. (See page 471.)

c.   Correct. Henry wanted the wealth of the monasteries, which moved him to seize them. (See page 471.)

d.   No. The monasteries were quite wealthy and not a drain on the English economy. (See page 471.)

19. a.   Correct. In Scandinavia, the monarchs had taken the lead in the religious reformation, which explains the influence of Luther. (See page 475.)

b.   No. Knox was critical to the reformation in Scotland not Scandinavia. (See pages 473, 475.)

c.   No. In Scandinavia, the monarchs had taken the lead in the religious reformation, which explains the influence of Luther. (See pages 473, 475.)

d.   No. Jesuits were Catholics and thus had little influence on the reformation in Scandinavia. (See pages 475, 478.)

20. a.   No. All Jesuit noviates took the traditional vows of poverty, chastity and obedience, but special monks took an additional vow of obedience to the pope; this special vow marks the Jesuits as distinctive. (See page 478.)

b.   No. All Jesuit noviates took the traditional vows of poverty, chastity and obedience; it was the vow of obedience to the pope that distinguished the Jesuits. (See page 478.)

c.   Correct. All Jesuit noviates took the traditional vows of poverty, chastity and obedience; it was the special vow of obedience to the pope that distinguished the Jesuits. (See page 478.)

d.   No. Pacifism is not really a part of the Jesuit system; indeed the Jesuits were quite aggressive in their protection of Roman Catholicism. (See page 478.)

21. a.   No. Although Luther did acknowledge the supremacy of the state this was not the result of his translation of the Bible. (See pages 461-2.)

b.   No. Actually Luther's argument that all vocations have equal merit in the eyes of God gave dignity to those who performed domestic tasks. (See pages 461-2.)

c.   Correct. The invention of the printing press and Luther's talent with the German language, as well as his belief that everyone should read the Bible, brought the message of the Bible to many people. (See pages 461-2.)

d.   No. In reality, Luther's message and spirit brought many more people into churches. (See pages 461-2.)

22. a.   Correct. This marriage made the Austrian house of Habsburg, already the strongest ruling family in the empire, an international power. (See pages 462-3)

b.   No. France was able to emerge as a leading continental power because of the conflux of the religious wars in Germany and the Habsburg-Valois wars. (See pages 462-3 and Chapter 13.)

c.   No. The marriage did not involve England, and only later was Spain affected. (See pages 462-3.)

d.   No. The Austrian Habsburgs were already the most powerful ruling house in Germany. (See pages 462-3.)

23. a.   No. Knox was a follower of the man who wrote the *Institutes*. (See pages 473, 467-9.)

b.   No. Although Luther started the Protestant Reformation and wrote many things, he was not the author of the *Institutes*, who was the most influential in the spread of the Reformation. (See pages 467-

9.)

c.   No. Zwingli, an early Protestant reformer and was a follower of Luther, but he did not write the *Institutes*. (See pages 456, 467-9.)

d.   Correct. Calvin wrote the *Institutes* and was the most responsible for the internationalization of Protestantism. (See pages 467-9.)

24.   a.   No. The pope was influenced by Catherine's nephew Charles V, Holy Roman Emperor, who had just invaded Italy. (See page 471.)

b.   Correct. Charles V was the nephew of Catherine of Aragon; this relationship did indeed complicate Henry's plan to divorce her. (See page 471.)

c.   No. Catherine's nephew was the Emperor Charles V, not the King of France. (See page 471.)

d.   No. Catherine, a Spanish princess, was not related to any members of the English parliament but was the aunt of Emperor Charles V. (See page 471.)

25.   a.   No. Although Calvin's government did try to regulate the lives of the Genevans rather closely, the Index was not published by his Consistory. (See pages 467-9, 480.)

b.   No. The princes did not publish the Index, which was a tool of the Counter-Reformation. (See page 480.)

c.   Correct. The Index was published in Rome by the Sacred Congregation as part of their effort to combat Protestantism. (See page 480.)

d.   No. The Anabaptists were both too unorganized and too tolerant to publish such an Index. (See pages 469-70, 480.)

Chapter 15

1. a. Correct. The search for gold, as well as the desire to Christianize the Muslims, discover an overseas route to the spice markets of India and find the mythical Prester John were all objectives of Portugese exploration. (See pages 506-8.)
   b. No. Actually it was the desire to convert Muslims to Christianity that was one of the objectives of Portugese exploration. (See pages 506-8.)
   c. No. The Portugese were searching for overseas routes to the spice markets of India, not North America. (See pages 506-8.)
   d. No. Even though Constantinople had fallen to the Turks in 1453, its reconquest was not a motive for Portugese exploration. If they had desired this, Constantinople's location was well-known. (See pages 506-8.)

2. a. No. The Netherlands were part of the patrimony of the Habsburg dynasty which did not rule France. (See page 494.)
   b. Correct. The Netherlands were part of the patrimony of the Habsburg dynasty, which also ruled Spain. (See page 494.)
   c. No. Elizabeth I of England was not the overlord of the northern Netherlands; indeed she tried to help the Netherlands in their revolt against their overlord. (See page 494.)
   d. No. Florence, although a rich trading city, was not the overlord of the northern Netherlands. (See pages 494.)

3. a. No. North American racist attitudes generally were transplanted from European homelands: from England to the English colonies in the New World, for example; South America could not then be the origins of such beliefs. (See page 518.)
   b. No. Spain did not have much of a colonial base in North America; other European states were the breeding ground of this racism, not Spain. (See page 518.)
   c. No. England's larger, more populous colonies, located in agricultural zones in which slave labor could be used efficiently gave it the lead over France as the origins of North American racist attitudes, which were generally transplanted from European homelands to their colonies in the New World. (See page 518.)
   d. Correct. England, which had the most populous colonies in North America, spread the racist attitudes from the mother country to her colonies. (See page 518.)

4. a. No. French diplomacy during the Thirty Years' War revolved around the policy of helping the Protestant enemies of the Habsburgs. (See page 499.)
   b. No. Indeed French policy, devised by Cardinal Richelieu, was designed to weaken the power of the Holy Roman Emperor. (See page 499.)
   c. No. Spain was ruled by a relative of the Holy Roman Emperor and an ally, and thus was an enemy of France. (See page 499.)
   d. Correct. French policy under Cardinal Richelieu was designed to weaken the power of the Habsburg emperor; allying Catholic France with the German Protestants was a means to that end. (See page 499.)

5. a. No. The war between England and Spain did drag on for years. (See pages 496-8.)
   b. No. Being sunk and dispersed was not the Armada's objective; its objective had been to transport troops across the channel. (See pages 496-8)
   c. No. Actually the destruction of the fleet effectively halted any attempts by Philip II to reimpose unity on Western Europe. (See pages 496-8.)
   d. Correct. The Spanish had been unable to conquer the Netherlands up to that point; the destruction of the Armada, and Elizabeth I's continued support, insured that the Spanish would be unable to conquer their rebellious province. (See pages 496-8.)

6. a.   No. France, although a Catholic state, was not interested in the role of international defender of Catholicism; when the situation demanded, the French allied with Protestants against other Catholic states. (See pages 498-501.)
    b.   Correct. Spain under Philip II considered itself the international defender of Catholicism. (See pages 498-501.)
    c.   No. Italy was still a polyglot of political entities, mainly independent city-states and small kingdoms; it would not become a nation until the 1860s. (See pages 498-501.)
    d.   No. England had undergone something of a Protestant Reformation under Henry VIII; the English people had become increasingly Protestant since. (See pages 498-501 and Chapter 14.)

7. a.   Correct. Columbus's primary motive was the discovery of a sea route to India. (See pages 508-9.)
    b.   No. Although a deeply religious man, Columbus did not yet know of "Americans" in need of Christianization. (See pages 508-9.)
    c.   No. Spanish desire to control the New World was not a motive for Columbus. (See pages 508-9.)
    d.   No. Actually Columbus was attempting to circumvent the Mediterranean in his voyage. (See pages 508-9)

8. a.   No. Although the Spanish were responsible for much of the early exploration of the New World, they were not the first. (See page 502.)
    b.   Correct. Under Eric the Red and Leif Ericson, the Vikings discovered Greenland and the eastern coast of North America in the ninth and tenth centuries. (See page 502.)
    c.   No. Although many Italians participated in the exploration of the New World, they were not the first. (See page 502.)
    d.   No. The English were late-comers to the exploration of the New World and were far from being the first. (See page 502.)

9. a.   Correct. During the sixteenth century the Spanish crown divided its New World possessions into four viceroyalties in order to improve administration. (See page 512.)
    b.   No. Spain, like the other European colonial powers, followed the economic policy of mercantilism: colonies existed to serve the needs of the mother country; native industries were not part of mercantilism. (See page 512.)
    c.   No. *Corregidores* were Portugese colonial officials, not Spanish. (See page 512.)
    d.   No. Through the institution of the viceroy, the Spanish crown held direct and absolute power over the colonies. (See page 512.)

10. a.   No. The spice trade of the Indian Ocean had long been under the control of the Muslims, not the Spanish. (See pages 504-5.)
    b.   No. The English would not be a player in this area of the world for many years. (See pages 504-5.)
    c.   Correct. The Muslims had controlled the spice trade in the Indian Ocean for many years; the Portugese had to fight them in the attempt to gain control of it. (See pages 504-5.)
    d.   No. The French would not play a role in this region until the seventeenth century. (See pages 504-5.)

11. a.   Correct. The conquests of Cortez and Pizarro, in Mexico and Peru, opened up rich new sources of silver mines to be exploited by the Spanish. (See page 510.)
    b.   No. As Cortez said, he had come to find gold; neither men were overly concerned with missionary fervor. The spread of Christianity was a side-effect of the quest for riches. (See page 510.)
    c.   No. Both Cortez and Pizarro were land-based explorers/conquerors and thus did not contribute to further exploration of the Pacific Ocean. (See page 510.)
    d.   No. Both Cortex and Pizarro explored in the New World, not Africa. (See page 510.)

12. a. No. There is some controversy on the relationship between European inflation and the importation of precious metals, but it seems unlikely that this importation alone caused the inflation. (See pages 511-2.)

b. Correct. Spain did become increasingly dependent upon this source of revenue, resulting in general economic and social decline. (See pages 511-2.)

c. No. Although prices did rise, this was not necessarily connected to the influx of gold and silver. (See pages 511-2.)

d. No. Actually the reverse is true; Spanish reliance on this source of wealth depressed other economic activities while its expenses incurred as a result of its aggressive foreign policies greatly damaged the Spanish economy. (See pages 511-2.)

13. a. No. The Treaty of Westphalia dealt with the Thirty Years' War, not French-papal relations. (See pages 488-90, 499-501.)

b. No. This treaty ended the dynastic wars between the Habsburg and the Valois. (See pages 487-90.)

c. Correct. The Concordat of Bologna, as well as recognizing papal supremacy over a universal council, also established Catholicism as the official state religion of France. (See pages 488-90.)

d. No. The Edict of Nantes, issued by Henry IV of France, granted French Huguenots freedom of religion. (See pages 488-91.)

14. a. No. Henry III was involved in the War of the Three Henrys, but it was his assassination that helped pave the way for a solution to the civil war. (See pages 490-1.)

b. No. Francis I, the Valois monarch who was a great patron of Renaissance art, had signed the Concordat of Bologna, establishing Catholicism as the state religion of France. (See pages 488-91.)

c. Correct. Henry of Navarre, later Henry IV, had converted to Catholicism in order to be crowned king; his astute, pragmatic intelligence helped end the civil-religious wars in France. (See pages 490-1.)

d. No. Charles IX, was the child-king who was dominated by his mother Catherine de' Medici; during this time the seeds of the religious-civil strife in France were sown. (See pages 490-1.)

15. a. No. Its heavy moral emphasis did appeal to the educated middle classes. (See page 492 and Chapter 14.)

b. Correct. Calvinism was a strict religion which attempted to root out ostentation and leisurely living, stressing moderation. (See page 492 and Chapter 14.)

c. No. Calvinism's intellectual emphasis appealed to the educated middle classes. (See page 492 and Chapter 14.)

d. No. This aspect of Calvinism's message was perhaps most appealing to the educated and successful middle classes. (See page 492 and Chapter 14.)

16. a. No. Versailles was the palace built by Louis XIV, the great French monarch, outside Paris. (See page 496 and Chapter 16.)

b. Correct. The Escorial was not only the palace of the Spanish monarchs but also a monastery for Jeromite monks and the tomb for deceased Habsburgs. (See page 496.)

c. No. The Escorial, not Tournai, was the palace of the Spanish monarchs; it also housed a monastery and burial grounds. (See page 496.)

d. No. The Escorial, not Hampton Court, was the palace of the Spanish monarchs. (See page 496.)

17. a. No. Actually the opposite is true; the Treaty of Westphalia sounded the deathknell for the Holy Roman Empire as a true political entity. (See pages 499-501.)

b. Correct. The Treaty to Westphalia, which left political power in the hands of more than 300 local rulers, gave the *coup de grâce* to the Holy Roman Empire as a viable state. (See pages 499-501.)

c. No. The recognition of Catholicism and Lutheranism had been effected by the Religious Peace of Augsburg in 1555. The Catholics had attempted to reimpose it, but the Treaty of Westphalia also recognized Calvinism. (See pages 499-501.)

d. No. The recognition of the independence of the United Provinces of the Netherlands was one of the provisions of the Treaty of Westphalia. (See pages 499-501.)

18. a. No. Las Casas was the Spanish bishop who advocated the introduction of African slaves into the New World. (See pages 517-20.)

b. No. James I was the Catholic monarch of Scotland and later England. (See pages 518-20.)

c. No. Calvin, although he did have a rather pessimistic view of mankind, believed quite strongly in God and was not a skeptic. (See pages 518-20 and Chapter 14.)

d. Correct. Michel de Montaigne, in his writings, expressed doubt that total certainty or definitive knowledge is attainable. (See pages 518-20.)

19. a. No. The Church had always had an uneasy stance on the issue of slavery; enslavement of Africans was not strictly forbidden by church law. Las Casas immediately regretted his suggestion. (See pages 517-8.)

b. No. Having witnessed the wholesale death of enslaved Indians and the hardiness of African slaves on the plantations of the Canary Islands, Las Casas believed the Africans better suited to the work and conditions.(See pages 517-8.)

c. No. Having witnessed the wholesale death of enslaved Indians and the hardiness of African slaves on the plantations of the Canary Islands, Las Casas believed the Africans better suited to the work and conditions. (See pages 517-8.)

d. Correct. The Native Americans did not rebel, but suffered terribly under the conditions of slavery. (See pages 517-8.)

20. a. No. Diaz was the first to round the Cape of Good Hope. (See page 503.)

b. No. Prince Henry, although of undeniable importance to the Age of Discovery, was not an explorer himself. (See page 503.)

c. Correct. Vasco da Gama, on an expedition in 1497-9, reached India and returned with samples of Indian products, touching off the Portugese conflict with the Muslims for control of this trade. (See page 503.)

d. No. Hernando Cortez was a Spanish, not Portugese, explorer who extended Spanish control in Mexico. (See pages 503, 510.)

21. a. No. Elizabethan refers to the literature produced during the reign of Elizabeth I in England (1558-1603.) (See pages 520-3.)

b. No. Jacobean refers to the literature produced during the reign of James I in England (1603-1625.) (See pages 520-3.)

c. No. Skepticism was a school of thought based on doubt that absolute certainty can be attained; it was not an artistic movement. (See pages 518-23.)

d. Correct. The baroque style of art was very emotional and exuberant, reaching the souls of ordinary church-goers. (See pages 521-3.)

22. a. No. Actually the appearance of gunpowder greatly democratized warfare in Europe, a person's social status was of little concern to a bullet or cannonball. (See page 487.)

b. Correct. As gunpowder tended to have a democratizing effect, it weakened the idea of warfare as an ennobling affair. (See page 487.)

c. No. The appearance of gunpowder had little impact on the necessity of governments' use of propaganda; the size of wars at the time, however, did demand a greater marshaling of resources, entailing the use of propaganda. (See page 487.)

d. No. Actually the introduction of gunpowder (along with muskets and cannons) fundamentally altered the nature of warfare up to modern times. (See page 487.)

23. a. No. The ten southern provinces, known as the Spanish Netherlands, would become the present-day Belgium; the present-day Netherlands emerged from the United Provinces. (See page 491.)
b. No. Bohemia is the heartland of present-day Czech Republic in central Europe and is not part of the geographical area known as the Netherlands. (See page 491.)
c. Correct. Present-day Belgium was once the Spanish Netherlands, eventually gaining their independence from Spain in the late eighteenth century. (See page 491.)
d. No. Schleswig is a German-speaking province located at the base of the Danish peninsula, not part of the Netherlands. (See page 491.)

24. a. Correct. The Thirty Years' War ravaged Germany so much that it was described as the "sand pit" of Europe; it was greatly depopulated by this conflict. (See pages 498-502.)
b. No. Although France did compete in the last stage of the Thirty Years' War, very little fighting actually took place in France. (See pages 499-502.)
c. No. Although some fighting did occur in eastern Europe, the vast majority of the war was waged elsewhere. (See pages 499-502.)
d. No. Spain was allied with the Holy Roman Empire in this conflict, but very little actual fighting took place in Spain. (See pages 499-502.)

25. a. No. The concept of slavery was already well-known to the Europeans long before the Turks captured Constantinople. (See page 516.)
b. No. The fall of Constantinople ended the flow of white, not black, slaves into Europe. (See page 516.)
c. Correct. With the fall of Constantinople, Europeans were forced to look to Africa to supply their demand for slaves. (See page 516.)
d. No. Slaves were exported to the "Indies," that is the West Indies, but were not exported from the Indies. (See page 516.)

1.   a.   No. Although mercantilism certainly was geared to the international competition rampant in Europe it was an economic system, not a military system. (See pages 539-41.)
      b.   Correct. One of the major components of mercantilism -- along with the importance of gold and silver bullion and land -- was a favorable balance of trade. (See pages 539-41.)
      c.   No. All of the European countries, France included, practiced mercantilism; in France the finance minister Colbert gave his name to the system of Colbertism. (See pages 539-41.)
      d.   No. Mercantilism was an economic system in which state power was measured in bullion reserves, balance of trade and agricultural wealth. (See pages 539-41.)

2.   a.   No. French peasants tended to be Catholic, not Protestant, which was an urban religion. (See page 541.)
      b.   No. Louis XIV was a devout Catholic; further, there was no power behind the throne after the dismissal of Cardinal Mazarin. (See page 541.)
      c.   No. Actually the French Protestants added greatly to the wealth of France. (See page 541.)
      d.   Correct. As in other areas where Protestantism had become popular, it was adopted by successful business people. (See page 541 and Chapter 14.)

3.   a.   Correct. By leaving Spain to his French heir, thus making possible the union of the French and Spanish crowns, Charles II had endangered the balance of power in Europe. (See page 545.)
      b.   No. Naming a Spanish heir to the throne would not have endangered the European balance of power and thus not have resulted in the War of the Spanish Succession. (See page 545.)
      c.   No. Eugene of Savoy was a leader of the allied opposition to France during the war. (See page 545.)
      d.   No. The war resulted from the threatened union of the French and Spanish crowns brought on by Charles II's naming of his French heir to the Spanish throne. (See page 545.)

4.   a.   No. Although London would become the financial and commercial capital of Europe in the eighteenth century, it did not have that honor in the seventeenth century. (See pages 556-9.)
      b.   No. Hamburg was a rich and important city but never the financial and commercial capital of Europe. (See pages 556-9.)
      c.   No. Paris was a very important urban center but never the financial and commercial capital of Europe. (See pages 556-9.)
      d.   Correct. Amsterdam, reflecting the wealth of the Netherlands during the seventeenth century, was the financial and commercial capital of Europe. (See pages 556-9.)

5.   a.   No. Despite the large and prosperous middle class, England was not the most centered on middle-class interests. (See pages 555-9.)
      b.   No. The Spanish middle class was quite small, hence Spain was not the most middle-class country in Europe. (See pages 555-9.)
      c.   No. While France did have a substantial middle class, the concerns of the aristocracy and royalty dominated the state. (See pages 555-9.)
      d.   Correct. With the prodigious wealth enjoyed by the Netherlands - even their workers were the highest paid in Europe - middle-class interests dominated the state. (See pages 555-9.)

6.   a.   Correct. James II was a staunch Catholic and believer in divine-right kingship; it was the production of male heir, presumably to be raised Catholic, which sparked the Glorious Revolution. (See pages 553-4.)
      b.   No. Oliver Cromwell was the ruler of England under the Commonwealth, running England more like a military dictatorship; he was a Protestant and tolerant of all religions except Roman Catholicism. (See pages 552-4.)

c.   No. Archbishop Laud had been supported by James I and Charles I before the English Civil War; while not Catholic, Laud was believed to be trying to lead the English back to Catholicism. (See pages 551-4.)
d.   No. William III had been invited, along with his wife Mary, to replace James II; William was a Dutch Protestant. (See pages 553-4.)

7. a.   No. In an absolutist state, sovereignty is vested in the monarch alone; representative assemblies, in theory, have no place. (See pages 531-2.)
b.   No. As with the case of sovereignty, accountability was to the monarch and no one else, despite the use by these monarchs of middle-class bureaucrats. (See pages 531-2.)
c.   No. In an absolutist state sovereignty is vested in the monarch alone; supression or cooptation of the aristocracy is very often a hallmark of absolutist states. (See pages 531-2.)
d.   Correct. In the struggle for political supremacy with internal and external foes, absolutist monarchs raised and kept standing armies, to free themselves from feudal restraints. (See pages 531-2.)

8. a.   No. Despite stop-gap solutions, the French government was never able to solve its chronic financial shortcomings. (See pages 534-6.)
b.   Correct. Richelieu's highly effective centralized adminstration, with its *intendants* and *généralités*, was the crowning achievement of his career. (See pages 534-6.)
c.   No. Actually Richelieu believed that Protestantism often served as a cloak for political intrigues; he suppressed the Huguenots. (See pages 534-6.)
d.   No. Richelieu's clerical status notwithstanding, the French Catholic Church had been allied with the state since Francis I's signing of the Concordat of Bologna in 1516. His foreign policy precluded Rome's support. (See pages 534-6 and Chapter 13.)

9. a.   Correct. This quotation implies total royal jurisdiction and formed the intellectual foundation for Stuart divine-right absolutism. (See page 549.)
b.   No. The Stuart monarchs did not care much for constitutionalism; the quotation implies total royal jurisdiction over every aspect of life. (See page 549.)
c.   No. The English Parliament of the seventeenth century would never have considered the idea of democracy; the quotation was uttered by James I as he lectured the House of Commons. (See page 549.)
d.   No. Constitutionalism implies constraints upon the power of governmental institutions; the quotation implies royal jurisdiction with no constraints whatsoever. (See pages 549.)

10. a.   No. Actually the Long Parliament (1640-1660), reacting to the Charles I's arbitrary and despotic measures, enacted legislation that limited the power of the monarch. (See page 551.)
b.   No. Parliament tended to be dominated by men with Protestant, even Puritan, leanings and opposed the efforts of Archbishop Laud and Charles I to further, seemingly, Catholicism. (See page 551.)
c.   No. Actually the English Civil War was fought between the King and his supporters and Parliament and its supporters. (See page 551.)
d.   Correct. Responding to Charles I's arbitrary and despotic policies, the Long Parliament enacted legislation designed to limit the power of the monarch. (See page 551.)

11. a.   No. Parliament had written a constitution for the new state, but Cromwell tore it up. (See page 552.)
b.   No. Democracy was a form of government that no one, in the seventeenth century, would consider instituting. (See page 552.)
c.   Correct. Cromwell used his New Model Army to regulate the English state, in almost all aspects of life. (See page 552.)

d.   No. Though some of Cromwell's policies were similar to those of absolutist monarchs, Cromwell's government did not have a royal personage empowered with executive authority. (See page 552.)

12.   a.   No. Creation and control of royal standing armies was a typical tactic of absolutizing monarchs. (See pages 532, 537-8.)
b.   No. State bureaucracies, such as the one created by Richelieu, were instrumental in reducing the local power bases of the nobility. (See pages 534-8.)
c.   No. Absolutizing monarchs were not reluctant to use their coercive powers to control rebellious nobles; Louis XIV's requirement that nobles spend part of the year at Versailles was coercive. (See pages 537-8.)
d.   Correct. Although monarchs did attempt to control religious groups in their states, this effort was, by this time, more directed at the middle classes than the nobility, as the example of the compromise over the Canal of Two Seas indicates. (See pages 541, 537-8.)

13.   a.   No. Long a symbol of aristocratic independence, Richelieu had many nobles' castles leveled. (See pages 534-6.)
b.   No. Richelieu crushed aristocratic conspiracies ruthlessly, as in the case of the duke of Montmorency. (See pages 534-6.)
c.   No. Although a few nobles held important offices, by far the majority of the state's officials were members of the middle class or minor nobility. (See pages 534-6.)
d.   Correct. Actually Richelieu introduced the institution of *intendants* (building on the work of Philip Augustus); these state-appointed officials held wide-ranging powers over the locality they administered. (See pages 534-6.)

14.   a.   No. Although Louis XIV had established a permanent standing army, it was not spread across the countryside of France to prevent aristocratic rebellion. (See pages 537-9.)
b.   Correct. In his attempt to control the French nobility, physically and psychologically, Louis forced the nobles to spend some part of each year at Versailles. (See pages 537-90.)
c.   No. Louis did not visit his nobility, they were required to visit him; Louis was able to keep close tabs on them through his secret police, army of informers and practice of opening mail. (See pages 537-9.)
d.   No. Even though some members did meet in their local assemblies, Louis did not force the nobles to participate in a national assembly, which had not met since 1614. (See pages 537-9.)

15.   a.   No. Crucial to the success of Louis XIV as an absolute monarch, both domestically and politically, was his establishment of a modern standing army, complete with standardized weapons and uniforms. (See pages 536-7.)
b.   No. Part of the military reforms of Louis and his minister of war Le Tellier was the establishment of a commissariat to feed the troops. (See pages 536-7.)
c.   Correct. As part of the reforms of Louis and Le Tellier, the French army even had an ambulance corps to care for the wounded. (See pages 536-7.)
d.   No. Critical to the maintenance of a permanent standing army was the institution of a rational system of recruitment, training and promotion. (See pages 536-7.)

16.   a.   No. Actually, by the terms of the Peace of Utrecht, the British Empire expanded greatly. (See pages 539-40.)
b.   Correct. As the War of the Spanish Succession was the result of the danger to the balance of power, the peace of Utrecht also represented this principle, setting limits to which any one power could expand. (See pages 539-40.)
c.   No. In reality, the treaty completed the decline of Spain from Great Power status. (See pages 539-40.)

d.   No. The Peace of Utrecht actually marked the end of French expansionist policy (for a few decades); Louis's 35-year quest for glory had exhausted and nearly bankrupted France. (See pages 539-40.)

17.   a.   Correct. The lack of any real administrative and economic base, coupled with the decadence of the Habsburg dynasty, caused Spain to fall from the ranks of the Great Powers. (See page 543.)
b.   No. If anything, industry and trade underwent contractions not overexpansion. (See pages 543.)
c.   No. Even though slavery was the prevalent form of labor in the Spanish colonies, this did not cause the decline of the absolutist state. (See pages 543.)
d.   No. The Spanish middle class rather than growing was actually lacking, a situation aggravated by the expulsion of the Jews. (See pages 543.)

18.   a.   Correct. The Scottish revolt sparked by Laud's attempt to impose the *Book of Common Prayer* on the fiercely Congregationalist Scots lead to the English Civil War. (See page 551.)
b.   No. Laud's attempt to impose the *Book of Common Prayer* on the fiercely Congregationalist Scots sparked a revolt which would eventually lead to the English Civil War. (See page 551.)
c.   No. Rather than ignore it, Laud's attempt to impose the *Book of Common Prayer* on the fiercely Congregationalist Scots sparked a revolt which would lead eventually to the English Civil War. (See page 551.)
d.   No. The Scottish revolt sparked by Laud's attempt to impose the *Book of Common Prayer* on the fiercely Congregationalist Scots would eventually lead to the English Civil War. (See page 551.)

19.   a.   No. Thomas Hobbes in his *Leviathan* had argued that sovereignty derived from the people who transferred it to the monarch by implicit contract; the monarch then had absolute power. (See pages 552, 554.)
b.   No. William of Orange was not a political theorist but the Protestant husband of Mary who had been invited by Parliament to assume the throne abdicated by James II. (See pages 553-4.)
c.   Correct. Locke, in his *Second Treatise on Civil Government*, argued that men set up civil government in order to protect life, liberty and property; later paraphrased by Jefferson in the Declaration of Independence. (See page 554.)
d.   No. Edmund Burke was a conservative political theorist who criticized the French Revolution; he did not maintain that government's sole function was to protect life, liberty and property. (page 554 and Chapter 21.)

20.   a.   No. Having thrown off an absolutist government, the United Provinces instituted a relatively weak government. (See pages 554-6.)
b.   No. Although the provincial estates held virtually all power, the federal assembly handled matters of foreign affairs but did not possess sovereign authority. (See pages 554-6.)
c.   Correct. After winning independence, the United Provinces were governed by strong local Estates with a weak federal Estate. (See pages 554-6.)
d.   No. The United Provinces were ruled by strong local assemblies which were dominated by wealthy merchants; democracy was not considered. (See pages 554-6.)

21.   a.   Correct. All of these aspects -- fishing, world trade, and banking -- contributed to the vast wealth of the Netherlands. (See pages 556-7.)
b.   No. The economy of Spain, not the Netherlands, was based on the exploitation of Peruvian silver mines. (See pages 556-7 and Chapter 15.)
c.   No. Although the Netherlands was famous for some of their exports (diamonds and linens from Holland, pottery from Delft), the Dutch economy was based primarily on fishing, transport and banking. (See pages 556-7.)

d. No. Actually the Calvinism of the Dutch looked favorably on successful businessmen, based on the concept that all callings have merit in God's eyes and that success is a sign of election to receive salvation. (See pages 556-7.)

22. a. Correct. The wars with France and England in the 1670s hurt the economy; the War of the Spanish Succession was a costly drain on manpower and finances; the peace marked the beginning of Dutch economic decline. (See page 559.)
b. No. The Dutch East India Company did involve the Dutch in imperialistic exploitation of parts of East Asia and Latin America, but with great success. (See pages 537-9.)
c. No. Actually the practice of religious toleration attracted many talented individuals and much money to the Dutch cities. (See pages 556-9.)
d. No. The adoption of Calvinism was natural for the successful middle classes of the Netherlands and Calvinism reinforced their quest for business success. (See pages 556-9.)

23. a. No. Walpole served after the Glorious Revolution, which marked the end of absolutism in England. (See page 554.)
b. No. Under Walpole the practice of a cabinet which worked with and was responsible to Parliament developed. (See page 554.)
c. No. The *stadholder* was an executive office in the Netherlands, not England. (See page 554.)
d. Correct. With the supremacy of Parliament after the Glorious Revolution, the idea that the cabinet should be responsible to Parliament developed. (See page 554.)

24. a. No. London's river is the Thames, not the Amstel. (See page 556.)
b. Correct. The Amstel River was Amsterdam's link with its world trading system. (See page 556.)
c. No. Paris's river in the Seine, not the Amstel. (See page 556.)
d. No. Amiens would become an important industrial city in France in the nineteenth century; it was not served by the Amstel River. (See page 556.)

25. a. Correct. Cervantes's masterpiece *Don Quixote* chronicled the misadventures of an idealistic and impractical soldier, who has been said to represent declining Spain. (See page 548.)
b. No. *Tartuffe*, a satire on religious hypocrisy, was written by the French classicist Molière. (See pages 542-3, 548.)
c. No. *Te Deums* are religious hymns of thanksgiving, traditionally composed and performed to commemorate great events, such as those composed by M.-A. Charpentier for Louis XIV. (See pages 542, 548.)
d. No. *Phèdre* was one on the tragic dramas written by the French playwright Jean Racine. (See pages 542-3, 548.)

Chapter 17

1. a. No. The Mongol invasion and conquest of the Kievan state was critical for the political future of the Russians, but the Mongols were not the first to unify them. (See pages 000.)
b. No. The Turks would have a great deal of impact on the future of the Russian state, but never ruled it. (See pages 000.)
c. No. The Romanov dynasty ruled Russia from the end of the Time of Troubles in 1613 until the Russian Revolution in 1917. (See pages 000.)
d. Correct. In the ninth century, in the quest for international trade, the Vikings moved into the Slavic lands and declared themselves the rulers of the eastern Slavs. (See pages 000.)

2. a. No. Royal monopolization of most aspects of economic activity actually retarded the rise of urban capitalists, a development with profound implications for the future. (See page 580.)
b. No. Cossacks were runaway serfs who joined together in free groups and outlaw armies. (See page 580.)
c. Correct. The Tsar's monopolization of most aspects of economic activity contrasted sharply with the West and had profound implications for the future. (See page 580.)
d. No. The Tsar's monopolization of most aspects of economic activity contrasted sharply with the West and had profound implications for the future. (See page 580.)

3. a. No. Peasants did not really even control their own small strip of land much less the law courts. (See pages 565-8.)
b. No. Unlike the western monarchs that had established royal legal systems, the eastern rulers had been unable to curtail the manorial courts. (See pages 565-8.)
c. No. Church courts were limited to jurisdiction over clerical matters and canon law. (See pages 565-8.)
d. Correct. The dispensation (and control of justice) by the noble landowning class was one aspect of the dominant position of the nobility in eastern Europe. (See pages 565-8.)

4. a. Correct. Brandenburg, the core of the Hohenzollern's lands, is located in the north European plain, without natural frontiers and poor land, mostly swamp and sand; the quote also refers to its general weakness. (See page 572)
b. No. Although Hungary was ruled by the Habsburgs, the traditional emperors of the Holy Roman Empire, it was not part of the Empire. (See pages 571-2.)
c. No. Sweden was not part of the Holy Roman Empire. (See page 572.)
d. No. Even though the ruler of Austria was usually the Holy Roman Emperor, Austria, located in southern Germany, was not referred to as the "sandbox," a region in north-central Germany. (See page 572.)

5. a. No. Ivan IV, the Terrible, conquered the khanates of Kazan and Astrakhan, adding new territories to Russia and crushing the remnants of Mongol power. (See pages 579-80.)
b. No. Little aroused fear in Ivan the Terrible; in an awe-inspiring ceremony he had himself crowned Tsar at age 16. (See pages 579-80.)
c. Correct. Ivan the Terrible completed the monopolization of most economic activity, which had profound implications for the future of Russia. (See pages 579-80.)
d. No. The process of transforming the nobility into a service nobility was completed by Ivan the Terrible. (See pages 579-80.)

6. a. Correct. One feature of Peter's "westernization" of Russia was the compulsory education for young, male nobles away from their home. (See page 584.)
b. No. Under Peter, Russian serfdom became even harsher, with higher taxes and arbitrary assignments to work in government-owned mines and factories, or in the construction of Saint

Petersburg. (See pages 584-5.)

c. No. The establishment of a merit-system bureaucracy, the Table of Ranks, was perhaps the greatest of Peter's innovations. (See page 584.)

d. No. Peter I was an autocrat; he would never have created an independent parliment; even though the idea of "state interest" was introduced, Peter decided what that interest was. (See pages 584-5.)

7. a. No. Gothic art had expressed the spirit of the High Middle Ages and had long since been supplanted. (See pages 585-6 and Chapter 11.)

b. No. Romanticism is an artistic movement of the late eighteenth and nineteenth centuries. (See pages 585-6 and Chapter 23.)

c. No. Impressionism is an artistic movement of the second half of the nineteenth century. (See pages 585-6 and Chapter 25.)

d. Correct. Baroque, growing out of the Catholic reformation, attested to the power and confidence of absolute rulers, employing line and color to evoke drama and emotion. (See pages 585-6.)

8. a. No. *Boyars* were the hereditary nobles in Russia, not Prussia. (See pages 572, 579.)

b. Correct. The *Junkers*, who dominated the estates of Brandenberg and Prussia, were land-owning nobles. (See page 572.)

c. No. The Vikings were the raiders from Scandinavia who had terrorized Europe in the eighth and ninth centuries and founded the Kievan state in the ninth century. (See page 572 and Chapter 8.)

d. No. Elector was the title of the ruler of Brandenburg which referred to his position as one of the seven electors who chose the emperor. (See page 572.)

9. a. Correct. The stronger political position of the eastern nobility, increased at the expense of the ruling monarchs, made it difficult to resist the nobility's demands regarding serfdom. (See pages 566-7.)

b. No. Actually the economic argument does not seem true, as the same set of economic factors led to the virtual disappearance of serfdom in the west. (See pages 566-7.)

c. No. The stronger political position of the eastern nobility, increased at the expense of the ruling monarchs, made it difficult to resist the nobility's demands regarding serfdom. (See pages 566-7.)

d. No. The stronger political position of the eastern nobility, increased at the expense of the ruling monarchs, made it difficult to resist the nobility's demands regarding serfdom. (See pages 566-7.)

10. a. No. Peter did enlist the Cossacks in his army, as a special unit, but they were not ennobled *en masse*. (See pages 580, 584.)

b. Correct. Reacting to the increasing demands of the service nobility, many Russian peasants fled southward, joining to form free groups and outlaw armies. (See page 580.)

c. No. Reacting to the increasing demands of the service nobility, many Russian peasants fled southward, joining to form free groups and outlaw armies. (See page 580.)

d. No. The Turks did rule part of southern Russia, but troops did not settle there; with the increased demands of the service nobility, many Russian peasants fled southward, forming free groups and outlaw armies. (See page 580.)

11. a. No. The conflict did begin over Habsburg attempts to suppress Protestants, but after the defeat at White Mountain the Bohemian nobility was decimated, the survivors fled into exile. (See page 568.)

b. Correct. After the defeat of the native nobility at White Mountain, Emperor Ferdinand II rewarded the motley crew of aristocratic soldiers of fortune with the confiscated lands. (See page 568.)

c. No. Actually conditions for the Bohemian peasantry worsened, as labor dues and taxes both increased. (See page 568.)

d. No. The Battle of White Mountain decimated the Bohemian nobility; the survivors fled into exile. (See page 568.)

12. a. No. After the Thirty Years' War, the Habsburgs, having suppressed Bohemia and then centralized Austria, turned their attention to the consolidation within their state, not Northern Italy. (See pages 569-72.)

b. No. The Thirty Years' War had destroyed the authority of the Holy Roman Emperor; as a result the Habsburgs turned inward and eastward. (See pages 569-72.)

c. Correct. After the Thirty Years' War, the Habsburgs, having suppressed Bohemia and then centralized Austria, turned to the consolidation of their position in Hungary, the third major part of their holdings. (See pages 569-72.)

d. No. After the Thirty Years' War, the Habsburgs, having suppressed Bohemia and then centralized Austria, turned to the consolidation of their position in own state. (See pages 569-72.)

13. a. No. As a consequence of the very real threat posed by the Turks, the Magyar nobles were able to manoeuver between the Turks and the Austrians, maintaining a great deal of autonomy. (See pages 571-2.)

b. Correct. By a combination of fierce nationalism, strong Protestantism and often allying with the Turks, the Magyar nobility was able to retain a great deal of autonomy. (See pages 571-2.)

c. No. Never decisively triumphant, the Hungarian nobility, by virtue of their strong Protestant faith, frequent alliances with the Turks and their nationalism, was able to retain considerable autonomy. (See pages 571-2.)

d. No. The retention of considerable autonomy, especially when one considers the fate of the Bohemian nobles after their revolt, is hardly inconclusive. (See pages 571-2.)

14. a. No. Peter the Great was the Russian tsar, not the ruler of Prussia. (See pages 574-5, 582-3.)

b. Correct. Frederick William I, with his mania for tall soldiers and militaristic disposition, was called "the Soldier's King." Building upon the work of Frederick William the Great Elector, he was responsible for the establishment of much of the structure of Prussian absolutism. (See pages 574-5.)

c. No. Ivan IV was a Russian tsar, not a Prussian king. (See pages 574-5, 579-81.)

d. No. Elector Frederick III was the father of Frederick William I; his claim to fame was gaining the title of king but otherwise did little to advance absolutism in Prussia. (See pages 574-5.)

15. a. No. The Vikings had long since been assimilated into the native Russian population by the time the Moscow princes asserted their dominance. (See pages 576-8.)

b. No. Although the rulers of Muscovy, such as Ivan IV, did make strategic marriages, this was not the crucial factor in their emergence as the dominant princes in Muscovy. (See pages 576-8.)

c. Correct. The princes of Moscow were able to consolidate their position by serving the Mongol Khan and eventually establishing their independence. (See pages 576-8.)

d. No. The House of Ruiruk had long since been eclipsed as an important element in the political process. (See pages 576-8.)

16. a. No. France was much too far from Russia to be an external threat at this time. (See pages 576-8.)

b. Correct. The Russian monarchy developed during the period known by the term "Mongol Yoke"; the princes of Moscow were able to consolidate their position by serving the Khan and eventually establishing their independence. (See pages 576-8.)

    c.   No. Actually the Prussian monarchy developed after the Russian. (See pages 574-5, 576-8.)

    d.   No. England was much too far from Russia to be an external threat at this time. (See pages 576-8.)

17.   a.   Correct. After the disruptive reign of Ivan the Terrible, who had killed his only son in a fit of demonic rage, Russia was engulfed in the chaotic Time of Troubles, brought on by the disrupted succession. (See pages 580-1.)

    b.   No. The Turks did not cause the Time of Troubles; which was the result of the disrupted succession after Ivan the Terrible. (See pages 569-71, 580-1.)

    c.   No. The Mongols did not cause the Time of Troubles; which was the result of the disrupted succession after Ivan the Terrible. (See pages 580-1.)

    d.   No. The Time of Troubles was not caused by crop failures but the disrupted succession after Ivan the Terrible's death. (See pages 580-1.)

18.   a.   Correct. Crucial to Peter's modernization of the Russian military and civilian bureaucracy was his resurrection of the concept of "service nobility" by which the Russian nobility was made to serve the state, for life. (See pages 584-5.)

    b.   No. Peter established a fleet in the Baltic Sea, but without a port on the Atlantic, he did not establish an Atlantic fleet. (See pages 584-5.)

    c.   No. Quite the contrary, Peter knew he needed talented people and recruited them wherever he could find them, including foreigners and even commoners. (See pages 584-5.)

    d.   No. Peter was the focus of both civilian and military power, being the absolute autocrat of Russia. (See pages 584-5.)

19.   a.   No. The peasants were certainly losers in the development of east European absolutism but they were not alone. (See pages 566-8.)

    b.   Correct. With the so-called "second enserfment" and the subjugation and repression of the towns, the peasantry and the middle classes were the clear losers. (See pages 566-8.)

    c.   No. Although the nobility did concede (or have taken from them) their political position in the state, they retained broad local powers. (See pages 566-8.)

    d.   No. Although the nobility did concede (or have taken from them) their political position in the state, they retained broad local powers; the clergy continued to exercise influence and own many serfs. (See pages 566-8.)

20.   a.   No. Rakoczy did lead a Hungarian revolt against the Habsburgs in 1703 but did not besiege Vienna. (See page 570.)

    b.   No. Actually the Russians were allied with the Austrians and attacked the invading forces as they retreated from Vienna. (See page 570.)

    c.   Correct. The Turks and the Austrians were bitter enemies; in 1683 they besieged Vienna in a last attempt to topple the Christian empire. Their defeat started the long decline of the Ottoman Empire. (See page 570.)

    d.   No. The Turks besieged Vienna in a last attempt to topple the Christian empire; their defeat started the long decline of the Ottoman Empire; Frederick William was too involved in the consolidation of his state. (See pages 570, 572-3.)

21.   a.   Correct. The victory at Poltava marked Russia's emergence as a European power while it reduced to Sweden to a second-rate power. (See page 584.)

    b.   No. Although Peter did wage war against the Turks, the Turks were not the Russian foe at Poltava. (See page 584.)

    c.   No. Poltava was the main battle of the Great Northern War, but Russia was not at war with Prussia at that time. (See page 584.)

d.   No. While Russia and Austria would be involved in many battles, Poltava was not one of them. (See page 584.)

22.   a.   Correct. Gothic cathedrals were built during the High Middle Ages, not the age of absolutism. (pages 585-6 and Chapter 11.)
b.   No. The alliance between the baroque and absolutism is exemplified in the paintings of Rubens, with his voluptuous style, and excelled in glorifying monarchs (his paintings of Marie de' Medici are an excellent example.) Royal palaces were also adorned in the baroque style. (See pages 585-6.)
c.   No. Royal cities, such as St. Petersburg, exemplified the power of the monarch. (See pages 585-7.)
d.   No. Royal cities, such as St. Petersburg, usually featured broad, impressive avenues (traversed by speeding carriages) and monumental royal buildings, all designed to exemplify the power of the monarch. (See pages 585-7.)

23.   a.   Correct. After the Battle of White Mountain, in which the native Czech nobility was decimated, Emperor Ferdinand II rewarded his officers (a collection of aristocratic soldiers of fortune) with their lands. (See page 568.)
b.   No. On the contrary, after the Battle of White Mountain and the installation of Habsburg henchmen as the Bohemian nobility, Bohemia was thoroughly subjugated. (See page 568.)
c.   No. After the Battle of White Mountain and the installation of Habsburg henchmen as the Bohemian nobility, Bohemia was thoroughly subjugated. (See page 568.)
d.   No. The Czech revolt had been inspired, in part, by religious concerns; after the revolt had been suppressed (and the Thirty Years' War concluded) Protestantism was wiped out in Bohemia. (See page 568.)

24.   a.   Correct. These were the three main sections; Austria was the ancient home of the Habsburgs; Bohemia and Hungary had been added through fortuitous marriage alliances. (See page 571.)
b.   No. Prussia was part of the patrimony of the Hohenzollerns; Bohemia and Hungary had been added to the Habsburg patrimony through fortuitous marriage alliances. (See page 571.)
c.   No. Brandenburg was part of the patrimony of the Hohenzollerns; Bohemia and Hungary had been added to the Habsburg patrimony through fortuitous marriage alliances. (See page 571.)
d.   No. Silesia was a part of Bohemia which was one of the main components of the Habsburg dynastic state. (See page 571.)

1. a. Correct. Indeed, territorial acquisition, especially her participation in the three partitions of Poland (suggested by Frederick the Great to maintain the balance of power) was perhaps Catherine II's most notable achievement. (See pages 616-9)
   b. No. Catherine II's power was derived from the Russian nobility who put her on the throne and they would not have allowed the abolition of serfdom; whatever personal belief she may have had concerning the emancipation of the serfs was destroyed by the Pugachev Rebellion. (See pages 616-9.)
   c. No. This area was one in which Catherine II acted on her "enlightened" beliefs, although the religious toleration was limited. (See pages 616-9.)
   d. No. Many historians have argued that Catherine's reputation as an enlightened despot derives from her contact with and sympathetic and monetary support (as in the case of Diderot) of the *philosophes*. (See pages 616-9.)

2. a. No. These monarchs were committed to reform, to strengthen their states. (See pages 614-5.)
   b. Correct. Democracy would not become a major factor in Europe until the nineteenth century and in central and eastern Europe, the late nineteenth century; while interested in reform, these monarchs retained power. (See pages 614-5.)
   c. No. Monarchs such as Catherine II and Frederick II were certainly exponents of the cultural values of the Enlightenment, sponsoring education reforms and subsidizing (and of course reading) Enlightenment authors. (See pages 614-5.)
   d. No. Monarchs such as Catherine II and Frederick II ascribed to the belief in the use of Reason to examine the world, a belief which rejected religious authority and was thus very secular. Both were relatively religiously tolerant as well. (See pages 614-5.)

3. a. No. Both of these persons were women and in that age women were generally excluded from such serious professions; Mme. du Châtelet was a notable exception. (See pages 608, 613-4.)
   b. No. As both Geoffrin and Deffand were women, they were excluded from leadership roles in religion. (See pages 613-4.)
   c. Correct. Both Mmes. Geoffrin and Deffand were mistresses of salons where *philosophes* gathered to discuss the new ideas of the day. (See pages 613-4.)
   d. No. Both of these people were women, which obviated their chances to become any type of leader. Further, serf leaders, with notable exceptions such as Pugachev, were anonymous. (See pages 613-4.)

4. a. No. While many of the scientists of the Scientific Revolution had been university professors, the *philosophes* were drawn from all professions of the educated elite. (See pages 607-10.)
   b. No. Most *philosophes* distrusted the people (the workers and the peasants) and put their faith in reform-minded monarchs like Frederick II and Catherine II. (See pages 607-10, 614.)
   c. No. Most *philosophes* viewed religion rather skeptically, and when they did believe in God, it was a detached, aloof "clock-maker" God rather than the "superstitious" God of Catholicism. (See pages 607-10.)
   d. Yes. The *philosophes* attempted to spread the ideas of the Scientific Revolution; because of the censorship in France they resorted to indirect attacks using satire and Aesopian language. (See pages 607-10.)

5. a. No. Upper-class women, rather than being excluded, were critical in the spread of Enlightenment thought through their sponsorship of intellectual salons. (See pages 612-3.)
   b. No. In fact the material improvement of life in the seventeenth and eighteenth centuries reinforced the Enlightenment. (See pages 612-3.)
   c. No. Although government officials participated, people from all professions of the educated

elite participated in the Enlightenment. (See pages 612-3.)

    d.   Correct. Indeed the literature and the conversational style prevalent in the salons of Enlightenment Europe were noted for witty conversation. (See pages 612-3.)

6.   a.   No. Her actions and generous support of the *philosophes* indicates that Catherine II did not believe them dangerous; the *philosophes* were not generally revolutionaries but reformers. (See pages 616-7, 619.)

    b.   No. Catherine II never freed the serfs (this would have to wait until 1861); her reliance on the nobility to retain her throne and the carnage of Pugachev's Rebellion quashed any notion she may have entertained along these lines. (See pages 616-7, 619.)

    c.   Correct. Her acquisition of territory -- Poland, the Caucasus, and other parcels -- was perhaps the greatest accomplishment of her reign. (See pages 616-7, 619.)

    d.   No. Catherine II, like other "enlightened monarchs" believed absolute monarchy to be the best form of government. (See pages 614-7, 619.)

7.   a.   No. Medieval thought placed man, and thus the earth, at the center of God's universe; all other heavenly bodies, including the sun, rotated around the earth. (See pages 595-6.)

    b.   Yes. Medieval thought, buttressed by the Aristotelian view of the universe, placed man and thus the earth at the center of God's creation; all other heavenly bodies rotated around this center. (See pages 595-6.)

    c.   No. Medieval thought placed man and thus the earth at the center of God's universe; all other heavenly bodies, including the moon, rotated around the earth. (See pages 595-6.)

    d.   No. Heaven, according to medieval thought existed beyond the crystal spheres which contained the heavenly bodies; these bodies rotated around the earth, the center of God's universe. (See pages 595-6.)

8.   a.   No. The center of the Aristotelian universe was the earth. (See page 595-6.)

    b.   No. The Aristotelian view fit neatly with Christian theology. (See pages 595-6.)

    c.   No. As the center of the Aristotelian universe, the earth would not have moved. (See pages 595-6.)

    d.   Correct. According to the Aristotelian view, updated by Ptolemy, the planets and stars rotated around the earth in perfect crystal spheres in perfect orbits. (See pages 595-6.)

9.   a.   No. Actually it was just the opposite; the sun-centered universe suggested a universe of enormous size, perhaps infinite. (See pages 596-7.)

    b.   No. Putting the stars at rest - their seeming movement being simply a result of the earth's rotation - Copernicus destroyed the main reason for believing in crystal spheres moving the stars around the earth. (See pages 596-7.)

    c.   No. By characterizing the earth as just another planet, Copernicus destroyed the basic idea of Aristotelian physics: that the earthly world was quite different from the heavenly one. (See pages 596-7.)

    d.   Correct. If in the course of a year the earth moved around the sun and yet the stars appeared fixed, then the universe was unthinkably large, even infinite. (See pages 596-7.)

10.   a.   No. Galileo, although an accomplished mathematician, was famous for his consolidation of the scientific method, not the use of mathematical equations to prove his theories of astronomy. (See pages 597-8.)

    b.   Correct. Johannes Kepler's three Laws of Planetary Motion (based on Brahe's accumulated data) were the first such mathematical equations. (See pages 597-8.)

    c.   No. Brahe was more famous for his observations and collection of data (and his alchemy). (See pages 597-8.)

    d.   No. Newton's synthesis of the Scientific Revolution did indeed contain many mathematical equations, but it was not the first. (See pages 597-600.)

11. a.   Correct. All three of these men advocated systems of belief - the atheism of d'Holbach, the utopianism of Condorcet, and the anti-rationalism of Rousseau - which rejected other belief systems. (See pages 610-1.)
b.   No. Social satire had been an intrinsic feature of the Enlightenment from the beginning. (See pages 610-1.)
c.   No. Actually the late Enlightenment was more hostile to religion, exemplified by d'Holbach's radical atheism. (See pages 610-1.)
d.   No. Enlightenment *philosophes* had early supported absolute monarchs such as Frederick II and Catherine II, but later attempted to limit the absolutist powers of Louis XV. (See pages 610-1.)

12. a.   Correct. Rousseau, somewhat sensitive, came to believe that his *philosophe* friends were plotting against him and broke with them in 1750s; he was passionately devoted to individual freedom, but rejected rationalism in favor of spontaneous emotion. (See page 611.)
b.   No. Voltaire, although sometimes at odds with his contemporaries, was much too rationalistic to have influenced the Romantic movement, which embraced emotion and spontaneity. (See pages 608-9, 611.)
c.   No. Diderot, like Voltaire, was much too rational, too "enlightened" to have influenced the Romantic movement which rejected the "cold" rationalism of the Enlightenment. (See pages 609, 611.)
d.   No. Condorcet's fanciful utopianism was built on a rational view of human progress, not the emotional spontaneity endemic to the Romantic movement. (See page 611.)

13. a.   Correct. The salons of enlightened women, where people from the various elites met, were the breeding grounds of Enlightenment discussion; two of the most famous were those of Mmes. Geoffrin and du Deffand. (See pages 613-4.)
b.   No. Salons, not lecture halls (which tended to be the preserve of conservatives) were the gathering ground to discuss the ideas of the Enlightenment; people from the various elites could meet in a social setting to discuss the newest ideas. (See pages 613-4.)
c.   No. As the Enlightenment was presenting ideas that undermined the authority of French absolutism it would have been unlikely for Versailles to serve as such a gathering ground. (See pages 613-4.)
d.   No. Although Enlightenment *philosophes* could be found at the University of Paris, its relationship with the royal government precluded it becoming such a gathering ground; it would not have been able to gather people from any but the academic elite. (See pages 613-4.)

14. a.   No. Territorial acquisition, usually the result of war, was not considered to be an enlightened policy; further, Frederick II (of Prussia) seized Silesia from the Habsburg Empire. (See pages 615-6.)
b.   Correct. Frederick II was able to fashion an enlightened reputation for himself through such external trappings as poetry-writing; he did improve the life of his subjects, through the reform of the bureaucracy and legal system; he *did not* free the serfs, though. (See pages 615-6.)
c.   No. He did preserve the social and political ascendency of the Prussian nobility, but this was not an Enlightenment concept; indeed, the Enlightenment attacked such artificial inequalities. (See pages 615-6.)
d.   No. After the War of the Austrian Succession (in which he seized the rich province of Silesia) Frederick II tried to avoid war, but had little success until after the Seven Years' War. (See pages 615-6.)

15. a.   Correct. The huge peasant rebellion led by Emelian Pugachev, who claimed to be the

murdered Peter III, effectively destroyed any notion Catherine II may have entertained about freeing the serfs. (See pages 616-7.)

b. No. The Russian urban working class was almost non-existent, and would not become a revolutionary force until the late nineteenth century. (See pages 616-7.)

c. No. Poland would rebel against Russian rule, but not until 1832. (See pages 616-7, 619.)

d. No. This response is fictitious; the rebellion which hardened Catherine's position on serfdom was Pugachev's Rebellion. (See pages 616-7.)

16. a. No. Actually, under the regency of the Duke of Orleans and in subsequent years, the French nobility regained much of its power. (See page 621.)

b. No. Judicial positions remained the preserve of educated elites. (See page 621.)

c. Correct. The debts incurred by Louis XIV in the building of Versailles and his aggressive foreign policy, coupled with the deficiencies of the taxation system, were a severe problem which would continue to worsen throughout the century and was one of the causative factors in the outbreak of the French Revolution. (See pages 621-2.)

d. No. With the death of the Sun King, French absolutism began to recede as the nobility, especially during the regency of the Duke of Orleans, reasserted itself. (See page 621.)

17. a. No. Joseph II was an Austrian emperor, and ruled after that war anyway. (See pages 615, 619.)

b. Correct. Determined to rebel against his dead father and to expand his state, Frederick II of Prussia seized Silesia, setting off the War of the Austrian Succession. (See page 615.)

c. No. While important in establishing Prussian absolutism, Frederick William I rarely used his army; he was the father of Frederick II who did seize Silesia. (See page 615, and Chapter 17.)

d. No. Louis XIV was the great absolute monarch of France. (See page 615 and Chapter 16.)

18. a. No. Hungary was part of the dynastic patrimony of the Habsburgs and thus part of the Habsburg Empire (Austria) and was not partitioned by Prussia, Austria and Russia. (See pages 617-9.)

b. No. Although Sweden had ceased to be a major power, its geographical location protected it from such a partition. (See pages 617-9.)

c. No. Brandenburg was part of the dynastic patrimony of the Hohenzollerns, the ruling house of Prussia and thus not subject to being partitioned. (See pages 617-9.)

d. Correct. The partitions of Poland, suggested by Frederick II to maintain the balance of power threatened by the impending defeat of the Ottoman Empire by Russia, wiped it off the political map of Europe, attesting to the danger of failing to form a centralized government. (See pages 617-9.)

19. a. No. The geocentric theory of the solar system was postulated by Nicolas Copernicus, not Francis Bacon. (See pages 595-6, 602.)

b. No. The notion of logical speculation was the prevailing philosophic trend of medieval scholars. (See page 602.)

c. Correct. Francis Bacon formulated the philosophy of empiricism which is based of the collection of data acquired through observation and experimentation. (See page 602.)

d. No. Bacon was uninterested in mathematical reasoning; analytic geometry was formulated by Rene Descartes. (See page 602.)

20. a. No. Darwin was the mid-nineteenth century biologist responsible for the theory of evolution. (See page 797 and Chapter 24.)

b. No. David Hume was the English philosopher of the late Enlightenment whose carefully argued skepticism was too have a profound long-term influence. (See pages 597, 611.)

c. No. Newton is famous for his synthesis of the Scientific Revolution, not the collection of data. (See pages 597-600.)

d.   Correct. Tycho de Brahe, a wealthy man and alchemist, built a great observatory from which he compiled a massive amount of data; it was left ot his assistant Kepler to utilize this data. (See page 597.)

21.   a.   Correct. The Parlement of Paris served as the high court of France responsible for the registration of laws (ruling on their "constitutionality"); it had been staffed by men of middle-class origins who had subsequently become nobles. (See page 621.)
b.   No. Actually the Parlement of Paris played a key role in the reduction of the absolutist regime in France by their opposition to Louis XV and Louis XVI. (See page 621.)
c.   No. Louis XV and his minister Maupeou had actually abolished the Parlement and banished its ministers to the provinces; when Louis XVI replaced Louis XV, the Parlement was recalled. (See page 621.)
d.   No. Actually the crux of the conflict between the King and the Parlement was the problem of finances and tax reform; the Parlement refused to register various proposals in an attempt to lessen royal power and preserve their tax-exempt status. (See page 621.)

22.   a.   Correct. Despite her devout Catholicism, Maria Theresa (following in the footsteps of many of the monarchs of the High Middle Ages) realized that the influence of the church was detrimental to royal power. (See page 620.)
b.   No. Actually, Maria Theresa, although not averse to needed reforms, detested the Enlightenment, especially its anti-Catholic stance. (See page 620.)
c.   No. Maria Theresa's government attempted to improve the lot of the agrarian population by limiting the power of the lords over the serfs. (See page 620.)
d.   No. Despite the loss of Silesia, Maria Theresa was able to preserve her state during the attempted dismemberment envisioned during the War of the Austrian Succession; she almost succeeded in regaining Silesia in the Seven Years' War. (See page 620.)

23.   a.   No. After the death of Louis XIV France was ruled by a regent, the Duke of Orleans, who supported the position of the nobility *vis-à-vis* the monarchy, thus eroding the power of French absolutism. (See pages 621-2.)
b.   No. Indeed, after the death of the Sun King, the Enlightenment, despite the half-hearted attempts at censorship, flourished. (See pages 621-2.)
c.   Correct. During the regency of the Duke of Orleans, the nobility was able to enhance its power; the growing power and influence of the Parlement of Paris was able to curtail the absolutist power of Louis XV. (See pages 621-2.)
d.   No. Although enlightened absolute monarchs ruled in many places in Europe (Prussia, Austria and Russia, for example) France did not see the emergence of an enlightened absolutist regime. (See pages 621-2.)

24.   a.   Correct. The idea that the world consists of two fundamental entities, the physical and the spiritual, is the core of the school of thought styled Cartesian dualism. (See page 602.)
b.   No. These two, water and air, are elements of the Aristotelian view of the universe. (See page 602.)
c.   No. Reason and passion more closely resemble the competing forces within the human psyche identified by the psychological pioneer Sigmund Freud. (See page 602 and Chapter 28.)
d.   No. Deduction and induction are two types of reasoning; induction was stressed by Francis Bacon (empiricism), deductive reasoning was employed by Descartes, but is not one of the two elements of Cartesian dualism. (See page 602.)

Chapter 19

1.   a.   No. Actually the Dutch population was quite urbanized, which (along with the scarcity of land) forced Dutch agriculture to be very efficient. (See pages 633-4.)
    b.   No. The Dutch would provide examples for the improvement of English agriculture. (See pages 633-4.)
    c.   Correct. The population growth and urbanization of the Netherlands called forth the innovations in Dutch agriculture. (See pages 633-4.)
    d.   No. One of the key features of the so-called Agricultural Revolution was the elimination of the "open-field" system. (See pages 630-1, 633-4.)

2.   a.   Correct. The imbalance between spinning and weaving is indicative of the production bottlenecks that plagued the cottage system. (See pages 642-4.)
    b.   No. With the growth of population and lessened demand for agricultural labor, there was no shortage of labor in the cottage industry. (See pages 642-4.)
    c.   No. Actually it was just the opposite; one of the problems of the industry was the lack of quality control. (See pages 642-4.)
    d.   No. Demand was not lacking; indeed increased demand caused the production bottlenecks that were a problem. (See pages 642-4.)

3.   a.   No. At this time, the Atlantic Economy was booming. (See pages 651-2.)
    b.   No. The eighteenth century saw a vast expansion of the cottage system of textile production. (See pages 642-4.)
    c.   No. The Agricultural Revolution and the enclosure movement had greatly curtailed the amount of common lands and open fields. (See pages 635-6.)
    d.   Correct. The eighteenth century saw both an increase in population and greater productivity in agriculture. (See pages 638-40.)

4.   a.   No. The enclosure movement had the opposite result, with more land available for a fewer number of landowners. (See pages 635-7.)
    b.   No. Actually well-off tenant farmers, often financed by wealthy landowners, were presented with more opportunities. (See pages 635-7.)
    c.   Correct. By 1815 a tiny minority of wealthy landowners in England owned the vast majority of the land, which they leased to tenant farmers. (See pages 635-7.)
    d.   No. Although the landless laborer was not necessarily created by the enclosure movement of the eighteenth century, he nevertheless could not hope to purchase his own farm. (See pages 635-7.)

5.   a.   No. Actually livestock farming was greatly improved with the introduction of scientific methods of breeding. (See pages 631-3.)
    b.   Correct. The elimination of the open-field system was necessary for farmers interested in scientific farming to control their experiments and then increase their productivity. (See pages 631-3.)
    c.   No. Rotation of fields, an ancient practice, was updated and expanded with new crops and longer schedules. (See pages 631-3.)
    d.   No. The use of nitrogen-restoring crops, such as old standbys like peas and beans and newcomers like turnips and potatoes, continued to be employed by European farmers of the eighteenth century. (See pages 631-3.)

6.   a.   Correct. The combination of oppressive landlords, demanding both money and labor, and poor harvests prevented peasants from realizing a profit on their land. (See pages 630-1.)
    b.   No. The plague had disappeared by the eighteenth century, probably as a result of the

A92

migration of the brown rat into Europe. (See pages 630-1, 638-9.)

c.   No. In reality the demands of landlords were quite exacting and drained off any profit the peasantry may have realized. (See pages 630-1.)

d.   No. Even though crop rotation is an ancient method, its use did not prevent the peasants from earning a profit. (See pages 630-1.)

7.   a.   Correct. Mercantilism advocated close state control of and cooperation in the economy. (See pages 645-6.)

b.   No. In England, the view was that state power and personal profit should both be served by mercantilistic policies; in most other states, governmental power was put above the needs of private interests. (See pages 645-6.)

c.   No. Mercantilism, along with close regulation of the economy, also advocated governmental assistance to private industry in order to increase the power of the state. (See pages 645-6.)

d.   No. Mercantilism, on the contrary, was an economic system that featured close government control of the economy. (See pages 645-6.)

8.   a.   Correct. With the population growth and urbanization of these two countries the necessity for increased agricultural efficiency was apparent and met by the adoption of these methods. (See pages 633-5.)

b.   No. Russian agriculture remained unchanged up to the twentieth century. (See pages 631, 633-5.)

c.   No. Agriculture in eastern Europe, as in Russia, remained unaffected by the innovations in western Europe. (See pages 631, 633-5.)

d.   No. These new methods were adopted at on the mainland part of the continent, not Scandinavia. (See pages 631, 633-5.)

9.   a.   No. Urbanization was a key factor in creating a market for commercial farming. (See pages 633-5.)

b.   Correct. The combination of a densely populated, urbanized society and a relatively weak nobility encouraged and allowed Dutch farmers to adopt new techniques and crops. (See pages 633-5.)

c.   No. The openness of both the political and economic structures of the Netherlands enabled the Dutch farmers to innovate freely. (See pages 633-5.)

d.   No. The large, urbanized, and relatively prosperous Dutch population provided a strong market incentive for the adoption of scientific, commercial farming. (See pages 633-5.)

10.   a.   No. Prior to 1700, European population growth was rather slow and erratic, not steady. (See page 637.)

b.   No. Actually population growth was slow and erratic; the age of marriage was not young, being in the upper twenties. (See page 637.)

c.   No. War, famine and disease all contributed to the slow and erratic growth of the European population. (See page 637.)

d.   Correct. Population growth was rather slow and erratic as a result of the cyclical pattern of growth, a factor of subsistence agriculture and demographic crises such as plague or famine. (See page 6373.)

11.   a.   Correct. Medical science did not provide a vaccine against the plague in 1718. (See pages 638-9.)

b.   No. Isolation of carriers of the disease did indeed impede the spread of the disease. (See pages 638-9.)

c.   No. The supplantation of the black rat (the carrier of the flea that carried the bacillus that caused the plague) by the brown rat was crucial to the plague's disappearance from western

Europe. (See pages 638-9.)

d.   No. Government quarantine of ships arriving at Mediterranean ports from the East also helped lessen the incidence of the plague. (See pages 638-9.)

12.   a.   No. France would become England's great rival in the eighteenth century. (See pages 644-7.)

b.   Correct. The Netherlands, with their vast shipping networks and imperial holdings, were the major maritime competitor that the Navigation Acts and even war were aimed at. (See pages 644-7.)

c.   No. Spain had already declined so much by the mid-seventeenth century that she was no major competitor to anyone. (See pages 644-7 and Chapter 16.)

d.   No. Denmark was not England's competition, but another small, rich, northern European state. (See page 644-7.)

13.   a.   Correct. The Seven Years' War was the decisive round in the Anglo-French colonial conflict, with the English emerging as the winners, dominating both North America and India. (See page 647.)

b.   No. Although the war was something of a stalemate in Europe, France lost in the colonial competition with England for dominance in North America and India. (See page 647.)

c.   No. Although the war was something of a stalemate in Europe, France lost in the colonial competition with England for dominance in North America and India. (See page 647.)

d.   No. By the Treaty of Paris (1763), France not only ceded its holdings in North America to England and Spain, but also gave up most of its holdings in India, paving the way for British domination on the subcontinent. (See page 647.)

14.   a.   Yes. The cheapness and availability of land coupled with the very expensive cost of labor inhibited the growth of industry in North America. (See pages 647-51.)

b.   No. Actually, North America was relatively prosperous, based on agriculture and extractive industries. (See pages 647-51.)

c.   No. Most settlers in North America were very industrious, but devoted their energies to agriculture. (See pages 647-51.)

d.   No. Actually North America was a very important market for the manufactured goods of the home country, England. (See pages 647-51.)

15.   a.   Correct. As a result of the cheap land, scarce labor and newly discovered cash crop, tobacco, African slaves were imported into the British colonies in North America to such an extent that by 1774 the ratio was 1:4. (page 000.)

b.   No. As a result of the cheap land, scarce labor and newly discovered cash crop, tobacco, African slaves were imported into the British colonies in North America to such an extent that by 1774 the ratio was 1:4. (page 000.)

c.   No. As a result of the cheap land, scarce labor and newly discovered cash crop, tobacco, African slaves were imported into the British colonies in North America to such an extent that by 1774 the ratio was 1:4. (page 000.)

d.   No. As a result of the cheap land, scarce labor and newly discovered cash crop, tobacco, African slaves were imported into the British colonies in North America to such an extent that by 1774 the ratio was 1:4. (page 000.)

16.   a.   No. The population of the colonies grew rapidly, from both immigration (including slaves) and natural increase. (See pages 647-51.)

b.   No. The British colonies in North America enjoyed the highest standard of living in the world at that time. (See pages 647-51.)

c.   No. The abundance of land and scarcity of labor, coupled with a growing European market, greatly stimulated the growth of slave-based agriculture in this region. (See pages 647-51.)

d.   Correct. Slavery notwithstanding, the colonies exhibited a remarkable degree of economic equality. (See pages 647-51.)

17.   a.   No. British mercantilistic policies did not prevent the exportation of products from England to the continent. (See pages 644-7.)
b.   Correct. Britain's mercantilistic policies were a form of economic warfare aimed at the Netherlands; by the end of the seventeenth century, Dutch shipping and commerce had greatly diminished. (See pages 644-7.)
c.   No. Indeed, the Navigation Acts stipulated that the colonists buy all their European goods through Britain. (See pages 644-7.)
d.   No. The Navigation Acts forced colonial planters to ship their goods on British ships but also guaranteed them a market. (See pages 644-7.)

18.   a.   No. At the time that the new farming methods were being introduced into England, the independent farmer was beginning to disappear. (See pages 635-6.)
b.   Correct. Profit-minded tenant farmers, often well-financed by wealthy landowners, exploited the new agricultural methods to the fullest extent that they could. (See pages 635-6.)
c.   No. Large landowners usually leased their land to tenant farmers; these commercially-minded tenant farmers did use the new methods extensively. (See pages 635-6.)
d.   No. The new agricultural methods required large tracts of land and sizable amounts of money, neither of which were available to small landowning wage laborers, if any existed. (See pages 635-6.)

19.   a.   Correct. The *creoles*, people of Spanish blood who had been born in the New World, dominated both the economic and political systems of Latin America. (See pages 652-4.)
b.   No. The Indians of Latin America were relegated to the role of impoverished peasantry. (See pages 652-4.)
c.   No. *Mestizos*, the offspring of Spanish men and Indian women, comprised the middle group in Latin American society. (See pages 652-4.)
d.   No. The Habsburgs were the ruling dynasty of Austria, not the dominant political and economic group in Latin America. (See pages 652-4.)

20.   a.   No. *Mestizos* were the middle grouping in Latin American society; they did not dominate the economic system. (See pages 652-4.)
b.   Correct. The *creoles*, people of Spanish blood born in the New World, dominated Latin American society. (See pages 652-4.)
c.   No. Mercantilists were people who believed in the economic system of mercantilism; they were not landowners in Latin America. (See pages 652-4.)
d.   No. Warlord is generic term often used to refer to any large landowner in a violent era. (See pages 652-4.)

21.   a.   Correct. Vermuyden was hired by the English to direct large drainage projects in Yorkshire and Cambridgeshire, a process which involved the construction of a large canal, the "Dutch river," to drain the swampy areas. (See page 634.)
b.   No. No doubt many such canals were constructed in the Netherlands, but the novelty required to earn a name such as the "Dutch river" eliminates this response; Vermuyden is representative of the English adoption of Dutch methods. (See page 634.)
c.   No. The novelty of the name "Dutch river" precludes this response; Vermuyden was hired by the English to direct drainage projects which required construction of large drainage canals. (See page 634.)
d.   No. England was the first place to adopt Dutch techniques of land reclamation; Vermuyden had been hired to direct drainage projects in Yorkshire and Cambridgeshire. (See page 634.)

22.   a.   No. France and England would later become colonial and commercial rivals, but France was not the initial target. (See pages 645-7.)
       b.   No. By the time of the Navigation Acts, Spain had already become a second-rate power and was not the target of these mercantilistic measures. (See pages 645-7.)
       c.   No. Actually, it was believed that the Navigation Acts would help the American colonists by providing a guaranteed market for their products. (See pages 645-7.)
       d.   Correct. The wealthy Dutch, with their extensive shipping, commercial, banking and imperial networks, were the initial target of the Navigation Acts. (See pages 645-7.)

23.   a.   No. The *asiento* refers to the monopoly on the West African slave trade, not the Isthmus of Panama. (See pages 646-7.)
       b.   No. The *asiento* refers to the monopoly on the West African slave trade, not Nova Scotian fishing rights. (See pages 646-7.)
       c.   No. The *asiento* refers to the monopoly on the West African slave trade, not Mexico. (See pages 646-7.)
       d.   Correct. As a result of the Peace of Utrecht, Spain was forced to cede the very lucrative *asiento* to England, adding greatly to England's dominant position in world trade. (See pages 646-7.)

24.   a.   No. Actually France was forced to cede Louisiana to Spain. (See page 647.)
       b.   No. Although Spain did receive Louisiana, this was compensation for the loss of Florida; she did not regain the *asiento*. (See page 647.)
       c.   Correct. Even though the war in Europe was a stalemate, England was able to emerge from it as the dominant colonial power, having secured North America and India. (See page 647.)
       d.   No. Actually the Navigation Acts were not seriously modified until after 1786; indeed, free trade rights were one of the causes of the American Revolution. (See page 647, and Chapter 21.)

25.   a.   Correct. Part of the mercantilistic Navigation Acts assured the colonial planters a market for their products in the mother country, which also aided in the retention of a favorable balance of trade. (See pages 645-7.)
       b.   No. Actually colonial producers in the British Empire had exclusive rights to the home market. (See pages 645-7.)
       c.   No. Mercantilism tried to avoid importing such products; colonies were used to supply the mother country with raw materials and agricultural products. (See pages 645-7.)
       d.   No. Although English merchants could send one shipload of goods to the Spanish colonies, the English market for such goods was the preserve of producers from within the British empire. (See pages 645-7.)

1.   a.   No. There was no lack of meat for rich Europeans; poor Europeans, the vast majority, however were not so fortunate. (See pages 671-4.)
     b.   Correct. Europeans of all classes suffered from insufficient consumption of fruits and vegetables. (See pages 671-4.)
     c.   No. For most Europeans bread was a staple of their diet, especially for poorer Europeans; however white bread lacks much of the nutritional content of whole grain breads; insufficient consumption of white bread was not a problem. (See pages 671-4.)
     d.   No. Most Europeans, especially the rich, were able to consume as much wine as was good for them. (See pages 671-4.)

2.   a.   No. A nuclear family consists of the two parents and the immediate offspring. (See page 661.)
     b.   No. A conjugal family consists of the two parents and their immediate offspring. (See page 661.)
     c.   No. The industrial family is sometimes a term synonymous with nuclear family, that is, the parents and their children. (See page 661.)
     d.   Correct. The extended family, described by this question, was once believed to be the prevailing family institution in pre-industrial Europe; modern research has proven this wrong. (See page 661.)

3.   a.   No. In some areas of Europe, couples needed the approval of the landlord or local noble to get married, in Austria and Germany there were legal restrictions well into the nineteenth century. (See pages 661-2.)
     b.   Correct. Marriage was controlled by both law and custom as well as the desires of parents. (See pages 661-2.)
     c.   No. Prior to 1750, no doubt some marriages were based on romantic love, but the vast majority certainly considered more mundane aspects, such as the dowry. (See pages 661-2.)
     d.   No. Indeed the relatively late age of marriage was the result of the couple waiting until they could support a family. (See pages 661-2.)

4.   a.   No. Actually, the bubonic plague had virtually disappeared from Europe by the early eighteenth century. (See pages 666-7 and Chapter 19.)
     b.   No. While foundling hospitals did deal with children, their purpose was not related to the treatment of smallpox. (See pages 666-7.)
     c.   Correct. With the increase in illegitimate births, many infants were being abandoned or killed and the foundling hospitals were established to take care of these children. (See pages 666-7.)
     d.   No. Rich women had other sources, such as expensive midwives and doctors, and did not need to rely on the charity of the foundling hospitals. (See pages 666-7.)

5.   a.   No. Indeed indifference and brutality were quite common in the attitude and behavior of parents, a result of the appalling infant mortality rates. (See pages 667-8.)
     b.   No. In the their need for labor, early English factory owners were provided with cheap labor in the form of pauper children by English authorities. (See pages 667-8 and Chapter 22.)
     c.   Correct. Doctors, like everyone else, urged parents to avoid becoming emotionally attached to their children, who were so unlikely to survive. (See pages 667-8.)
     d.   No. Infanticide by parents had decreased greatly, but abandonment had replaced it and was so common that foundling hospitals were set up to alleviate the problem; wet nursing was so deadly that it was called a "putting-out industry of death". (See pages 667-8.)

6.   a.   No. Actually medical science, despite the promise of Enlightenment principles in the medical

profession, was of little help in improving the health of Europeans in the eighteenth century. (See pages 674-9.)

b. Correct. The medical profession, with few exceptions such as that achieved by surgeons and in the singular case of the efforts against smallpox, did very little to improve the health of Europeans in the eighteenth century. (See pages 674-9.)

c. No. Surgery, with some improvements, would still have to wait until the nineteenth century to undergo significant advances. (See pages 674-9.)

d. No. Preventive medicine in the eighteenth century did not really do much to improve the health of the people. (See pages 674-9.)

7. a. Correct. The surprisingly late age of marriage was probably a function of economic constraints, especially the availability of land. (See pages 661-2.)

b. No. Contrary to previous beliefs, Europeans were discovered to marry rather late, in their late twenties. (See pages 661-2.)

c. No. Even though many men and women did not marry, the great majority of people did marry. (See pages 661-2.)

d. No. Actually the late age of marriage and the restrictions on divorce precluded this. (See pages 661-2.)

8. a. No. Modern research has proven that the typical European family lived together in the nuclear unit. (See pages 661-2.)

b. No. One of the most significant and distinctive characteristics of the European family was the late age of marriage. (See pages 661-2.)

c. No. Given the late age of marriage, it would be logical to assume that there would be many unmarried relatives. (See pages 661-2.)

d. Correct. Actually the extended family was a rarity in Europe and may never have existed there at all. (See pages 661-2.)

9. a. No. The overwhelming reason for the postponement of marriage was the necessity to be able to provide for a family. (See pages 661-2.)

b. Yes. The necessity to be able to provide for a family, which usually meant being able to acquire enough land either through inheritance or purchase, was the major reason for the postponement of marriage. (See pages 661-2.)

c. No. The need to be able to provide, economically, for a family, not a legal restriction on age, was the greatest reason for the postponement of marriage. (See pages 661-2.)

d. No. Actually as the eighteenth century progressed and young people were able to earn a living by working in cottage industry, the age of marriage went down. (See pages 661-2.)

10. a. No. As more young people moved to cities the traditional restraints on behavior broke down, resulting in a much higher rate of illegitimate births. (See pages 664-5.)

b. No. Being able to earn a living in cottage industry or as a worker in a town meant that people did not have to wait to inherit or buy enough farm land to support a family. (See pages 664-5.)

c. Correct. Actually in the second half of the eighteenth century there was a growing trend of marriage among cottage workers and later factory workers for reasons of romantic love. (See pages 664-5.)

d. No. Unions based on love were increasingly the pattern for cottage, and later factory, workers. (See pages 664-5.)

11. a. No. Laws, such as those in Germany, designed to prevent the marriage of poor people, were often disregarded by young couples who simply lived together and produced illegitimate offspring. (See pages 662-4.)

b. No. With the rise of cottage industry more and more young people moved away from the village with its traditional checks on promiscuous behavior. (See pages 662-4.)

c.   Correct. The French Revolution did not repress sexual freedom; indeed it promoted freedom of thought and action. (See pages 662-4 and Chapter 21.)

d.   No. With the increase of rural to urban migration there was a lessening of traditional controls on young people. (See pages 662-4.)

12.   a.   No. Actually, due to the appallingly high rate of infant mortality, children were more often ignored and brutalized. (See pages 667-8.)

b.   No. Most commentators and authorities recommended stern discipline, a recommendation that was generally followed. (See pages 667-8.)

c.   No. Children were generally ignored, brutalized and unloved, a result of the very high infant mortality rate. (See pages 667-8.)

d.   Correct. Children were caught in a vicious circle: they were ignored, brutalized and unloved because they were likely to die and they were likely to die because they were ignored, brutalized and unloved. (See pages 667-8.)

13.   a.   Correct. The churches, Protestant and Catholic (sometimes at the prodding of the state), contributed most to popular education; in Protestant countries the belief that everyone should read the Bible gave impetus to this trend. (See pages 668-9.)

b.   No. Although the state did play a role in education, especially Prussia which was motivated by the idea that a literate population could better serve the state, churches were the greatest sponsor of education. (See pages 668-9.)

c.   No. Although private tutors did indeed offer educational opportunities, these were very limited in number and catered exclusively to the richest people. (See pages 668-9.)

d.   No. Most parents were uneducated themselves. (See pages 668-9.)

14.   a.   No. In reality, patients were crammed into wards, packed three or more to a bed, passing diseases to one another. (See pages 677-8.)

b.   No. The hospitals were crowded, filthy establishments with no real concern for more than rudimentary, if that, sanitation. (See pages 677-8.)

c.   No. Actually patients were crammed into wards, with three or more sharing the same bed. (See pages 677-8.)

d.   Correct. Indeed, the nurses were generally old, ignorant, greedy and often drunk. (See pages 677-8.)

15.   a.   No. Starvation has not yet been conquered, but the European diet did improve in the eighteenth century. (See pages 673, 678-9.)

b.   Correct. The conquest of smallpox - which had replaced bubonic plague as the most terrible of the infectious diseases - by Dr. Edward Jenner through vaccination was the greatest achievement of medical science. (See pages 678-9.)

c.   No. Scurvy was a dietary ailment caused by a deficiency in vitamin C, which was alleviated by the improved diet. (See pages 672, 678-9.)

d.   No. Cholera has not yet been conquered; it was a problem in western Europe until well into the nineteenth century. (See pages 678-9.)

16.   a.   No. The cottage system was a system of industrial manufacturing. (See pages 665-6 and Chapter 19.)

b.   No. Infanticide is the practice of killing new born children; although many infants died as a result of the practice described in the question, that was not necessarily the intended result. (See pages 665-6.)

c.   Correct. Wet-nursing was the practice whereby many new mothers sent their infants to the countryside to be suckled by a peasant woman. Many children did die as a result of this practice.

(See pages 665-6.)

d.   No. Overlaying refers to the accidental or purposeful suffocation of infants sleeping in their parents bed. (See pages 665-6.)

17.   a.   No. Even though many Europeans did not consume enough vegetables during the winter, they were a staple of the diet, being called "poor people's food". (See pages 671-2.)

b.   No. Indeed beer was a popular drink, enjoyed by most Europeans. (See pages 671-2.)

c.   No. Dark bread was literally the staff of life in eighteenth-century Europe. (See pages 671-2.)

d.   Correct. Milk was rarely drunk; people believed it to cause various ailments except in the very young and very old. (See pages 671-2.)

18.   a.   Correct. The greatest dietary problem was the insufficient consumption of vitamins A and C, from not getting enough green vegetables and milk, especially in the winter months. (See page 672.)

b.   No. The lack of vitamins A and C (from green vegetables and milk) was the chief dietary problem. (See page 672.)

c.   No. Actually the over consumption of meat by the rich caused them problems such as the gout; lack of vitamins A and C, however, was the greatest dietary problem. (See pages 671-2.)

d.   No. Europeans consumed sufficient sugar, even too much; the lack of vitamins A and C was the major dietary problem. (See pages 672-4.)

19.   a.   No. If an operation was suggested, whether performed in a hospital or not, the patient was in serious trouble. (See pages 674-8.)

b.   No. If one needed drugs, these could be purchased from an apothecary without entering the hospital, which was always a good idea. (See pages 674-8.)

c.   No. Whether the hospital consciously followed Galen's theory - that wounds be encouraged to fester for example - was academic, given the filth and overcrowded conditions of the hospitals. (See pages 674-8.)

d.   Correct. Unless one was merely looking for a place to die, staying out of the hospital was perhaps the best prescription. (See pages 674-8.)

20.   a.   No. Education in Britain was carried out by the church, not the state. (See page 669.)

b.   Correct. In 1717, Prussia, motivated by both the Protestant idea that every believer should read the Bible and that a literate population could better serve the state, made attendance at elementary schools compulsory. (See page 669.)

c.   No. In France in 1682, Christian schools had been established by the church, not the state. (See page 669.)

d.   No. Austria lagged behind the rest of Europe in universal education. (See page 669.)

21.   a.   No. Austria was a Catholic state; the Catholic church did not advocate individuals reading the Bible. (See page 669.)

b.   No. Although both the Church of England and dissenting congregations established "charity" schools for the poor, it was Scotland which created an effective network with excellent results. (See page 669.)

c.   No. France was a Catholic state; the Catholic church did not endorse the practice of individuals reading the Bible. (See page 669.)

d.   Correct. Presbyterian Scotland's staunch religious beliefs led to the establishment of an effective network of schools for rich and poor alike, with excellent results. (See page 669.)

22.   a.   No. The growing popularity of white bread led to a nutritional decline as the coarse bran and the germ were milled and sifted out of the flour. (See page 674.)

b.   No. Actually it was just the opposite; the production of white bread resulted from the removal of the most nutritional parts of the grain. (See page 674.)

c.   No. This development had little impact on the supply of bread other than the fact that people began to eat less bread. (See page 674.)

d.   Correct. With the removal of the bran and the germ to produce its whiteness, white bread lost almost all nutritional value. (See page 674.)

23.   a.   No. Actually, believing masturbation caused insanity, parents, churches, and schools all waged relentless war on masturbation by males. (See page 678.)

b.   No. In general, masturbation by males was roundly reviled and castigated; female masturbation was of little interest. (See page 678.)

c.   Correct. Indeed the general belief was that masturbation not only caused insanity but also acne, epilepsy and premature ejaculation and therefore had to be prevented. (See page 678.)

d.   No. The prevalence of warnings and unbelievable treatments - mittens, straitjackets and the like - attests to the fact that masturbation was not unknown in the eighteenth century. (See page 678.)

24.   a.   Correct. The Reformation era had increased the power of Catholic monarchs over their churches; Spain, for example, took firm control of church appointments and the Inquisition, creating a national church. (See page 680.)

b.   No. The Catholic monarchs limited the power of the church, they did not attempt to change the basis of belief. (See page 680.)

c.   No. The Catholic monarchs certainly reduced the level of allegiance to the pope by creating national churches but they did not sever all ties. (See page 680.)

d.   No. Catholic monarchs followed the Protestant lead in curtailing the power and influence of the church, not in caring for the poor. (See page 680.)

25.   a.   No. As a result of the effective participation in the game of politics for so long, the Jesuits had created a broad coalition of enemies which almost completely destroyed the order. (See page 680.)

b.   No. The Jesuits were expelled from both Portugal and France, with their properties confiscated. (See page 680.)

c.   Correct. The Jesuits were expelled from Spain and France (Portugal as well) as a result of the actions of the broad coalition of enemies they had created over the years. (See page 680.)

d.   No. Actually the Jesuits were very involved in politics, which almost destroyed their order; their property was confiscated in France after they were expelled. (See page 680.)

Chapter 21

1. a.   No. Eighteenth-century liberals did not believe that people should be economically equal, but that all should have an equal chance at economic success, without benefit of special privileges conferred by birth. (See pages 691-2.)
    b.   No. Eighteenth-century liberals stressed equality of opportunity, with personal liberty and identical rights, not equality in property holding. (See pages 691-2.)
    c.   Yes. Liberals believed that all men should have an equal chance to succeed, without benefits conferred by birth. (See pages 691-2.)
    d.   No. Race and sex were not much considered by most eighteenth-century liberals who stressed equality of opportunity for European males. (See pages 691-2.)

2. a.   No. The delegates of the Third Estates, joined by some members of the First and Second, voted to call themselves the National Assembly in June 1789, the third event on the list. (See pages 694, 700.)
    b.   No. Louis XVI was executed in January 1793, for treason, part of the radical "second revolution"; this is the last event on the list. (See pages 694, 707.)
    c.   No. The American Bill of Rights, drawn up to allay fears of a too powerful Federal government, was promulgated in March 1789, the second event on the list. (See page 694.)
    d.   Correct. The Seven Years' War ended in 1763, 26 years before any of the other events on this list. (See page 694 and Chapters 18 and 19.)

3. a.   No. The aristocrats who fled France were known as the *émigres*; the Jacobins were revolutionary radicals. (See pages 706-7.)
    b.   No. Jacobins were revolutionary radicals, named after their political club, and were committed to the revolution; indeed when Louis XVI was guillotined the members of the Legislative Assembly were all Jacobins of a sort. (See pages 706-7.)
    c.   No. There were some priests among the ranks of the Jacobins, but the term applies to a much broader group of people. (See pages 706-7.)
    d.   Correct. The Jacobins, named after the Jacobite monastery they met in, were all firmly committed to the liberal revolution; they eventually split into two competitive wings. (See pages 706-7.)

4. a.   Correct. In June 1789, the delegates to the Third Estate decided to call themselves the National Assembly, with the purpose of writing a constitution for France. (See pages 699-700.)
    b.   No. Louis XVI had only grudgingly called the Estates General, much less establish the National Assembly, an act he was forced to accept. (See pages 699-700.)
    c.   No. Although some aristocrats agreed with the establishment of the National Assembly, it was the creation of the Third Estate. (See pages 699-700.)
    d.   No. The *sans-culottes* would have a tremendous impact on the course of the revolution, but they did not establish the National Assembly. (pages 699-700, 708.)

5. a.   No. In an attempt to meet the financial burdens that had toppled the monarchy, the Assembly nationalized church lands and sold them off to raise money. (See page 704.)
    b.   No. One of the earliest acts of the Assembly was to issue the Declaration of the Rights of Man, which was the clarion call of the Revolution. (See pages 703-4.)
    c.   No. The establishment of the metric system, abolishing the hodgepodge of medieval weights and measures in France, was indicative of the rationalism of the Enlightenment that so many of the delegates adhered to. (See pages 703-4.)
    d.   Correct. The Reign of Terror was ushered in by Robespierre and the Mountain in 1793; it was a repudiation of the ideals of 1789, exemplified by the Declaration of the Rights of Man and Citizen. (See pages 703-4, 708-10.)

6. a.   No. In his famous pamphlet, Sieyès argued that the nobility was a tiny over-privileged minority, which did not deserve to rule France. (See page 700.)
    b.   No. Sieyès argued, in his famous pamphlet *What is the Third Estate?*, that neither the clergy nor the nobility should rule France, but that the Third Estate, dominated by the middle classes should rule. (See page 700.)
    c.   Correct. In his famous pamphlet, *What is the Third Estate?*, Sieyès argued that the true strength of France lay in the Third Estate, which should rule. (See page 700)
    d.   No. Sieyès had argued that the Third Estate, which represented the "people" of France, that is all those who were neither noble nor clergy, should rule, not the king; this estate was dominated by the middle classes. (See page 700.)

7. a.   No. In 1789, Sieyès argued that the people, that is the Third Estate should rule; by 1799 he was calling for a strong authority figure at the top. (See page 712.)
    b.   No. In 1789, Sieyès had argued that the leaders of the Third Estate, in the name of the people, should rule; by 1799 after a decade of turmoil, Sieyès was calling for a military strongman. (See page 712.)
    c.   Correct. Sieyès exemplified the evolution in political thinking; ten years of turmoil had created a yearning for a strong leader. (See page 712.)
    d.   No. Actually the Directory's incompetence and corruption had added to the desire for a strong military ruler. (See page 712.)

8. a.   Correct. The National Assembly, which had declared its intention to write a constitution for France, founded a constitutional monarchy, although the king had very little power. (See pages 703-4.)
    b.   No. Actually the collapse of the absolute monarchy had led to the Revolution. (See pages 703-4.)
    c.   No. A republic was founded once the King had been executed in January 1793; the first government established by the constitution of the National Assembly was a constitutional monarchy. (See pages 703-4, 706-10.)
    d.   No. Actually a military dictatorship was the last form of government established by the Revolution, with Napoleon's coup in 1799. (See pages 703-4, 712-8.)

9. a.   No. Burke was an English conservative who attacked the excesses of the French Revolution while defending the English monarchy and aristocracy, not the Catholic church. (See page 705.)
    b.   No. Burke's *Reflections on the Revolution in France* was a defense of European conservatism; he predicted that events in France would lead to chaos and tyranny. (See page 705.)
    c.   No. Burke's *Reflections on the Revolution in France* was a defense of European conservatism, and the English aristocracy and monarchy, in response to the early stages of the French Revolution. (See page 705.)
    d.   Correct. Burke's *Reflections of the Revolution in France* was an intellectual defense of European conservatism in general and the English aristocracy and monarchy in particular. (See page 705.)

10. a.   No. Liberalism attracted support from the educated elite and substantial classes throughout Europe; the elite favored its views on private property and individual liberties. (See page 692.)
    b.   No. Liberalism was highly attractive to the members of the middle class, with its ideals of private property, individual liberty, and equality of opportunity. (See page 692.)
    c.   Correct. Liberalism lacked strong support from the masses; they did not worry about theoretical and political questions, being too busy with the daily struggle. (See page 692.)
    d.   No. Liberalism found broad support among the educated elite, being the political manifestation of the Enlightenment. (See page 692.)

11. a. No. Eighteenth-century liberals did not demand a communistic sharing of the wealth but the equal opportunity for all to get rich. (See pages 691-2.)
 b. No. Eighteenth-century liberals did not advocate or believe that economically-based classes should be abolished, only that legal distinctions and privileges be abolished, granting everyone equal protection and opportunity. (See pages 691-2.)
 c. No. Indeed eighteenth-century liberals believed in the idea that men should "pull themselves up by the bootstraps" and were not overly fond of social welfare systems; they believed that economic liberty would solve all social problems. (See pages 691-2.)
 d. Correct. Eighteenth-century liberals believed that all men deserved an equal chance, without the interference of legal distinctions and privileges; this is the core of liberal economic and political theory. (See pages 691-2.)

12. a. No. Actually , the Stamp Tax was quite moderate; indeed the Americans, with the highest standard of living in the world, paid the lowest taxes in the British Empire. (See page 693.)
 b. No. The people living in England had been paying a variety of taxes for years; Americans objected because they had not been consulted. (See page 693.)
 c. No. Actually the cost of administering the Stamp Tax had nothing to do with American objections to the tax. (See page 693.)
 d. Correct. The Stamp Tax was indicative of the key political issue, that of sovereignty; with its imposition, without consent, Britain apparently denied the local authority of the American colonies. (See page 693.)

13. a. No. Actually the American Revolution was seen as the physical embodiment of the Enlightenment and inspired many Europeans. (See page 696.)
 b. Correct. The French government, at the urging of foreign minister Vergennes, supported the Americans, hoping to embarrass the English. (See pages 694-6)
 c. No. Actually both Locke and Montesquieu, in both the Declaration of Independence and the Constitution, display their influence on the American Revolution. (See pages 692, 696.)
 d. No. Actually the Revolution was not supported by all of the colonists, with many, the Tories, remaining loyal to England. (See pages 694, 696.)

14. a. No. Peasant revolt in the countryside was a result, not a cause of the outbreak of revolution. (See pages 699-700, 702.)
 b. No. The death of Louis XVI was caused by the Revolution; he was guillotined in 1793. (See pages 699-700, 707.)
 c. Correct. The aristocratic attempt to turn the financial woes of the monarchy into a political victory, exemplified by the Assembly of Notables' refusal to agree to be taxed, led to the calling of the Estates General. (See pages 699-700.)
 d. No. Actually the rash actions of the Revolution, when the Legislative Assembly declared war on Austria and Prussia, prompted foreign invasion. (See pages 699-700, 706.)

15. a. Correct. In 1808 a coalition of Catholics, monarchist and patriots, supported by England, rebelled against Napoleon's attempts to make Spain a French satellite. (See page 717.)
 b. No. Russia was never part of the Grand Empire, being only an ally. (See page 717.)
 c. No. Prussia, only an ally, would remain loyal until the rout of Napoleon in Russia in 1812. (See page 717.)
 d. No. Italy was not the first to revolt against Napoleon's rule. (See page 717.)

16. a. Correct. Prior to 1765, the Americans enjoyed "benign neglect;" the expenses of the Seven Years' War, however, caused England to regulate the colonies more closely. (See page 693.)
 b. No. English policy toward the American colonies had always been generally tolerant and

benign, save for a short period in the 1690s. (See page 693.)

c.   No. Actually the Americans, with the highest standard of living in the world, payed the lowest taxes in the British Empire. (See page 693.)

d.   No. The American colonies had never been under the direct control of the East India Company, which did control India and had received a monopoly on the tea trade with the colonies. (See page 693.)

17.   a.   Correct. The peasantry, not surprisingly, bore the brunt of the tax burden in France. (See pages 000.)

b.   No. The bourgeoisie did not enjoy the tax exemptions that the aristocracy and clergy did, which was one of their major complaints. (See page 698.)

c.   No. The clergy was exempt from taxation, only responsible for a voluntary donation. (See page 698.)

d.   No. The nobility, owning 25% of the land, were taxed very lightly. (See page 698.)

18.   a.   No. It was the cost of bread, not the desire for political representation, that motivated the Parisian population in the summer of 1789. (See pages 700-2.)

b.   Correct. The rising cost of bread, taking as much as half (or more) of one's wages, motivated the people of Paris to revolutionary activity. (See pages 700-2.)

c.   No. It was the high price of bread, not the murder of Marat by the Girondin supporter Charlotte Corday, that motivated the people of Paris. (See pages 700-2.)

d.   No. It was the high price of bread, not the allegedly repressive nature of the King's regime exemplified by the Bastille, that motivated the Parisian population. (See pages 700-2.)

19.   a.   No. The trend toward urbanization was not directly or greatly accelerated by the Revolution. (See pages 702-3.)

b.   Correct. The revolutionary land settlement and the sale of church lands presented the French peasantry with greater land ownership. (See pages 702-3.)

c.   No. The peasantry, after the abolition of feudalism in August 1789, would become a force for order and stability, but did not exert active political power. (See pages 702-3.)

d.   No. With the abolition of feudalism and the sale of confiscated church lands, the French peasantry achieved a substantial gain. (See pages 702-3.)

20.   a.   No. Actually the National Guard, commanded by Lafayette, protected the Royal Family as best they could from the people who wanted to reduce the Queen to an entree. (See pages 703-4.)

b.   No. Despite the fact that the Jacobins, including Robespierre and the radical Mountain, would eventually condemn the Royal Family to death, they were not the ones who said this. (See pages 703-4, 706.)

c.   No. This wildly vitriolic hatred of the Queen was not the expression of the revolutionary committees. (See pages 703-4.)

d.   Correct. The women of Paris, especially the market women, enraged by the high cost of bread and the luxury of the Court, further inflamed by the hateful rumors about the Queen, expressed their hatred in such words. (See pages 703-4.)

21.   a.   No. The Revolutionary Army was too busy fighting France's external enemies. (See pages 708-10.)

    b.   No. Secret police were indeed utilized by the Committee of Public Safety which attempted to rid France of any internal opposition to the Revolution. (See pages 708-10.)

    c.   No. The mob was present in the revolutionary tribunals, but the Committee of Public Safety had taken on the task of ridding France of any internal foes of the Revolution. (See pages 708-10.)

    d.   Correct. Robespierre and the Committee of Public Safety attempted to created "civic virtue" by the use of revolutionary terror. (See pages 708-10.)

22.   a.   Correct. Indeed Mary Wollstonecraft made the logical if radical conclusion that the ideals of the French Revolution should be extended to women. (See pages 705-6.)

    b.   No. Actually Edmund Burke argued this; Wollstonecraft attacked this view and argued that the ideals of the Revolution should be extended to women. (See pages 705-6.)

    c.   No. Actually Wollstonecraft, in addition to arguing that the ideals of the Revolution should be extended to women, attacked Burke's defense of the English society. (See pages 705-6.)

    d.   No. Wollstonecraft argued that women should not limit themselves; they were completely capable of managing businesses and entering politics. (See pages 705-6.)

23.   a.   No. Actually the reverse is true; the revisionists have argued that the nobility and the bourgeoisie actually had converging political and economic interests. (See pages 698-9.)

    b.   No. Actually, according to the revisionists, the nobility was a fluid and relatively open class. (See pages 698-9.)

    c.   No. Actually the opposite is true; the revisionist argue that rather than locked in inevitable conflict, the nobility and bourgeoisie shared both political and economic interests. (See pages 698-9.)

    d.   Correct. Reinforcing the long held view that the Old Regime had ceased to correspond with social reality, the revisionists have argued that the nobility and the bourgeoisie shared political and economic interests. (See pages 698-9.)

24.   a.   No. Actually the Congress of Vienna was charged with the reconstruction of Europe after the devastation of the wars of the Revolution and Napoleon. (See page 715, and Chapter 23.)

    b.   No. Frederick William III of Prussia attacked Napoleon after his reorganization of the Holy Roman Empire, which had alarmed the Prussians. (See page 715.)

    c.   No. The Continental System was the device which Napoleon installed to bring Britain to its knees by cutting off all trade between the continent and the English. (See page 715.)

    d.   Correct. Napoleon, as he conquered Europe, attempted to rationalize it; to that end he abolished the Holy Roman Empire and reorganized it into the German Confederation. (See page 715.)

25. a. No. The Treaty of Amiens was a diplomatic triumph for Napoleon and actually allowed him to consolidate his forces for the anticipated invasion. (See page 715.)

b. Correct. When Britain violated the Treaty of Amiens, Napoleon (looking for an excuse) decided to invade; in the process the French fleet was sunk by Lord Nelson and the British fleet at the Battle of Trafalgar. (See page 715.)

c. No. Actually the collapse of the Third Coalition was a victory for the French; the British victory at Trafalgar prevented the invasion. (See page 715.)

d. No. Actually the Treaty of Amiens had allowed France a chance to recover economically, besides Napoleon was rarely restrained by such considerations. (See page 715.)